THE RAPE OF BELGIUM

Belgium in 1914

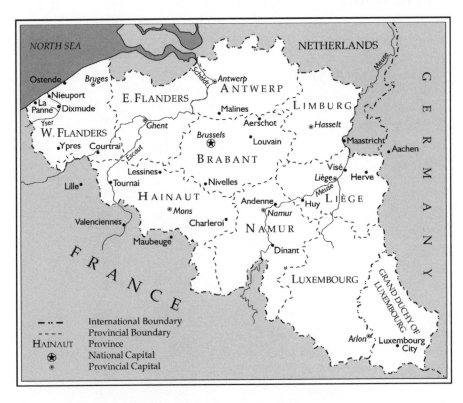

Source: United States Central Intelligence Agency, 1985

LARRY ZUCKERMAN

THE RAPE OF BELGIUM

The Untold Story of World War I

New York University Press • *New York and London*

NEW YORK UNIVERSITY PRESS
New York and London
www.nyupress.org

Quotations from the Hugh Gibson Papers at the Hoover Institution Archives, Stanford University, appear by permission of Michael F. Gibson.

Quotations from the David Theodore Nelson Papers at the Hoover Institution Archives, Stanford University, appear by permission of John P. Nelson.

Library of Congress Cataloging-in-Publication Data
Zuckerman, Larry.
The rape of Belgium : the untold story of World War I / Larry Zuckerman.
p. cm.
Includes bibliographical references and index.
ISBN 0–8147–9704–0 (alk. paper)
1. Belgium—History—German occupation, 1914–1918.   2. World War, 1914–1918—Belgium.   3. War and society—Belgium.   4. World War, 1914–1918—Evacuation of civilians.   5. World War, 1914–1918—Social aspects—Belgium.   I. Title.
D615.Z83   2003
940.3'493—dc22   2003015217

New York University Press books are printed on acid-free paper,
and their binding materials are chosen for strength and durability.

Manufactured in the United States of America

10 9 8 7 6 5 4 3 2 1

For Aaron and Jonah

Contents

Acknowledgments		ix
Note on Geography		xi
	Introduction	1
1	Your Neighbor's Roof	5
2	Marching through Hell	22
3	The Ghost of 1870	38
4	Belgium Does Not Ask for Pity	62
5	A Vague and Misty Unreality	78
6	This Poisoned Atmosphere	103
7	At Least They Only *Drown* Your Women	120
8	Hell's Premises	142
9	Taking Note of These Things	165
10	*Mort pour la Patrie*	183
11	Like a Thief in the Night	200
12	It Is Impossible That We Will Be Abandoned	218
13	A Trifle	242
14	A Popular Delusion	259
	Notes	277
	Bibliography	321
	Index	329
	About the Author	339

Acknowledgments

Writing this book would have been impossible without help from many people whom I have never met. Janet L. Polasky told me about José Gotovitch, who passed me on to Sophie de Schaepdrijver, who has since been a frequent source of aid and encouragement, and who read this book in manuscript. Not only did Professor de Schaepdrijver send me hard-to-find journal articles, she managed to photocopy a document from the Algemeen Rijksarchief/Archives Générales du Royaume in Brussels, an act of wizardry I can only marvel at. Jan D'hont of the Stadsarchief in Brugge put me in touch with Captain Graeme F. Boxall, MN (Ret.'d), who resolved ambiguities in the Charles Fryatt case for me. Guy Wuyds persuaded archivists at the Belgian Ministry of Foreign Affairs to search for dossiers on war crimes trials and make them available.

His nephew, Ruben Verbist, chased down elusive facts and gave me a survival guide to the Algemeen Rijksarchief, a bewildering place for foreigners. At the Rijksarchief, Luis Angel Bernardo y Garcia eased my way and introduced me to Cyriel Vleeschouwers, who unearthed wartime diaries widely believed lost, which form a crucial part of this narrative. Librarians at the Bibliothèque Royale Albert indulged my whims and kindly intervened before various microfilm rolls (and I) became unraveled. My thanks go to all these people.

Carol Leadenham at the Hoover Institution Archives at Stanford University answered myriad questions, went out of her way to see that I found the papers I needed, and helped me research permission to use photographs and archival material. She deserves my particular gratitude. Librarians at the University of Washington fetched materials, and the map librarians found me a good map; the Seattle Public Library borrowed rare books from other institutions.

Marie-Rose Thielemans answered my questions about King Albert's views of war crimes. Sally Marks counseled me on sources concerning the Paris Peace Conference; James F. Willis and Gary Jonathan Bass did the same regarding war crimes trials. Robert Hanks shared his expertise on Georges Clemenceau, and Richard Breitman gave me a helpful hint about connecting the Holocaust to German crimes against Belgium. Ruth Harris advised me on French propaganda, and David Owen Kieft offered tips on other sources. My appreciation goes to all, and to anyone I have forgotten, none of whom are responsible for my errors.

Special thanks go to my wife, Helene, who shouldered double duty during my periodic absences, and to our two children, who also did without me at those times. All three listened to my daily bulletins about Belgium and endured my moods.

Finally, I must thank my agent, Ed Knappman, who found me my editor. Deborah Gershenowitz was interested in this book before she had read it, and her encouragement and enthusiasm ever since have meant much to me. Without her, and the staff at New York University Press, this book would not have been published with as much thought, care, or respect.

Note on Geography

Belgium in 1914 was divided into nine provinces, three of which—Liège, Namur, and Antwerp—shared their names with their principal cities. Major population districts were called arrondissements, and the next rung down the ladder was the canton. But the most important division in 1914 was the commune, which, through a burgomaster and a communal council, wielded powers associated in other countries with a central government.

These pages refer to places as an English-speaking reader in 1914 would have heard of them, so that several towns and cities known today by their Flemish names (Leuven, Brugge, Ieper) appear in their French equivalents (Louvain, Bruges, Ypres).

Introduction

IN AUGUST 1914, the German Army invaded Belgium because the granite-block roads of Flanders and Brabant seemed to lead to Paris as veins lead toward the heart. The attack violated a treaty that the German chancellor likened to a "scrap of paper," prompting many foreigners to conclude that Germany did not respect international law. When the invaders shot thousands of Belgian civilians and looted and burned scores of towns, the news shocked a world that had taken European culture for granted. Allied propagandists invoked the "rape of Belgium" to claim that justice lay on their side, though they often argued the case by telling fables about "barbarians" who had done unspeakable things to women and children.

The killings and burnings deserved notice not least because they resulted from the invaders' delusion that Belgian civilians had fired at them, setting off a controversy that persists today. But less well known is that the rape of Belgium lasted more than fifty months under an occupation that kept seven million people in fear for their lives, liberty, and property. The real rape had nothing to do with atrocities, authentic or imagined, but with routine terror and the mind-set that condoned it, which put German crimes on another level. In this book, I show why the crimes matter, what legacy they left, and why they offer a new way to look at the First World War.

Before August 1914, Belgium had been the world's sixth-ranked industrial power, but the Germans plundered it so thoroughly that it never regained its former place. The Belgian labor force had been known for skill and the willingness to produce for modest wages; the Germans deported more than a hundred thousand workers to make weapons and tortured the majority who refused. Belgium had been Europe's second-oldest democracy; the Germans jailed thousands of people on contrived charges, including the failure to inform on family or neighbors. Such methods scorned even the prewar era's supple legal standards and were what a later generation would have recognized as totalitarian. Occupied Belgium was a forerunner of Nazi Europe.

Consequently, I argue that there was no question where justice lay, and that the Allies were correct to say that Germany menaced law and the world order. Britain's decision to fight was the right one, whereas American neutrality appears misguided if not craven. Had Woodrow Wilson wished above all to make the world safe for democracy, he would not have ignored Belgium for almost three years while lecturing both sides about morality. He would have asked for war no later than autumn 1916, when the labor deportations began, recognizing that Belgium was a more compelling issue than the sinking of American merchant ships.

That said, however, neither the press nor government in Britain or the United States grasped what the occupation meant. Britain seldom cited the crimes of occupation to make the case against Germany more persuasive, and as a neutral, the United States avoided discussing them altogether, a stance that rarely changed, even after America declared war. Public discourse about Belgium in both English-speaking countries remained stuck on 1914, even as Belgians under German rule were being punished for protesting excesses that had occurred daily ever since.

I have focused on Britain and the United States because each power protected Belgium, whether as a belligerent or, in neutral America's case, as the nominal sponsor of a private relief effort. That two nations knowing nothing of invasion should be Belgium's guardians emphasized how crucial it was for outsiders to comprehend the occupation. France had endured invasion too and understood implicitly what German rule meant, but the French had their own troubles to worry about, including a battlefield death toll more than thirty times the size of Belgium's.

Ignorance of, or lack of concern for, the Belgian occupation surfaced in 1919, when the victors gathered at Paris to talk peace terms. British leaders in particular sought to deny Belgium the reparations that had long been promised and to reserve them for Britain and France alone. Political convenience had much to do with this, but the maneuver nevertheless undermined Britain's claims that it had fought to uphold the rights of small nations and would sign no treaty that disregarded them. Britain had also pledged to try war criminals, but the government never backed the idea wholeheartedly. Partly at French insistence, the Treaty of Versailles called for systematic war crimes trials, the first treaty ever to do so, but the plan fell apart when the victors did not enforce it. As a compromise, Germany was allowed to hold a few trials, but the court dealt so leniently with the defendants that France and Belgium withdrew from the proceedings.

The failure to prove the crimes of occupation encouraged the growing belief that Belgium's ordeal had either ended in 1914 or never happened, and that the German Army had behaved no worse than any other. The obsession with 1914 that had served the Allies during the war now worked against them in the twenties and thirties, as critics of all stripes picked apart the atrocity stories to argue that the German menace had been greatly exaggerated. In their hands, martyred Belgium seemed a shameful lie, the war a cynical exercise, and the Treaty of Versailles an insult to moral principle.

Perhaps nothing could have rescued the Allied cause from the conviction that the war had been futile. Even so, the victors owed a reckoning to those who had sacrificed in their name, and deciding not to obtain one had dreadful repercussions. When a new round of occupations began in 1939, the world was seeing them as if for the first time, unaware that Belgium's experience had offered a warning. Likewise, the Nazis were able to dismiss initial reports of the Holocaust by recalling the charges Germany's enemies had made about Belgium during 1914–18 and cautioning people not to be gullible.

The misperceptions of Belgium therefore injured more than one country and lasted far beyond the First World War. In the following pages, I aim to show how this blunder came about and how it has shaped attitudes toward the war ever since.

I

Your Neighbor's Roof

THE FIRST WEEKEND of August 1914, the streets of Brussels buzzed with a rare electricity. Café conversations seemed louder than usual, and regulars who had never exchanged more than a nod or a *bonjour* threw aside formality and pulled their chairs closer to discuss the latest news.[1] How many classes of reservists would be called to the colors? What about Austria's ultimatum to Serbia? Would there be a general European war? Around the city, some people talked anxiously of killing, as if war had already started, but the soldiers seemed calm, promenading the boulevards with cigarettes in their lips and fiancées on their arms.[2]

The most agonizing question was what France and Germany would do with their gathering armies, some 3 million combat troops combined. Belgium's population totaled 7.5 million, and its field army mustered only 123,000. Heavy fortifications on both sides of the Franco-German border deterred an attack across the Rhine, but Belgium offered a route by which either neighbor could turn the other's flank. If an invader adopted this strategy—which would violate Belgian neutrality—no matter who won the battle, Belgium would lose lives, perhaps land, maybe even its independence. Strain filled the air, already thick and heavy from a midsummer heat wave, and nerves yielded alternately to panic and euphoria.

Headlines urged CALM,[3] even as merchants were causing panic by refusing paper money, which prompted hordes to descend on the Banque Nationale and carry away suitcases bulging with coins.[4] When the army mobilized the night of 31 July–1 August, church bells and trumpets in every town roused reservists from bed. Come morning, a Saturday, customs agents went house to house collecting the black, yellow, and red Belgian flag to put up along the border and on churches and public buildings.[5]

Brussels, as the American journalist Richard Harding Davis fondly described it, was an "imitation Paris" of parks, tree-lined boulevards, and arches, of "lakes gay with pleasure-boats" and "haunted forests, where your taxicab would startle the wild deer."[6] But the capital showed a different face that weekend. In parks, officers stopped horseback riders, handed them receipts, and led away their mounts. Automobile owners lost their vehicles, and the Parc Cinquantenaire, a monument to the late King Leopold II's imperial dreams, soon held cars, horses, cannons, and caissons.[7] The German military attaché professed surprise at the warlike preparations, saying, "We couldn't do better!"[8]

A patriotic delirium spread like an infectious fever. A Ghent University student who enlisted described the ovation for recruits at the train station, where bystanders sang "La Brabançonne" or "De Vlaamse Leeuw" (The Flemish Lion)—the two national anthems—and a few wearing national costume shouted, "Long live the war!" The young student thought this was "stupidity," so with all his strength, he yelled, "Long live the homeland!"[9]

The night of 1 August, sleep was difficult, when anybody bothered. On a square bordering a large barracks in Brussels, an immense crowd milled nervously about, silent except for an occasional murmur or sob, waiting, waiting—for what, they were not sure. As if from nowhere came a tumult, a pushing, and a file of reservists marched in, singing, shaking their bundles of belongings, hats, or handkerchiefs. The crowd made way, at first surprised, mute. Then they broke out into long, loud applause.[10]

Thirteen miles north of Brussels, at Malines, by eight o'clock, reservists had gathered in a widening stream, and gendarmes rang doorbells to summon others. Cars commandeered from a nearby factory raced through the streets, and a crowd thronged the main square. When the authorities unfurled the national tricolor from the town hall balcony, people removed their hats and cheered enthusiastically—and they were still there at 2:00 A.M. Those who could not fit in the square brought their nervous energy to the cafés, jam-packed even at that hour.[11]

Where many Belgians had found public ways to let off steam, their king, Albert, had stayed indoors to write a letter. Albert had German roots, through his Saxe-Coburg-Gotha grandfather and his Hohenzollern mother, and he had married a Bavarian duchess, Elisabeth of Wittelsbach.[12] Having heard that afternoon that the French government had promised to respect Belgian neutrality but that the German minister in Brussels had dodged the question, Albert decided to appeal directly to his Hohenzollern cousin, Kaiser Wilhelm II. To help him draft a note, he summoned a veteran Foreign Ministry official to the palace.

Albert's letter put law before family, stressing Belgium's fidelity to its international duties and reminding Wilhelm of Bismarck's praise for Belgium's "correct and impartial attitude" during the Franco-Prussian War of 1870–71. The king supposed that Germany meant to treat Belgium with that same regard but had preferred not to say so publicly. Still, given "the bonds of kinship and friendship" between the two monarchs, Albert wanted "to write to you and beg you, in these critical hours" for "the guarantee that our neutrality will be respected." He closed by saying that he was confident of obtaining this.[13]

The calm assurance was like Albert, but the letter was not his alone, for the Foreign Ministry secretary later credited Elisabeth's sound advice, and not just because Albert lacked her fluency in written German. She displayed "a sure judgment and that peculiar tact which often makes women better psychologists than men," though she spoke "softly, almost timidly," voicing her opinions as questions. When the letter was done, the queen suggested the text be translated, brought a dictionary, and put it on an armchair next to her. As Albert looked on, she knelt before a low table on which she wrote her translation, sometimes stopping to explain why she had chosen a particular word, repeatedly moving her husband aside to use the dictionary.[14]

Women of that era, even queens, seldom steered their husbands, and the striking contrast between the pair made the scene more poignant. They were the same age, thirty-eight. But Albert was a tall, blond athlete of shy manner who often wore thick pince-nez, which accented the appearance of diffidence, whereas the more outgoing Elisabeth, known as the "little queen," was dark, thin, and sickly. One can just see the giant peering myopically over her shoulder as she knelt in unintended supplication, behavior that other European monarchs would probably have called improper and unregal. But neither "the frail little woman with the lion heart," as an American diplomat described her, nor her husband lacked courage or self-respect.[15] They, the parents of three, were simply pleading with his relations for every family in Belgium.

Their subjects, meanwhile, were trying not to see that their nation might be facing extinction. Throughout that weekend, the Belgians continued to believe in miracles, trusting the treaty that guarded their neutrality and the premise that no harm should come to them because they bore no blame for European tensions. That a Serb had murdered an Austrian archduke meant nothing to Belgium, which had no quarrel with Germany or Austria-Hungary and no special sympathy for their enemies, the Triple Entente of France, Russia, and Britain. Culture linked Belgium to France, but only for Walloons, who numbered less than their Flemish compatriots, and both groups suspected French designs. Britain had sometimes acted as Belgium's guardian, but not as an ally, and Belgium was forbidden to join alliances anyway. Belgians thought that by what was right and proper, their country should be able to stand aside if Europe chose to go berserk.

Their wish to escape the calamity found expression in their belief in law, which had shaped Belgium's history as an independent country. From Caesar to Wellington, many great captains had fought there, a curse of geography that had made Belgium a rag doll for neighbors to squabble over. The pattern repeated itself after Napoleon's defeat in 1815, when the victors awarded the prized toy to the Netherlands, hoping to deny it to the French. But the Belgians had never liked foreign rule, and in 1830, they revolted, sparked by a theatrical performance in Brussels that roused the audience to take to the streets. After the rebels gained the upper hand, in July 1831 the British insisted that Leopold of Saxe-Coburg-Gotha, a German prince with English connections, be placed on the Belgian throne. A month later, though, the Dutch attacked, and Leopold asked for French troops, who drove the Dutch out but showed no urge to leave. The four other great powers—Austria, Britain, Prussia, and Russia—pressured France to withdraw, and after the French agreed, the five drafted treaties that made Belgium a perpetually neutral state, guaranteed its territory, and mapped its borders.

But the Dutch rejected the settlement, which left Belgium's boundaries unstable and its survival uncertain. The five powers, led chiefly by British Foreign Secretary Lord Henry Palmerston, spent eight years trying to preserve their troubled creation. Palmerston saw a viable Belgium as a bulwark against a western European aggressor, and he also wished to keep Antwerp, which Napoleon had called a pistol pointed at England's heart, out of unfriendly hands. The result was three documents known collectively as the Treaty of 1839—in whose terms the Belgians had no say—which essentially pledged the Netherlands, Belgium, and the five powers to uphold the 1831 neutrality articles.[16]

As the price of Dutch agreement, the Treaty of 1839 returned certain lands to the Dutch king as his personal possessions. The transfer angered the Belgians, who hated to yield territory to their oppressors, more so when the inhabitants had taken part in the revolt. But the border revision injured more than dignity and had a purpose other than appeasing the Dutch. The five powers preferred to weaken the new country because they reasoned that conquerors would hesitate to seize what they could not hold. So to the southeast, Belgium gave up most of the Grand Duchy of Luxembourg, the remnant forming a Belgian province also called Luxembourg. The Grand Duchy had never been a massive obstacle, but now, if a hostile army occupied it, Luxembourg the Belgian province and Namur province to the west would be defenseless. This strategic area contains the Belgian portion of the Ardennes. North of Luxembourg lies the province of Liège, whose capital city of that name, built where the Meuse bends to the southwest, commands the entrance to the Meuse Valley. "Whoever is master of the Meuse, is master of Belgium," wrote a highly regarded nineteenth-century military expert, but his axiom did not begin to tell the story.[17] Only a hundred miles separate the French border city of Maubeuge from Aachen (Aix-la-Chapelle), and the line between them passes through Liège and Namur city, the two chambers of Wallonia's heart. The Treaty of 1839 removed a major artery, because north of Liège province, the powers snipped off part of Limburg province, where the Meuse runs almost north-south. The surgery shortened the Prussian Rhineland's frontier with Belgium but put a crucial stretch of the river in Dutch hands. The Dutch controlled the right bank adjacent to Limburg and both banks at Maastricht, depriving the Belgians of a barrier to the east and restricting their access to river traffic.

In the west, the Belgians coveted the Dutch territory of Flemish Zeeland (Dutch Flanders), a sparsely populated district through which the Scheldt flows before reaching Antwerp and, further downriver, Ghent. Though Flemish Zeeland had not joined the revolt, the Belgians wanted it, because if the Dutch held both banks of the

Scheldt, they could deny Antwerp and Ghent passage to the North Sea. Should Belgium be attacked, a navy trying to reach Antwerp to offer aid—presumably Britain's—would also be blocked. But the five powers did not cede Flemish Zeeland, instead writing treaty clauses that hindered the Dutch from closing the North Sea outlet to damage Belgian trade.

Belgium, therefore, began life exposed at three corners and squeezed between two ancient opponents, France and Prussia, which might resume their dispute at any time. The Belgians reacted by fortifying Antwerp in 1859, and Liège and Namur in the 1880s, thinking that masonry alone might discourage an invader. But even these steps went forward only after fierce debate in Parliament. Neither major party, the Catholics nor the Liberals, supported defense spending or strengthening the army, and toward 1900, a third, growing bloc in Parliament, the Socialists, voted against anything that looked military. Voices within the dominant Catholic Party called for reform, but conservative Catholic newspapers supposed that there was no point in having an army when any invader would be too strong to resist.[18] Older-line Catholics also worried that the barracks would corrupt young men and expose them to atheistic ideas.

Building the forts may even have hurt in the long run, because once the bricks had been laid and the guns placed, the issue of self-defense faded away, leaving behind a sense that Belgium was secure. Antwerp symbolized this feeling. The notion arose that the city could not be captured, and that should an invasion come, the army need only retreat within its walls and wait for help. By 1900, alarmists were warning that Belgium must have an army capable of weathering invasion at least until that help arrived, and that advances in weaponry had made the forts obsolete.[19] But though the country received its first conscription law worth the name in 1909, the saying went around that the army was the only one whose destiny was to not fight.[20] As one soldier later recalled, "Let's face it, the Belgian Army was strictly for parade."[21]

Sunday afternoon, 2 August, Brussels looked magnificent under brilliant blue skies. Men and women sang songs and promenaded with armfuls of flowers, and buildings everywhere displayed tricolors, some so large they dwarfed the windows showing them. The patrons jamming the cafés, seeking refreshment in the heat, wore tricolor rosettes in their buttonholes and hats, and men of all ages and social classes enlisted at barracks and military hospitals. Not everything was a party, though, for food sellers raised prices, and angry crowds overturned potato carts and stole the merchandise.[22] Around three o'-clock, a special edition of Le Soir hit the streets, and the terrifying headline confirmed a rumor: GERMANY DECLARES WAR ON RUSSIA. But beneath that appeared: GERMANY WILL RESPECT BELGIAN NEU-TRALITY: REASSURING WORDS FROM THE GERMAN MINISTER IN BRUSSELS.

Minister Karl-Konrad von Below-Saleske explained that his government had made no formal pledge because, in his opinion, none was needed. "The idea has always prevailed with us," he said, "that Belgian neutrality would not be violated. . . . German troops will not cross Belgian territory." He added: "Maybe you will see your neighbor's roof burn, but the fire will spare your house."[23] The minister did not name the neighbor, though probably he meant France. But he might as well have been talking of the Grand Duchy, which the Germans had occupied overnight, despite denials from their Brussels military attaché.[24]

Like Belgium, the Grand Duchy was neutral, but by the 1867 Treaty of London was neither obliged nor allowed to defend itself, and its army was a police force just large enough to supervise about a thousand square miles of territory. The Grand Duchy also had a superb railway network, transferred to German administration from French in 1871, but on condition that the rail lines not be used for military purposes. The German invasion violated this proviso, but the Treaty of London offered weaker international protection than the Treaty of 1839, allowing the Grand Duchy's guarantors to claim that they were not bound to uphold the law individually, only in concert.[25] In practice, that meant none would fight, a comment on power politics and the relative values of European real estate.

A hundred thousand soldiers were thus poised to slice open Belgium's underbelly, but paradoxically, the news inspired hope in Brussels.[26] People said that if the Germans had intended to attack both the Grand Duchy and Belgium, they would have done so at the same time. Optimists further concluded that if the Germans attacked France, they would strike south of the Meuse, perhaps even south of the Ardennes, crossing only the southernmost portion of Luxembourg province or skirting Belgium entirely.

Hopes rose again when Below-Saleske requested a meeting that night with the Belgian foreign minister, Julien Davignon, whose cheerfulness was a byword. "So much the better," Albert's secretary remarked, supposing that the meeting would "clarify our international situation" and provide the awaited guarantee.[27]

That night, the Brussels air was hot and muggy. People left their windows open, hoping for a breeze, but instead they let in vague, faraway noises—those of marching men, cars racing, field guns rumbling over pavement.[28] At the Foreign Ministry, the staff put aside etiquette and worked in shirtsleeves.[29]

Promptly at seven, Below-Saleske entered Davignon's office. The only published account of the meeting, reported secondhand, says that the German minister looked pale, and that he walked unsteadily and leaned on a table, putting a hand to his chest.[30] "What's wrong?" Davignon asked. "Are you ill?"

"I climbed the stairs too fast, it's nothing," Below-Saleske replied. He added that he had brought a confidential note, which he handed over.

Davignon read it and turned ashen. "No, it's not possible!" he exclaimed, letting the note fall to the floor.

Right after Below-Saleske left, still wobbling, Davignon's son and private secretary, Henri, pushed open the door. "My father had the pallor of a dead man," he wrote later.[31]

A few minutes past seven, an American diplomat saw Below-Saleske being driven away. Sweat stood out on the minister's forehead, and he stared straight ahead, holding his hat in his hand as he "puffed at a cigarette like a mechanical toy, blowing out jerky clouds of smoke."[32]

Meanwhile, Davignon was slumped in his chair, telling two colleagues, "It's horrible, it's dreadful. A worse misfortune couldn't have befallen us."[33] He handed them the paper, which they began to translate—it was in German—and to copy. Charles de Broqueville, the tall, midfiftyish minister of war and cabinet leader, joined them and heard the note read. "Well, Mr. Minister, are we ready?" someone asked.[34]

"Yes, we're ready," he replied, saying that the mobilization had gone well. "Tomorrow night, the army will be in a condition to march; tomorrow morning, even, if absolutely necessary. But we don't have our heavy artillery." The Belgians had placed orders with Krupp, but the guns had never arrived. What de Broqueville of course did not say, but what everyone knew, was that his four sons—all his children—were serving with the army.[35]

One diplomat went out to grab dinner at a nearby restaurant. He later recalled his anguish in the brilliantly lit room among gay, carefree diners who had read the papers and thought Belgium safe. "For my part, I felt crushed by the weight of what I knew, the secret that would be revealed the next day, and would cause such a rude awakening to those around me. I asked myself if I was the victim of some nightmare, or if I was really awake."[36]

The German note that had stunned him was easily summarized: "Reliable information" showed that French forces intended to march through the Meuse Valley via Namur to attack Germany.[37] The German government feared that despite Belgian goodwill, Belgium would not be able to repel the French, putting Germany in danger. "It is essential for the self-defence of Germany," the note continued, "that she should anticipate any hostile attack" by invading first. However, the German government would "feel the deepest regret" if Belgium regarded the move "as an act of hostility," given that "the measures of Germany's opponents force Germany, for her own protection, to enter Belgian territory." Therefore, if Belgium kept "an attitude of friendly neutrality towards Germany," the German government promised to evacuate Belgium and guarantee its territory and independence when peace was concluded. Moreover, Germany would pay cash for all necessaries, plus an indemnity to cover damage.

But if Belgium resisted, whether by manning the Meuse forts or by destroying tunnels, bridges, or railroads, Germany would, "to her regret, be compelled to consider Belgium as an enemy." If so, Germany would have no obligations toward Belgium, and "the decision of arms" would shape the two countries' future relations. The German government hoped that matters would not go so far, in which case "the friendly ties" that bound the two neighbors would "grow stronger and more enduring."

The Belgians had twelve hours to respond.

The night of 2 August, the palace was brightly lit and under heavy guard.[38] Between eight and nine o'clock, the cabinet ministers went in, mounted a huge marble staircase and turned down a long corridor, whose many windows were hung with crimson draperies. Walking past silent lackeys in red-and-gold livery, they entered a room containing a long table, on which a red cloth had been laid. Inkwells and blotters lay at every place.[39]

What happened next, in the most crucial moment in Belgium's brief lifetime—and a rare instance when Belgians affected world events—remains vague. That was partly by design because until 1916, Belgian cabinets took no minutes, to preserve the illusion that all decisions were unanimous. But that night, Georges Helleputte, minister of agriculture and public works, penciled cryptic notes that narrate much, if not most, of the proceedings.[40] Rediscovered only in 1981, his transcript defies complete decoding, for it is mostly phrases and words, not complete sentences, that emerge with certainty. Even so, Helleputte's scrawl reveals more than his colleagues would probably have wished.

At 9:15, with the king presiding, Foreign Minister Davignon recounted his conversation with Below-Saleske and read the ultimatum. Helleputte did not record the cabinet's reaction, but the conversation may have become heated and chaotic, because de Broqueville seems to have tried to restore order. The cabinet leader brought up the military situation, and he mentioned that "ministers of state" would soon be joining the group, a reminder that time was short. Albert took that as a cue and spoke at what, for him, was probably some length. He appears to have said that the ultimatum was unacceptable; stated the size of the field army and garrison forces; and invited the generals present, his protegé and de Broqueville's, to give their views.

It was typical of Belgian politics that king and cabinet leader favored different generals. By the Belgian constitution, the king commanded the army, but only during wartime, and every other royal act required a minister's signature. Belgian war plans deployed the army close to Antwerp, a strategy that Albert had tried to change. In 1913, he had named General Louis de Ryckel chief of the General Staff, and de Ryckel had drawn up a scheme to defend the Meuse.[41] But de Broqueville had overruled Albert on constitutional grounds, and when he replaced de Ryckel with General Antonin de Selliers de Moranville, in effect, he had committed Belgium to conceding the Meuse crossings.

That became clear at the cabinet meeting, because de Selliers said that the army could do little against "a superior force." Liège and Namur "must defend themselves with their garrisons," whereas the field army would retreat, giving battle when "a good position" offered itself. This would mean yielding the Meuse gateway and much of Wallonia and its heavy industry in return for husbanding resources to hold Antwerp. But de Ryckel replied, "It is not acceptable to let him [the enemy] cross our territory without having been absolutely forced to." He objected to withdrawing before they knew how superior the invaders' strength was, and he envisioned dealing blows, not just absorbing them. He proposed deploying virtually the whole army along the Meuse, from where "we can take the offensive" when an opening presented itself. After the retreat to Antwerp, the army could still attack and "harass" the German advance, which, he said, was intended not to conquer Belgium but to cross it.

There was little love lost between the generals, who fell to bickering over how to feed the lone brigade that de Ryckel wanted to assign to Antwerp. Perhaps amid the tension, the pettiest aspect of his plan was easier to speak of than whether Belgium would live or die. As if to refocus on that larger picture, Albert said, "If we resist, we must hold them on the Meuse." But when that statement did not stop the argument, the king addressed the cabinet: "What is the opinion of the ultimatum?"

Once again, Helleputte's notes leave no trace, but apparently a consensus voted to resist. His next entry, at ten o'clock, mentions the arrival of the ministers of state, mostly ranking parliamentarians invited to participate in meetings known as Crown Councils. The rising star among the newcomers was the Liberal leader Paul Hymans, raised to the post that day as a gesture to unity, along with Emile Vandervelde, the Socialist chief, who was not in Brussels that night. Small, dapper, and intellectual, the suave Hymans was a brilliant jurist and speaker whose temper sometimes got the better of him. Despite his support of defense, he had always mistrusted military experts who predicted doom, and, as an admirer of German science and education, had never expected the Germans to attack.[42]

On entering the conference room, Hymans wrote later, unaware of the ultimatum, he saw Frans Schollaert, a fellow minister of state whose face was distorted with emotion.

Hymans said that they had to hope that the war between France and Germany would not involve Belgium.

"What!" Schollaert exclaimed, turning on him. "Germany is going to invade us!"

Hymans paled and felt as if he'd gotten punched in the chest.[43]

The figure who dominated the Crown Council was Charles Woeste, the seventy-seven-year-old Catholic Party patriarch who had been minister of state since 1891 and the staunchest opponent of army reform. After Davignon reread the ultimatum and de Broqueville reviewed military matters, less than nine hours remained to answer the Germans, but Woeste argued as if he wished to turn back the clock. He insisted that the government must reply that no French troops had invaded Belgium, and that the ultimatum was based on a mistake. Asking Belgium's guarantors to help would achieve nothing, because that would be "appealing to France and Germany," and if "France is beaten, we will be lost" too. England could do little, and the Belgian Army could not hold the Germans by itself. "We can fight for the honor of the flag," Woeste remarked, adding that "doing nothing is not possible." But he repeated his conviction that contesting the facts was the best course, and he warned, "We must try to attempt to resist [while] not putting Germany on our backs."

Schollaert commented that that was all very well, but there would be "cannon fire," and Belgium would have to respond in kind. However, his words did not sway Jules Greindl, the seventy-nine-year-old former minister to Berlin. Until 1912, when Albert maneuvered to replace him on the pretense of ill health, Greindl had spent a quarter century faithfully believing German assurances. He had long favored army reform, but he had expected a different enemy, for on being summoned to the Crown Council, he had asked, "What, have the English landed?"[44] Now, he said, "The emperor"—meaning Wilhelm—"always told me we must have confidence in him," adding that the kaiser was "a very honest man," and that he, Greindl, was "staggered" by the ultimatum. Albert agreed that they all were, and Greindl went on to discuss his chief worry. "If we are allied with France, we risk annexation. Victorious, they will annex us."

Hymans retorted that Woeste's plan to contest the excuse of French invasion was dishonorable and illegal. Helleputte's notes are maddeningly elusive here, but Hymans seems to have declared that to yield would put Belgium in the wrong regarding France. "Germany proposes an alliance," Hymans said, and his words imply that if Belgium accepted, France could invade and demand an indemnity, which he called "a humiliating proposition." He also cited the Treaty of 1839: "This alliance [would mean] tearing up with our hands the treaty and [would be] a betrayal of our duty to Europe." Besides, no one knew who would win the war.

"We would betray the country in accepting this," Hymans declared. "Small nations may be mutilated but live. The army may be beaten, but we must resist an action that will revolt the world. We must say no and do our duty."

Perhaps emboldened, Louis de Sadeleer, another minister of state, began throwing around words like *abomination* and *felony*, and spoke of showing the Germans that they were "brigands." But though Woeste agreed with the sentiment, accusations were what he wished to avoid, and his reasoning evoked what a later generation would have called appeasement. "To shout this in Germany's face is to forget that we are a small country," he remarked. "We will have shouted in vain, there is no more Europe." Germany, he warned, would treat Belgium as an enemy; better to retreat to Antwerp instead of fighting for every inch.

But the tide appeared to be turning. Schollaert, clambering up the rhetorical heights, said that Antwerp was "the refuge" where Belgium would live "after the torment," and he spoke of paying the Germans "violence for violence" and "avenging Belgian honor." With that threat in the air, de Selliers noted that "a neutral that defended itself did not put itself in a state of war." That he should have said so seems odd, but to a government concerned about losing its position and its independence, the comment made perfect sense. International law guaranteed that a neutral could repel invasion yet retain its status and rights, an issue that proved to be important later.[45]

Jules van den Heuvel had "two words to add to what has been said." Van den Heuvel was neither a politician, a soldier, nor a diplomat, but as Belgium's most respected international lawyer, he carried weight. He said that Belgium must maintain legality before all the guarantors, which meant making an effort at self-defense. How far Belgium had to go to satisfy the law was no easy question, and he asked whether sacrificing the army was necessary. But he said, "We cannot content ourselves with protest," and "to retreat would violate our neutrality."

Woeste, perhaps sensing that he was under attack, said, "I am not saying that [we should retreat]. We must protest."

But van den Heuvel nailed down the point. "The army must defend not only our rights but those of the guarantor states."

Helleputte's notes end there, and the deliberations probably did soon after, for three men were chosen to draft a reply to Germany in the remaining hours. Significantly, they were Minister of Justice Henry Carton de Wiart and the two others who had spoken most cogently about the legal issues, van den Heuvel and Hymans.

The document reflected their views.[46] The German attack was "a flagrant violation of international law" that "no strategic interest" could justify. If the Belgians acquiesced, they would "sacrifice the honour of the nation" and "betray their duty towards Europe." Having participated "for more than eighty years in the civilisation of the world," they "refused to believe" that Belgium had to forgo neutrality to remain independent. But if Germany persisted, the Belgian government would "repel, by all the means in their power, every attack upon their rights."

After the meetings, de Broqueville stayed up working in his office. His secretary, Louis de Lichtervelde, wrote later that the cabinet leader looked pale from fatigue, and that the distress he had been trying not to show left him short of breath.[47] A Flanders newspaper had once derided the sleek de Broqueville as a "beautiful fashion plate" and a "pretty prime minister," teasing him for plumage that stood out among the somber crows in the halls of Belgian government.[48] But he had gone on to do what no one else had done, guide an army reform bill through Parliament in 1913.

Now, he asked de Lichtervelde to help him pack documents for safekeeping, some to go to Antwerp in case the Germans captured Brussels. When the two men pulled files relating to the 1913 army law from an armoire, tears formed in de Broqueville's eyes. "Tell me that I worked so hard and that I come too late!" he exclaimed.[49]

Come morning, a noise rose from the streets. A diplomat who had also worked all night said, "It was like an extraordinary murmur, swelling gradually as it passed along," a sound that came from newspaper hawkers calling out headlines, "the exclamations of surprise and anger" from passersby, the terrible news passed from mouth to mouth.[50] The street fronting the Foreign Ministry quickly filled, and everywhere crowds hurrahed the tricolor and cursed Germany.[51]

On 3 August, Albert received an answer from his cousin. "If I have felt myself compelled to make so grave a demand," the kaiser cabled, "it was with the most friendly intentions towards Belgium. . . . [T]he possibility of maintaining our former and present relations still lies in the hands of Your Majesty." Albert reportedly said, "What does he take me for?" and scribbled a reply on the back.[52] Nothing would have led Albert to suspect that Belgium "would be cruelly forced to choose, before all Europe, between war and the loss of honor, between the respect for treaties and failing to recognize our international duties."

The question of the hour was where Britain stood. The obligation to France under the Triple Entente divided government and country, but Belgium was another matter, about which Foreign Secretary Sir Edward Grey spoke to the House of Commons that afternoon. If Germany violated Belgium, Grey said, Britain must fight. He stressed the "honour and interest" in sustaining the treaty and raised the menace of one power dominating the Continent. If Britain stayed neutral while Germany conquered, Grey said, Britain would "sacrifice our respect and good name and reputation before the world, and should not escape the most serious and grave economic consequences." When he finished, the House applauded long and warmly.[53]

The next morning, 4 August, at six o'clock, Below-Saleske presented a declaration of war. At eight, as German patrols were crossing the Belgian border, the Belgian minister in Berlin, Napoléon Eugène Beyens, called Foreign Secretary Gottlieb von Jagow. Jagow readily agreed to meet at that early hour, but, according to Beyens, seemed surprised that the Belgian came to protest and ask for his passport. To that, Jagow replied, "But I don't want to break off my relations with you that way. We will perhaps have more to talk about." Beyens thought Jagow looked disappointed.[54]

In Brussels, *Le Soir* promised that BELGIUM WILL DEFEND ITSELF TO THE UTMOST. "Right is on our side," the paper said, "and the guarantors of our neutrality will help us make it triumph."[55] Feelings ran high as a huge, excited crowd waited by the palace for the royal family: The king was to address Parliament before he went to lead the army. With keen anticipation, people yelled, ran about, shook hands with perfect strangers, and chanted patriotic slogans.[56] The only troops left to keep order were the Garde Civique, composed of little-trained volunteers not liable for military service, and they too could not contain their enthusiasm. They shouted, "Long live the king!" or "Long live Belgium!" and raised their hats, tall bowlers with feathers stuck in the band, atop their rifles.[57]

In Parliament, Albert spoke wearing a lieutenant-general's uniform, with boots, spurs, sabre, and white gloves. The queen and their children sat behind him, on golden chairs. Quoting the revolutionaries of 1830, Albert asked: "'Are you unshakably determined to maintain intact the sacred patrimony of our forefathers?'" And the deputies sprang up, hands raised as if to swear an oath, and shouted: "Yes! Yes! Yes!" Then the king uttered words that would be famous: "A people that defends its existence cannot die."[58]

After the king left, the crowd outside called for de Broqueville. He came out to the balcony and said, "From the bottom of my Belgian heart, I cry: This is an abominable murder attempt that cannot be carried out with impunity. . . . There is one thing to which we will never submit, and that is domination." And when he shouted, "Long live the king! Long live Belgium!" the crowd replied, "Down with the Germans! Down with the murderers!" Some men cried, "To arms!" and went off, in procession, to enlist.[59]

That afternoon, as German diplomats prepared to close their Brussels legation, one exclaimed: "Oh, the poor fools! Why don't they get out of the way of the steam roller? We don't want to hurt them, but if they stand in our way, they will be ground into the dirt. Oh, the poor fools!"[60]

Meanwhile, in Berlin, Chancellor Theobald von Bethmann Hollweg was telling the Reichstag that German troops had occupied the Grand Duchy "and perhaps have already entered Belgian territory." The chancellor, a tall, awkward, schoolmasterish man who often used words nobody understood, expressed himself clearly that day. "The wrong—I speak openly—the wrong we are thereby committing we will try to make good as soon as our military aims have been attained," he said. However, necessity knew no law, and "he who is menaced, as we are, and is fighting for his all can only consider how he is to hack his way through."[61] That night, pleading with his friend the British ambassador, he likened the Treaty of 1839 to a "scrap of paper," a phrase that would haunt its author to the grave.[62]

But on the afternoon of 4 August, Brussels knew nothing of this. Brand Whitlock, the American minister, was trying to keep his patience while a rich American expatriate was pestering him, mostly with her own troubles but also with horrifying rumors. Though the war had begun only that morning, she professed to know that German "barbarians" were killing women and children on sight in eastern Belgium. "That is buncombe," Whitlock replied. "You know they are not savages."[63]

HIS MAJESTY ALBERT I, KING OF THE BELGIANS,

King Albert had German blood in his veins but no illusions about the danger of a German invasion. Under Belgian law, the king commanded the army, but only during wartime, which turned planning for war into a political tussle between crown and cabinet. Hoover Institution Archives

2

Marching Through Hell

DURING THE INVASION'S FIRST HOURS, German cavalry crossed the frontier near Aachen and headed west, seeking to secure the Meuse bridges north of Liège. Around noon, they reached Visé, a town of twenty-two hundred on the right bank, only to find that Belgian troops had blown up the bridge and were shooting from the opposite shore. Belgian witnesses said that the resistance angered the Germans, who accused the townsfolk of having participated, a violation of the laws of war.[1] Shouting, *"Man hat geschossen!"* ("Someone has shot!"), the soldiers burned houses, fired into windows, and shot or bayoneted a dozen passersby, killing seven. They broke down doors, smashed armoires, and tore apart fireplaces or any nook or cranny where they suspected snipers or weapons might be hidden.

By late afternoon, the killing and destruction in Visé had ended, but Belgian statements assert that the tension remained. The curé said that on the square fronting his church, he asked a group of tired Germans why they did not quench their thirst at a nearby pump. "That water is poisoned," they replied. "That's town water and supplies everybody," the curé answered, but when they did not believe him, he drank first to calm their fears.

The action at Visé does not appear in official German testimony, but the British and American presses reported the German Army's account, through Dutch sources.[2] "Civilians caught by the Germans firing on them were executed," went one typical bulletin. Another said that "several women took part in the resistance," and a Berlin paper later alleged that a sixteen-year-old girl had been shot for mutilating German corpses.

What happened at Visé merits mention chiefly because it came so soon after German troops crossed the frontier. But many such confrontations occurred, especially during August, though they lasted sporadically into late October. By 8 August alone, the fifth day of war, ten or more civilians had been killed in each of twenty-one incidents. Total casualties for the five days reached 850 deaths, and thirteen hundred buildings had been deliberately destroyed.[3]

These events marked the start of what the Germans named "the Belgian people's war," what Belgian sympathizers labeled "the rape of Belgium," or what skeptics simply called war, terrible but familiar. The controversy over whether the Belgians had ambushed the Germans or the Germans had massacred the Belgians profoundly shaped feelings about the war. For many, Belgium defined a struggle between justice and lawlessness, civilization and barbarity. To a world that could not even have imagined death camps, bombed-out cities, or ethnic cleansing—or, in August 1914, the trench warfare that would soon bleed Europe—Belgium was a terrible shock. What had happened there challenged the axiom that cultured Europeans did not behave like savages.

Consequently, the question of what had actually taken place assumed great importance, as did the related issues of who had broken what laws, and for what motives. Did justice lie with both sides, one side, or neither? Were the treaty violation and the invasion violence cut from the same cloth, and, if so, who was responsible? Had the Germans plotted to destroy Belgium, or had the Belgians conspired to entrap Germany?

Six miles west from the German border and nine miles east from Liège lay Herve, a town of about forty-seven hundred. There, on 6 August, said a German soldier, he came upon Belgian troops holding three German hussars prisoner, while a fourth hung dead from a tree, his ears and nose cut off. The witness and his comrades disarmed the Belgians and took them prisoner. "We were all convinced that this had been done by villagers," he said. Another soldier concurred, adding that when he passed through Herve again, "we were fired at from cellar gratings and windows." Ordered to disarm the villagers and take them prisoner, "we forced our way into the houses and carried out the order." When the firing did not stop, "six guilty Belgian peasants were shot by order of an officer." A third witness swore that west of Herve, while the firing was going on, he noticed that "girls of eight or ten years of age, armed with sharp instruments, were busying themselves with the German wounded." He found out later, he said, that the girls had cut the soldiers' earlobes off.[4]

Of Herve, Belgian civilians said that during the late afternoon of 4 August, a car full of German officers entered the town and hailed two men. Reports disagreed over whether the officers shot them when they tried to run or before they had the chance, and whether the troops that subsequently occupied Herve began pillaging right away or the following day.[5] But in any case, the Germans allegedly executed twenty-two civilians on 6 August and more the next day, started looting, and burned Herve on the eighth. The fires lasted three days, left thick, black smoke in a red-tinged sky, and made more than a thousand people homeless.[6] Thirty-eight died from German bullets altogether.

Meanwhile, angry Belgians in several cities had been beating up resident Germans and smashing windows of houses and businesses thought to be German property. Hugh Gibson, secretary at the U.S. legation in Brussels, noticed that a restaurateur named Fritz had posted a large blackboard that read, "Fritz Is Luxembourgeois But His Establishment Is Belgian."[7] Gibson, sensing the mood, expected that "incidents may happen at any moment that will entail grave consequences."

Two days later, Gibson barely prevented such an incident. With the exit of German diplomats, the legation had agreed to represent German interests, and hundreds of Germans squeezed into its offices to ask advice. Drawn by the commotion, a mob of Belgians had gathered to shout insults. Gibson happened to look out the window just as one German, "a poor little worm of a man," was leaving, and when "he reach[ed] toward his pocket as though for a revolver," the crowd attacked. Gibson and the legation lawyer, a Belgian, rushed out and managed to "pull him back into the Legation before they did away with him," but "we nearly had our clothes torn off in the bargain." The crowd beat on the door, the Garde Civique was called, and only then did order return.[8]

When the Belgian government decided to expel resident Germans, the Garde Civique was again deployed to protect them. But in Brussels, the departure went smoothly. Gibson wrote that the Germans endured no worse than hooting, and he overheard the Garde Civique pitying them. "But it's unfortunate, all the same," they said. "Look at these poor people; it's not their fault there's fighting."[9] At Antwerp, the expulsion was more abrupt, but the American consul there said that though the German women and children had suffered "cruel hardships," no one had caused them bodily harm.[10]

Back in the war zone, innocent Belgians were being uprooted too. A Dutch correspondent said that Visé's story was written in the faces of hundreds of men, women, and children fleeing the town. They "had taken off their shoes and boots, on account of the scorching heat. . . . The aged were supported, the babies carried."[11] Most of the refugees bore parcels on their backs or under their arms, "seemed tired to death, had dark red faces, and betrayed great fear and nervousness." At his approach, the column stopped, and the women and girls crept behind the men, who doffed their caps. Their actions puzzled him until he realized that they had taken him for a German officer, perhaps because of his Norfolk jacket, leggings, knapsack, and water bottle. And when a car carrying German officers sped past, the people dropped to their knees and put their hands up.

What these Belgian refugees and thousands of others had left behind may be imagined from a description by Walter Bloem, a reserve captain in a Brandenburg regiment. Battice, a village that neighbored Herve and had burned the same day, was "completely gutted," Bloem wrote, with nothing left of houses but empty window frames, through which he saw "roasted remnants of iron bedsteads and furnishings."[12] Broken household utensils scattered the streets, dogs and cats scavenged in the ruins, and "in the market square stood the roofless, spireless church." Later, Bloem's company came to a village still ablaze, where passing through "was like marching through Hell. The scorching glow almost stifled us." Cattle bellowed in a barn; chickens with singed feathers rushed crazily about. Two peasants lay dead by a wall; Bloem was told they were *francs-tireurs,* or civilian snipers, found with rifles in hand. "A suitable revenge and a just punishment," he said.[13]

Liège fell on 7 August when a staff liaison officer assigned to the invasion spearhead, General Erich Ludendorff, banged on the citadel gates to demand surrender, a gesture that made his reputation. Berlin rejoiced, misreading the dispatch and thinking that the forts ringing Liège had also yielded, when they had not. Nevertheless, the government used the triumph as an excuse to prod the Belgians to negotiate. Through neutral channels, Berlin sent a message regretting that the Belgians should have wanted war, though granting that their army had "upheld the honour of its arms by its heroic resistance to a very superior force."[14] But "to spare Belgium the further horrors of war," Germany was ready "for any compact with Belgium which can be reconciled with their arrangement with France." (Those horrors now included a tactic that had once belonged to science fiction, for on 6 August, a zeppelin had bombed Liège, the first aerial attack in history.) In return, Germany promised to "evacuate Belgium as soon as the state of war will allow her to do so."

The Belgian government rejected the offer, and the public mood was defiant, not least because of reports about Herve, Battice, and Visé. When *Le Soir* spoke of the "vile savages" who had throughly shot up and destroyed Visé, the paper added an exclamation point, which revealed that such cruelties were new enough to shock.[15] The Brussels press also waxed eloquent about two Belgian soldiers who had supposedly killed seventeen cavalrymen[16] and about the twenty thousand dead the Germans had lost before Liège[17] (more than four times the real figure).[18]

The Bruxellois, entertaining the martial spirit, greeted one another with "The forts still hold!" echoing the headlines, and *"Les Uhlans se rendent pour une tartine"* (Uhlans [cavalrymen] surrender for a slice of bread and butter).[19] A victory announcement brought French and Belgian flags to café terraces, where patrons sang "La Brabançonne" and "La Marseillaise." But when Red Cross cars brought in a hundred wounded men from Liège, they received a "discreet ovation."[20]

On 12 August, the German Army deployed siege guns at Liège so large that each needed thirty-six horses to drag it, in two parts, through the streets, which trembled under the weight. The shells measured 420 mm, and on impact they threw debris a thousand feet in the air.[21] The Germans turned these monsters on the forts, bludgeoning them one by one, so that by 16 August, the Meuse Valley lay open, and the invaders poured through by the tens of thousands. They marched under a constant sun, and wherever they stopped, the odor of unwashed men permeated the village.[22] A popular expression said the fields turned gray, from the uniforms, and the soldiers raised huge clouds of dust, the clumping din of hobnailed boots being audible for miles.[23]

Richard Harding Davis, who marched with them one day—an escapade that nearly cost him his life when his hosts accused him of spying—marveled at the speed.[24] For five hours, they kept up a steady trot, on roads paved with rough-hewn granite blocks. "The men did not bend the knees," the American journalist wrote, "but, keeping the legs straight, shot them forward with a quick, sliding movement, like men skating or skiing. The toe of one foot seemed always tripping on the heel of the other." Many men fell out, only to be flung back into the ranks, where they marched on, "partly comatose." Whenever the column halted, soldiers dropped as if clubbed, tumbling asleep onto road, grass, or fields.

As the soldiers advanced, Berlin warned Brussels that the civilized world would judge Belgium for its brutalities, and that the German Army would take stern measures to protect itself "against the unloosing of popular passions."[25] These reportedly rose once more at Visé, where firing broke out on the night of 15 August; the Germans retaliated by burning six hundred homes. Paul Oskar Höcker, a captain who commanded a reserve company, rode through Visé three hours after the fires started and said the place had a "terrible beauty," with charred ruins and roofs cracking in bundles of flame. The noise scared the horses, embers burned the soldiers' cheeks, eyes watered from smoke, and the air was scarcely bearable.[26]

The Belgians claimed that Visé burned because drunken soldiers had fired and begun shooting one another before they recognized their error. When they did, they shouted, *"Man hat geschossen!"* and turned their weapons on the populace, killing sixteen civilians. For two days, the Belgians said, the soldiers pillaged Visé street by street, loading the loot onto trucks bound for Germany, and set fires, which they helped along with naphtha pumps and disks made of incendiary material. Afterward, they rounded up 631 "suspected francs-tireurs," including women and children, and sent them to Germany as prisoners of war.[27]

The Belgian Army was battered and reeling. Forced to give up his defensive position in eastern Brabant, Albert ordered a retreat to Antwerp on 18 August, which the army handled with skill, gaining time to regroup.[28] The withdrawal was particularly serious, given the Allied positions at the time. The British Expeditionary Force, mobilized on 4 August, had taken two weeks to cross the Channel and would not be ready to begin operations until 20 August. Only on that date did French headquarters decide to move its northernmost armies into southern Hainaut, Namur, and Luxembourg, beginning to realize the danger to the French left, but even then, few troops faced the main thrust of the invasion. Albert's retreat did make the Germans divert four divisions to cover Antwerp, but the Belgian withdrawal left Brussels open, and the government fled to Antwerp. Davis, now back in Brussels, wrote that the Bruxellois seemed unperturbed, as if two weeks of glory had gone to their heads. When they heard rumors that the Germans had shelled and occupied Louvain, Albert's recently abandoned headquarters, they said that the Germans would not bombard an unfortified town and were still at Liège anyway.[29]

The next morning, Brussels awoke to cars streaming in from the provinces, the traffic making a noise "like the steady roar of a gale in the rigging, and it spoke in abject panic." Some refugees came on carriages with servants, who still wore their livery of striped waistcoats and silver buttons. The less-well-off arrived on bicycles, with bundles strapped to their shoulders, or on foot, carrying their children. The peasants, "old men in blue smocks, white-haired and bent, old women in caps, the daughters dressed in their one best frock and hat," rode high-wheeled carts drawn by large draft horses. Those who could not find room to ride, wrote Gibson, walked alongside, carrying whatever the carts would not hold. "It was the most depressing sight so far." Many were crying, and "all looked sad and broken. . . . Their crops are rotting in the ground and many of their houses are already in ruins. . . . Even the wounded and the dead are not so pitiful."[30]

By ten the next morning, the streets were empty and the houses closely shuttered, "as though the plague stalked," Davis said. When the Germans marched in, he watched for two hours, got bored, and went back to his hotel, only to return. "The thing fascinated you, against your will. . . . No longer was it regiments of men marching, but something uncanny, inhuman, a force of nature like a landslide, a tidal wave, or lava sweeping down a mountain." He noticed "no halts, no open places, no stragglers," and "not a strap was out of place." The infantry sang, taking three steps between each line of song, and "the stamp of iron-shod boots" reminded Davis of "the blows of giant pile-drivers."[31]

Gibson remarked that nearly all the men were freshly shaven, their uniforms brushed, and that "they swaggered along," trying "to show that they were entirely at home and that they owned the place." The officers looked at the crowd "in their best supercilious manner," their men copying the pose, as if to say, "'Now do you realize what your little army went up against when it tried to block us?'" No foreign army had occupied Brussels since Napoleon's time, and no European capital had endured a victory march since 1870. Gibson wrote that "the humiliation has been something terrible," that the Belgians had a greater sense of municipal pride than anyone, "and I think it hurts them more than it could possibly hurt any other people."[32]

Within twenty-four hours, they learned another cost of being occupied. The army imposed a "war levy" on Brussels of 50 million francs ($10 million), payable in three days, and of 450 million francs more on Brabant. The capital extracted a promise that its sixteen communes would never pay to lodge troops. But Brussels was also to deliver almost a million francs' worth of food, and if the occupiers did not receive the supplies on time, the Bruxellois would be penalized twice the market value in cash.[33] That day, the German government began debating how much to take from Belgium as a "war contribution," and over the coming weeks, the Foreign Office worked up figures.[34]

The effort to obtain money followed a pattern. Shortly after the Germans entered Liège, they demanded the keys to the vault at the Banque Nationale. The director refused, so they locked his family, employees, and him in the bank, and after they released him, he found that they had forced his office safe and stolen almost six million francs. Similar raids occurred at eight other branches, where the threat of personal violence usually worked, though at Neufchâteau, the Germans said they would burn the town too if they did not get the cash.[35]

The ten days between 8 August and the army's withdrawal to Antwerp had seen only a few, isolated outbreaks of violence, the most remarkable of which had been the second episode at Visé.[36] But the retreat seemed to presage a rash of reprisals, including several large-scale executions. The first mass killing happened at Aerschot, an eastern Brabant town of eight thousand, near where the Belgian rearguard had fought. The next evening, 19 August, the Germans accused the burgomaster's fifteen-year-old-son of murdering their commander as part of a franc-tireur uprising. As punishment, they burned almost four hundred buildings; shot 156 civilians, including the burgomaster and his son; and expelled another thousand toward Louvain.[37]

The next three mass executions all happened in Namur province. On 20 August at Andenne and Seilles, towns that straddled the Meuse east of Namur city, the Germans again charged an uprising, for which they executed 262 with firearms and axes and burned more than 200 buildings. The civilian burial party had to collect limbs and entrails.[38] Two days later, at Tamines, west of Namur city toward Charleroi, the toll was 384 dead and 240 buildings.[39] On 23 August came the turn of Dinant, a picturesque riverine town in southern Namur. There, German soldiers accused the townsfolk of having fought alongside French troops and retaliated by killing 674 people, deporting an unknown number, and destroying 1,100 buildings.[40] Dinant witnessed the invasion's bloodiest scene, but not the most infamous, not the one cited as Exhibit A, either of rape or a "people's war." That dubious, tragic distinction belonged to a different place.

Sixteen miles east of Brussels lay Louvain, a Brabantine city of forty thousand founded in the eleventh century and known for its Gothic architecture. The inhabitants earned their livings brewing beer, making lace, manufacturing church ornaments, and teaching at the Catholic University, which dated from 1425. A "clean, sleepy, and pretty" town, said Davis, Louvain offered the visitor "narrow twisting streets and smart shops and cafés," a splendid Gothic hôtel de ville, or town hall, and the fifteenth-century church of St. Pierre.[41] The university, Belgium's most influential, had educated many of the country's political and intellectual leaders. Its library, the Halles de l'Université, was three centuries old and held about 230,000 volumes, including 800 ancient manuscripts and books. A center of Catholic learning, Louvain was also renowned for classical literature, law, and science, and its professors edited thirty periodicals, mostly in these fields.

German troops entered Louvain on 19 August, hours after the local contingent of Garde Civique had disbanded and shipped its weapons to Antwerp. The rumors of bombardment were false, and for almost a week, German columns passed through Louvain without disturbance. As a precaution, garrison forces took prominent people hostage, posted notices threatening harsh penalties for any hostile act—in case Aerschot had not sent the message—and searched for arms but found none.[42] A Dutch visitor said that on 21 August, he saw soldiers come running when they heard drums, thinking they heralded an execution, but went away, disappointed, when they found it was only a proclamation being read.[43] A senior officer remarked on the city's "quietude and peace."[44]

On 25 August, four Belgian divisions dashed out of Antwerp and attacked south of Malines between Brussels and Louvain, a diversion to aid the French and British making a stand at the Sambre River and the Mons Canal. The sortie kept the Germans occupied until word came on 26 August that the British had retreated from Mons, whereupon the Belgians withdrew to Antwerp.[45] Their action would have furnished only a footnote to a celebrated battle, save that on the evening of 25 August, they advanced within six miles of Louvain.

That night, the garrison sent a detachment to bolster the German lines, and when this unit returned to Louvain, firing began near the train station, on the edge of town. The Belgians maintained that the shooting came first from nervous sentries, perhaps men from a Landsturm battalion, a third-line unit of reservists, who formed a large part of the garrison. But the sentries were not the only ones; soldiers inside Louvain shot wildly in reply, spraying the streets with lead. Bullets flew most thickly in the fashionable quarter, the half mile between the train station and the Grand'Place, where the hôtel de ville and the church of St. Pierre stood.[46] Less than ten days before, Davis had admired the neighborhood's gracious, red-roofed houses and their flower gardens, where pear trees spread their laden branches like candelabra.[47] Now, said the Belgians, soldiers fired from windows, killing or wounding one another and provoking a furious counterfire.

Machine guns accented the fusillade with their dreadful tac-tac-tac. Clarions and whistles sounded, and riderless horses dashed through the narrow streets. Other horses, hitched to caissons, dragged them madly about until they hit an obstacle, or a bullet hit the horses themselves. Soldiers broke down doors, hauled people out, and either shot them or sent them to the train station, where a firing squad or detention awaited. Sometimes the civilians endured mock executions before the real sentence was carried out. Priests were particular targets, and two had lighted cigars applied to their faces before being shot.

Wherever the Germans suspected francs-tireurs, they burned the houses, launching incendiary fuses onto rooftops from devices that looked like broom handles, or tossing firebombs the size of soccer balls through windows. To speed the flames, sometimes the soldiers first soaked the curtains with naphtha and broke up furniture for kindling. So rapidly did the fires spread that weeks later, burial parties found charred remains of entire families in cellars, where people had sought refuge when the shooting started. Within an hour of the first shots, smoke and flame rose above Louvain. The fire ascended in thick columns, and a whirlwind of sparks marked the sky, which glowed red in every direction. Walls were heard to crumble and windows blow out. Tremendous cracking noises echoed like explosions.

One Belgian testified later that he opened his door to two soldiers who rushed upstairs despite his insistence that no one was there. He heard firing from upstairs, and the two came back down. As they passed him on their way out, more soldiers came and accused him of shooting, saying that they had seen him fire. The first two soldiers said nothing, and the newcomers fired at him. But they missed, and he managed to hide from further danger.[48]

Another man was less lucky. He said that when the barrage began, he tried to carry his wife, who had given birth to their second child two days before, to safety. But when the firing grew particularly intense, he paused on the stairs, and while they waited, bullets struck them both. He sensed that he was wounded only slightly, but he felt warm liquid drench him, and when he lit a match, he saw that his wife's skull was smashed and her throat mangled. He left her and exited through the roof. When he returned a few hours later for the children, he found the newborn safe in his crib and his four-year-old daughter crouching, terrified, by her mother's body, soaked in her blood. The soldiers took the man away and deported him to Cologne.[49]

Meanwhile, at the hôtel de ville, a general was haranguing Emile Schmit, a lawyer and city official.[50] Max von Boehn commanded the Ninth Reserve Corps, to which the garrison belonged, and he had just been driven into the city and was livid at having been fired on. Unless Schmit could stop his fellow citizens from fighting, Boehn said, the other hostages and he would be hanged, the city razed, and a fine of twenty million francs imposed. Boehn left, and Major Walter von Manteuffel, the ranking officer, drafted a proclamation repeating the threat. Under heavy guard and with drums beating, Schmit, other hostages, and Manteuffel walked where the fusillade had done its worst, stopping every hundred feet to have the warning read in French and Flemish. Burning debris, corpses, and equipment littered the cobblestones, but not a shot rang out during the half-hour march.

Schmit saw soldiers shaking their fists in priests' faces until Manteuffel intervened, but the major did not reprimand a Landsturm surgeon who pointed to a dead comrade and exhorted his unit to vengeance. The man's life, the surgeon shouted, "was worth more than that of all the inhabitants of this city, more than the whole city itself."

Back at the hôtel de ville, Schmit saw the sky filled with fire-rimmed bits of paper. The wind blew a few inside his office, and he realized from what had been printed on them that they came from antique manuscripts. The Halles de l'Université, the famous library, was no more.

When Manteuffel came to see him, Schmit pleaded that the troops had made a terrible mistake. They had found no weapons in Belgian hands, and Manteuffel had seen for himself that no civilians had fired. Manteuffel shook his head, saying that Boehn had given his orders, so Schmit suggested conducting autopsies on the dead soldiers to prove whose bullets had killed them. Manteuffel hesitated, then agreed. But an hour later he returned, saying that his men had "had to set fire to one of the most beautiful houses behind the church." They had found a cache of German cartridges there, which implied that Belgian francs-tireurs had used German ammunition.

"So autopsies would be useless?" Schmit asked.

"That's self-evident," Manteuffel replied.

And when Schmit pressed the point, suggesting that autopsies were a golden opportunity to show that Louvain was a nest of francs-tireurs, Manteuffel changed the subject.

For another three days, the Belgians said, the shooting recurred sporadically, but the burning never stopped. Soot hung in the air, and the heat was unbearable. The Germans destroyed more than a thousand homes in Louvain proper, one-seventh of the housing stock but one-quarter of the building surface area. Besides the Halles, a school of commercial sciences burned, as did a second library with two hundred thousand volumes, the Hall of Justice, a theater, and part of the church of St. Pierre.[51] The Germans had also disabled the city's water pump and torched the water company headquarters, but the destruction and the high demand had reduced the pressure so much that probably little would have been saved had the system been working.[52]

Soldiers broke into stores and houses to steal shoes, food, lingerie, and cigars. A few robbed a musical instruments store and emerged with mandolins and violins, which they played in the street.[53] In the outer districts, people hung white flags from windows, in vain—doors and windows were broken in, walls riddled with bullets.[54] Gibson, who visited on 28 August, wrote that entering the town, "we began to see ghastly sights—the poor civilians lying where they had been shot down as they ran—men and women, most of them old. All sorts of wreckage scattered over the street, hats and wooden shoes, German helmets, swords and saddles, bottles and all sorts of bundles which had been dropped and abandoned when the trouble began."[55] The soldiers Gibson met had hardly slept and "were nervous and unhappy and shook their heads with real feeling at the horrors through which they were passing." Some were drunk on looted wine.

An officer told him that every house was to be destroyed. "Not one stone is to be left on another," Gibson wrote. "The Hôtel de Ville was to be battered to pieces . . . and the rest of the town systematically burned."[56] Manteuffel had ordered the city evacuated prior to a bombardment because, as one rumor went, a Belgian barber had cut a German officer's throat. But the bombardment never came; those few civilians granted the right to remain spoke of hearing only two cannon reports, and no shells landing. Many heavy blasts followed, but they were explosions to blow open safes, thirty or forty of which were later found empty. After the blasts, officers directed horse-drawn wagons house to house to take furniture, clothes, bedding, and wine. When the soldiers had removed what they wanted, they piled up curtains, hangings, and furnishings and set fire to them, pillaging that continued well into September, despite Manteuffel's promises and his posted orders.[57]

The army's report on Louvain disputed virtually all of this. The Germans charged that the civilians had "remained in secret communication with Antwerp," knew of the Belgian attack toward Louvain, expected it to recapture the city with British help, and were thus prompted "to take part in the fighting."[58] That the garrison was undermanned further encouraged the civilians, who must have carefully planned an uprising "to annihilate the Germans during their retreat through the town" but had masked their intentions through a show of friendliness.[59]

The fighting could not have been spontaneous because it lasted for days, which "points to the fact that the authorities had a hand in the organisation" and that the populace "readily received" the "insurgents" and "offered hiding places" to them.[60] Three hundred rifles were said to have been found in a church, priests preached armed resistance, "and it is certain that some of them even took direct part in the fighting."[61] The francs-tireurs appeared to have employed machine guns, and they used explosives that some witnesses identified as grenades.[62]

Not only did the uprising persist after the proclamation, which showed the francs-tireurs' fanaticism, they disregarded the Red Cross banner by firing on hospitals and medical staff.[63] A few even cut up German wounded, and others poured hot tar on the troops.[64] But despite these provocations, the Germans observed the law and shot only those people whose guilt they had proven, who numbered more than a hundred at the train station alone.[65] The soldiers had had to use fire to defend themselves, and it was unfortunate that the flames spread, but "the magnificent town hall was saved through the efforts of our troops."[66]

In retrospect, the soldiers said, the symptoms of uprising had been obvious. Toward evening, before the attack, they had noticed the streets fuller than usual with "a very large number of young people," or, as one described them, "young, strong people."[67] The civilians conversed with one another before going inside suddenly, drawing curtains and shutters, which made one captain who observed them "uneasy."[68] His anxiety seemed justified when shortly after dark at 8:00 P.M., he and other soldiers saw a rocket, "a swarm of small bluish balls of light that descended on us without making any noise and were then extinguished." Several swore later that this rocket must have been "the sign for the inhabitants to begin firing at once," because "suddenly and unexpectedly we were terribly fired at from the surrounding houses, from windows, attics, and particularly from the roofs."[69]

From Boehn on down to Landsturm privates, the soldiers agreed that they faced "murderous fire"[70] that only civilians could have produced because, as one said, "to judge from the sound, the firing did not come from military rifles."[71] Luckily, the Belgians fired too high, or they would have done more damage. A few witnesses spoke of darkness, noise, and confusion obscuring everything, but many others testified that they saw the Belgians shoot from rooftops or through closed shutters, and a couple thought these structures had been altered for the purpose.[72] Francs-tireurs also fired from windows, visible by the lamplight in the rooms or because of muzzle flashes.[73]

A captain who said he witnessed a great deal from where he lay wounded under a baggage cart recounted that the soldiers burned houses with kerosene lamps, by igniting gas fixtures, or with liquid benzine on hand from supply columns. When the smoke got too strong, the francs-tireurs came out, often holding their weapons. "I clearly saw muskets, revolvers, military rifles, and other firearms. . . .

The francs-tireurs were to a man evil-looking figures such as I have never in my life seen before; they were shot by the German sentries standing below."[74]

Boehn stressed repeatedly that many were soldiers in disguise, as proven by the identification disks they carried. A German soldier who had acted as an interpreter during the questioning of suspected francs-tireurs confirmed this serious breach of the laws of war.[75] Boehn also noted that many of the guilty wore "disarranged work-men's clothes" and had "delicate hands" and "exceptionally fine and superior underclothes," which proved that they were not workmen at all. Moreover, none of the inhabitants recognized them.[76] Another soldier reported having heard of a hundred young men speaking various languages who had arrived in Louvain the day the attack began, and how an innkeeper had wanted nothing to do with these men, who looked like trouble.[77] Several witnesses said that Belgians had confessed to the uprising and had blamed the Garde Civique, priests, or soldiers in civilian garb.[78] The army concluded from the evidence that Belgian treachery ran deep.

Belgian reports said that Louvain's punishment included the deportation of 650 civilians to Germany, including women and children.[79] As the first trains left the station, witnesses remarked that two officers were writing postcards. Most of the deportees were gone a week, but some were imprisoned from one to five months. When the trains reached Germany, the Belgians were exhibited like beasts at every station. Many wore shabby work clothes, which onlookers apparently took as proof that they were brigands. Crowds screamed hate and insults, brandished canes and umbrellas, and tried to hit the Belgians, especially the priests. One deportee said later that so many Germans filled the stations that the deportations must have been announced. He also said that when the prisoners were fed in transit—their only meal in forty-eight hours—they were made to run between lines of officers, who beat them with their fists and the flat of their sabers.[80]

Gibson wrote that after Manteuffel gave his order to evacuate Louvain, a "great column of dull gray smoke" covered the city, and the road to Brussels was "black with frightened civilians carrying away small bundles."[81] Belgian sources said that soldiers beat any man wearing a religious habit, prompting some priests to abandon their soutanes and borrow workers' clothes.[82] But twenty-five priests were herded onto the Tervueren road toward Brussels, where, at one point, the Germans kept them in a fenced-in meadow and threatened to shoot them. One priest noticed, just in time, a soldier trying to plant a cartridge in his pocket.[83] However, a young Jesuit was found with a diary in which he had written that the Germans at Louvain were like the barbarians who had destroyed the library at Alexandria.[84] The soldiers let him confess for a half minute before they shot him and threw him into a shallow grave. "A dead dog would not have been treated so brutally," remarked a witness. The other priests were warned that in case of a shot, a false move, or any disturbance, the others would meet his fate. To assure the civilians' good behavior, the priests were made to lead the column and to preach peace and calm in every village.[85] It was a strange, terrible procession that reached Brussels, reminding one bystander of the French Revolution's persecutions. Carts and wagons jammed with priests, lay brothers, and Jesuits, including eminent theologians, trundled down the boulevard as soldiers walked alongside, shouting, "Swine! Swine!" The Bruxellois froze in mute horror, and the men removed their hats.[86]

Brand Whitlock and the Spanish minister interceded, and to placate these representatives of neutral powers, the Germans released the priests. Whitlock wrote later that Monsignor Jules de Becker, the rector of the American College in Louvain, visited the next morning to thank him. De Becker, a dignified man with silver hair, cut a striking figure in his black soutane and red sash. He had seen his father's and brother's homes burned, friends and colleagues murdered—it was he who later made the comment about the dead dog—and hundreds of hostages herded together at the railway station. The monsignor explained all this to Whitlock calmly, logically, from beginning to end. But when he tried to speak of the university, his voice stuck on the word *library*. "*La biblio*—," he stammered, and bowed his head and wept.[87]

3

The Ghost of 1870

AUGUST 1914 REAFFIRMED THE ADAGE that when nations prepare for the next war, they are haunted by the last one. Before a shot
was fired, before the ultimatum had been written, the Franco-Prussian
War of 1870–71 had beguiled Germans and Belgians alike. That war
had seen a lightning-quick triumph over the French Army, which the
Germans intended to repeat, and a civilian uprising afterward, which
they wanted to avoid at all costs. The Belgians remembered 1870 as a
war between neighbors who had respected Belgium, a miracle that
proved the transcendent power of law. Both conclusions derived from
false premises, and they explain why the ultimatum and invasion unfolded as they did.

Ever since 1870, German strategists had considered the possibility
that Germany's location would eventually involve the nation in a
two-front war. For twenty years they had assumed that they should
begin that war in a defensive posture, east and west, because 1870
was exceptional, and they could not expect lightning to strike again.[1]
But in 1891, Alfred von Schlieffen became chief of the General Staff,
and he believed that duplicating 1870 was both feasible and essential.[2]
Schlieffen said that war must be short or risk ruining the finely tuned
industrial economies that supported it; that victory came only through
the offensive; and that decisive victory resulted from destroying the
enemy's attacking power. When France and Russia signed a military
alliance in 1894, Germany's danger of a two-front war increased, but
Schlieffen took little notice of politics. He devised his strategy as if it
had been a theoretical problem of time, space, and movement, the solution to which would permit Germany to defeat France and Russia in
sequence.

The chief of staff lived up to the Prussian stereotype in that he
spoke little, wore a monocle, and spent his rare hours of relaxation

reading military history to his daughters. But he also believed in original sin and inherent human weakness, and he spared no one, even the kaiser, whom he derisively called "Willy" in the privacy of his own home.[3] Perhaps this was what led Schlieffen to search more than fourteen years for a technical answer to a puzzle that in the end hinged on unpredictable human frailties. Schlieffen knew railroads, which ran like clockwork when properly managed, and they had drawn his eyes westward.[4] In a memorandum he wrote shortly before his retirement in 1905, Schlieffen sketched out how the German Army could attack France through Belgium, which had Europe's densest rail system.

Violating the neutrality of Belgium, the Grand Duchy—and, in his original scheme, Holland—held political, legal, and moral implications, but these did not concern him. The violations were "necessary," and "as long as no other expedient can be found, one has to make the best of these difficulties." Schlieffen feared that "if we respect the neutrality of Luxembourg and Belgium . . . France will not show the same consideration but will immediately attack" Germany by the same route.[5]

His logic invoked the doctrine of necessity, which, in law, released a perpetrator from blame or granted the right to take an action that overrode conflicting rights or laws.[6] Jurists everywhere discussed necessity, but from 1870 onward, German writers had pushed the idea the furthest. They called urgent necessity *Kriegsraison*, differing from *Kriegsmanier*, the laws and customs of war, binding in ordinary circumstances. *Kriegsraison* allowed a government to disobey the law "if the accomplishment of the war-aim, or the escape from extreme danger, is hindered by sticking to it." Self-preservation mattered above all, and the state alone could judge whether the situation warranted the act.[7]

Kriegsraison was aggressive even by the loose standards of 1914. The Hague Conventions of 1899 and 1907 on land warfare, which Germany had signed, allowed necessity leeway but narrowed its use and forbade it as a right. Most military manuals followed suit, as with the 1914 American edition, in which necessity "justifies a resort to all the measures which are indispensable" yet "not forbidden by the modern laws and customs of war."[8] The eminent English expert John Westlake had argued that *Kriegsraison* stressed victory by any means, an outlook that jurists should not encourage, and that self-defense had its limits.[9]

You might kill in self-defense, Westlake said, but not someone other than your attacker so as to "throw on him, rather than bear yourself, the consequences of a fatality in which neither was at fault."[10]

By definition, *Kriegsraison* involved caprice. War is extraordinary, and any belligerent might decide that its needs were urgent, in which case the law vanished. Nothing prevented applying *Kriegsraison* to gain a perceived tactical advantage. Reserving that right created volatile prospects in a state like Germany, where the military lay beyond civilian control. Bethmann, the highest-ranking civil official, did not know when he addressed the Reichstag on 4 August that German troops had entered Belgium that morning. He could not have quashed the ultimatum had he tried, and he did not, having accepted Moltke's reasoning about the invasion and the generals' power to infringe on policymaking.[11] His assertion that necessity knew no law—at which many Reichstag deputies shouted approval—suggested that the doctrine did not appeal only to soldiers.[12]

By contrast, French President Raymond Poincaré had told his generals in 1911 that France could not invade Belgium, and he overruled their objections. He was trying to placate the British, who had insisted that France must not violate Belgium before Germany did, and he warned the Belgians that they could keep France out altogether only by making the German Army respect their territory.[13] Nevertheless, necessity did not rule unchallenged, and a politician had kept the generals in line.

Kriegsraison's urgency paralleled the feeling in Germany that enemies had plotted to "encircle" and destroy it. Many foreigners treated these suspicions as fantasy, but what outsiders said did not matter. (Ironically, King Albert was one foreigner who thought the Germans had a good case.)[14] This mind-set viewed attack as the means to break the stranglehold, and if the route went through Belgium, so be it; as Bethmann said, the Germans only had to consider how to hack their way through. To a desperate Germany, the resistance of the people being hacked might appear evil or unfair, as if opposition could have no motive besides thwarting Germany. Schlieffen described Belgium this way in a memorandum he wrote from retirement in 1912: "This country is regarded as neutral, but in fact it is not. More than thirty years ago [Belgium] made Liège and Namur into strong fortresses to prevent Germany from invading its territory, but towards France it has left its frontiers open."[15]

However, his plan (which his successors refined but left unchanged in essence) worsened the problem he was trying to solve. He calculated that the huge Russian Army would need six weeks to take the field, the amount of time that had sufficed in 1870 to smash the French. To exploit that interval, he foresaw deploying the bulk of German forces westward, beating France, and shifting them to meet the Russians. But even if France fell on schedule, the Russians would advance toward Germany's lightly defended eastern border. How far they got would depend on whether Germany's Austrian ally could distract them, and in 1914, the Austro-Hungarian Army, of unsure reliability, also had Serbia to deal with. Therefore, the longer Germany took to defeat France, the more time that gave Russia to barge through the back door, which posed great military and psychological risks.

Then there were the political objections that Schlieffen and his successors called irrelevant. The Germans talked as if only the Treaty of 1839 protected Belgium, but they overlooked the law of neutrality. Since the late eighteenth century, the community of nations had accepted that a neutral, in return for the right to remain at peace, must do nothing to aid any belligerent and must require all to respect its borders.[16] As a standard English text commented in 1909, allowing "passage for the sole and obvious purpose of attack is clearly forbidden."[17] Moreover, a neutral that failed to take reasonable measures to prevent violations became "an active offender" liable for damages if the injured party demanded them.[18] This provision was what Hymans seems to have spoken of during the Crown Council when he warned what France would do if Belgium accepted the ultimatum.

The Fifth Hague Convention of 1907, which laid down the rights and duties of neutrals, followed the tradition in sum. Neutral territory was inviolable, whereas neutrals must forbid crossings and were absolved from committing a hostile act if they repelled an attack—another issue that emerged at the Crown Council. Nowhere did the Fifth Convention say that either a neutral or a belligerent might invoke necessity.[19] That was suggestive, but the German military manual current in 1914, *Usages of War on Land* (1902), went further. A belligerent must refrain from attacking a neutral "even if the necessity of war should make such an attack desirable." But if a neutral did not stop one belligerent from marching through, that belligerent's opponent was free to do battle on neutral territory, and a neutral that disregarded its duties had to "give satisfaction or compensation."[20]

Even by the Germans' own lights, therefore, to demand an open road through Belgium was illegal and unreasonable. The ultimatum expected the Belgians to breach their neutrality for Germany's benefit, in return for "more enduring" ties. The note did not say what they were, but to have accepted the offer would have meant putting Belgium at Germany's mercy while offending Britain and France. No matter which side won the war, Belgium could lose its independence if the victor imposed annexations or political or economic controls.

Curiously, the note appears to allude to the law of neutrality with the claim of "reliable information" regarding a French attack via the Meuse, as if the Belgian failure to repel the incursion would justify a preemptive strike. But no "reliable information" existed; thanks to Poincaré's intervention in 1911, the French General Staff was preparing to attack Alsace. Even had the French had been aiming for the Meuse, only superb intelligence could have discovered this, because the ultimatum was written on 29 July, before France had mobilized. Had the Germans truly known that the Meuse was in peril, they could have openly alerted the other guarantors and Belgium, embarrassing the French. That the Germans were dredging up a pretext was even clearer from the ultimatum's previous drafts, which had offered Belgium territory at French expense, wording that Below-Saleske had deleted on Berlin's orders.[21]

The note infused cynicism with insults. National honor was a powerful concept in 1914, but even without that, the Germans presumed that the Belgians could be bought for German friendship, money, or French territory. Closer reflection would have revealed that the Belgians had always thought that theirs was the country menaced on two sides. But the ultimatum's authors apparently saw no absurdity in arguing that to defend itself, Germany must attack Belgium.

The Germans failed to anticipate how the Belgians—and most foreigners—would view this reasoning, but lack of insight alone does not explain why Germany violated Belgium. Among the many, complex motives must be contempt. Perhaps no one had stated the feeling more bluntly than Friedrich von Bernhardi in *Germany and the Next War* (1912), a saber-rattling tract that Allied propagandists later dissected with enthusiasm. He argued that weak nations did not have the same license to live as powerful ones, each nation had its own concept of right, and none would submit to international law, a subservience he equated with dishonor. "There never have been, and never will be universal rights of men," he wrote. Following that logic, he ridiculed Belgian neutrality, "contrary to the essential nature of the State."[22]

Arguments still rage over how much authority Bernhardi's ideas exerted outside German nationalist circles. He was respected enough to be considered a candidate to succeed Schlieffen, and his book went through six printings by 1914, embarrassing less truculent Germans, who were quick to say that all countries had their raving militarists.[23] This was true, but the question of whether Bernhardi started the First World War has obscured the currents beneath his argument. His disdain for Belgium cannot be dismissed as one man's prejudice because others expressed the same or related ideas, both concerning the ultimatum and subsequent German policies in Belgium.

Bethmann's remark about a "scrap of paper" was one example, though again, the debate over this phrase has focused on its effect, not its content. The effect was immediately noticeable, especially in Britain, which, unlike any other belligerent in 1914, faced no threat of invasion and fielded a volunteer army. "Scrap of paper" justified the war in three, plain words, and a few British recruiting posters used them as a headline, below which appeared a replica of the treaty, including signatures.[24] Few people had studied the law, but "scrap of paper" made the violation concrete and provided a reason to enlist.

In his memoirs, Bethmann wrote that by repeating "scrap of paper," the British ambassador had divulged a phrase from a private conversation and taken it out of context.[25] But even if so, the chancellor had used the expression to plead that nothing so trifling as a treaty could bring Britain and Germany to blows in a world war. The argument overlooked that no matter what Britain did, Belgium was the injured party and the invasion was still a crime, and Bethmann's incredulity that Britain could hold Germany responsible underlined the point. Further, to say that only great powers mattered and that small ones did not possess the same right to exist was to restate Bernhardi.

Not that the Germans sent the ultimatum because they scorned the Belgians. Rather, the Germans could have sent the note—particularly *that* note—only to people they disdained, and they could have expected compliance only from a society they pictured as different from their own. The Germans themselves would never have tolerated the ultimatum, yet they supposed the Belgians would.

■

When France and Prussia fought in 1870, the Belgian Army mobilized, one hundred thousand strong, to guard the border. In September the Prussians won a crushing victory at Sedan, six miles from the frontier, but the only soldiers who crossed into Luxembourg province were Frenchmen fleeing for their lives. The war dragged on through winter 1871, as the French government urged civilians to rise, and almost fifty-eight thousand heeded the call as francs-tireurs.[26] Of what followed, a German officer wrote, "Atrocious attacks are avenged by atrocities which remind one of the Thirty Years War."[27] But Belgium's danger had lasted only six weeks and was improbable to begin with.

"The miracle of 1870" proved to many Belgians that France and the now-unified Germany would respect a combination of the treaty, the Belgian Army, and British guarantees, the latter reaffirmed in 1867.[28] For the Belgians to trust that the miracle would recur required faith and complacency, but above all, an inward focus. To most Belgians, foreign affairs mattered less than local politics. Following a tradition of self-government that dated from the Middle Ages, each of Belgium's 2,636 communes exercised broad powers over schools, public works, charity, factories, and even the militia.[29] Conscription was a curse, partly because of ideals of individual liberty, and as recently as 1909, a recruit could buy a replacement. A Belgian general said that this made Belgium the laughingstock of Europe.[30]

Consequently, in August 1914, Belgium fielded an army little larger than that of 1870, whereas French and German combat forces had quadrupled. That did not prevent a Brussels newspaper from declaring on mobilization day that neither neighbor would invade for fear of engaging the Belgian Army, reported at twice its size.[31] The remark underscored how far behind Belgium had fallen in military manpower. Had the Belgians begun in 1903 to conscript annually the same proportion of their population as Germany, 0.4 percent,[32] by 1914, they could have assembled a field army of 360,000—respectable, but less than half the invading force that the Germans threw against them. Whether that would have deterred an enemy committed to attacking in the West is an open question.

Moreover, to enlarge the army might have meant choosing between guns and prosperity. Starting in 1900, the economy grew a healthy 3 percent per year, and in 1913 produced 4.4 percent of the world's commerce, which placed Belgium sixth. Antwerp surpassed Rotterdam, Hamburg, and London to become the world's second-busiest port, behind New York. Belgium exported more per capita than Germany or the United States, chiefly coal, steel, machines, glass, and textiles. Industry employed more than 40 percent of the work force, compared with 25.5 percent in Germany. Many mines and mills used up-to-date machinery and processes, and in key fields, the work force received on-the-job training.[33]

But this growth depended on cheap labor. Wages averaged 30 percent less than in France, and 20 percent less than in most of Germany, whereas the Belgian workday was longer.[34] The number of Belgian men in their prime, ages twenty to thirty-four, was small, only about 900,000 by the 1910 census.[35] If the military conscripted 30,000 every year, the cost in lost productivity would likely be bearable. But to call up 360,000, plus 70,000 to garrison the forts, would cause strain, maybe enough so that the Germans would conclude—as Schlieffen did—that the Belgians could not afford to fight.

The issue, therefore, was one of sacrifice. When Hymans argued for de Broqueville's army bill in 1913, he charged that the word *homeland* never evoked anguish in Belgium as it did elsewhere, and that the concept echoed only to the sound of orchestras on feast days or in public merrymaking.[36] These were harsh words but probably no kinder than those German nationalists would have used. Comparing national experiences suggests where their contempt for Belgium may have come from. Germany had earned unification through war and will, whereas Belgium owed its life to diplomats who had cobbled it together. When Germans saw menace in Britain's navy, they taxed themselves to build battleships, whereas Belgians talked about an independence they refused to spend money on, let alone defend with their lives. Germany had become an industrial power on its own muscle, whereas Belgium had fattened off a peace it did nothing to keep. As a minor German diplomat said in July 1914, "Would you rather [instead of going to war] that we should sink to the level of Belgium?"[37]

How foreigners perceived that level had much to do with Albert's uncle and predecessor, Leopold II. A tall man with a limp that piqued his vanity and, later, a bald head and a Saint Nicholas beard, Leopold had envisioned Belgium as a colonial power, Brussels as a world capital, and the army as a powerful force. When the good burghers in Parliament rejected these ideas, he went as far as he could on his own. He obtained the Congo as his personal property, plundered it, and used the profits to remodel Brussels, amuse himself, and amass a fortune.

But when the international outcry over his methods in the Congo grew loud enough, in 1908 an embarrassed Parliament voted to buy the colony and make it Belgian. Leopold demanded and received a stiff price.

No German king would have had to rebuild his capital from his own pocket. No German king would have sold his country a colony or used the occasion to extract a ransom. According to a suspiciously secondhand but evocative anecdote, a German general said that if Leopold had been alive in 1914, he would have sold the invasion routes too. The late king would have pointed to a map, the general thought, and asked for either one billion or two billion francs, depending on where the Germans wanted to cross.[38] The general had misjudged Leopold, who signed the law forbidding the purchase of conscription substitutes on his deathbed, when he could hardly hold a pen.[39] But buying substitutes struck Germans as crass, and in 1914, they seemed not to know—or pretended not to know—that it had ended.[40]

As Jagow had told Beyens in Berlin, there must be something to talk about; the Belgians could not really intend to fight. General Otto von Emmich, who commanded the invasion vanguard, brought a notice repeating "formal guarantees" that if the Belgians stood aside, his troops would behave themselves and "show themselves the best friends" of the Belgians, for whom "we feel the greatest esteem." The proclamation did not speak of the ultimatum, of which his troops knew nothing, but mentioned the bottom line, that his men would pay in gold for food.[41] Berlin's offer to negotiate after Liège fell implied that the Belgians must have an "arrangement with France," as if they could not have decided to resist on their own account but must have been pushed or bribed. The notion of an unworthy, venal enemy who had no honor again suggests contempt.

The conspiracy theory lived a hardy life throughout the war, and it is easy to see why. To accept that the Belgians had defied Germany with open eyes and ungreased palms would have led to asking whether the German General Staff had underestimated the Belgians' will to resist and misperceived their motives. Germans might have had to wonder whether the Belgians had answered the legitimate call of self-defense, and if so, how Germany could say the same when the battle was taking place on Belgian soil. If Belgium had not plotted against Germany, one might even have to think about where the conspiracy had occurred and what its extent was. But it was simpler to widen the encirclement theory to include Belgium and ascribe the decision to resist to a secret pact. Once the invasion began, allegations of francs-tireurs confirmed the treachery, whose motives now appeared to include irrational hatred and evil character.

The year 1870 left a deep impression on German thinking about how the next war would be waged, what problems should be expected, and how soldiers should behave. Four manuals on tactics published between 1906 and 1910 assumed that a civil population would rise against an invader and advised measures patterned after those of 1870.[42] A government ordinance of 1899 gave army officers the power to execute anyone out of uniform who worked to "assist the enemy power or cause damage to the German forces or their allies." The edict required legal process and a written record under normal circumstances but allowed summary judgment if civilians were caught in the act. The rule left three loopholes: discretion concerning normal circumstances; what constituted aiding the enemy; and the leeway to mete out a capital sentence even if the culprits had not taken up arms. The government reissued this ordinance on 2 August 1914.[43]

The most sweeping (and best-known) statement of principles was *Usages of War*, the 1902 manual that embraced "every means of war" essential for victory, prohibiting only those that were not, which again gave commanders wide license. The only restraints, voluntary and self-imposed, were "chivalrous feeling, Christian thought, higher civilization," and considerations of "one's own advantage," meaning the likelihood of reprisals. "Custom and conventionality" determined the laws of war, not international legal codes or humanitarian ideals, "which not infrequently degenerated into sentimentality and weak passion" and contradicted "the nature of war and its object."[44]

Normally, said *Usages of War*, a hostile populace enjoyed protection, but the manual described exceptions, all of which recalled 1870. Should civilians join the fighting, disobey the army, or injure the soldiers, "there can no longer be any talk of violations of . . . immunities," and civilians would answer to martial law. In such cases, officers must employ "the necessary means of defense and intimidation" because "the ordinary law" did not suffice.[45] The invaded country's government had the right to raise civilian volunteers, but francs-tireurs who appeared singly or in small groups could be executed.[46] Martial law could replace the judicial system "if the behavior of the inhabitants makes it necessary."[47] "War treason," any act that imperiled authority "through deceit or through communication of news," also demanded "the most ruthless measures" in response.[48]

An occupier could require nothing that "can be construed as an offense against one's own Fatherland or as a direct or indirect participation in the war."[49] Even so, the inhabitants' seven major duties included building or repairing trenches, bridges, and railways. Another was to furnish hostages, who could be placed on trains so that francs-tireurs would hesitate to wreck them.[50] In 1870, this "was the only method which promised to be effective against the doubtless unauthorized, indeed the criminal, behavior of a fanatical population."[51]

However, 1870 had also shaped The Hague Conventions. The Fourth Convention of 1899 and its 1907 sequel were the first successful attempts to modify necessity, and though the wording was often vague—the kind the signatories would accept—the law was moving in a distinct direction. Some rules allowed room for necessity, whereas others deliberately omitted it.[52] The 1907 preamble revoked "the arbitrary judgment of military Commanders" in favor of "the usages established between civilized nations, from the laws of humanity, and the requirements of the public conscience."[53] What this meant for a given case was open to interpretation, but officers had to consider limits. As the American manual for 1914 saw things, "the infliction of suffering for the sake of suffering or for revenge" and acts that made "the return to peace unnecessarily difficult" were banned.[54]

The Fourth Convention outlawed any "general penalty, pecuniary or otherwise" as punishment for "acts of individuals for which [the populace] cannot be regarded as collectively responsible."[55] A British interpretation allowed them anyway, to chastise "illegitimate warfare,"[56] whereas the American manual permitted fines but not summary executions.[57] But even if such flexible readings showed the soldiers' reluctance to abandon their right to use whatever force they wished, the Fourth Convention had limited the grounds on which they could apply it by changing the definition of "illegitimate warfare." Francs-tireurs must now be treated like uniformed soldiers, provided they wore visible insignia, carried their weapons openly, and obeyed a recognized leader.[58] This was the convention's only rule in which consideration for civilians depended on their conduct.

Pillage was absolutely forbidden, and property of religious, scientific, educational, or cultural value must be protected from damage. Requisitions were legal, but the occupying soldiers could demand only their immediate needs, only in proportion to local resources. The army could not compel the populace to take part in military operations or sign an oath of allegiance, and must respect "family honour and rights."[59] There was nothing about taking hostages, a practice that most authorities called illegal, and those who accepted it specified that hostages must not be punished or, at worst, might be imprisoned.[60]

German jurists noted the contradictions between the Fourth Convention and *Usages of War*.[61] The convention had set no deadline by which a signatory had to rewrite its code, though Britain and France had already done so. Whether changing codes would have changed warmaking was also debatable, considering that during the Boer War (1899–1902), Britain had herded civilians behind barbed wire (which led to the term *concentration camp*) and put hostages on trains. Nonetheless, the German military was ignoring accepted restraints, declaring that they lacked authority and betokened weakness in a soldier. The German Army would therefore employ the methods of "defense and intimidation" that its predecessor had used in 1870. The phrase mixed two ideas—that attack was the best defense, and that an invading army was beset by hostile forces wearing civilian clothes.

The invasion design encouraged this mind-set. On paper, the plan worked like the jaws of a trap. The upper jaw, the right wing, stretched north from the Grand Duchy at mobilization and would attack Belgium from both sides of the Meuse, through East Flanders and Brabant north of the river, and Liège, Limburg, Namur, and Luxembourg provinces to the south. (Estimates vary as to the number of troops committed to Belgium in 1914, but eight hundred thousand is a reasonable figure.)[62] By the twenty-second day, the right wing was to reach the Franco-Belgian border; in another nine days, to occupy a west-east position along the Somme and the Meuse rivers. From there, these forces would swing south, and the vanguard would outflank Paris.

The lower jaw, the German center and left, extended south at mobilization from the Grand Duchy through Alsace and Lorraine, the two provinces annexed from France in 1871. If the French tried to reconquer them, all the better, for anything that diverted their manpower from the thrust toward Paris suited German aims. But whatever the French did, the center and left were to drive west, not just hold Alsace-Lorraine, so that by the forty-second day, the jaws would snap shut on the French Army.[63]

The logistics staggered the imagination. Mobilization alone required moving more than three million men and six hundred thousand horses in eleven thousand trains in thirteen days—or 312 hours, as the General Staff reckoned them.[64] The precision reflected the common wisdom that losing twenty-four hours to an opponent would cost ten to twelve miles of territory.[65] But Belgium was the world's most densely populated country, with more than 250 people per square kilometer.[66] If civilians disrupted the campaign, the delay could be disastrous, and the knowledge that this was so could prompt field officers to retaliate with a brutal hand if they saw—or presumed—popular resistance.

Schlieffen had wished to avoid putting reserve units in the front line, partly because reservists could not keep the pace of regulars, but the need for numbers left him no choice.[67] However, to yank men out of civilian life and fling them into battle on top of fifteen- or twenty-mile-a-day marches was sure to inflict a physical and mental toll. Further, aside from officers who had served in 1870, nearing retirement age if not past it, or a small cadre of veterans from colonial wars, few soldiers had seen combat. Even Ludendorff could later write that he would "never forget hearing the thud of bullets striking human bodies."[68]

Almost six hundred thousand men, their horses, and equipment had to pour through Liège and just south of it, a small, thickly populated area where the soldiers' nerves and inexperience could easily spark confrontations.[69] Schlieffen's notion to invade the Netherlands would have spread out the attack more, but his successor, Helmuth von Moltke, worried that if the campaign did not end on schedule, a neutral trading partner with access to the North Sea would be useful. From his retirement, Schlieffen agreed, but the change did not matter.[70] In any version, the plan heightened the usual stresses of war. The invaders had to march like demons, protect the eastern border by slashing west, pass among people who could turn on them, and engage the enemy. This explains how the Germans could outnumber the

Belgian Army by almost seven to one, yet act as if they were surrounded.

So it was that on 7 August, a Düsseldorf paper described a "perfidious attack" by Belgian civilians—"friends of France"—who allegedly ambushed a German column.[71] The same day, the *Kölnische Volkszeitung*, which represented the Center Party and its Catholic membership, spoke of Belgians in Brussels and Antwerp ambushing German residents in their midst. For a week, the paper ran headlines like: BELGIAN VIOLENCE AGAINST EXPELLED GERMANS; PERSECUTION OF GERMANS IN BELGIUM; THE BELGIAN BARBARIANS. Vague sources claimed that mobs had verbally abused, beaten, maimed, and robbed resident Germans while authorities watched or joined in, sometimes as the victims were being expelled.[72] Other newspapers imitated the theme, and the *New York Times* was soon (skeptically) quoting bulletins that at Antwerp, crowds had stripped women naked and dragged them by the hair through the streets, while police and soldiers looked on.[73]

Walter Bloem, the reserve captain who portrayed burned-out Battice, wrote of reading the papers on 8 August while waiting for orders to cross the frontier. He said the press spoke "of priests, armed, at the head of marauding bands of Belgian civilians, committing every kind of atrocity, and putting the deeds of 1870 into the shade."[74] The comparison was meaningful coming from Bloem, a best-selling author whose novels about 1870 were said to be the kaiser's favorite family reading matter.[75] A scene from a book Bloem published in 1912 suggests the German revulsion at francs-tireurs: "One had long ago forgotten how to distinguish between human and animal. . . . A captured enemy was nothing more than a wild, malicious beast."[76] After Bloem and his company read of Belgian attacks, "sentries found later with eyes pierced and tongues cut off, of poisoned wells and other horrors," they took precautions. Their first night in Belgium, they bedded down with loaded rifles and fixed bayonets and forced the civilians to drink from wells before they themselves did.[77]

Even when bullets did not fly, the invaders vented their hostility. They defecated on the floors of houses they pillaged,[78] threw hostages into pigsties or chicken coops, swore at the Belgian flag, and beat suspects called before military courts.[79] One Namur man was beaten and

Felix Schwormstädt envisioned this ambush of a supply column for the *Illustrierte Zeitung*, Leipzig, in late August 1914. Two houses are already burning, but that has apparently not deterred this franc-tireur. University of Washington Library

his house destroyed because a soldier who had stolen a bottle from his cellar said the wine had been poisoned. The court freed the man—a rare acquittal—ruling that the wine had gone flat, after which the soldier bringing the complaint thrashed him again.[80]

Peril hung in the air. The moment the Germans came to a place, they took hostages—usually the burgomaster, priest, and other notables—whose lives or property would answer for any offense. The Belgians were so unnerved that even young, able-bodied men and women were said to have "sat whole days in a chair, or [lain] abed" from fear, or smiled "nervously and desperately" as they offered soldiers cigars.[81] At one Flemish town, as an unending line of soldiers marched in, silent onlookers heard a single cry: "We are lost."[82]

Well that person might have said so. The soldiers suspected everyone, regardless of age or sex, and every activity. They punished possession of arms with death, but if a town had locked away weapons, a safeguard that many burgomasters took, that must mean the Belgians had planned to attack. The name tag attached to each firearm supposedly proved a person's involvement.[83] The Belgian Ministry of the Interior and communal authorities repeatedly exhorted the populace through proclamations and newspaper notices not to provoke the soldiers and, above all, not to fight.[84] But the Germans shrugged these off. At Andenne, for example, an officer threw a proclamation on the ground without reading it, saying, "That's just paper with ink."[85]

Raising carrier pigeons was a favorite Belgian sport, and some people said gambling on the races was a national vice.[86] But when Paul Oskar Höcker, the captain who had ridden through Visé, happened on pigeons near Liège, he said that francs-tireurs used the birds to communicate. When he saw villagers making weapons in their living rooms, he assumed that the pigeons carried messages about arms deliveries from secret workshops.[87] Höcker did not know that arms manufacture was an ancient craft in Liège, that the workshops were not secret, and that the workers seldom assembled entire weapons, only parts, and would have had no way to equip francs-tireurs.[88]

Other Germans accused the Belgians of having designed their homes to prepare for a franc-tireur war. The story went that each house—and church steeple—had loopholes in the walls, which movable metal flaps covered on the outside, and which reached the inside through a metal tube. The franc-tireur stuck a rifle through the tube, shoved the flap aside, and *voilà!*[89] In fact, the holes accommodated scaffolds, for ease in painting.[90]

The atmosphere of intense suspicion that prevailed from the first shows that the Germans were capable of seeing provocation everywhere, so that the problem is deciding how much provocation Belgian civilians offered. Someone, somewhere probably fired, whether from poor judgment, rage, or the realization, once a firebomb smashed the window, that the Germans were going to kill him. The Belgians admitted that this might have happened on rare occasions. But the Germans never proved a single franc-tireur guilty, let alone the charges of uprisings. Recent research has found plausible German testimony concerning a half-dozen cases of sniping, the only such evidence to come to light, but the Germans gave no proof, and the incidents were unconnected.[91] Isolated potshots could not justify repeated terror—the Germans named about 50 places where incidents occurred, and the

Belgians, more than 700, though the number included many that did not involve killing.[92] A recent study has corroborated 484 episodes that led to at least one civilian death.[93]

At first, Belgian tactics may have inadvertently contributed to German distrust. The Belgians often posted cyclist troops as sentries, who, if they spotted a German patrol, fired a volley and sped away. That was fair game, though the invaders despised the hit-and-run tactics and assumed that the cyclists were francs-tireurs. But sometimes, sentries fired from houses or behind them, and when the Germans advanced, they found no soldiers, or said that they saw only civilians running away.

That the main Belgian forces had left the border regions undefended perhaps encouraged the notion that the civilians had been told to do what the soldiers could not. After all, if the Belgian government had expected invasion, deploying the army on the Meuse would have made the most sense. But whatever honest confusion the Germans may have labored under should not have lasted past the first skirmishes, and if the invaders saw deceit rather than ineptitude or caution, that was their error.

Also, the Germans appeared to take sudden noises for gunshots, like a car backfiring or a tire bursting.[94] A Limburg priest told of a day when kids blew up a bottle of water as a prank. Soldiers came running, searched a nearby barn, found a child's weapon, and would have shot the farmer except that an officer intervened. But the incident still ended badly when the soldiers seized unthreshed rye to make beds and let their horses trample the potato fields and eat sheaves of oats.[95]

The Belgians believed that such excesses proved that the soldiers were looking for any excuse to take what they wanted and, if necessary, raised the alarm to get it. Whether that was true or not, the soldiers were careless with their weapons. Emmich himself acknowledged the fault on 5 August, writing that "the outrageous and nervous shooting of one's own troops is a crime." He ordered rifles to be kept unloaded after dark, and prohibited firing during those hours except under an officer's direction.[96] Nevertheless, mistakes continued, and if an unexplained shot rang out, the Belgians were doomed, unless they could persuade the army to investigate, which seldom happened.[97]

One reason for the carelessness was alcohol. Skeptics doubted that the world's most disciplined soldiers would drink too much, whereas

Allied sympathizers were sure they did. But prejudices aside, the German Army exhibited a powerful thirst. Gibson said the way the soldiers "cleaned out the wine of the country was a revelation to everybody," as they plundered whole cellars and loaded onto carts what they could not drink.[98] Weeks after reprisals at Eppeghem, Whitlock saw "black bottles, bottles, bottles, littered, thousands of them, of the wine that the soldiers had been guzzling"; at Malines, he noticed "bottles on window-sills, doorsteps, everywhere."[99] The day of the bottle-bursting in Limburg, hundreds of soldiers spent a day drinking and lay on the ground, soused. The officers did not seem to mind and even joined in.[100] Following a night's shooting and burning at Huy, the commanding major's report said that apparently intoxicated soldiers "in quite incomprehensible fear of enemy attack opened fire," making an "absolutely shameful impression."[101] Aerschot, the Belgians said, began the same way.[102]

The Belgian claim to innocence looks even stronger in the details of individual encounters and the lengths to which the Germans went to misread them. Louvain was a perfect example of bizarre accusations, starting with the notion that "insurgents" had timed their attack to coincide with Albert's sortie from Antwerp. After all, he had abandoned Louvain only the week before, could not have held it had he recaptured it, and had he left Antwerp unguarded, he would have risked losing the city—and West Flanders—in the bargain. To assert that Louvain was undermanned and presented a tempting target was pure fiction because the Germans had more than fifteen thousand troops there; that the soldiers seemed not to know this suggests both confusion and a stubborn belief in their peril.[103] The civilians' abrupt departure from the streets at dusk had a benign explanation—a curfew—and the garrison occupied the stylish part of town, so of course these particular civilians were well-heeled.[104] That they appeared able-bodied did not suggest a conspiracy, as with an influx of strangers. Rather, military service was not universal.

For that matter, a roster of 209 Belgians who died at Louvain listed only 6 not from the area, and not one was a soldier.[105] If the Germans had found Belgian Army identification disks, as they purported, they could have published the numbers as proof. But they never did,[106] though at Aerschot and Andenne too, they asserted that soldiers had taken part in uprisings.[107] One Belgian witness saw the rocket that supposedly presaged the attack, but he spoke of German soldiers making "luminous signals"; otherwise, soldiers in battle outside the city might have fired it.[108] The charges of mutilating wounded bodies rested on hearsay (never verified by doctors), as did the allegations that the Belgians had confessed to the uprising. No priest was ever proven to have fought, and German churchmen tried to debunk these charges, the only aspect of the franc-tireur war to raise serious doubts in Germany.[109] The Germans indeed saved the hôtel de ville, their headquarters, but they had put it in jeopardy by setting fire to the church of St. Pierre, which sits directly across a narrow street from it. Moreover, they mentioned their efforts to preserve the hôtel de ville to deflect outrage that they had burned a library containing medieval manuscripts.

Francs-tireurs always seemed to have a well-stocked arsenal. The Germans heard machine guns many places besides Louvain—Aerschot, Andenne, Dinant—though the Belgian Army had gone to war with only 102 of them.[110] Besides, civilians would not have known how to use sophisticated weapons, least of all grenades, which the army did not issue until 1915.[111] No German soldier testified that he himself had seen the 300 rifles in a church, and the story sounds as if it sprang from suspicion of priests and Catholicism.

Belgian marksmanship, or lack of it, was another refrain in German statements, for poor shooting was often thought to account for light losses, as at Aerschot and Andenne.[112] During three days of "fighting" at Louvain, the army suffered "several killed and wounded," whereas journals of two battalions noted a combined total of 5 wounded, one severely.[113] The *White Book*, the Ministry of War's 1915 report on the invasion, gave few precise numbers but implied that about 16 soldiers had died and some 36 been wounded in clashes with francs-tireurs. In May 1918, the ministry said that 626 soldiers had died in the "Belgian people's war," whereas Belgian sources said that more than 5,500 civilians had been killed.[114] By any measure, these figures suggest an unusual definition of combat.

German statements always had francs-tireurs surrendering with weapons in hand, forty at Aerschot alone.[115] One can imagine that a few here and there might have frozen when they realized they were caught. But none ever took one last soldier with him, and all kept the evidence that would certify their guilt—not that German Army justice required much. At Louvain, the Germans held between one hundred fifty and two hundred drumhead trials in no more than six hours, so that each defendant, on average, had at most three-and-a-half minutes to justify himself.[116] Those who escaped the firing squad were deported. The Belgians estimated that during the invasion, more than thirteen thousand people were brought to Germany as prisoners of war, most of whom spent at least six months in captivity.[117]

No uprising occurred at Louvain, nor is there proof that any Belgians fired, period.[118] Few Belgian witnesses were in a position to testify that they saw Germans shoot at one another, yet only friendly fire can explain the tremendous fusillade and the soldiers' impression that the bullets came from everywhere.[119] The Germans' refusal to consider that they had made a mistake led them to inflict a penalty that would have been excessive anytime but was worse for being groundless. They were ready to see francs-tireurs, so they saw them. Some soldiers were so incensed, they appear to have taken revenge, which officers allowed or encouraged in the form of tortures, mock executions, the destruction of religious and educational treasures, and organized pillage.[120] Deporting civilians en masse, including those found innocent, ridiculed the laws the Germans pretended to observe. As the soldier who had acted as interpreter during the trials said, the civilians "must have rendered themselves suspect in some way, otherwise they would not have been examined at all."[121]

It seems incredible that the army could justify hundreds of rampages based on a delusion that never wavered. Belgian reports quoted open-minded officers who served amid the ruins of Louvain but many more who insisted that the army had acted in self-defense. A few officers are known to have doubted the franc-tireur legend, but they kept this to themselves or told only trusted friends.[122] The most outspoken skeptic was the Berlin Socialist daily *Vorwärts*, which decried calls for retaliation against Belgian civilians on 23 August, even before Dinant, Tamines, or Louvain. The paper reasoned that franc-tireur stories were secondhand, that the Belgians thought they were defending their homes, and that Germans must not put "our struggle in the wrong in the eyes of all the world." Working-class soldiers should remember "their brethren on the other side," after all.[123]

These objections were highly unusual. Anecdotal evidence suggests that Germans who wondered about the terror presumed Belgian guilt and questioned only the severity of punishment.[124] Just as many anecdotes confirm that Germans thought the Belgians were swine, deserved whatever the army dished out, and that claims of violations were spiteful assaults on German honor.[125] Without fear of contradiction, the *White Book* could declare that Louvain was noteworthy less because an old city had been destroyed than because foes abroad had tried to use the case to "prejudice public opinion against the Germans."[126]

The pot was calling the kettle black. The magistrate who took the German depositions on Louvain acknowledged having spoken phrases that appear in the testimony, such as "murderous fire," as if he had led the witnesses.[127] His successor asked key Belgian witnesses to testify, and they complied, but they accused him of rewriting their statements, which they refused to sign.[128] Likewise, Belgians in Liège province complained that in early 1915, investigators asked them leading questions or tried to intimidate them.[129] In the end, the *White Book*'s Louvain section included only one statement from a Belgian (who said he had seen nothing).[130] What appears to be a rough draft of the *White Book* suggests that the authors deleted testimony that no weapons had been found at Louvain or Andenne and revised statements that departed from the official line.[131]

Many facts vanished altogether. The report did not mention incendiary devices, as if the army had not equipped the soldiers with fire-starting in mind, or pillage, except to deny that anyone had loaded loot on military transports. The *White Book* said nothing about deportations or bank extortions and seldom assigned a figure to civilian losses. Tamines, the second-bloodiest reprisal, did not appear. Nor did the information that Visé and Dinant had been almost wiped off the map, nor that German troops at Aerschot had smashed or burned the church altars, confessionals, harmonium, and wooden Gothic statuary.

Nevertheless, none of this proves that the soldiers in the field knowingly lied. The army had invented francs-tireurs and believed in them implicitly; the press, writers like Bloem and Höcker, and the *White Book* merely reinforced the legend. At Louvain, Gibson spoke with "decent looking fellows" who "all seemed fully convinced of the truth of what they told us" and were "very bitter against the civilian population." Gibson decided that the civilians had shot, thought he had seen them in the train station square, and wished "the Louvain business" could "be brought home" to the Belgians "in some striking way" so that they would desist.[132] He was wrong, because for once, German reports admitted that troops had traded fire near the station the day he had visited.[133] But if a skeptical outsider could accept the franc-tireur accusation, the soldiers could do the same.

One may yet ask how intelligent, often highly educated people could credit—and repeat—tales that young girls collected pails of German eyeballs. Rumors about mutilation exerted such pull that some wounded soldiers refused treatment from Belgians, and at least a few insisted so long that they got tetanus, or their wounds became wormy.[134] When Höcker let a civilian barber shave him, the captain laughed privately at having allowed a Belgian to hold a blade to his throat.[135] But to the *White Book* witnesses, mutilation stories were no laughing matter.

No country willingly admits that its army has committed brutalities. But in Germany's case, the franc-tireur myth served a purpose, reliving encirclement and sustaining the belief that the nation had gone to war to break its enemies' chokehold. Hostile civilians in Brussels and Antwerp had set upon resident Germans in their midst; elsewhere, they had killed soldiers. The *White Book*'s insistence that the citizenry had welcomed the soldiers warmly, only to turn on them, pointed to a shameful betrayal, much as Belgium had welcomed Germans to Brussels and Antwerp, only to beat and expel them. All this treachery had an ancestor: the Belgian diplomacy that had feigned neutrality, only to align with the Entente at Germany's desperate hour. In this light, invading Belgium looked almost like justice, whatever foreigners said about the sanctity of treaties.

Still, to execute civilians and burn their homes was shocking, which explains why the Germans decided that the Belgians were less than civilized and therefore merited the treatment. The crowds who struck at deportees in train stations seem to have shared this opinion, as if respect or mercy should not apply to such vile creatures. Höcker called franc-tireurs "rabble,"[136] and the officer at Louvain who said they were "evil-looking figures" wrote a newspaper account in which he termed them the "scum of the earth."[137] The army noted that the Landsturmers, fathers of families, did not hesitate to execute their Belgian counterparts who broke the law, as if that expressed the enormity of the crime.[138] But the francs-tireurs wore another face too. The statements about their wealth or fine clothes reminded people that where Germany conscripted everyone, rich and poor, Belgium let men avoid service if they had money.[139] Such cowards were naturally the type to turn franc-tireur.

Meanwhile, many Belgians thought the Germans had planned the terror, if only because it began right away, unlike the case in 1870, and because the invaders carried fire-starting materials that seemed to have no other purpose. But no high-level order for terror has ever surfaced, and the confusion and whim that often shaped local events would suggest the lack of one. Moltke issued a general order on 27 August discussing enemy forces, including francs-tireurs, noting that "only with emphatic measures against the population can a national uprising be nipped in the bud."[140] But he was saying nothing new, and by then the worst brutalities had occurred, which may mean that he was merely justifying them.

The strongest case for planning concerns Dinant, where several sources, including a subsequent inquiry among German prisoners of war, imply a prior intent to destroy the town.[141] That objective may have applied elsewhere too, but Höcker, who admitted that he hunted francs-tireurs, seems to have been alone in saying so, and he did not reveal what his superiors told him to do if he found any.[142] The Belgians claimed that the Germans openly discussed plans to destroy places—Louvain was supposedly the subject of ten such threats—but anyone can spread a rumor.

When a German officer told Gibson in early September 1914 that the army had wielded deliberate terror, the only part that surprised the American was the officer's frankness.[143] But he might have been bragging, and what stands out about this conversation is that no one else reported one like it. The most serious published evidence—said the Belgians—came from Bloem, who, in February 1915, wrote that the army had planned collective punishments as a deterrent. "Can anyone imagine that the capital of Belgium would have tolerated our moving about and governing within its walls as if we were at home had it not trembled before our vengeance and if it still did not tremble today?" he asked.[144]

The *Kölnische Zeitung*, which published Bloem's essay, was a semiofficial paper with ties to the Foreign Office, and censorship was such that he could not have written without approval. Even so, what a novelist-turned-captain said might have carried more weight had a higher authority ever repeated it. The timing may have mattered most, because his article ran when the *White Book* was being prepared. Consequently, he may have been reassuring everyone in the meantime that the army had mastered all and had intended the terror.

Nevertheless, what he said stands as evidence that official Germany would have rather confessed to wanton violence than concede a human inability to control events. After the war, a British officer who detested both the terror and the Allied propaganda about it commented on this quirk of character. Germany's rulers "could not even be content to say it was an act of moral beauty to sink the *Lusitania* or to burn Louvain. They must go on to boast that these scrubby actions were pieces of sound, hard thinking," which incurred not only revulsion at their cruelty but a "still more universal distaste for pedants."[145]

But the terror occurred so often and with such merciless precision that to say it happened out of the blue does not satisfy, either. The Germans crossed the border prepared to fight the armies that met them as well as a mental image of Germany struggling to breathe, and they were angry that the Belgians had chosen to bar their way. In that sense, the terror did not have to be planned or ordered, and once the cycle of outbreak and accusation gathered steam, the machine ran by itself. The Germans could have stopped it had they seriously examined their purposes or actions, but instead, they raised willful ignorance to a science that identified scaffold mountings as loopholes.

Belgium's critics later quibbled about how small a fraction of Louvain had burned and asserted that all invading armies cut a swath of misery. So they do, but the danger that Germany posed came as much from the psychology of terror as from the terror itself and cannot be reckoned in a census of deaths and blackened buildings. It takes a certain outlook to destroy a Louvain rather than admit that a few nervous sentries shot at their friends, what sentries have done throughout history. Thousands of Belgians died or were left homeless because the German Army never made mistakes.

4

Belgium Does Not Ask for Pity

ON 23 AUGUST, the Germans put Dinant to the torch and captured Namur after only a four-day siege. The next night, they repeated their aerial feat over Liège by sending a zeppelin to bomb an Antwerp residential district, killing ten people and wounding many more. The attack incensed the Belgians, who thought the target pattern revealed an attempt to kill their leaders as they slept, including the royal family. One bomb tore a hole in the cobblestones four or five feet deep and twenty feet square.[1]

Then came Louvain. The sack of a city whose cultural stature had granted no protection was disturbing, and the thoroughness of the destruction, which reports exaggerated, increased the horror. Albert was said to have remarked, "They will destroy Brussels,"[2] a fear that recurred periodically in false rumors that the capital was aflame.[3]

Tension rose with a feeling of helplessness. Namur's loss was bad enough, but the French and British armies, having come to Belgium only within the past week, were already leaving, hoping to regroup on French soil. With the Belgian Army clinging to Antwerp, the future looked bleak, but the Belgians insisted that the war had not ended. On 27 August, de Broqueville told Gibson that he was willing to sacrifice his sons' lives, his own, and his fortune if need be. However, "he was *not* prepared"—and as he said this, his eyes flashed and he banged the table—"to admit for a minute the possibility of yielding to Germany."[4]

But that night, the Belgians reached a decision that looked as if they were admitting that they could not keep the Germans from reducing their country to ashes, and that maybe no one could keep Germany from winning the war. They resolved to send a mission to Washington, to present documentary evidence of German violations to President Woodrow Wilson and the American people.[5] Two days later, with Entente blessings, five envoys led by Minister of Justice Henry Carton de Wiart sailed to London, their first stop on the journey. A second boat carried Queen Elisabeth, the royal children, and two hundred million gold francs from the Banque Nationale, with engraving plates used to print banknotes.[6]

From London, Carton de Wiart announced that his colleagues and he wanted simply to submit documents that showed "the truth about the German army's disregard of the laws of God and man."[7] He wrote later that the mission wished to reveal "Belgium's exact situation" in the war and "to bring to light" legal and moral issues that "would interest all nations concerned with law and the pledged word."[8] But after hearing the envoys speak, a *New York Times* correspondent guessed that the Belgians harbored a "secret hope" to cause "a spontaneous outburst of indignation which may bring some definite results." They did not anticipate that the United States would protest on Belgium's behalf but were thinking to provoke an outcry, or at least, by disclosing certain facts, to shape the "ultimate settlement at the end of the war."[9]

Why the Belgians rushed off to talk about settling a war destined to last years may sound strange in retrospect, but in late August 1914, it seemed as if the war might end very soon. The Germans were closing in on Paris, the French government was debating whether to leave, and the generals were squabbling about whether to defend the city. If Paris fell and France asked for peace, Germany might dictate punitive terms as in 1871, and Belgium could not expect to emerge intact. In effect, the Belgians were looking for a new guarantor, because the Entente had not done its job, and Hymans, who played a major role in the mission, confessed as much to Theodore Roosevelt. In late September, he told the former president that the Belgians hoped the American people would exert moral pressure against the terror and defend Belgian independence and territorial integrity at a peace conference.[10]

American sentiment was generally favorable to Belgium but unlikely to lead to action. The violation of neutrality had touched American hearts because a small country had chosen to resist a mighty aggressor.[11] The press also liked Albert's stoicism, his manly decision to fight, and what they saw as his common touch, a unique tribute from a nation that scorned monarchy and ascribed the war to imperial blood feuds.[12] Belgium alone among the embattled nations was said to bear no blame for the conflict. However, the admiration remained abstract.

Few Americans desired even a protest, and little backing for entering the war existed outside the Eastern social aristocracy, strongly pro-British, and several prestigious universities.

Perhaps none of that would have mattered had the person the Belgians most needed to persuade been more encouraging, but Wilson acted as if the United States must stay far above the fray. At a 3 August press conference, he had voiced pride "that America, if nobody else, has her self-possession and stands ready with calmness of thought and steadiness of purpose to help the rest of the world. And we can do it and reap a great permanent glory out of doing it, provided we all cooperate to see that nobody loses his head."[13]

Wilson's words suggested that America was superior to and more sensible than war-mad Europe, which put the president at a distance from the moral issues at stake. He also wanted to mediate peace, which he thought the best approach to salve the war's wounds, and the details of legal violations did not change his mind.[14] He was not alone. The *New York American,* part of the Hearst empire, waited almost a month to comment on Louvain, only to say that the uproar over a cultural landmark was misplaced. The way to protect art treasures from warfare "is not to make protests to neutral countries, but to stop the war."[15]

The president's neutrality policy followed logically from his personal views. On 18 August, he said that the "spirit of the nation" would be decided by public discourse, and that "every man who really loves America" would show "impartiality and fairness and friendliness to all concerned." Dividing America "in camps of hostile opinions" would cost peace of mind and might keep the country from fulfilling its duty as a mediator. America and Americans "must be impartial in thought as well as in action" and "put a curb" on any speech or transaction "that might be construed as a preference" for one side over the other.[16]

Nothing in the laws of neutrality said that a neutral must speak or think of each belligerent in the same way or be equally friendly to all. Wilson's formula was restrictive to the point of being ascetic, based on the apparent premise that unfettered speech would endanger the country, even during peacetime. Yet his friend Colonel Edward M. House wrote that the address earned "universal approbation," even in the Republican press, and the comments suggest that editorialists saw virtue in austerity.[17]

The newspapers assumed that the speech to be muzzled was that of menacing foreign influences. In lauding Wilson, the *Washington Post* warned against "schemes . . . concocted by brilliant, audacious, and desperate men" to drag the United States into war.[18] The *Chicago Tribune* cautioned against "treason" should "Americans of foreign ancestry . . . cultivate here . . . the race prejudices and jealousies of the old world."[19] But even where such suspicions found no voice, Wilson drew praise for keeping the war as far away as he could. As the *Christian Science Monitor* said, the president's stand "has the possibility of minimizing as far as may be the fact that war exists."[20] What effect his policy might have on speech went almost unnoticed. A notable dissent came from the *Wall Street Journal*, which remarked that war was hell, a person could not be neutral about that, and "either way, you have a perfect right to express your opinion."[21]

Consequently, the Belgians needed to stir up a conversation that few Americans wanted to have and that many might resent as a provocation. But the Belgians held one trump card. Before Louvain, the *Washington Post* had advised its readers to "set off one story of barbarism against another, and let it go at that." After Louvain, the paper said that "the atrocity seems incredible, but there is no reason to doubt its truth."[22] The *New York Times*, which in early August had reported the franc-tireur debate from the German side, did the reverse after Louvain, remarking that much of the world's business was done on scraps of paper, and that breaking a contract entailed penalties.[23] The *Chicago Tribune*, which had previously waved away charges of German violations, now quoted an Amsterdam paper that even if civilians had fired, destroying Louvain was "a revelation of barbarity" that would bring "eternal shame" to Germany.[24]

What was more, the German response to Louvain played into Belgian hands. The *Berliner Tageblatt* charged that the guilt lay with Belgian civilians and their government, which was conducting a "hopeless" war in "bestial fashion." The *Vossische Zeitung* agreed, saying that all art lovers must lament what happened, but that the Belgians had been warned about franc-tireur warfare. "We are in a holy war, we fight for our existence, and since the Belgians have forced us, we must pay them in their own coin." The *Deutsche Tageszeitung* remarked that the German troops surely possessed "heavy hearts" when they had had to destroy the famous "Flemish" city, but that the Belgians' "treacherous, murdering way of war" deserved no mercy.[25] The tone of such comments created a poor impression abroad.

Not that the Belgians knew, but Louvain had moved Wilson too—in private. House wrote that the president "felt deeply the destruction of Louvain, and I found him as unsympathetic with the German attitude as is the balance of America," more critical, even, than House himself, whose sympathies lay with Britain.[26] Wilson feared that a German victory would hinder the chances of working out "a better international ethical code," and that the war "would throw the world back three or four centuries." He "was particularly scornful of Germany's disregard of treaty obligations" and "indignant" at the "scrap of paper" remark.

The Belgians had to get president and public to speak of the anger they preferred to keep hidden. Once that surfaced, the Belgians had to hope that they could make Americans believe that their own interests were at stake in Belgium, and that they should bend their neutrality policy accordingly.

But the Germans struck first. On 3 September, while the mission was at sea, Ambassador Johann von Bernstorff protested their "contemplated representations, which are groundless."[27] On the seventh, Wilson got a telegram from Wilhelm that denounced the French and British for having used dum-dum bullets, which the Fourth Convention outlawed, and condemned the Belgian government for having "openly encouraged" and "carefully prepared" a franc-tireur war.[28] Even women and priests were committing atrocities against wounded soldiers and medical staff; quelling the culprits had required stiff reprisals.[29] Regarding the destruction of towns and Louvain in particular, Wilhelm said, "My heart bleeds when I see that such measures have become unavoidable" and cost innocent people their homes and property.

But the Belgians were getting bad press even without his imperial help. On 6 September, the *Washington Post* ran an editorial, "Trying to Involve Us," which rejected any protest over The Hague Conventions and rebuked a British suggestion that the United States should question Germany about violations. The editorial predicted that the president would sidestep the dispute and warned that people who counseled him otherwise were "the enemies of peace, not its friends."

Whatever the country did to affront any belligerent would "lessen its friendly influence" with that nation and perhaps prolong the war.[30]

The next day, the *New York World* printed a wire from five respected American journalists saying that atrocity reports were "groundless." They had spent two weeks with the German Army, covering more than a hundred miles between Brussels and the French border, yet could not confirm one instance of "unprovoked reprisal." Soldiers had paid for purchases, respected property, treated civilians correctly, and stayed sober.[31] The telegram caused a stir; many papers reprinted it. The *Chicago Tribune* called the cable "highly gratifying"— not least because *Tribune* men were involved—and offered that if the Belgian charges had been true, "one would despair of civilization and culture."[32]

Even seasoned diplomats might have had trouble managing these problems, but none of the Belgian envoys possessed any diplomatic background. Rather, they were parliamentarians whose selection exhibited the Belgian fixation with domestic politics. Joining the aristocratic, elegantly mustachioed Carton de Wiart, who alone among them had ever held cabinet rank, were Louis de Sadeleer, Hymans, and Emile Vandervelde—a Catholic, a Liberal, and a Socialist. Rounding out the company was de Broqueville's secretary, de Lichtervelde, whose father had been minister to Washington and who just happened to give the Catholics a three-to-two majority. Hymans spoke and wrote fluent English, and his Protestant background would be an asset in American political and social circles. But the mission made mistakes that more practiced emissaries would have avoided.

When the Belgians landed in New York on 11 September, a reporter showed de Lichtervelde the published text of the kaiser's telegram and asked for comment. Hymans remembered that the young secretary blurted out, "He's a liar!"; Carton de Wiart recalled him saying, "But that's false!"; and de Lichtervelde recorded his words as "How is it possible for anyone to lie like that?"[33] The pro-Entente *New York Tribune* ran the headline BELGIANS GIVE LIE TO KAISER, and Carton de Wiart had to soothe the State Department, ruffled at this breach of etiquette.[34] De Lichtervelde had wished to rebut Wilhelm's charge that the Belgian government had ordered an uprising, but he might have known that he had to weigh his words. When the mission went south to Washington, he remained behind.

Hymans recalled that wherever the delegates went, people said, "God bless Belgium," and offered other sympathetic greetings, which touched him.[35] But one newspaper ran a story about Belgian atrocities, illustrated by a photograph of the German empress visiting blinded soldiers in a hospital. She was shown bending over to ask one man whether there was anything to do for him. His reply: "One thing, Your Majesty, give me a revolver so that I can put an end to my intolerable sufferings!"[36] German-American groups complained that receiving the Belgians would violate neutrality, and Senator James H. Lewis of Illinois, the Democratic whip, took the matter to Wilson in person.[37]

The Belgians had assumed that Wilson would see them, but until the kaiser's telegram, Secretary of State William Jennings Bryan had been wondering whether an audience would be proper. However, they were in luck, for Bryan decided that if Wilhelm could appeal to the United States, the Belgians could too.[38] So on 16 September, the Belgian minister in Washington, Emmanuel Havenith, escorted the envoys to the White House, where Bryan welcomed them. The meeting was awkward. He lectured them on the beauties of compulsory schooling, perhaps unaware that the issue had bitterly divided prewar Belgium as a church-and-state quarrel in which the envoys had taken opposing sides. Next, the secretary brought up his pet project, treaties of arbitration, by which nations promised to submit to fact-finding rather than go to war, and he urged Belgium to sign one. By the time Wilson sent for the visitors, they were chafing.[39]

In the East Room, the delegates stood before a thin, tall, stately, fifty-seven-year-old man in pince-nez and frock coat who wore a mourner's band around one arm. Wilson greeted them with "a cordial gesture and a professorial solemnity" that evoked his days as a teacher and college president. Carton de Wiart gave over the documents and spoke in Albert's name. "The American people has always displayed its respect for justice, its search for progress, and an instinctive attachment for the laws of humanity," he said. "Therefore it has won a moral influence that is recognized by the entire world. . . . Our faith in your fairness, our confidence in your justice, . . . generosity and sympathy—all these dictated our present mission."[40]

Wilson responded in kind. "You are not mistaken in believing that the people of this country love justice, seek the true paths of progress, and have a passionate regard for the rights of humanity," he said. He was proud to be allowed to represent such a people, and honored that the king of the Belgians should have turned to him in distress. Wilson promised his "most attentive perusal" and "thoughtful consideration" for the documents, but he added, "You will, I am sure, not expect me to say more." When the war ended, "The day of accounting will then come when I take it for granted the nations of Europe will assemble to determine a settlement." Until then, "It would be unwise, it would be premature" to make a final judgment.[41]

Hymans insisted later that the president had not discouraged them, though he conceded disappointment when Wilson answered Wilhelm the same day he received the Belgians, in almost the same words.[42] When the envoys compared the messages, though, they pretended to read greater sympathy for Belgium and were mollified.[43]

But the next day, the *Chicago Tribune* published its correspondent's report of his travels with the German Army. Newspapers across America picked up James O'Donnell Bennett's story under headlines like DID NOT SEE SINGLE ACT OF ATROCITY and ATROCITIES ARE LIES, SAYS AMERICAN WRITER: WORST BEHAVIOR OF GERMAN SOLDIERS IN BELGIUM WAS KISSING OF PRETTY GIRLS.[44] The copy was just as provocative. At Louvain, said Bennett, civilians had committed "the supreme outrage against laws of civilised warfare" when they "went mad" and "fired from ambuscade upon German soldiers." The punishment was "terrible," but "it was war." No civilian Bennett spoke to had witnessed sensational crimes, like rape or the killing of old men, women, or children—the "next village" was always where these acts had happened.[45]

Whenever the reporters asked about destruction, the Germans almost always replied that shells had done the damage. A few houses had been burned, but to chastise francs-tireurs. Germans and Belgians got on so well that signs on some houses proclaimed that "good people" lived there, and when one of those houses was attacked, "Go easy now," was added. The German Army, Bennett concluded, was "a superb machine," whose officers were educated, spoke "charming English," and engaged in elaborate courtesies. During the two-week march, he thought only one soldier behaved rudely, and only two could have been called drunk.

No one reading his account could have known that the Americans' travels took them through seven towns between Brussels and the French border that exhibited only the typical ruin of war. For all seven combined, the Belgians later charged no more than a few killings, broken windows, and small-scale pillage.[46] Because the Americans did not witness these acts, the relatively modest number of blackened buildings might have led them to believe the Germans' explanations, and at least two towns suffered no significant damage until after the journalists had left the area. Typical of both sides in August 1914, the Germans had kept the correspondents under virtual house arrest, so it is unclear how much of Bennett's story was shaped without his knowledge and how much resulted from his views.

Either way, the Belgians lacked the information to contest his findings, though that probably did not matter. The story knocked the Belgian delegation off the front pages and almost out of the press. The day after it ran, the *Tribune* remarked politely that Bennett had not disproved the evidence given to the president. But in the next breath—and with obvious relief—the paper dismissed all charges, German and Belgian, as exaggerated. Random crimes had occurred, but no more.[47]

Having failed to woo Wilson or answer their critics, the envoys spent two weeks saying and doing the right things, like laying a wreath on Washington's grave and visiting Independence Hall in Philadelphia. Vandervelde met Samuel Gompers, president of the American Federation of Labor, and addressed workers' meetings; university presidents honored the delegates with dinners. The envoys lobbied newspaper and magazine editors, and Hymans wrote an article for *The Outlook*, a weekly that boasted Roosevelt as a contributing editor.[48] In Cleveland, the Belgians breakfasted with the man himself, who said he would do what he could to help. Hymans said afterward that Roosevelt was "a man of enterprise, of initiative, of attack," an impression reinforced by his habit of showing his large, regular, white teeth like a carnivorous animal.[49] The former Rough Rider's love of a fight was legendary—unusual for a Nobel peace laureate—but though he saw justice in the Belgians' case, he wrote Rudyard Kipling that they had presented flimsy evidence. He sooner believed the five journalists, whom he knew, and he cited recent examples of wartime behavior he thought as brutal as Germany's or worse, including campaigns against the American Indians.[50] Coming from someone who was soon to prove himself Belgium's most influential friend in the United States, the skepticism was a bad omen.

Just before the envoys returned to Belgium, they published *The Case of Belgium in the Present War*, a book that indicted the German Army for violating Belgian neutrality, wielding terror, extorting money, bombing Antwerp, and using dum-dum bullets. Citing the Treaty of 1839 and the Fourth Convention, the tract also quoted Carton de Wiart's and Wilson's statements from the White House visit and reprinted reports on German crimes from a Belgian commission of inquiry—all this in 120 pages. Once that came off the presses, the Belgians had finished their work, and on 30 September, the delegation sailed for Europe, except de Sadeleer, who stayed in New York, trying to drum up publicity.

To fulfill "a duty of my conscience," de Sadeleer wrote an unofficial plea to Wilson, "dictated by the profound respect of the principles of justice which I have defended and honored all my life." He still believed "that one word" from the president would "prevent new crimes from being committed by the soldiers of the German Army" and "spare the lives of thousands of innocent people." The president seems not to have answered him.[51]

But in mid-October, Wilson wrote a private, confidential note to James W. Gerard, the ambassador in Berlin, asking him to protest the Antwerp bombing—a demarche that, six weeks before, Bryan and Wilson had agreed was useless.[52] Gerard was to speak unofficially to whatever key member of the government he judged most likely to listen. He was to say that the bombing, which had "no result except terror and the destruction of innocent lives," created a bad impression in the United States. Wilson asked Gerard to suggest that the president was trying to keep public opinion neutral, but that such acts "wholly nullified" his efforts.[53] Reportedly, no record exists in German Foreign Office files of such a message, so Gerard was discreet that way. But about a month later, Bryan denied rumors that the government had asked any belligerent to stop bombing, saying that the United States had only made inquiries about American lives and property but no objection to any military tactic.[54]

The maneuver raises the question of whether the envoys might have tapped American sympathy more adroitly. The answer is both no and yes. The mission could not have persuaded Wilson to involve himself because that would have contradicted his policy, and the tide of indignation the Belgians were hoping for did not exist. Sympathy lay largely in the Northeast, whereas isolationism held sway almost everywhere else. Louvain may have altered perceptions of the terror, but the change was neither universal nor permanent, as the *Chicago*

Tribune's brief flirtation with Germany's "eternal shame" implied. No matter what Americans thought about the terror, no outpouring of opinion suggested that they wanted the United States to act as Belgium's protector.

Nevertheless, the Belgians missed an opportunity they would never have again to offer clear, reasoned arguments, supported by evidence that forced open-minded critics to consider the case on its merits. But whether the Belgians aroused the United States was secondary. What mattered more was establishing Belgium as a nation of impeccable credibility whose injuries deserved consideration on legal and moral grounds. After all, the Belgians were not just speaking to America, they were placing their brief before the court of world opinion. What they said damaged their standing, with lasting consequences.

Much of the trouble stemmed from haste. The charges of terror focused on Aerschot and Louvain, but the commission of inquiry had spent no more than a week gathering evidence on Aerschot, and the Louvain report appeared on 31 August, when the embers had hardly cooled.[55] Assembled under pressure, the accounts would surely err on key details, facts would be sketchy, and discrepancies would emerge. Many eyewitnesses had left the country, so that the commission had had to question others who had fled but remained within reach, and who testified under vivid shock, when tales grew tallest. Without hard evidence, the commission accepted hearsay, which, as Roosevelt commented, was unconvincing. It was bad luck that Bennett made a splash, but the Belgians could have guessed that the Germans would try to head them off and should have waited to tighten their case.

They did not know that they could afford to, that the British and French armies would blunt the invasion at the Marne in early September, and that a decisive German victory would seem less imminent. But they could have supposed that their mission was hopeless to begin with. It was as if they were waving the treaty, unable to believe that the paper had failed, convinced that if they could only speak eloquently enough, they would yet be saved. A measure of their thinking was that just before they decided to send the mission, Davignon had instructed Havenith to press Wilson to name an American to the commission of inquiry.[56] The Belgians did not ask themselves why any neutral would do that, and the State Department recommended that the president reject the request as potentially compromising.[57] In their panic, the Belgians did not realize that time would help them.

As it turned out, they would not have had to wait long. During the Battle of the Marne, Albert had launched another sortie from Antwerp, during which the Germans evacuated Aerschot. Belgian forces briefly reoccupied the town, and the Ministry of Justice sent an investigator, whose report revealed rigorous observation and reluctance to speculate from unconfirmed evidence. Though he assumed that many rapes had taken place—the Belgian emphasis on crimes against women was notorious—he did not insist. He wrote of burned-out buildings whose remnants crumbled in a strong wind, of loose telephone wires tangled on the ground, of the massive, oak church doors that seemed to have been forced by a battering ram. He found the place of execution, where black clots of blood still lay, the pit where victims had been buried, and plundered houses littered with bottles and human waste and wrecked furniture. And he asked how a German colonel's murder—if murder it was—could have justified the verdict to massacre and destroy a town of eight thousand.[58]

These findings came too late to be anything but an appendix to *The Case of Belgium*, and nothing like them appeared in the three commission of inquiry reports. Neither the Aerschot nor the Louvain account conveyed the ferocity, the implacable suspicion, the intense fear, or the lethal sequence of accusation and punishment that marked the terror as unusual. An amazing number of details were accurate, given how quickly the commission had gathered them, but a few were plain wrong, and those would be the ones remembered. The Aerschot report, for instance, dismissed the colonel's death as a pretext, which it was, but even doubted that he had been killed, which undercut the townspeople's claim that the fatal bullet was German. Of Louvain, the commission said that the Germans had bombarded the city before burning it, and that most or all of Louvain—the report contradicted itself—had been destroyed. Within two months, Belgians under German occupation knew better, as crowds of sightseers visited the ruins on travel permits obtained from an administration that normally treated anyone who wanted to move about as a potential spy.[59] For decades, the Belgians could not shake the allegation that they had either lied about or exaggerated the damage to Louvain.

As Roosevelt implied, the commission had produced a mound of details, many of which seemed minor unless viewed as a whole. The first report devoted itself to minutiae, down to the number of oxen taken from a particular farm. The other two digressed from Aerschot and Louvain to speak of how many houses burned in this or that village, or how an officer had tried at gunpoint to extort a confession of sniping. These items and the haphazard way they appeared unwittingly suggested that the terror was random rather than systematic and had harmed relatively few people.

Further, what the Belgians said about those people suggested an intent to portray the enemy as morally depraved. In a charge widely quoted abroad, the first report said, "Young girls have been raped and little children outraged at Orsmael, where several inhabitants suffered mutilations too horrible to describe." The other two reports recounted how, for example, the invaders had tied a man to a tree and burned him alive, "probably" buried another alive, hacked the limbs off a third, and poured oil on a fourth and thrown him, alive, into a burning house. The Germans had also allegedly bayoneted an old woman—she had supposedly been found still holding the needle with which she had been sewing—and strung up and burned an old man. Besides that, there had been two gang rapes near Louvain, one of which involved a young girl whom soldiers had bayoneted in the breast.[60]

To judge from how many such stories the Belgian government dropped from the record, they were as dubious as they sounded. When the commission reprinted the first dozen reports in January 1915, the one on Orsmael did not appear. A reliable postwar inquiry cited no rapes as having happened there, though a Belgian soldier had been cut up, one of only five mutilation charges to withstand scrutiny.[61] A few sensational indictments remained, like that of the young girl raped and bayoneted outside Louvain, but for every charge verified, ten others had vanished without a word.[62] Publishing them hurriedly in August 1914 only cast a shadow on Belgian integrity, so that ever since, some historians have said that the terror existed more in propaganda than reality, and that Belgium hoodwinked the world.

The number of atrocity tales made every other German soldier out to be a deviant, a ludicrous idea and a distraction, for it implied that the terror resulted from a character defect rather than a disregard for law. *The Case of Belgium* magnified the blunder by reprinting the statements of commission witnesses, of which nearly one in four attested to rape, mutilation, or both, usually at second- or thirdhand, without corroborating testimony. Secondhand rape accusations were not necessarily false because few victims spoke for themselves or even let their names be published. But to rely so heavily on rape and mutilation to prove the case exploited the creed that no self-respecting man allowed defenseless women to suffer. The Belgians did not anticipate that evoking this code would whet an appetite for the lurid that would hold their cause captive and require them to provide juicy tidbits if they wanted their plight to make the papers.

The tone of the Belgian brief was almost as self-defeating. The preface to *The Case of Belgium* declared that "Belgium does not ask for pity; she asks for justice," but overall, the Belgian evidence gave the reverse impression.[63] The emphasis on victimhood, which the many anecdotes of martyred villagers represented, suggested "poor little Belgium" asking for charity rather than one sovereign nation approaching another to stand up for its rights. Belgian war victims needed food, clothing, and shelter, and money was welcome, but Belgium needed diplomatic action more, even if eliciting pity was easier than commanding respect. And as the Belgians would learn, the pity wore thin after a while.

To some extent, the Americans expected the Belgians to play the role of waif and rewarded them for it. When Lalla Vandervelde, the Socialist leader's English wife, visited in late September to raise money for relief, an American she met wondered why she was not dressed in mourning. The startled Mme. Vandervelde took the hint, dyed her wardrobe black, and in three weeks collected $300,000, a sizable sum for the time.[64] Then too, the United States almost invited appeal by casting itself as the guardian of liberty. Wilson's Fourth of July address had portrayed the nation as "the light which shall shine unto all generations and guide the feet of mankind to the goal of justice and liberty and peace."[65]

Some wartime Belgian investigators resisted the sentimental and the sensational. Maurice Tschoffen, a Dinant magistrate who had witnessed the massacre—his garden wall had been a place of execution—undertook a thorough inquiry and was so discreet the Germans never noticed until his work was published abroad. Fernand Van Langenhove, whose 1916 critique of the franc-tireur myth remains a classic, traced the German delusion as it evolved in the press and analyzed it with a keen sense of psychology.[66] Moreover, though the Belgians helped create the monster that demanded raw meat, recruiting officers and newspaper editors abroad saw its usefulness and fed it by hand.

For instance, a rumor about Aerschot arose in mid-September that had the Belgians admitting that the burgomaster's son had killed the German commander. He had done so, the yarn went, because the officer had announced he would sleep with the boy's beautiful elder sister. A London paper ran the story, a *New York World* correspondent also reported it, and the *New York Times* credited it without reservation.[67] In a well-known book published that autumn, the *World* correspondent remarked, "What the real truth is I do not know." But he professed to know that "young girls were dragged from their homes and stripped naked and violated by soldiers—many soldiers—in the public square in the presence of officers." Men and women "were unspeakably mutilated," and the Germans turned their bayonets on children.[68]

Less spectacular allegations appeared in the Hearst press, as when the *New York American* published a story about the documents Carton de Wiart had given Wilson under the subheadline CARRIED HALF NAKED WOMAN AWAY FROM HOME. A week later, the *American* quoted a New York doctor who claimed to have seen two "young and attractive" Belgian women from a wealthy family whose breasts had been hacked off by Uhlans.[69] This kind of story often appeared in London tabloids, in racier language, but the doctor caused a commotion by saying he wanted to bring the women to the United States to show what Germans did. A German-born peace activist and history lecturer at Columbia University wrote the State Department asking what would happen if the Germans brought over their women said to have been abused at Antwerp. "What vista of nastiness opens before our eyes?" he lamented.[70]

Nevertheless, regardless of what foreign journalists wrote, in August 1914 the Belgians rushed to publish stories that calm reflection would have revealed as incredible, not to say absurd. The Germans naturally accused them of lying, but there is no proof. Rather, much as the franc-tireur myth reaffirmed encirclement for Germans, for Belgians, rape and mutilation stories echoed what had happened to their country—Germany had violated Belgium and was now dismembering it. But the connection was more than metaphorical. The Belgians viewed the ultimatum and the invasion as savage acts, so if the invader had assaulted women and children too, that fit his barbarian profile. A typical expression of this attitude arose at Liège in late August, when the Germans ordered that doors remain unlocked day and night. The Belgians interpreted the rule as a plan to take advantage of the womenfolk, whereas the Germans were really trying to keep francs-tireurs from barricading themselves inside houses.[71] Both sides were thus showing too much imagination.

The sensational accusations also derived from a sense of insult. The terror was bad enough, but being blamed for it was worse; as the postwar inquiry remarked, the Germans had not only killed and burned, they had dishonored their victims.[72] The Belgians seethed over this and spoke of the need to disprove the lies that the Germans had spread about them. Van Langenhove noted that they had not only mocked the Belgians as heroic fools for attempting to resist a mighty invader, they had called the whole population cowardly and odious, even women, children, and priests.[73] These slanders must be answered, he said, but he knew how to do that without dealing in the same coin. The Belgian commission, at least at first, did not show the same restraint.

Painting the enemy as a demon is commonplace, but the Belgian rendering served a special purpose. As a people to whom law was sacred and nation-giving, the Belgians could depict the Germans as habitual lawbreakers and themselves as righteous victims. That contrast comforted them, particularly when the alternative was shame at having ignored their danger and then succumbing so quickly, of which German troops were a constant reminder. In part that explains the story, which came from both Belgian and Entente sources, that "in literal fact, it is Belgium which saved Europe" by deciding to fight.[74]

The grain of truth was that had Belgium accepted the ultimatum, the invasion campaign might have turned out differently. The invaders would have reached French soil more quickly and in fresher shape, particularly if they had been able to use Belgium's railroads. Could the main body of the French Army have wheeled westward in time to parry the thrust? Could the British Expeditionary Force have reached France soon enough to join in the battle for Paris, and would there have been one?

Belgium's military contribution during the invasion had more to do with the fact of resistance than with battles won. Rather, the Belgians had earned a moral victory by choosing to fight for their independence against murderous odds, which needed no embroidery. They had shown courage and devotion to principle; they did not need to be pure and noble as well.

5

A Vague and Misty Unreality

EVENTS IN BELGIUM had overtaken the mission to the United States even before the envoys landed. In his first proclamation as governor-general, Field Marshal General Colmar von der Goltz told the Belgians that the "hard necessity of war" dictated that punishment for hostile acts fell on innocent and guilty alike. Reasonable citizens must keep "unruly elements" from upsetting public order, but Belgians who went about their lives peaceably "had nothing to fear" from soldiers or authorities. "I ask no one to renounce his patriotic feelings," Goltz said, but he expected "reasonable submission and absolute obeyance" from all Belgians.[1]

That day, 2 September, Bethmann wrote to urge the occupation to court Flemish leaders and exploit their quarrel with the Walloons, to split Belgian loyalties and later, perhaps, divide the country geographically.[2] This policy, called *Flamenpolitik,* assumed that the Belgians had no nationality, and that the Latin Walloons and Germanic Flemish were irreconcilable. *Flamenpolitik* further supposed that Belgium had never been independent but had always leaned toward France, thanks to the dominant Walloon minority. Therefore, if encouraging (or pretending to encourage) Flemish aims reversed the trend, the Flemish would look to Germany, and Belgium would never again conspire with France. And even if a peace treaty required German withdrawal from Belgian territory, Germany would retain influence over the Flemish.[3]

Dismantling Belgium intrigued Bethmann, as it did other German leaders, and a week later, he proposed terms that Germany should demand in peace negotiations. He thought that Germany should annex Liège, perhaps Antwerp, and a corridor between them, which, aside from other benefits, would put strategic territory in German hands. But even if Belgium were "allowed to continue to exist as a state," the country "must be reduced to a vassal state," must grant naval bases at the Flemish seaports, and "must become economically a German province."[4]

This was an ambitious wish list, drawn up before the shock of the Marne had made itself felt. Yet throughout the war, the Germans never renounced the idea of controlling Belgium, either through annexations or as a satellite. Tradition had laid down that an occupant was a caretaker, replacing the former government only until a peace treaty disposed of the occupied region,[5] as *Usages of War* noted.[6] Occupiers could not annex conquests until the fighting ended, and the Fourth Convention forbade them to rewrite the laws wholesale.[7] But the German occupiers governed as if they had erased Belgium from the map and wished to redraw it in their own image.

Belgium was in disarray. Communications had stopped dead, no trains ran except for military purposes, and neither the post office nor the telephone service functioned. The Germans had prohibited all newspapers, as custom and the Fourth Convention allowed. An underground trade sprang up in foreign newspapers, and despite the rumor that anyone found with one would be shot, London penny papers continued to fetch as much as fifteen francs apiece, the equivalent of three dollars.[8] Once, Gibson bought a copy of *The Times* of London and carried it to lunch in his overcoat. The next night at the same restaurant he overheard an angry official complain about the *Amerikanischer Legationsrat*—Gibson—who had been seen there with an English newspaper. Gibson took the incident as proof that the occupiers maintained a well-informed spy network, but the official's fury also reflected how the administration viewed attempts to escape its control.[9]

In mid-September, the occupiers decreed that Belgian branches of foreign banks had to settle operations and call in their assets, which would be frozen. Belgian-based banks could not conduct affairs "in a fashion opposed to German interests," as in sending funds to unoccupied Belgium or to Germany's enemies. A former Reichsbank director, von Lumm, was appointed commissioner-general for all banks. He could examine their books, demand an inventory, watch over foreign transactions, or require any information, all at Belgian expense. The banks objected, but Lumm was ready to take them over, so they went along. Their protest to Goltz that the Fourth Convention protected private property and limited the occupant's powers changed nothing.[10]

Meanwhile, the occupation was discussing whether to install a so-cial security system patterned after Germany's in certain areas as a test. This looked like benevolence, because Belgian social security cov-ered only coal miners (and to a limited degree), the war having inter-rupted efforts to expand the program. But changing these laws ex-ceeded an occupier's powers, and the German goal was to make the labor market costlier, depriving Belgium of its chief trade advantage. As one official said, after the war the Belgians would have to keep the more inclusive system or risk "creating difficulties with the prole-tariat."[11]

The Germans never enacted this scheme, but it figured in secret peace talks, in memos from industrialists and occupation officials, and in draft peace treaties, the last written only three months before the war ended.[12] Even two Socialist Reichstag deputies who visited Brus-sels in September 1914 wondered why the Belgians had resisted when, had they stood aside, Germany would have granted them universal suffrage—which they lacked—and social insurance. When the Bel-gians asked where their national honor fit into that bargain, the visi-tors replied, "That is bourgeois ideology, for which socialists can have no use."[13]

The most pressing matter, however, was food, for even in a good year, Belgium produced a three-month supply of wheat and a fifth of its overall needs. When the war began, the Belgian government had tried to control food distribution, but that ceased when Brussels fell. The shortage worsened when the invasion disrupted the harvest, the occupiers shipped Belgian laborers to German farms, and requisitions cut into food stocks. Private citizens had formed charitable commit-tees in each province and in major cities, and every communal govern-ment had permanent offices to aid the poor, but supplies were run-ning low. After weeks of negotiation, Goltz allowed an American member of the Brussels committee to travel to London to buy food. But the army arrested him at the border, and by the time he reached London on 26 September, the $100,000 he had to spend would not have covered a fraction of the need.[14]

The Germans said that the threat of famine resulted entirely from the British naval blockade, which prevented food imports for Bel-gium as well as Germany. In listing food as absolute (rather than conditional) contraband, a British Order in Council of 20 August had departed from custom, but denying food or supplies to an enemy army was lawful.[15] Blockading a civilian populace struck the Germans as criminal, but that is open to debate. The army could always take less and let the civilians have more, and if the army took too much, the people had to decide what sacrifices they were ready to make.[16] The Germans naturally resented the attempt to set the army against the populace, but that was not what made the blockade legally questionable.

Rather, the blockade challenged the law through the manner in which it attacked the sources of German supply. Though the Order in Council said that a cargo must have a military destination to be liable to seizure, this safeguard existed on paper. Captains of blockading cruisers were encouraged to infer "from any sufficient evidence" whether a cargo had an *eventual* military destination, no matter where the vessel was bound.[17] By this logic, a cargo headed for a neutral port—Rotterdam, say—was fair game, because the ship's papers could not possibly prove to British satisfaction that the goods would stay in the Netherlands.

Dutch merchants did, in fact, conduct a brisk trade with Germany, including foodstuffs, but they had every right. Both custom and the Fifth Hague Convention protected neutral trade, whereas the assumption that a neutral would resell contraband to an enemy, known as the doctrine of continuous voyage, had limits. The 1909 Declaration of London had confined it to cases in which a vessel's papers confirmed the blockader's suspicions.[18] Britain had not signed the declaration, but to seize neutral cargos on presumption was to rewrite the rules; tacitly, Britain had invoked military necessity. Still, despite what the Germans claimed, the law the British were stretching—perhaps to the breaking point—protected neutral traders, not belligerents.[19]

In theory, the blockade would allow Britain to rescue Belgium by starving Germany, but only by starving Belgium too. What was more, Belgium would go under long before Germany did, because Germany typically imported an amount of food equivalent to only 10 percent of its annual calorie consumption.[20] But if that logic did not apply, politics did. Britain purported to be fighting to uphold the rights of small nations, Prime Minister H. H. Asquith having said so as recently as 4 September, whereas Belgium, in accepting war, had tried to fulfill a treaty that served British interests.[21]

The first week of October, the British agreed to let the shipment for Brussels sail, but bureaucratic tangles held it up, and the committee realized that one boatload would not be enough. On 14 October, reported Gibson, a German general told him that the Allies were "at liberty" to feed Belgium and would be responsible for whatever happened if they did not, including bread riots. If disturbances broke out, the "natural thing" would be to drive the populace behind barbed wire and let people starve.[22]

This veiled reference to Boer War concentration camps was a barb at the staff officer who had devised them, H. H. Kitchener—now Lord Kitchener, Britain's secretary for war. The general probably did not know that Kitchener opposed the relief, believing that The Hague Conventions required Germany to feed Belgium (they did not), and that relaxing the blockade would aid the enemy by freeing him of his obligation. Kitchener was even said to have remarked later that a famine would help the Allies, for Germany would have to divert troops to quell bread riots.[23]

All this time, the military struggle continued, and with it, the terror. On 4 and 5 September, after a skirmish with Belgian troops, the Germans bombarded, pillaged, and burned Termonde, an East Flanders town of ten thousand people.[24] No mass executions took place there, nor did the likes of Aerschot or Andenne recur anywhere, but shootings still followed skirmishes between German and Belgian patrols, and sometimes violence occurred where there had been no battle.[25] On 27 September, the Germans revisited a Limburg parish where, to the strains of "Die Wacht am Rhein" on an accordion, they burned and looted, taking food, drink, clothes, silver, blankets, and "absolutely all the razors."[26]

Two days later, punctuating weeks of siege, a thunderous barrage crashed into the forts and trenches protecting Antwerp. The German artillery numbered 173 pieces, including the sixteen-inch guns that had reduced Liège and Namur. To oppose them, the Belgians had one six-inch gun per mile of front, and only a single enemy battery lay within range.[27] Unless Allied help arrived quickly, Antwerp's defenders, sixty-five thousand in the field army and a garrison of eighty thousand, would have to abandon the city. And if that happened, the Germans might overrun West Flanders, the only major part of Belgium they did not hold. On 1 October, Asquith worried that

Antwerp's loss would be a "great moral blow to the Allies," a remark that revealed how Britons often viewed Belgium solely as a British concept.[28]

First Lord of the Admiralty Winston Churchill belatedly grasped the threat, but the raw, underequipped naval division he hustled into Antwerp could do little. The Belgians already outnumbered their attackers; they needed heavy artillery, which the Allies could not spare. Asquith fumed about fraying Belgian nerves, while deserters in twos, threes, and half dozens hurried along the roads west of Antwerp.[29] "Their eyes were glassy," wrote Edward Eyre Hunt, an American reporter. "Often they were breathless and staggered as they walked." One soldier approached him and demanded a suit of civilian clothes.[30]

In the city, "fear-frantic people" scrambled aboard scows, canal boats, rafts, any craft on which they might sail up the Scheldt. Along the river rose "a great murmur of mingled anguish and misery and fatigue and hunger from the homeless thousands adrift upon the waters." The forty-mile road to Ghent "was a solid mass of refugees," as was "every road, every lane, every footpath leading in a westerly or a northerly direction." And when the army retreated, the soldiers slogged the same routes. "White-haired men and women" clung to harnesses of horses hauling guns, and "springless farm wagons literally heaped with wounded soldiers with piteous white faces" leaked bloody trails. The din was dreadful. Wheels rattled, drivers cursed, the wounded groaned, women and children cried, and one heard "always the monotonous shuffle, shuffle, shuffle of countless weary feet."[31]

Antwerp yielded on 9 October. The Germans marched in without flags or music, wearing green sprigs in their coats. Hunt watched an "absolutely fearless" old woman harangue some soldiers in Flemish, "berating them like schoolboys." He guessed that they understood "about one word in six," but they accepted her tongue-lashing with good humor. And when the German flag ran up the cathedral spire, they yelled and broke into "Deutschland über Alles." Other soldiers looked around suspiciously, as if francs-tireurs lay in wait behind the shuttered windows. But many shutters concealed no residents except forsaken dogs, thousands of them, whose piteous howls from hunger accented the city's misery.[32]

Three days later, the Germans entered Ghent. A young girl who watched them expected them to sing, as she had been told they had at

These refugees from Antwerp numbered among the more than one million Belgian civilians who fled to Holland during the invasion. The occupation regime went to great lengths to persuade them to return. Hoover Institution Archives

Brussels. But these men said nothing, and their faces looked like masks, drawn with apprehension. Their rigid step and resemblance to machines frightened her, and she saw in the compact, gray-clad columns a force ready to explode, "like stored-up electricity."[33] They were heading west to the River Yser, from which their generals hoped to drive the Belgian Army into the North Sea. The future looked desperate. At Dunkerque, Vandervelde saw thirty thousand men from the Antwerp garrison in full flight and said that anyone might have thought that the army had collapsed, and the country with it.[34] But the Belgians dug in on the Yser, and when the enemy gained ground, the defenders opened the Yser sluices, halting the advance in mud that became a legend. The British official history, spare with commentary, credits "the determination of the King of the Belgians" for the stand.[35] Albert later said his troops had freely given "much more than what was ever extorted from the serfs in the Dark Ages."[36]

The victory, Belgium's most celebrated feat of arms during the war, preserved a foothold, but only just. The Germans controlled everything but a tiny corner of Namur province that the French held and a desolate sliver of West Flanders. The line marking that sliver ran southeast from Nieuport on the coast past Ypres, a name already soaked in blood, toward the River Lys and the French frontier. The modest seaside villa at La Panne that the king and queen borrowed for their home lay barely twelve miles from the Yser trenches at Dixmude. The cabinet left Belgium for the French port of Le Havre, whereas 1.4 million or perhaps even 2 million less distinguished Belgians, almost 27 percent of the prewar population, had also fled. More than a million civilians went to Holland, and so did thirty thousand soldiers, whom the Dutch interned, as the Fifth Convention required.[37]

The Germans tried to woo back the refugees by formally promising the Dutch government that any civilian could return unharmed, an assurance they repeated at Antwerp. "Young people have no cause to fear being sent to Germany, either to be enrolled in the army or to be employed at forced labor," and only soldiers would be considered prisoners. Burgomasters in Flanders posted similar notices, and the publicity brought a flood of refugees home, starting in late October. But some stayed put, whereas others went to France or Britain, joining those who had fled there directly. Until the war's end, 325,000 Belgians remained in France, and 162,000 in Britain.[38]

Just after Antwerp fell, the Germans published a memo unearthed in a Brussels archive detailing secret talks between the Belgian Major General G. E. V. Ducarne and the British military attaché, Colonel Nathaniel W. Bernardiston, in 1906. The officers had discussed what Belgian strategy might be if Germany invaded, and how and where Britain might send aid, an arrangement that supposed a nominal alliance and compromised neutrality.

Rather, that would have been the result had Ducarne and Bernardiston reached a binding agreement, and if Belgium had ceded Britain the right to send troops before hostilities broke out. But Ducarne stressed that the talks were informal, that British forces could not enter until a German violation, and that Belgium would defend itself against incursion from any quarter. A Belgian official penciled "Anglo-Belgian Conventions" on the dossier, but there were none. Admittedly, Belgium should not have planned strategy with any guarantor, but the talks concerned how to repel an attack, not launch one, and nothing came of them. In 1912, the British attaché's successor informed the Belgians that if invasion occurred, British forces would arrive whether Belgium had asked for them or not. The Belgians became so alarmed that Grey assured them the attaché had spoken out of turn, and that British troops would never come uninvited.[39]

From this thread, the Germans spun the tale that Belgium had invalidated the Treaty of 1839, and that the invasion was no breach. To make the Ducarne memo read better, they deleted the phrase that limited intervention until after a German attack, and changed the word *conversation,* which appeared in the text, to *convention,* which did not.[40] Bernstorff told the American press that despite the convention, Britain had forced the "unfortunate little country" into war and "left [it] to its own resources." By contrast, he said, Germany had heard of the talks and offered a better deal—another instance in which Germans pretended to have seen all rather than admit a mistake.[41] But the tale of seduction and abandonment persuaded nobody, not even the *Chicago Tribune.*[42] In Belgium, when the Germans handed out yellow pamphlets explaining how the country had betrayed itself, the Belgians tore them into scraps of paper and left them on the street.[43]

The accusation rested on what for Belgians was a painful, ludicrous paradox, for had Britain and Belgium prepared their strategy together, the invasion might have gone differently. Antwerp would have received more attention, perhaps become the concentration point for British troops, an idea that had gotten brief consideration anyway.[44] The Belgians, knowing where help was coming and what the British expected, might have chosen to defend the Meuse, but even if not, they would have had to plan more carefully. A real military agreement would thus have hampered the Germans more than their cartoon version allowed, but again, they insisted that the Belgians had betrayed them.

Still, Bernstorff had blundered onto a half-truth. When he said that Britain had abandoned Belgium, he was striking a posture, but many Belgians would have agreed, starting with Albert. The king never openly revealed how much the Entente had disillusioned him, and he wrote of this in his diaries only later. But he did tell Gibson in mid-September "with a great deal of feeling" that the Germans had invaded only a sixth of France but had taken nearly all Belgium.[45] Was he rebuking broken French promises of timely military aid? Three weeks later at Antwerp, when Albert realized the city would fall, he ordered the field army to withdraw, whereas he would stay with the garrison. His advisors were appalled, but a row with de Broqueville only hardened his resolve, and for a few days, he did not budge.[46] The man whose name was a byword for stoic determination, whose photograph adorned the wall of every Belgian home and inspired hope of liberation, had thought seriously about surrender.

At the last minute, the queen changed his mind, but why he relented remains as much a mystery as why he had wanted to stay. Giving himself up would have slapped the Allies in the face, but Elisabeth may have persuaded him that the blow would cost too much. Albert's liberty and Belgium's were at stake, and if he rebuffed the Allies, they might renounce their vows to Belgium. But whatever swayed him, the shock of the defeat left its mark. When Gibson visited the royal couple at La Panne weeks later to obtain the queen's signature on a relief appeal to the United States, he saw the pain on Albert's face. "I looked up at him once but could not bear to do it again—it was the saddest face you can imagine—but not a whimper from him."[47]

It is not certain whether Antwerp's loss was what convinced Albert that the Allies and Belgium fought for different goals, but once that belief took hold, nothing altered it. Unlike many of his ministers—if not most Belgians—Albert did not accept that Belgium must cast its lot with the Allies, whose fortunes would determine in what shape the country emerged from the war. The desire to remain aloof was the greatest irony in the Ducarne affair, because even after having been nearly swallowed whole, the Belgians were still talking about their neutrality. On 4 September, the Allies signed the Pact of London, by which each belligerent promised not to negotiate a separate peace. They did not invite Belgium to sign, for Belgium had never declared war and was technically not a belligerent, which cut two ways.[48]

On the plus side, Belgium could still play the blameless neutral, and the Allies would have to measure how much they asked from a country that was a so-called Associated Power, not a full partner. But that could affect what they gave in return, and Belgium wanted many things. Most Belgians, including Albert, thought that a just peace would see Belgium regain its independence and conquered territory and receive an indemnity. Albert never spoke of punishing Germany, but in January 1915, the commission of inquiry endorsed the idea, which made the Belgian government the first to do so.[49] Some politicians, like de Broqueville, Carton de Wiart, and Hymans, even dreamed of reversing the Treaty of 1839 to address the problem of vulnerable borders.[50]

To expect the Allies to enforce these terms because Belgium deserved them was asking a lot. Yet Belgium's alternative, forsaking the status of an Associated Power to become a full-fledged Ally, would have meant abandoning neutrality to join in wrecking German power. Albert doubted that France and Britain could beat Germany and worried that if they did, their greater strength would threaten Belgium anyway, which led him to favor a stalemate and negotiation. For this reason among others, in late 1914 he rejected the first of many requests to place Belgian troops under Allied command or to coordinate offensive operations, refusals that perplexed and angered Allied generals.[51]

By coincidence, the leader of another neutral country shared Albert's ideas, for in mid-December, Wilson reportedly said in a private talk that he favored a stalemate as providing the best chance for a just, lasting peace. That king and president had a similar outlook was curious, when Albert was so close to the war and Wilson far away, but the comparison went deeper. Alone among national leaders, they were convinced that only negotiation could and should end the struggle, and in taking that stance, they left German crimes off the agenda. Wilson's interviewer recalled his saying that "it might be well if there were no exemplary triumph and punishment," which reinforces how he preferred to address problems of peacemaking and leave those of warmaking aside.[52]

Antwerp's fall marked several profound changes that outsiders could not readily appreciate. To begin with, Belgium existed in several places, most of them not on any map—behind enemy lines, where the king was with the army, wherever the refugees lived abroad, and Le Havre. The occupation isolated most of Belgium, divided families, and separated leaders from one another and from constituents. With so much territory lost, Belgium seemed to belong to the occupiers, who, as if they had been waiting for this moment, began passing dozens of punitive decrees. More than ever, the Belgians needed to explain what was happening and to appeal to foreign sympathy and sense of justice.

But reaching out abroad had become more difficult, and not just because the Germans had sealed off the country. Belgium had earned and held the spotlight for more than two months because David had chosen to resist Goliath and had made the giant stumble at Liège. But after Antwerp, the Belgian Army slipped from view. The heroes of

Liège had delayed the invasion timetable by only two days, but they had faced the enemy alone; the heroes of the Yser were keeping the invaders back permanently, but they were fighting alongside the French and British. As Allied casualties rose and Liège faded into memory, Belgium's contributions faded with it. Belgian relief remained a popular cause—and Belgium, ever the noble waif—but German crimes under the occupation either went unnoticed or paled beside the invasion terror.

Foreigners had the impression that not a building stood in Belgium, and that seven million people wore rags and begged their food. The truth was less extreme but a picture of misery nonetheless. Women and children sat dumbly by roadsides[53] or groped among "the tumbled wreckage of roofs, walls and rafters."[54] Some hunted for bits of wood, whereas others poked among the rubble of their homes, hoping to find something worth keeping.[55] Gibson, who visited Visé in December, said he saw only two or three houses, an elderly man, two children, and a cat. The man had PRISONER-OF-WAR MUNSTER stenciled on his coat and had returned home that afternoon for the first time since mid-August. "He was standing in the street with the tears rolling down his cheeks and did not know where to go. He had spent the day wandering the neighboring villages trying to find news of his wife and had just learned that she had died a month or more ago."[56]

In places, people lived in pigpens and chicken coops, in cellars beneath their ruined homes, in lofts over cow stalls. One man "considered that he was doing well when the population of his poultry house was reduced from 22 to 16 refugees."[57] The fires had burned so hot that brick partitions had crumbled, leaving "no sign of beam or rafter . . . not even a charred end sticking in the wall."[58] The saving grace was that, except for Louvain, Malines, and Charleroi, the larger cities had escaped heavy damage. But if combat had scarred the country less than might have been expected, overturned locomotives still blocked the railroads, and the Liège forts looked "as if they had been shattered by a terrible earthquake."[59] Outside Antwerp, shellholes, barbed wire, empty trenches, and a torn-up tram line with twisted rails dotted the landscape, with "now and then a fresh grave by the roadside with a little new wooden cross above it."[60]

A tell-tale stench permeated the air where dead bodies had been buried in shallow trenches or where wheels of heavy artillery pieces had churned up graves.[61] Bethmann's private secretary wrote that he would never forget the drive from Brussels to Antwerp, and "the destroyed towns, trampled tomato fields full of dead cows, the plundered stores."[62] South of Antwerp, Hunt saw once-picturesque Flemish villages that were now "heaps of bricks and ashes." Shrapnel had pitted the whitewashed walls, "so that the bricks showed through red, like blood."[63] A German officer said of Flanders, "When one sees the wasting, burning villages and towns, plundered cellars . . . dead or half-starved animals, cattle bellowing in the sugar-beet fields, and then corpses, corpses, corpses . . . everything becomes senseless, a lunacy, a horrible bad joke of peoples and their history."[64]

"The national life was dead," said an American relief worker.[65] Travel was prohibited, as in one Namur commune, in which no male sixteen years or older could leave without a permit—obtainable in Brussels.[66] The ban hit a mobile population hard. Workers had always commuted by rail to city factories from towns and semirural villages; in 1906, it was thought that 125,000 people made such trips daily.[67] Train passes were cheap, and railways put businesses within easy reach of one another. Brussels was fifty minutes from Antwerp and Ghent, ninety minutes from Liège. Now, Brussels might have been ninety years from Liège. The relief worker said, "Distances assumed the proportions of the middle ages, the next town became a foreign land . . . and the outside world was but a vague and misty unreality."[68] The *New York Times* noted, "Antwerp is now a strange city of silence. The streets, avenues, quays, and stations are all curiously empty, and only here and there do you see a citizen scuttling along a pavement to dive into the cellar of some house."[69]

The fall of Antwerp let the Germans finish installing the machine that administered this stunned, mute country. Goltz, who reported directly to the kaiser, was a main cog but not the only one, for the contraption seemed designed to satisfy a love of intricacy and to keep bureaucratic rivalries well oiled. The occupiers split the country into three zones, the smallest of which, the *Operationsgebiet*, or zone of military operations, was only a few miles wide anywhere and fell under martial law. The next largest, the *Etappengebiet*, or zone of depots and communications, lay under military jurisdiction but supposedly respected civil law. The area included the two Flanders and the southern parts of Hainaut and Luxembourg provinces.

The rest (except Antwerp, under military governorship) made up the *Generalgouvernement*, or occupied area, where the governor-general held sway, from Brussels. The Generalgouvernement's boundaries shifted to accommodate changes in the Etappengebiet, but its structure never changed. German civil administrators served alongside the military, in ten departments with dozens of subsidiaries, in which Germans duplicated Belgian officials down to railway stationmasters. Presidents replaced provincial governors, and a civil commissioner oversaw every *Kreis*, formerly an arrondissement, the largest unit within a province. A province had a military governor too, a general who also exercised civil powers, over such matters as hunting, fishing, road building, waterways, and motor vehicles. Under him a *Kreischef*, a lieutenant-colonel, ran each Kreis.[70]

Consequently, Belgium was a military dictatorship in all but title, even if the rules varied by zones. Belgians in the Generalgouvernement could buy, sell, or barter, whereas their Etappengebiet neighbors could not, and Etappengebiet residents endured more house searches. But the military zone suffered the most, and routinely. For instance, as anyone who had read *Usages of War* might have anticipated, the administration imposed labor, as with the rebuilding of forts or bridges.[71] This happened occasionally in the Generalgouvernement, but the unfortunates who lived near the battle lines were regularly drafted for such purposes. In late October, the army fined Harlebeke, near Ypres, because its citizens would not dig trenches or make sandbags.[72]

The control the occupiers exerted allowed them to plunder Belgium at will, which they did with increasing thoroughness. A different administration might have considered the advantages in Belgian cooperation and let the world's sixth-ranked industrial power continue as a working organism rather than bludgeon it to death. How the Belgians would have responded is an open question, but just as the invaders had not weighed the political effects when shooting priests, the occupiers did not weigh them when pillaging private industry.

One motive for the policy was that Germany had not secured the material resources needed for a war lasting beyond a few months. By October, supplies like ammunition had run short, and the army had been forced to cancel offensives, which prompted the new chief of staff, Erich von Falkenhayn, to ask Bethmann several times in November to arrange a cease-fire.[73] To attempt to narrow the deficit, in October the occupiers entered idle Belgian workshops and factories to seize machines, machine tools, and raw materials, which they shipped to Germany. At Liège, they also took drive belts with which to make boots and harnesses.[74]

Though the Fourth Convention allowed leeway to seize or destroy property according to necessity, the rule was meant to assist combat or occupation forces under unusual circumstances, not to enrich the occupier's home industries.[75] The Germans had taken what the occupying army did not need, removed it from occupied territory, used it expressly for military operations, and had neither paid for it nor promised to. Moreover, taking machines and drive belts suggested that the Germans had no interest in seeing Belgian factories work again.

The general idleness afflicting industry had no visible cause, because battle had touched few factories. Combat in West Flanders had destroyed textile mills, industries at Liège and Namur had suffered mildly, and the invaders had flooded or obstructed several coal mines,[76] though even there, most mines resumed operation in October.[77] What kept the wheels from turning was the dearth of transport and communications and, especially, of raw materials. In late October, Goltz listed forty-four substances as "materials serving the needs of war," paralleling what the blockade called contraband. These included metals such as copper, lead, zinc, and nickel; chemicals like phosphates, nitrates, and certain acids; medical compounds; and cotton, wool, and other fabrics. No Belgian could export any of these unless a Brussels agent of the Ministry of War approved. But that officer could, in denying the request, decide that whoever owned the goods must cede them to Germany or to third parties, in which case Berlin would fix the price. Anyone who evaded the law would lose the goods and any chance of payment.[78]

Goltz's decree effectively deterred companies that refined, manufactured, or used the forbidden materials from exporting them or keeping stocks of them because of the likelihood that the Germans would seize them or impose their sale at low prices. Exportation slowed to a trickle, and in targeting metals, chemicals, and textiles heavily, the Germans were squeezing three vital industries. Within weeks, the list named more chemicals, threads, industrial remnants, lubricants, and rare woods.

From the second half of October until March 1915, the occupiers entered warehouses, seized millions of francs' worth of goods—on the list or not—and packed them off to Germany. This time, they gave receipts, agreeing to pay when Berlin settled the price. However, the requisition of so-called *Massengüter* ("bulk goods") resembled an enforced fire sale, with the buyers none too careful about the papers they issued in exchange.[79] Still, those whose property was being appropriated realized that they might see some money later, whereas refusal to cooperate only provoked reprisal. When the Cockerill steel mills in Seraing rejected an order to repair Antwerp's defenses, soldiers took machinery, one of Cockerill's many penalties for recalcitrance.[80] But even when punishment was not the purpose, the confiscation sometimes suggested a hidden motive. At Louvain, a well-known metalworks had to surrender equipment, which was sent to a competitor in Düsseldorf. The officers who supervised the transfer had connections to the competitor, whose director had toured the Louvain works before the war.[81]

Often, the Germans left a company's assets alone but sought to control its operations. In late November, Goltz decreed that a company was subject to surveillance if it was managed from enemy countries or sent revenue there, if enemy foreign nationals had an interest, or if German capital amounted to 10 percent or more of the total. The decree affirmed property rights but said surveillance was necessary to make sure businesses were not run "in a fashion opposing the interests of Germany or of occupied Belgium." Overseers had to approve all decisions. They could interfere in any property transaction or communication; examine the books, inventory, or shareholding records; obtain any information; and attend directors' meetings. The firm bore all costs and could be liquidated and sold to a German buyer.[82]

In early December, Berlin decided that Turkey, where Goltz had served as adviser, needed his expertise more than Belgium and sent General Moritz von Bissing in his place. Whitlock described the new governor-general as a seventyish man who had "the manners, the viewpoint and the intellect of a drill-sergeant," with a "cannon ball of a head."[83] He thought that Bissing's face, "shaved with a remorseless razor" except for a mustache, had a "sinister look," an impression strengthened by his "small cruel eyes, red and watery." He always wore "a number of gaudy decorations" and flew easily into rages—or, as Gibson said, he was the only German general who could strut sitting down.[84]

Among Bissing's first acts was to order the Belgian provincial councils, which had not met since the invasion, to approve a "war contribution" of 35 million francs a month, or 420 million a year. This was greater than Belgium's direct-taxation revenue for 1914, 354 million francs. To fund the contributions, every month, banks would buy special bonds with paper currency the provinces must guarantee, which would flood the country with weak paper.[85] Legal opinion had never discussed exactions this large, but though experts accepted levies, the only concept remotely similar, they usually enjoined the occupier to defray local expenses at most and to consider ability to pay. *Usages of War* for once agreed with Westlake, saying that an occupier could not recoup the cost of a war by taking private property, "even though the war was forced upon him."[86] Even Maximilien von Sandt, the occupation's chief civilian official, urged Berlin to demand less, to avoid awkward questions in the Reichstag and objections based on international law. He estimated that the contribution exceeded what the occupation needed by so much that roughly one-fourth of the money would wind up in the imperial treasury.[87]

Nevertheless, Bissing directed the councils to ratify the contribution, which had been raised to 480 million francs, or 40 million a month. He promised that if they did, he would ask for no more contributions, and that the *Massengüter* receipts would be paid promptly. Behind this carrot lurked a stick, for Lumm told the banks that if they refused to cooperate, he would confiscate their deposits. They consented to float the bonds.[88]

Besides machines, raw materials, and money, the occupiers were seizing food. In November and December, they ordered anyone who possessed any of five different kinds of grain, flour, potatoes, other vegetables, or livestock to declare them on pain of seizure.[89] The rest was simple. One Liège commune yielded up everything from livestock to fodder to blacksmiths' and carpenters' tools to fuel to clothes and shoes to butter, bacon, wine, coffee, and sausages.[90] The officer who had remarked on the war's "horrible bad joke" said of Passchendaele in late November that "only a month ago, this country might have been called rich; there were cattle and pigs in plenty." Now, requisitions had emptied the place. "We have taken every horse, every car; all the petrol, all the railway-trucks, all the houses, coal, paraffin, and electricity, have been devoted to our exclusive use."[91]

On 16 October, Whitlock cabled Wilson that "in two weeks the civil population of Belgium, already in misery, will face starvation."

Eleven days later, his alarm made front-page headlines in the *New York Times*.[92] By then, more than a million Belgians were said to be on the bread line, and the country had a three-week supply at most, less in Brussels. Namur had no flour, Flanders was running short because of having to feed the returning refugees, and famine was menacing the poorer parts of north Limburg. The head of the Belgian committee estimated that feeding his country would require eighty thousand tons of food every month, four times the original appraisal, to the tune of four million dollars.[93]

The only hope in sight lay with the shipment stalled in Britain since late September, which a new, American-run organization called the Commission for Relief in Belgium, or CRB, had finally arranged to sail to Rotterdam. The food reached Belgium via canal barge in mid-November. "As we entered the villages," said a CRB supervisor, "women and children sought refuge in the ruins of roofless homes, terrified lest we were some fresh visitation of the war." But when people saw the barges, they "came running to the banks of the canals, where they stared at our flotilla as if it were a mirage."[94]

The delivery staved off calamity, but the British cabinet balked at permitting more shipments. Asquith and Grey favored them, but Churchill, Kitchener, Home Secretary Sir Reginald McKenna, and Chancellor of the Exchequer David Lloyd George were opposed (though he changed his mind later). The naysayers noted that though the Germans kept their hands off the CRB food, they broke promises not to take native food, so that the relief was indirectly feeding Germany and helping to pay war contributions. In early December, the Admiralty asked British shipowners not to carry food to Holland and announced that the government's maritime insurance would no longer cover such voyages. The Admiralty rescinded the policy two weeks later, but the apparent attempt to smother the CRB in its cradle implied that leading officials had forgotten what the war was supposed to be about.[95]

The CRB's new director, an iron-jawed mining engineer named Herbert Hoover, reminded them. Hoover was the type to melt when he saw little girls curtsey their thanks on a soup line but chew out obstinate prime ministers, and he sank his teeth into Asquith. If the British were fighting for Belgium, Hoover warned, "they would be unable to substantiate this claim in history" or "to hold one atom of American public esteem."[96] Asquith allowed that he was not used to

These schoolchildren, like all seven million Belgians living in occupied territory, would have starved without the Commission for Relief in Belgium. Notice the American flag between the photographs of King Albert and Queen
Elisabeth (background, left) and the scale (background, right). Hoover Institution Archives

being spoken to that way, but he could not deny the reasoning, particularly when Britain wished to borrow American money and buy
American weapons. But though both Germany and Britain let the CRB
continue its work, neither side liked the relief, which constantly forced
Hoover to play one enemy against the other. Whitlock, who participated in the negotiations, later remarked, "It would be easier to feed
milk to a lamb in a cage between a lion and a tiger than to feed the
Belgians between the Germans and the British."[97]

What preserved the CRB but also put it in jeopardy was that each
side accepted it for opposing reasons. Where Britain saw the CRB as
politically expedient but a military handicap, the Germans believed
that the relief suited their military needs despite its political drawbacks. Goltz had approved the attempt to buy food in London because

he, like Kitchener, focused on the idea that bread riots would disturb order. Bissing, however, fixed on the relief as a rallying point for Belgian moral resistance.

Goltz might have come to share Bissing's view had he stayed long enough to see the Americans whom Hoover brought over as CRB delegates. There were only ten at first, Rhodes Scholars on leave from Oxford, and they never numbered more than thirty-five. But they drove cars that the Germans could not take, had moderate freedom to travel, and annoyed officers by talking with their hands in their pockets, revealing a lack of deference. "The German," one delegate heard it said, "stalks about Belgium as if he owned the country and the American as if he did not care who owned it."[98] This cheered the Belgians, who, as Hunt said, were "isolated and broken-hearted . . . starving for sympathy as well as for food."[99] The sight of Americans dashing about, seemingly untouched by regulations, gave rise to rumors that the United States had bought Belgium and must not let it starve.[100]

The wishful thinking was understandable. The blanket ban on travel was eased in parts of the Generalgouvernement, but to go anyplace, a person had to spend hours in line, answer questions, and buy a pass. Even then, the railroads served military traffic first, and what should have been short trips became long and unpleasant.[101] But the Belgians could not go far anyway, because visiting Germany required a passport, and Holland was forbidden territory. By spring 1915, a ten-foot-high fence armed with fifty thousand volts enclosed that well-patrolled frontier to keep able-bodied men from escaping.

Telegrams and telephone calls remained illegal, as did uncensored letters. All mail had to travel in unsealed envelopes, and sneaking letters in or out was a crime. So unrelenting was the rule that at Christmas 1914, a boatload of presents from American children waited at Rotterdam until the "charming, naive little notes" with the gifts were removed.[102] The eminent Belgian historian Henri Pirenne wrote later that the mail restriction also hurt those whose loved ones were soldiers and whose fate they could only guess at. Only prisoners of war in Germany could correspond with Belgium, and only with their parents, though other soldiers sometimes managed to put notices in Dutch papers. A secret network called *Le Mot du Soldat* ("The Soldier's Word") sent messengers between the front and the occupied area, but the Germans imprisoned or deported any they caught.[103] Pirenne knew the pain of silence. Having heard in December 1914 that one of his soldier sons, Pierre, had gone missing, he had to wait until August to learn that Pierre had been killed at the Yser.[104]

Before any artistic performance, the censor had to approve plays, recitations, poetry readings, films, slide shows, and songs. Whoever "distributed" them—a term that included leaving placards in cafés—without permission faced military justice. A decree ordered that any communication or work of art not expressly authorized was expressly banned.[105] Whistling or singing "La Marseillaise" or "La Brabançonne" could land you in jail, and the censors combed sheet music for traces of the melodies.[106] Religious processions were often forbidden, which meant that certain holidays could not be observed in the traditional way. But in places, processions were allowed if the worshipers paraded without banners, sang only religious songs, and caused no trouble.[107]

New regulations appeared every week. In late December, a burgomaster in Namur province griped to his diary—for which he could have been arrested—about having to carry out the most recent rules. Pigeon owners had to present a list of the birds. The pigeons could not be sold or allowed to fly. All carbide had to be inventoried. No one could travel by bicycle, on foot, by car, or otherwise without a pass that bore a photograph and the burgomaster's stamp. Vehicle passes were taxed, though the tax cost less if paid in gold. Soldiers' tombs had to have wooden or wire enclosures, with the man's name lettered in oil paint, black on white. The tombs had to be sketched, and the burgomaster had to present lists of the fallen, in alphabetical order.[108]

But the law that aroused the most resentment and defiance was that which put Belgium on German time. What the occupiers gained by setting the clocks an hour later remained a mystery, but keeping Belgian time was a "hostile demonstration." As the war lengthened, the decree expanded to cover clocks visible from the street through windows, but hardly had the Germans refined the rules than the Belgians resorted to new tricks. Defying threats, they kept their watches on Belgian time. They marked social invitations "H.B." ("*heure belge*"), though that became illegal too. In public documents, Belgian authorities referred to the "time as kept at the hôtel de ville," rather than admit to "German time." And nothing stopped patriots from doubting the loyalty of families said to live by the invader's hour.[109]

■

To an extent, the occupation reflected how the army at home treated civilians. The Law of Siege, invoked in Germany on mobilization, made a general a virtual dictator over each district. Like Goltz or Bissing, he reported to the emperor, had a military staff that served alongside civil servants, and had to maintain "public safety," a loose phrase that let him poke his nose into everything. The way district commanders applied censorship and protective custody annoyed even conservatives, and as districts did not coordinate policies, the law was a "maze of ordinances." Chance decided whether officers were trained administrators or could pick up the skills on the job. Some did not wish to, believing that civil servants were fussy.[110]

But if the occupiers exported a caricature of army rule, they also brought ideals of themselves as lords and masters. There were exceptions, like the Landsturmers, whom Scott Hurtt Paradise, a CRB delegate in Limburg, pitied as "nice old fellows" who "ought to be home making toys."[111] But Hunt thought the occupation had "a cat-and-mouse air," and that the "the army seemed to play with the country, and thoroughly to enjoy itself."[112] Some officers got caught up in the duty to impose order, a task they knew to be important because it was so distasteful. One German at Liège told a CRB delegate, "You see in war-time the military *must always* come first, and so we have a thousand things to contend with here. I would rather be back at the front, than worried to death here." The American thought the Belgians had "great freedom when one considers the tenseness of the situation," and he sympathized with the officer, who worked twelve hours a day, "dealing most of the time with excitable Belgians."[113]

Whatever the Germans' individual motives, however, the more they cracked down, the more stubbornly the Belgians resisted. By late autumn, except for the mines, the "whole country" was on strike "against any employment which may benefit the German occupation" (a situation that Hoover used to justify the relief to the British). Railway and postal employees refused to work, and one Brussels journal was said to have wrecked its presses rather than publish German bulletins.[114] At Christmas, the primate of the Belgian Catholic church, Desiré, Cardinal Mercier, wrote "Patriotism and Endurance," a pastoral letter in which he exhorted Belgians to observe only those laws that did not breach personal liberty, Christian conscience, or duty to Belgium.[115]

The message increased Mercier's considerable prestige, especially after the Germans decided not to arrest him, but the resistance he called for had old roots. Pirenne wrote that the occupiers' laws, beliefs, and manners grated on a people proud of institutions that respected personal dignity. The goose step, servility to officers, and passive, unquestioning obedience aroused mockery or anger. When soldiers paraded by, Belgians asked one another how many grandsons of serfs were passing.[116] On Brussels streetcars, which soldiers rode free, citizens turned their backs or refused to sit beside them. The Bruxellois left cafés if Germans entered, polite society ostracized women who consorted with Germans, and on the streets, Belgians avoided meeting German eyes.[117] Some patriots whispered about Belgians who did not show the correct attitude, and they called those who had fled the country *froussard*, meaning "yellow-bellied" or "chicken." One Belgian wondered wearily whether a quarrel between Belgians in Belgium and abroad would substitute for the petty squabbles that had been put aside out of national unity.[118]

"Patriotism was a cult," remarked Hunt.[119] People cherished medallions bearing the images of the royal family and named newborns Albert or Elisabeth.[120] The Germans had banned the Belgian flag, but shopkeepers used black, yellow, and red cord to wrap packages. These colors appeared in blouses and accessories, even as tassels on the chic, black silk caps that Brussels prostitutes wore, until the Germans outlawed such displays.[121]

Paradise described the Belgian attitude as hard-edged optimism. He said that a youth returning from a military prison might laugh off his travails while admitting that you could not love the Germans. A girl who shook her fist at them behind their backs seemed "half amused at her own display of emotion." Everyone said, "*C'est la guerre*" ("That's war"), but to comfort themselves—not, as the Germans said it, to excuse their excesses. The smile that accompanied the comments seemed to say, "We can laugh at all this misfortune now because very soon our turn will come."[122] They told jokes, like the one about the Flemish peasant who applied for a travel pass. "How long is this pass to be good for?" growled the German clerk. "How long are you Germans going to stay in Belgium, *mynheer?*" replied the peasant.[123]

The laws suppressing political activity, possibly excepting those restricting church services, violated neither the letter of the Fourth Convention nor custom. Military occupiers had always been granted the right to keep order, however they saw fit, and to exact obedience. Nevertheless, Goltz's first proclamation had promised not to interfere with the Belgians' natural loyalties, and many experts would have said that was only just. Though most had assumed that the populace must obey, if only to avoid punishment, some had taken a strong line about working against the country. One had even argued that "where certain acts are in themselves offenses against the laws of war, the inhabitants are bound to abstain from them."[124] By that rule, for example, railway and postal workers had the right (if not the duty) to resign. In that sense, Mercier's plea to disobey would have had legal support, though admittedly from American and English interpretations no German court would have recognized.

But Mercier's tract also offended for reasons that had nothing to do with law or the obligation to obey. He had counseled patience in the certainty that the Belgian Army would liberate the country, which implied that the Germans would lose the war. With this, Mercier had jabbed a weak spot, for the occupiers saw defiance in random remarks or gestures. Gibson observed in mid-November that they were "mighty busy doing pin-head things for people who have a war on their hands"—and that day, they arrested a little boy for imitating the goose step. The American legation lawyer, a Belgian, tried to intervene, presuming that the Germans would not jail a child, but they did, releasing him a few days later.[125] After "Patriotism and Endurance" appeared, a soldier in a Brussels café claimed that Paris was no more than a three-hour march away. The Belgian who explained his error to him spent twenty-four hours in jail and paid fifty marks (forty francs) for "having tried to discourage a German soldier."[126] His case was not unusual.

Perhaps the Germans were chastising the Belgians' motive for telling the truth, or for the smile that may have punctuated the bad news, but that says something. The law let the Germans punish, but some experts had addressed the difference between having power and feeling compelled to use it. Prewar British and American manuals had held that because occupation was temporary, "the occupant should not exercise all the powers he enjoys. He should do only those things necessary for the purposes of the war, the maintenance of order and safety, and the proper administration of the country."[127] In arguing against war treason, the catch-all category that let an occupier call disheartening talk a crime, Westlake had warned that he must not intrude "the notion of moral fault" into whatever he judged to hurt his interests. Such a sense of injury "serve[d] only to inflame his passions" and made it less likely that he would observe just limits on necessity.[128]

An administration that saw hostility in wristwatches set to a forbidden hour or tassels on prostitutes' caps had crossed into a psychological domain like that in which Germany viewed the terror. Just as the invaders had burned cities because they imagined that armed civilians had shot at them, the occupiers jailed or fined unarmed civilians they suspected of sneering. For once, the suspicion was correct. But to assume that derision could hurt an army of 250,000 men that had the country in a hammerlock and its people scared to death was to grant that German authority had limits after all.

Sometimes the way they demanded to be taken seriously had funny consequences. At 11:00 P.M. on 31 December, the citizens of Antwerp heard such a hullabaloo, with big guns booming at the forts and small arms firing, that they fled to their cellars, fearing a bombardment. Then down the street marched a band, followed by soldiers singing "Die Wacht am Rhein" at the top of their lungs. Hello, 1915.[129]

6

This Poisoned Atmosphere

WHEN WHITLOCK TRIED TO DESCRIBE the occupation in early January 1915, he could not quite explain why, but he knew that what he was seeing made the invasion violence pale by comparison. The contempt for rights and dignity cut deepest, he thought. "Somehow, I do not know exactly how, the very air is poisoned with militarism, one has a constant sense of personal discomfort . . . one cannot voice one's own thoughts. There is a menace everywhere, and in this poisoned atmosphere one suffocates."[1]

Whitlock's instinctive revulsion suggested that Belgium had a new story to tell, even more compelling than that of the scrap of paper or Louvain. He was witnessing a regime that placed production, consumption, livelihood, and property at the service of the state. Law bowed to arbitrary notions of necessity, which outweighed claims of individual right. To enforce its will, the occupation outlawed free expression, put political, economic, and social relations under surveillance, and applied terror, often for imaginary or minor offenses.

The reason Whitlock had trouble defining this regime was that the word that came closest, *totalitarian,* did not enter the English language until 1926. The Belgians were lucky that the occupation lacked certain features that would mark Stalinist Russia or Hitler's Germany, but people in parts of Nazi-occupied Europe would have recognized Belgium as familiar.

The system's outlines emerged in the laws decreed in January and February 1915 to realize a pet project, keeping Belgian manpower from serving the enemy. The threat existed in that young Belgians crossed the Dutch border and went from Holland to France or Britain to enlist in the Belgian Army—some thirty thousand of them, or roughly twenty every day on average.[2] But the numbers deceive, because a large proportion made the trip in late 1914 or early 1915, before the Germans imposed stricter border controls. In January, Gibson alleged that more than two thousand had gotten out simply by visiting a country home belonging to a friend of his, where caves on the property ran under the frontier.[3] Whether that report was accurate or not, the job got much tougher once the Germans' paid informants and military police began breaking up escape networks, and the high-voltage fence ringed the border.

A volunteer from Liège province learned this firsthand. One day in March, he bade his mother good-bye—quietly, so that the two Germans living with them would not hear—and left with a few gold coins and sandwiches in his pockets. The first safe house on his route turned him away because the Germans had been snooping around, but he found other marooned escapees, and they slept in a train station without getting arrested. The next day, they located a secure network at Herstal that sent them on to Visé. At Visé, he nearly missed his rendezvous, because all the houses on the street had been burned, and only after careful inspection did he see a staircase leading into a basement. He crossed the border one midnight in a heavy rain, lying down to avoid the sentries' lights, by which he picked his way, fearful of meeting a stray dog or a patrol. But he got to Holland, as did fifteen of his group from Herstal, and when they reached London, a crowd cheered them. He was seventeen years old.[4]

His group at Herstal had totaled thirty, but he never found out what had happened to the other fifteen, whether they had gotten scared, lost, arrested, or killed. The ratio speaks to the impressiveness of thirty thousand escapes, and how badly the Germans wanted to keep Belgians out of the Yser trenches. But the number represented only a fraction of those of military age, and the work force was mostly idle.

The Germans considered anyone who tried to leave to be a criminal. In late January, they announced that border guards would shoot, and that captured escapees would be sent to Germany as prisoners of war, neither of which were questionable methods. But a proclamation also said, "Anyone who aids or favors the prohibited passage to Holland of a Belgian liable to military service will be treated in accordance with the laws of war." By this decree, family members who failed to prevent an escape would be punished, a tactic used in 1870–71.[5]

At that time, the German occupiers had demanded that each French locality supply lists of able-bodied men, who were told not to leave the district. If they did, their families and the municipal authorities were held liable. Since then, the Fourth Convention's "family honour and rights" clause had arguably prohibited any tactic that set spouses, parents, and children against each other. But even if not, tradition respected national sympathies. In 1908, an American lawyer had condemned the practice of 1870, which he called "violence to the most laudable feelings of patriotism" and cited the Fourth Convention's rule against coercing civilians to work against their country. He also quoted a Belgian expert to say that acts that injured an occupier but were not illegal, such as escapes, could not be punished at will. The right to punish depended on the power to prevent the act, but if the escapee evaded capture, the power was lacking. Picking on his family, the American said, was "especially improper."[6]

Nevertheless, the Germans began deporting the parents of young men who had escaped. One such scene unfolded in February at Hasselt, a Limburg town about fourteen miles from Maastricht, as Scott Hurtt Paradise watched. "There were old white-haired men and women among them, and they were weeping and clinging to their friends as well they might." A large crowd followed them, "muttering and crying, but there was nothing to be done, and finally the old people were herded into the station like cattle, a few friends called out 'good luck,' and it was over."[7]

In April, the occupiers took another leaf from 1870 and required certain classes of people to show continuous residence by reporting periodically to a registration office, or *Meldeamt*. Those liable included Belgian militiamen, members of the Garde Civique, Germans not subject to military service, returned civil or military prisoners, enemy foreign nationals older than fifteen (male or female), and anyone else thought suspect. All had to present a special card at the Meldeamt at least once a month—by November 1918, one Liège commune had held forty-two registrations—and to obtain approval for any trips or changes of domicile. The authorities threatened the parents of anyone who missed a registration with fines or imprisonment if he failed to appear at the next call, and the violators themselves faced those penalties as well as deportation. Sentences were meted out without trial and sometimes merely on suspicion.[8]

To the Germans, keeping Belgians in Belgium was only half the battle; making expatriates return from France and Britain was the other half. Why the occupation bothered is unclear, because the expatriates had acquired a bad reputation, largely for their reluctance to enlist, and Belgian conscription laws were loose and difficult to enforce abroad. In February, when the Le Havre government lowered the draft age to eighteen from twenty-five and limited exemptions, so many Belgians tried to flee to Holland or Switzerland that France and Britain sealed their borders.[9] Of those who remained, some of the wealthy ostentatiously pursued pleasure, whereas many poorer refugees went on relief rather than find work.[10] The ill feeling that resulted obliged the British and Belgian expatriate presses to try to repair the damage. But in a sense, the Belgians could not win, because British trade unions worried that if unemployed, skilled Belgians found jobs, they would displace British workers by accepting lower wages.[11]

Consequently, the Germans might have done better to let the refugees stay where they were, but that was not how Bissing saw things. In January, he decreed that any expatriates who stayed abroad after 1 May would be fined ten times the rate of taxation, financed through the sale of their goods—which violated the Belgian constitution—and threatened that their houses would be used to quarter troops.[12] The Germans claimed that the measure redistributed the tax burden so that the well-to-do paid their share,[13] whereas Le Havre warned that refugees might lose their liberty if they returned.[14] Within Belgium, the communes, which were to collect the tax and keep half the money, dragged their feet for so long that the Germans let the matter drop. This was perhaps the only case during the entire occupation when popular resistance nullified a hated law.

No such permissiveness tempered the quest for usable goods. For industrial materials alone, 1915 witnessed twenty requisition decrees, many of which struck not just businesses but, for the first time, householders. Hungry for copper, the Germans entered private homes to take brass and copper door and window fastenings, doorbell wiring, and plaques under letterboxes and outside professional offices. Some people hid their fixtures, replacing them with wood, but that worked only until the Germans got around to searching gardens, cellars, and armoires; they even felt the beds.[15] Thanks to the verb *repasser*, which means "to iron" and "to go back across," the joke went around Brussels that the Germans were taking all the clothes irons (*fers à repasser*) so that they could go back across the Meuse.[16] Other goods they listed early that year included walnut trees—for rifle stocks and airplane propellers—fuels, fats, sugars and their sources, rubber, tires, and eleven different metals. As before, the owner had to declare possession, and if the inventories were honest, the occupiers paid by weight or volume, never generously. If they discovered any irregularities, they seized the goods without payment, often taking other property as well.

Two million Belgians were said to be on soup lines in early 1915,[17] yet native-grown food was not safe from requisition. "It makes one furious and it makes one sick," wrote Whitlock in early January, when he learned that seizures had taken place days after renewed pledges that they would stop. "The fact is that one cannot believe a word they say."[18] The requisitions imperiled the CRB, a strain that increased in February, when Germany announced unrestricted submarine warfare, permitting U-boats to sink any target on sight. After intense haggling, the CRB gained protection for vessels that bore easily recognized markings, sailed agreed-upon routes, and observed myriad formalities. However, on 10 April, a submarine torpedoed *Harpalyce* in the Channel, drowning seventeen crew members, including the captain. Despite eyewitnesses and photographs testifying that *Harpalyce* had carried a CRB banner visible at five miles, the Germans said that nothing had distinguished the vessel from any other merchantman. Only more hard bargaining kept the relief going.[19]

The occupation's economic measures started to cut deeper. In mid-February, Bissing granted Lumm the power to sequester Belgian businesses if surveillance did not safeguard German interests. Whereas surveillance left a company in Belgian hands, under sequester, it belonged to the occupiers, the proprietor and shareholders no longer having rights. The business paid all costs. By October 1915, the Germans were supervising more than 350 Belgian companies, having sequestered about one-fifth of these. As with surveillance, the targets were usually companies in which enemy foreign nationals held a significant portion of the capital, revenue, or seats on the board of directors.[20]

Another February decree forbade any exports, not just of forbidden goods, without special permission. Over time, the law changed to permit exceptions, as the Germans opened or closed the export pipeline to suit their needs.[21] Following the practice in Germany, in April they created offices to manage consumption of coal, oils, gas, water, and electricity and to redistribute each to aid the war effort. Another agency oversaw the gathering and shipment of raw materials to Germany; others bought or amassed vegetables, fruits, and products that the *Massengüter* had not touched. Special bureaus controlled matches, tobacco, butter, salt, and food oils.[22] But the most important agency regulated coal production and diverted nearly the entire output to Germany, to the occupying army, and to trade with Holland, Switzerland, and Scandinavia. This commerce yielded foreign exchange and bought raw materials that the blockade had denied Germany. The Germans parceled out deliveries to different sources as political and economic policies dictated, but the Belgian populace—and factories that would not work for Germany—always came last.[23]

Amid all this, German newspapers never missed an opportunity to praise the occupation's successful efforts to "revive" the Belgian economy. "If Belgium is not a desert today," declared the *Frankfurter Zeitung* in early March, "if its mines, its factories, its enterprises function to a certain extent, if its cities are habited, if, in the localities where destruction spread, the inhabitants were saved from the worst, they owe this to the German government, against the will of their own government." Further, the American relief would have been impossible without active German support. Another journal said that prewar Belgian farmers had grown rare fruits, shrubs, and flowers for export but ignored basic domestic needs, a typical lack of foresight that went along with the Belgian habit of chasing after money. Luckily for Belgium, the article said, the Germans were there to redirect efforts toward producing necessaries, for which the Belgians were duly grateful and reaping the happy results.[24]

Even as the public was reading these tidings, Bissing was circulating an official letter about relations with Belgium. He wished "to advance the interests of Germany alone . . . with the greatest possible ruthlessness and with no unworthy lenience . . . and to lay the foundations for the future conclusion of peace." He intended "to use Belgium in one way or another for the expansion of Germany's power," and he deplored the thinking that this was a "temporary, wartime thing." He did not call for annexation, but "the population must be trained to respect order and discipline and be brought nearer to Germandom."[25]

The judicial system felt the impact. One February decree transferred the jurisdiction for property crimes such as forcible theft and pillage that involved German nationals from communal courts to arbitration tribunals consisting of two German judges and one Belgian. The immediate goal was to manage cases against Belgian mobs that had destroyed German property in the August disturbances. The tribunals' decisions lay beyond appeal, and the German judges could outvote their Belgian colleague, who could be replaced if he made a nuisance of himself.[26] A second decree created other tribunals for tenant-landlord cases, before which the principals had to appear, virtually always without counsel. This prevented expatriates from protecting their property, part of the campaign to force them to return.[27]

A third law let military governors, Kreischefs, and commandants (in charge, respectively, of provinces, arrondissements, and communes) fix punishments for offenses, subject only to a maximum penalty that rose with each rung on the administrative ladder. These officials could also pass sentences and punish third parties of their choice, whether communities or family members, if the guilty were absent. Further, the officials could issue decrees, which meant they held legislative, executive, and judicial powers, and the public knew of the laws only when the authority chose to post them.[28] A Namur province burgomaster told his diary that his commune's commandant always referred in a decree to three previous ones by number and date, without mentioning the gist, and that he often wrote in German.[29] German was also the language of military courts, whose proceedings were summary and secret, and before which no defendant had the right to examine the prosecution's charges.[30]

The rules of evidence did not apply. Whitlock wrote that German judges said, "We will presume that," if the prosecution lacked proof.[31] He heard of a Belgian railway official named Lenoir who had bragged once too often in a bar about the information he was supposedly sending to Le Havre. Whitlock believed Lenoir could have known nothing important and that the Germans had no proof, but they tried him anyway, at Ghent. The story went that at eleven one morning they condemned him, and at five that afternoon, having had no visitors, not even a priest, "he was led out before his coffin" and shot. His wife was deported.[32]

The Belgians were taking all this with a brave face and taut nerves. Paradise remarked in December 1914 that, contrary to his expectations, Belgium did not seem to have been robbed blind and was not enduring "a sort of half-life at the point of the victor's bayonet." Even so, "the people were plainly very much frightened, only spoke of the Germans in whispers," and observed curfews faithfully. Seven weeks later, he was saying that because many people had no work, "they have learned to stand calmly on the street corner, or in front of their ruined houses and wait." At night, villages were "dark and silent, because when one has no oil for the lamp one must perforce go to bed with the sun." Those Belgians who lacked food or money, which included many formerly well off, found soup kitchens that would give them "a little soup, a half loaf of whole wheat bread, and perhaps a few beans or some rice." On these, they would exist for another day.[33]

Belgium was not starving; another CRB delegate who had worked in a New York City settlement house thought that he had seen more distress and hunger there than in Antwerp.[34] Even so, by April, Paradise was writing that the strain had grown so great that when people made speeches of gratitude to the United States, "every one present, men and women . . . suddenly burst into tears." He noticed "a quality of savage bitterness" where "there used to be only courage and optimism," and he remarked, "The Lord help any German when he *retreats* through Belgium."[35]

The Germans could not help sensing the tension, but they professed not to know where it came from, which seems hard to believe yet makes perfect sense. To understand the Belgians' reaction would have required the ability to see a problem from someone else's viewpoint, and the occupiers lacked that gift. After the war, when a former high-ranking occupation official explained the friction between Germans and Belgians, he wrote as if his side had displayed nothing but goodwill. The Belgians had simply subscribed to different beliefs about liberty, government, and the purpose of the state; disliked interference; were irrevocably hostile to the German administration because of French influence; and allowed "continuous agitation" to fan "aversion and distrust." And so on.[36]

This was the official wartime line, restated in 1927 to justify Germany after the fact, but daily dealings revealed similar attitudes. Pirenne wondered how longtime friends and fellow historians from Germany could visit, see the destruction (and sometimes write articles endorsing the regime), yet expect relations with him to remain unchanged. "It is curious from a psychological point of view," he told his journal, "that experience exerts no effect on credulity."[37] Americans, said one CRB supervisor, sometimes met German officials who "complained"—he stressed the word—"that the Belgians did not seem to 'like' them, in fact that they seemed to hate them." He thought the German grievance resulted partly from vain efforts to penetrate higher Belgian society.[38] One day at Hasselt, Paradise saw a German band concert in a public square that, to him, illustrated the divide between conqueror and populace. Soldiers "armed to the teeth" kept the crowd of "sullen Belgians" moving, while the musicians, "big, husky hussars, each with an immense sabre dangling at his side," were playing "Love Me and the World Is Mine" with "an earnestness which brought tears to their eyes." Paradise commented, "I nearly died laughing at them."[39]

In late April, burgomasters received a questionnaire that asked whether the number of unemployed had grown recently and whether relief had made them less likely to work.[40] A month later, with Bissing's consent, forty-four German companies formed a cartel to hire Belgians to fill jobs in German war industries. The *Deutsches Industriebüro* (Office of German Industry) acted as a clearinghouse to match requests for skilled labor with Belgians willing to sign contracts. Originally hoping to find 3,600 laborers, chiefly miners and metalworkers, the cartel set up offices in various cities, sent recruiters, and spread stories about rosy working conditions. The contracts, which the army enforced, usually stipulated a three- or four-month term and the same salaries and benefits that German workers enjoyed.

For the twelve months beginning July 1915, Belgian sources say, about eighteen thousand workers signed with the cartel, whereas the German figure runs almost 11 percent higher.[41] The difference in reporting underscored a power struggle, because the attempt to employ Belgian labor collided with the passive resistance. Burgomasters made problems over providing the certificates of moral character that the cartel required applicants to have, and the clergy and workers' circles spoke against signing up. Factory owners who had the money paid their skilled employees a partial salary to keep them bound and forestall their departure for Germany, where they might find life more appealing.[42] The Comité National de Secours et d'Alimentation (National Committee of Assistance and Feeding), which distributed food under CRB protection, withdrew aid from any family in which a member signed a contract.

The German administration saw the Comité National and its forty thousand Belgian workers as a threat, not least because the CRB had obtained for them the right to attend meetings. In German eyes, the Comité National had a political agenda, for, besides opposing the labor cartel, it withheld support from women who consorted with Germans.[43] Further, most aid recipients had to pay a nominal price for their food, which, after clever management, allowed the Comité National to expand and fund other relief activities (which the Germans impeded but took credit for).[44] The occupiers therefore perceived the Comité National as the hub of resistance through which the Belgians could imagine the occupant had ceased to be "master in his own house."[45] The phrase, written after the war, suggests how far apart conqueror and populace had been; the Belgians had never stopped thinking it was *their* house.

But labor was the most critical issue, and Bissing made it clear he would tolerate no interference. In spring 1915, he focused on the railroads, which the occupation had to maintain because Belgian railwaymen would not. He believed that they could afford to strike because of the relief and, he suspected, because Le Havre was smuggling money into Belgium. (His hunch was probably correct, because during a trip to France that Hoover took in March, several Belgian cabinet ministers tried to enlist him as a courier. He declined.)[46] Accordingly, Bissing had workers from two state railway arsenals arrested and imprisoned for refusing to repair track or restore lines to operation. When 190 men proved incorrigible, they were deported.[47]

These punishments broke German promises that civilians would never be put to forced labor and arguably breached the Fourth Convention concerning war work, but that was not all. Bissing's maneuver showed what could happen to anyone who would not sign with the cartel. The message came through even more loudly in the Etappengebiet, where the commanding general rejected the pretexts of patriotism and The Hague Conventions and charged that troublemakers were out to "create difficulties" between the populace and the military. He warned that he would hold the communal authorities responsible should such friction continue, and that he would curtail certain liberties if necessary.[48]

Where labor fit into the occupiers' economic vision surfaced during a meeting of German officials and industrialists that Bissing convened in Brussels in June. The governor-general declared that his administration always kept the Fatherland's welfare foremost in mind, a remark intended to counter the impression that Germany was cultivating Belgium as a Garden of Eden. He said that the Belgian economy must be revived, for "I am of the opinion that a squeezed lemon has no use, and that a dead cow gives no milk."[49] But he and the occupation officials who spoke after him insisted that whatever stimulation Belgium received, German industry would not suffer, and that Belgian competition would never threaten German interests. Belgium merely had to be rich enough to support the occupation army and contribute to the cost of the war.[50]

The industrialists wanted guarantees. They noted how potent a rival prewar Belgium had been because of cheap labor, low taxes, and the absence of social security, and they complained that Belgians refused to work for them. Spokesmen from the textile, cement, and glass industries were adamant about export controls, because they saw the chance to regain ground they had lost to Belgian companies before the war. Bissing assured them that Belgium would not export, that the cartel would provide the workers, and that the Comité National would not stand in the way. He did not like to use force, he said, but he had done so before and would again if he had to.[51]

These promises ran counter to what he had led Belgian industrialists to believe, that they could negotiate with Britain to resume exports. The Belgians' model was a Dutch operation, *Nederlandse Overzeetrust,* known by its initials as NOT, under which Dutch merchants could continue to trade while obeying blockade rules. The NOT certified that no Dutch company or a neutral intermediary sold contraband to Germany and posted bond worth several times the cargo so that violations would be pointless. The Belgians had asked for permission to talk to Britain about a NOT under which they could import raw materials and export finished goods, and which the Comité National would supervise.[52] Bissing could not have liked the sound of that, but he had encouraged the Belgians' efforts.

Now, at the June economic meeting, he was telling German industrialists that Belgium would lie dormant. A week later, he wrote Whitlock that the relief must not let workers "refuse remunerative labor," and the next month, a conference of jurists gave the governor-general grounds to act.[53] Ignoring the Fourth Convention requirement that the occupier must protect life and property except under unusual circumstances, the jurists said that law did not shield civilian rights.

The occupation was like a "despotic State" in which the conqueror conferred and applied laws at the pleasure of the military, whose authority derived from the emperor. (It may not be a coincidence that around this time, Bissing wrote the burgomasters that he held the power that had once resided in the Belgian government.)[54] Force took precedence over law; war had nothing to do with constraints, of which the occupier was the sole judge.

Luckily, said one jurist, that judge was unshakable, and Germans could be sure that their leaders would not let themselves be swayed by "petty juridical scruples." A renowned law professor offered that it would be "narrow-minded" and "criminal" to wish to limit the army when national existence was at stake.[55] This professor had been among those in Germany who had once criticized *Usages of War* for contradicting The Hague Conventions.

If Bissing had been asking for a legal excuse to do what he wanted, generals in other jurisdictions did not bother. When the directors of a factory at Renaix, East Flanders, refused to make cloth for sandbags, the Etappengebiet authorities threw them in jail for eleven days, imposed a 7:00 P.M. curfew, and forbade virtually all travel. In Menin, West Flanders, no women, children, or families could receive relief unless their men worked regularly on military projects and other imposed labors.[56] Anyone who refused had no recourse to assistance.

As part of the campaign to break the passive resistance, the administration imposed an early curfew in Brussels on 1 August to commemorate the first anniversary of Germany's entry into the war.[57] To mark the occupation's first year, Whitlock grieved as if for a lost love. "We have not heard the ring of a hammer or of a trowel in a year," he wrote, "what music it would be!" The shops were depleted, soap, toothbrushes, cigarettes, and many medicines had become scarce, and he saw no new styles of clothing. People dragged themselves around the streets, "staring aimlessly," and soldiers were everywhere, "tramping stolidly, stupidly, brutally along, in their heavy hobnailed boots." But above all, he railed against the "Machiavellian or Borgian crimes . . . the attempts at slow poisoning and corruption of the minds of those they would enslave."[58]

Two days later, Bissing decreed that anyone who declined work "in the public interest" that fit his profession and that the German authorities had ordered would face imprisonment. Anyone who aided him, such as by offering relief, would be jailed and fined up to ten thousand marks, and if that party were an organization, its leaders would be held responsible. Tribunals or military authorities would judge all infractions, though refusal to work "will be valid if it is admissible under international law." Another decree warned that anyone who lied about his employment in response to an official inquiry risked a heavy fine and a prison term. Anyone receiving public or private relief who refused an offer to work would be punished, as would any person or organization encouraging his refusal. Belgian courts would prosecute under this article, and, as before, international law was an acceptable defense.[59]

Bissing had given his administration vague, menacing powers. Who would decide what employment suited the public interest? If the Comité National were held liable for having aided workers who rejected employment, how would the relief survive? Would German courts, especially military tribunals, honor a refusal based on international law? Would the jobs involve a military purpose or public works? Public works had proven their worth, especially in an agricultural, forested province like Luxembourg, where they absorbed ten thousand people, or almost all the adult unemployed. These projects shrank the relief rolls and cost the communes little because the Comité National paid most of the expense. But the new decrees outlawed assistance for anyone who turned down a job with public works, which looked like an attempt to set communal authorities against the committee.[60] Moreover, in late July, Bissing had promised Whitlock that he would never use the Comité National "to force the Belgian population" to work for the army "contrary to the stipulations of the Hague conventions."[61]

A test case arose over the Lessines quarries, a Hainaut concern that produced porphyry, a rock useful in making macadam that Germany had imported before the war. Not only were the Lessines quarries the nearest to the Flanders battlefront, they had been closed since the invasion, which made them a target. In August 1915, the quarry directors were told to resume operations and that the output would go only toward repairing Belgian roads. The directors agreed, provided they had guarantees, and they suggested that neutrals should oversee distribution. When the Germans said no, the directors held firm, whereupon the Germans seized the quarries, told the quarriers to return, and threatened those who did not. When the quarriers resisted, a tribunal sentenced the foremen and seven directors to deportation, eighty-one other workers to prison terms in Belgium, and the town to an afternoon curfew. Then the occupiers reopened the quarries in September, employing Germans, Russian prisoners of war, other foreign laborers, and a few Belgians who relented.[62]

The remaining directors appealed to Bissing in October, saying that "great misery prevails among the working population," and that "masters and workmen would embrace with joy the opportunity to resume work which would not be opposed to their patriotic duty." But when the military had rejected their request for guarantees, they believed their fears were confirmed, and now that the quarries were working again, the Belgians had "received proof" that the macadam was being "shipped toward the German lines." Accordingly, international law and the August decrees supported their refusal.

Not so, replied Bissing. His decrees were "efforts to induce the workmen to earn a regular salary," so instead of protesting, the directors should be asking the military to force the men to comply. Besides, even if the macadam did not serve only occupied Belgium's needs, as with "the repair of important military roads" or use in exceptional cases for the army, "this is no reason for refusing to produce it." Because the occupiers did not employ the macadam "primarily for military undertakings of war, the workmen do not take part in operations of war against their country." As for the sentences, the military authorities had warned the workers, whose stubborn opposition merited severe penalties.[63]

As 1915 drew toward a close, the screws tightened. A decree made harboring a former Allied soldier punishable by forced labor or death, even if the defendant was a family member. Two more decrees threatened fines, imprisonment, or forced labor for failing to inform against any offender, and the authorities' belief that a person must have known about an infraction was grounds for accusation. Under this law, three Luxembourg men were jailed for having failed to denounce people they knew to have helped a French aviator and would-be army volunteers cross the Dutch border.[64] Meanwhile, the governors of the Etappengebiet ordered that anyone who refused work on any project the military required would be jailed for a year and subject to deportation. Neither Belgian law nor international covenants were a defense, and the commune where the crime had taken place would be held responsible as well as the individual violator.[65]

The strain of occupation provoked mean behavior. A Namur province burgomaster wrote that never had he seen as "many rifts, as much animosity, hatred, rebelliousness, speculation, or weakness!" Farmers, workers, and merchants "in great number" gave themselves over to greed. The unemployed refused to work for the commune because they claimed the right to public assistance, and people who should have been self-sufficient demanded relief. And when two cabarets were turned into brothels for the Germans, Belgians, including married men, went there. A Limburg priest wrote that public morals remained solid until mid-1915, when people began speculating in food. When he preached against them, he was deported. He also said that many young men who should have been with the army spent their time playing skittles, and that the Germans seemed to take special pleasure in seducing Belgian soldiers' wives—he knew of six cases.[66]

In mid-October, Lumm told the Belgians that the receipts for the *Massengüter* would now not be paid until after the war, because the Allied attempt to starve the Belgian population and destroy the country economically relieved any obligation. He argued this from Article 53 of the Fourth Convention, which said that war matériel need not be reimbursed until after the peace—and, said Lumm, any goods the Allies denied Germany must be war matériel.[67] So when Bissing summoned the provincial councils in November to approve a second war contribution of 480 million francs, Antwerp and Brabant refused, recalling Bissing's promises. Lumm told them that if they did not vote the new contribution within twenty-four hours, he would take over the Banque Nationale. The councils gave in.[68]

Whitlock had compared the occupation with slow poisoning for the purpose of enslavement. Yet to outsiders, especially in Britain, the most infamous crime that took place during 1915 involved a single volley from a firing squad, and the victim they mourned was not even Belgian. In October, the Germans executed Edith Cavell, a fifty-year-old English nurse who had freely admitted that she had used her Brussels clinic to shelter hundreds of Allied soldiers lost behind enemy lines, enabling them to escape. Her actions had abused her immunity under the Red Cross banner and betrayed a trust because the Germans could have interned her as an enemy foreign national. Still, the indictment accused her of conducting escaped prisoners to the enemy, though she had never left Brussels, and the men had never been captured. What law she had broken and whether she had deserved to die were therefore unclear, which may explain the occupation's subsequent decree that made harboring an enemy soldier a capital offense.

Executing a sister of mercy was sure to cause an uproar, but Traugott Martin von Sauberzweig, the military governor of Brussels, refused to hear pleas for clemency from American and Spanish diplomats. When the neutral press treated Cavell's death as an atrocity, Berlin pretended that she had been a spy and had, among other trespasses, smuggled dynamite to blow up bridges.[69] That only made matters worse. The British had no trouble turning the gallant nurse into a symbol of their cause; her death was yet another crime against a woman that confirmed that Germans were uncivilized brutes. A statement she wrote in her last hours became famous: "I realise that patriotism is not enough. I must have no hatred or bitterness toward any one."[70]

The furor obscured several facts of Belgian life. Eight women numbered among the 1,135 Belgians who worked for escape or intelligence networks and paid the death penalty, not counting escapees shot or electrocuted trying to cross the border. One woman, Louise Derache, died months before Cavell did.[71] The British labeled Cavell's sentence judicial murder and called attention to her trial, in which the court had allowed her no reasonable chance to defend herself. These complaints had merit, yet, trumpeted afterward, they overshadowed the judicial terror that all Belgians lived with. For the twelve months after her death, German courts convicted more than 103,000 Belgians, almost 20,000 of them women.[72] But when Belgian authorities tried to apply the law, they got nowhere. The same month as Cavell's execution, the Germans prevented the Ghent police commissioner from pursuing a case involving the seduction of minors to debauchery because the evidence might compromise army officers.[73]

That one person's execution could eclipse a country's sufferings highlighted how hard it was for the Belgians to get their point across to people who had never been invaded. Edith Cavell was instantly recognizable to Britons, who knew a person like her or could imagine that they did, whereas the seven million people trapped in Belgium were foreigners. Ironically, however, the British never realized that their claims against Germany would have been more persuasive had they stressed what was happening to a nation of Belgians instead.

For one thing, the ambiguities of Cavell's case invited dispute, whereas the pervasive threat of the occupation offered firmer ground. Moreover, to place Cavell above an invaded, subjugated population implied that she embodied their struggles, and that, through her, Britain had suffered them too. This was straining a point, for the British government had freely chosen to fight, a decision that not every Briton had supported and that needed more justification than one woman's execution. It was only human that her death struck a deeper chord in Britain than the terrors under which millions of Belgians lived, but in the long run, the emphasis did not serve Britain's cause.

7

At Least They Only *Drown* Your Women

SHOCK AND ANGER OVER the invasion terror gave voice to a radical idea, that warring nations could not break the law with impunity and must pay. The day before Louvain burned, the *Times* of London declared that "by every law of honour and right," Belgium should have "the first claim to compensation and indemnity" in a peace settlement.[1] Five days later, the paper ran an editorial about Louvain titled "The March of the Hun" and refused to apologize for its immoderate language. "Even Attila had his better side. He spared Milan. . . . The wickedness of this abominable act shall be expiated to the uttermost when the day of reckoning comes."[2] The *Manchester Guardian*, which had opposed entering the war, said nothing about penalties but spoke of saving Belgium from "Prussian domination," which showed how much the political landscape had changed in only about three weeks.[3]

The popular movement to punish Germany, which gained momentum throughout the war, also faced opposition, partly because the British government hesitated to commit itself on Belgium's behalf, and because little or no precedent existed. Traditionally, an indemnity was what a loser paid a victor, as with France in 1871 and, more immediately, Brussels under occupation. Britain eventually endorsed compensation for Belgium, but at first, Asquith thought to ask the House of Commons for a message of "sympathy & laudation," because the Belgians "are really gallant fellows."[4]

In early November, he announced that Britain would fight until "Belgium recovers in full measure all and more that she has sacrificed," but, typical of British war aims pledges, the terms remained vague.[5] Not until late March 1915 did Britain refine them, when Grey named an "essential condition" as the "restoration of Belgium" to independence and "free possession of her territory; and reparation to her, as far as reparation is possible, for the cruel wrong done to her."[6] But still, the announcement was ambiguous, and British leaders left it that way.

In May 1915, a French commentator suggested that an indemnity—above and beyond restitution—would be "the best legal sanction for the injured parties," inviting judgment of German methods.[7] The focus on world opinion reflected the common belief that public censure was the strongest, if not the only, way to defend international law. The only sanction The Hague Conventions specified was to hold a belligerent "liable to make compensation" for how its armed forces behaved, which paralleled the legal concept that held states responsible for the conduct of persons.[8] The covenant did not say what the liability entailed or mention prosecutions. As for the neutrality violation, that carried no defined penalty, because the Treaty of 1839 never referred to one, and, moreover, waging aggressive war was not a crime.

No one anticipated holding a state culpable for war crimes—to apply a term little used then—and enough peace treaties included reciprocal amnesties so that some jurists took them for granted.[9] American and British military manuals provided that enemy soldiers might be punished for gross offenses, but not if they followed superior orders, in which case the commanders were liable—on capture.[10] Legal textbooks cited the American Civil War case of Captain Henry Wirz, who had commanded the Confederate prisoner-of-war camp at Andersonville, Georgia, and been accused of causing many prisoners' deaths. The victors had considered his offenses flagrant enough to fall outside a general amnesty, and a federal tribunal convicted and hanged Wirz. But this instance and a few others stood as exceptions to the presumption—and preference—that each belligerent discipline its own lawbreakers.

General opinion also assumed that "civilized" armies would never practice brutalities associated with less cultured nations. The *Chicago Tribune* spoke to this just before Louvain, noting that Germany was unlike the Balkan states, where the populace was "ablaze with race and religious hates and grudges centuries old."[11] The comment evoked the Balkan Wars of 1912–13, whose cruelties had prompted the Carnegie Endowment for International Peace to conduct an inquiry. After the Belgian envoys landed in New York, the *Tribune* dismissed their case on principle. "Nations cannot be convicted upon evidence of brutal acts by individuals," for if so, "any Mississippi town would have the character of the whole United States in its keeping. The burning of one negro, in such a case, would be sufficient excuse for a world combination in the name of civilization against such a country."[12]

That the paper could draw this analogy hardly a half century after the Civil War was startling, more so to minimize a scourge that American law enforcement seemed unwilling or unable to abolish. As recently as 1901, more than a hundred lynchings had happened in a single year, and the figure generally remained in double digits until the mid-1930s.[13] Yet, rather than admit that Americans nurtured "race and religious hates and grudges"—or that German soldiers had vented theirs on Belgian priests and churches—the *Tribune* ascribed this vice to other, presumably inferior, peoples. Unwittingly, the editorial was also inviting the comparison between a lynch mob and German troops, both of whom wreaked violence under the pretext of justice. Americans, the paper implied, need not concern themselves with either posse.

But few people who wanted Germany punished had thought through how to go about it. After Louvain, the *Times* printed letters that agreed that the responsible parties should face justice, even the kaiser, but the devil lay in the details. One respondent supposed that the court would be neutral and that the measure would apply to all belligerents, "though there appears to be no reason to apprehend that we or our Allies would be at all incriminated." The comment illustrated what critics have since labeled "victor's justice," the idea that trying your beaten enemy is "might makes right" wearing judge's robes.[14]

Santiago Pérez Triana, a Colombian international lawyer and delegate to the Second Hague Conference, contended that victor's justice offered a tool for change. "Where action is possible, no matter how forlorn, inaction becomes complicity," he wrote. He argued that fair, correct trials would serve German interests, placing the blame where it belonged rather than leave the nation culpable. The Allies could make prosecution a war aim, requiring delivery of offenders and providing for extradition, and neutrals should demand that all belligerents obey these terms, which, if stated immediately, might deter criminal abuse.[15]

This letter, which anticipated how the Allies of the Second World War would proceed, mapped out unknown territory. Pérez Triana had stressed the need for political and legal machinery, but the goverments acted piecemeal, if at all. The French convicted several captured German soldiers in October 1914 of "plundering in an armed band" and four others of having followed orders to take no prisoners. Early the following year, they convicted two more, one for plunder, one for arson. But France had not sought international participation, and the trials prosecuted crimes long outlawed in military manuals rather than loopholes the Fourth Convention had closed. When the Germans took reprisals on French prisoners, the two governments parleyed secretly, later agreeing to defer all punishments until the war ended.[16] Moreover, a leading French jurist argued that no nation would consent to "an abdication of all dignity" in handing over its soldiers, and penalizing a defendant who had followed orders was "excessive." You could still punish, because the Germans had behaved like "bandits," but you could not call that justice.[17]

Many people thought the destruction of Louvain's art warranted action. A London newspaper wrote that to punish "the infamy of Louvain," the Allies must cross the Rhine and destroy German war industries.[18] The *New York Tribune* applauded a statement in the London press that if the Allies won, art should be taken from Germany to replace what Louvain had lost. Destroying German art would be a "poor revenge," the paper said, but "the shifting of beauty . . . to a nation better able to honor it would be a just punishment and a just recompense." An American art critic even supposed that Louvain had contained "more beautiful works of art than the Prussian nation has produced in its entire history."[19]

This argument obscured the case. The ill-fated library had held fewer treasures and ranked lower among European collections than the Belgians claimed, and Louvain by no means outclassed Prussia, let alone Germany, in artistic achievement. Thanks to pressure from German art historians, in 1915 Berlin even sent an expert to identify treasures in occupied lands that should be protected.[20] But to tot up how many manuscripts had burned and use the answer to affirm or deny that Germans were barbarians missed the point. The real questions were why cultured people had set the fires and how the crime could be remedied, if at all.

The British playwright Jerome K. Jerome addressed them in an essay that the *New York Times* reprinted in late September. Jerome urged restraint about atrocity stories, most of which he doubted, and said that the guns should do the talking. No one could have argued with that, but Jerome extended the thought to the crimes themselves. He ascribed Louvain to "some criminal lunatic strutting in pipeclay and mustachios [who] was given his hour of authority and took the chance of his life. If I know anything of the German people, it will go hard with him when the war is over, if he has not had the sense to get killed."[21]

Belief in German remorse held tremendous power, and not only because religious ethics emphasize repentance and reparation. If one officer had burned Louvain, that meant not having to suspect his subordinates, his superiors, or his country, and if the Germans punished him, all was resolved. Their redemptive act would keep esteem for Germany intact and erase Louvain's most frightening implication, that European civilization may not have merited trust. The *Chicago Tribune*, in the editorial that referred to lynchings, alleged that neither side in Belgium had engaged in more than casual, arbitrary violence. Similar to Jerome, the paper cast German perpetrators as "demented or intoxicated, escaped from discipline, crazed by the sight of the slaughter of comrades, or infuriated by battle." And in asking whether the burning of Louvain was necessary, the editorial wondered whether "hasty acts of great severity [have] been such as will make Germans themselves apologetic."[22]

But the German public had called the arsonists heroes. Among soldiers, to have helped quell the "uprising" was such an honor that some were prouder of the wounds they had received there than in combat. Others pretended that they had served at Louvain when they had not.[23] The day Jerome's essay was republished, Belgian Freemasons asked their German brethren to push for an international inquiry into the invasion. Only two of seven lodges replied, rejecting the plea, demanding to know where Freemasonry had been when the Entente had forced the war on Germany, and saying that they would never doubt the army's word.[24]

Three days later, on 30 September, a naval staff officer at German headquarters in France told his diary that he had taken advantage of a visit by Bethmann to recommend creating an international court at The Hague to verify Allied charges. That way, Germany could have them corrected and avoid discredit "in the eyes of the whole world." Bethmann had agreed and promised to speak to Foreign Secretary

Jagow about it. But Jagow declined, "because we already have too much on our conscience," a rare instance of a high official openly admitting the possibility of wrongdoing. What he meant "I was never able to discover," the officer wrote. "Presumably he meant the unavoidable shootings of Belgian partisans due to war psychosis."[25]

This comment is tantalizing; who suffered from psychosis? Most likely the officer was talking about the Belgians, whom he had portrayed as combatants destined for punishment, which would have fit the German belief that the populace was crazed, and that Belgium was insane to resist. Whatever the officer was saying, however, Jagow's refusal to act disappointed him, because he thought that "a resolute clearing up of the atrocity stories would have profited us."[26]

But if Jagow had questions about army conduct, Germany's great minds did not. In early October, the Nobelist playwright Gerhart Hauptmann said that Germany, not the Allies, was fighting for civilization and to liberate Europe.[27] This moved his French friend Romain Rolland, a pacifist and admirer of Germany, to publish an open letter in reply. Rolland said that invading Belgium had aroused disgust, that German "ferocity" against an innocent nation was shameful, and that "you wage war against the dead, against the glories of centuries" by bombarding Malines and burning Louvain. "But who are you and by what name do you wish to be known now, Hauptmann, you have denied the name of barbarian? Are you the offspring of Goethe or of Attila?" Rolland challenged Hauptmann to protest against "the Huns who command you," saying that if he did not, he could not defend his own liberty and had no business talking about Europe's.[28]

Within days, Max Planck, Wilhelm Roentgen, Hauptmann, and others—ninety-three of Germany's scientific, artistic, and intellectual élite—issued a manifesto to which about four thousand professors eventually signed their names. The statement blamed the Belgians, adding that the Russians had killed German women and children, and that the French and British armies had employed dum-dum bullets. "Can any one point to an example of our ferocity?" the declaration asked. Like Hauptmann (and the German press), the Ninety-Three condemned the presence of nonwhite soldiers in the Allied armies as a crime against civilization, "letting loose mongrels and niggers on the white race." Doubting that any nation could equal Germany in loving art, the manifesto said nevertheless that "the preservation of art is not to be bought at the price of German defeat." Germany's "hypocritical foes" alleged that they fought against militarism, not culture, "but without German militarism German culture would long ago have been trodden into the earth." As for Rolland daring Hauptmann to disavow Germany's military leaders, the Ninety-Three proclaimed: "The German Army and the German people are one."[29]

The manifesto prompted a few objections within Germany, including ten signatories who withdrew their names, saying that they had been misinformed about the contents.[30] But the spectacle of Europe's finest minds hurling vitriol when months before they had been friends and colleagues was just one of the affair's disturbing aspects. Genius had displayed virulent race prejudice, and celebrated practitioners of the scientific method had taken libelous myths on faith. Leading thinkers had excused the destruction of a university town and embraced the military as culture's guardian. These startling expressions of allegiance made Rolland's question about the relationship between master and servant in Germany worth asking in a different way. Who was guilty for Louvain—only the leaders, or also those who had followed them without protest?

Maurice Maeterlinck, the Belgian writer whose remarks had originally set Hauptmann off, proposed an answer. He warned that once the war ended, "the unfortunate German people" would be cast as victims, and that "the Germany we know that is so sympathetic and cordial" bore no blame, only "hateful, arrogant Prussia." Maeterlinck passionately disagreed. All Germans were responsible, for governments reflected "the private morality and mentality of the nation." They had not been deceived because deception needed a willing partner, "and it is not intelligence that Germany lacks." Individual Germans were innocent in that their leaders led them astray, but as a society, they were subconsciously guilty. No experience, bitter lesson, or progress could prevail on this criminality, which must be punished, not pardoned.[31]

Maeterlinck was saying that critics must look past charming surfaces, that German crimes derived from a psychological process, and that forgiveness could not reform people who thought themselves innocent. But holding an entire populace culpable for war crimes would be difficult even when murder occurs on an industrial scale, and the invasion saw nothing like that. There was also no mistaking his vengeful tone, which would have troubled people to whom punishing war crimes seemed vindictive. Some thought Belgium must turn the other cheek and set an example, paving the way for a German apology.

Even Belgians—those who had fled German rule, that is—could not agree about whether punishment was just. In late October, *L'Indépendance Belge,* the expatriate newspaper in London, carried an article by a Belgian senator who questioned whether his people should "demand an eye for an eye." They had borne their sufferings stoically, and they must continue to or risk becoming "criminal in their turn" by punishing the criminals. Shame and disapproval would be reprimand enough, and he anticipated that much as certain German officers privately voiced their horror, all Germany would one day wake up.[32]

The senator had stepped on a hornet's nest. One man wrote in to say that Belgians did not derive comfort from stoicism but the "certainty, the absolute confidence" that "the German crime would not go unpunished." Another compared war to a duel, whose result normally had to be accepted without complaint, and that had the Germans observed the rules, the former enemies could have reached an understanding after the war. But the crimes changed that, and without sanctions, the victims could not forgive. A third respondent said, "The German leaders, hateful and conscious destroyers, those who are the directors of the masses, deserve the punishment inflicted on the worst criminals."[33]

Talk of hatred unnerved even generals. Writing in a journal devoted to Christian thought, Lord Frederick Roberts, the former Boer War commander, urged fellow Britons to "keep our own hands clean and . . . fight against the Germans in such a way as to earn their liking as well as their respect."[34] Roberts was an old soldier, but the era shared his perspective. The First World War killed more than five thousand combatants daily, on average—roughly equivalent to the entire Belgian civilian death toll in 1914—yet amazingly few commentators wrote about hate or frankly assessed its importance. To talk of avenging Louvain by wrecking Krupp or to call the foe barbarians evoked the language of hatred, but the shallow, borrowed kind, the type that left many who got swept up in it feeling ashamed afterward.

Ironically, one person who contemplated enmity without flinching was a churchman. Cardinal Mercier's archdiocese was Malines, and when he preached in the cathedral that German shells had partly destroyed, the partition of rough boards and brick that screened the worshipers from the damage lent pathos to his sermons. If he forgave the Germans, he did not say so, nor did he expect them to see their sins unless someone like himself pointed them out. The cardinal's flair for publicity, like the car in which he traveled—a first for a Belgian bishop—evinced a dash of modernity, and so did his views on the war crimes.[35]

Like Albert and de Broqueville, Mercier was unusually tall, over six feet—so much for "little" Belgians—and his thin, ascetic face with deep-set, humorous, gray eyes suggested the gentle scholar.[36] The appearance was deceptive. While traveling abroad in early September 1914, he told the Paris paper *Le Temps* that what was happening was not war but "the outcome of hate." The Germans were taking revenge for the stigma of having violated the treaty. Thinking that they could frighten history into forgetting their crime, they were outpouring their "rage against God, against His temples, against art, sacred or secular, and still more against God in the massacre of helpless women and children." The invaders were "savages" who had committed "crimes against the rights alike of Heaven and humanity" while presuming to invoke the hand of God as they destroyed innocents.[37]

Nothing in this referred directly to the subconscious, but Mercier's reasoning followed Maeterlinck's in one respect. The cardinal was making the novel interpretation that the Germans had struck out of deep-seated fear and rage that the Belgians, by choosing to resist, had held a mirror up to them. This idea had a powerful, if grim, significance. If the invader had dealt out terror to avoid having to face the treaty violation, he was unlikely to admit either crime, because the guilt would be too great. Therefore, the Germans would not atone, and the Belgians would not forgive. Mercier's argument was uncommon, and what he expected both sides to do, he did not say— for now.

When Theodore Roosevelt first heard of the invasion, he wrote private letters in which he waved away the Treaty of 1839 and refused to challenge Germany's necessity in violating it.[38] By late September, he was sounding like the former president who had sponsored the Second Hague Conference and was annoyed that the United States had forsaken "his" treaty. He told the Belgian envoys that had he been president, he would have protested the invasion as a breach of neutrals' rights under the Fifth Convention and asked all neutrals to join in enforcing it.[39] He told his friend the British ambassador the same, adding, "I would not have made such a statement unless I was willing to back it up" with willingness to go to war.[40]

Roosevelt's change of heart may have come from outrage at the invasion, a chance to score off Wilson, a growing belief that America must join the Allies, or all three. Whatever the case, he had traveled far since August, and in the process, found grounds to protest that would not have compromised neutrality. Had he stopped there, he might have exposed a weakness in Wilson's policy, but by linking protest to intervention, Roosevelt raised the stakes. Cutting out diplomatic pressure as an option left two choices, keeping quiet or declaring war. Since American opinion would have accepted only one of them, framing the issue that way would not have helped Belgium and would have confirmed the wisdom of recoiling from unpleasant problems around the globe.

But Roosevelt had a grander idea. In an essay the *New York Times* published in early November, he drew on his Nobel acceptance address of 1910 and proposed to enforce Hague with a "posse comitatus," an international tribunal backed by armed force. Roosevelt conceded that his plan would be hard to work out but asserted that the world had no choice, because "merely to trust public opinion without organized force back of it is silly." Nations must not shrink from punishing wrongdoers, and he attacked the Wilson administration for not having protested the invasion. He urged the United States to ascertain the facts, particularly about the levies, Aerschot, and Louvain, and to act if the findings warranted.[41]

The "posse comitatus," a League of Nations by a Latin name, was so provocative that the *New York Times* ran an editorial the same day of twice the usual length. The paper chided Roosevelt for not saying whether the United States should protest or fight, and rejected both. War was impossible, not least because joining a European conflict would breach the spirit of Washington's Farewell Address and the Monroe Doctrine. The country had, "in the light of reason," no cause to fight for The Hague Conventions and no means. As for protest, "how faint and colorless and feeble" a note would have been "compared with the unsparing denunciation that the whole American people have pronounced upon Germany for her savage treatment of the Belgians!"[42]

Still, thanks largely to Roosevelt's muckraking, the State Department was obliged to face the problem. In late January 1915, chief counsel Robert Lansing wrote Secretary Bryan that the department had been receiving daily inquiries asking why the United States had kept silent about the invasion. Lansing, who opposed a protest but objected to the failure to explain, argued that Germany's breaching the Treaty of 1839 had been a purely political act, and "that national safety may justify a nation in violating its solemn pledges." If necessity had not compelled the violation, the act was morally wrong, but no nation could judge another's motives or necessities, and "international ethics" did not "furnish an excuse" to do so.[43] Two weeks later, he wrote that Belgium had lost its neutrality by deciding to fight. As for war crimes, those could be sorted out after the war, but, as with neutrality, the United States had no basis on which to speak.[44]

These memos took on greater meaning in June, when Bryan resigned and Wilson named Lansing to replace him. The president chose him partly because he saw him as someone who had few ideas of his own and would defer, but that was not entirely true. The tenets Lansing expressed derived from his long-standing belief that sovereign nations behaved as they wished until physical force or public opinion persuaded them to act otherwise. Legal remedies for war crimes did not exist.[45]

Lansing's statement did not anticipate that the Germans might push the point, for in February came their announcement that they would start unrestricted submarine warfare. At the time, Germany possessed too few submarines to mount an effective blockade, and since Britons despised these weapons on principle, in Britain the announcement was interpreted as an underhanded attempt to terrorize merchant seamen into refusing to sail. On 8 March 1915, Churchill directed the Admiralty to say that captured submarine crews would be treated as criminals, not prisoners of war, and though the government soon retreated from this position, the threat stirred opinion.[46] Several letter writers told the *Times* that the miscreants should stand trial in a British civil court, and the debate expanded to consider who was responsible, officers or also those who had followed their orders.[47]

The Germans retaliated against British prisoners of war, already reported in the British press to have been stripped of their clothes in bitter weather, overcrowded in their barracks, or subjected to blows and insults. Public outrage boiled over, and in late April, Asquith condemned "this horrible record of calculated cruelty and crime," promising that at war's end, Britain would "exact such reparation . . . as it may be possible for us to do" from those proven guilty.[48] The *Times* approved "Mr. Asquith's emphatic declaration of the Government's intentions," though the prime minister had not said how he would pursue them and had made no commitment except not to forget the wrongs.[49] Whatever he had in mind, however, the *New Statesman* wanted the method applied to "the officers who ordered the butcheries at Louvain, Dinant, and elsewhere," along with those responsible for submarine warfare, poison gas, and other crimes.[50]

Six days later, a German submarine torpedoed the British liner *Lusitania* off the Irish coast, killing almost 1,200 people, including 128 Americans. The *Irish Times* declared that Germany must be treated like a "mad dog,"[51] but for the first time, a German act had shaken the United States. Though fewer than one in a hundred American newspapers demanded war, even the *Chicago Tribune* and the *Washington Post* allowed that war was possible and rejected as inadequate the German defense that the ship had carried munitions in the cargo.[52]

A few pro-Allied papers compared the sinking with the invasion, like the *New York Tribune*, which published a drawing of a widowed Belgium comforting a weeping Miss Columbia. The caption read: "At Least They Only *Drown* Your Women."[53] But Wilson said that the country must set "a special example" by remaining at peace, "the healing and elevating influence of the world." His next words earned praise at home but irked the Allies: "There is such a thing as a man being too proud to fight. There is such a thing as a nation being so right that it does not need to convince others by force that it is right."[54] The *New York Tribune* ran a cartoon of Albert, facing front with one hand on Wilson, in profile, above the words: "The Man Who Was Not Too Proud to Fight."[55]

The clamor rose even higher when, on 13 May, the English-speaking press excerpted the *Report of the Committee on Alleged German Outrages,* known as the Bryce report, Britain's official account of the invasion. "We know that there are no depths of moral degradation and other brutishness to which the Germans are incapable of descending," the *Irish Times* remarked. Even the *Manchester Guardian* said that to "a campaigner hardened to warfare among savages," the report "would read like a hideous nightmare. It should be in the hands of

every eligible man who still wonders where his duty lies."[56] BRYCE
FINDS GERMANS WAGE FIENDISH WAR ran the *New York Tribune* headline, referring to Viscount James Bryce, who had led the inquiry.[57]
Wellington House, a British propaganda agency, and a New York review each surveyed the American response and remarked how newspapers linked the report to the *Lusitania*.[58] The *New York Herald*, for
one, had said that the two together ended any hope that German
atrocities had been exaggerated.[59] The *Washington Herald* spoke of
"frightfulness" (translating *Schrecklichkeit*, what the Germans called
the invasion terror) and said that the authorities who unleashed it on
Belgium were the ones "who sank the *Lusitania* and murdered 115 [*sic*]
Americans."[60]

In Germany, the *Norddeutscher Allgemeine Zeitung*, official in all but
name, defended the army. Atrocity stories abroad grew like "a
Hydra," and as soon as you struck one head off, a pair grew in its
place, while "the poisonous sap of slander spread over everything."
The paper would not have expected a nation "that possessed a spark
of fair play and sense of justice" to purvey such "filth and lies" and
wondered where British outrage had been when Belgian francs-tireurs
had killed German soldiers.[61]

No document about Belgium stunned the British and American
publics like the Bryce report or enjoyed its circulation. Wellington
House shipped forty-one thousand copies to the United States alone
and sent speakers to discuss the contents. In Britain, patriotic groups,
including those soliciting enlistment and Belgian relief funds, promoted the report and handed out copies. By June, Wellington House
had overseen translations into ten languages; more followed.[62] Because of the publicity and Britain's official oath that every word was
true, the report came to represent the Belgian case, an endorsement
that went awry.

The problem began with the report's methods. The preface said that
the investigators had taken more than twelve hundred statements
from refugees and Belgian and British soldiers, but few of them de-
posed under oath because their examiners had lacked the power to
administer one. The testimony gave no witnesses' names and few
identifying details, though the original papers were said to show
them, a defect that the *Norddeutscher Allgemeine Zeitung* fastened on.
The committee said that anonymity would protect relatives still in Bel-

gium, but that could not have applied to everyone, British soldiers especially.[63]

The preface also contended that the committee had deleted hearsay and anything "palpably irrelevant" or implausible, which explained why the report printed only 350 statements recounting crimes against Belgian civilians. However, if witnesses had seen a dead body on a doorstep or a woman "who has the appearance of having been outraged," what the witnesses later learned about these incidents was allowed. Most people would call this hearsay, but the committee, which included prominent jurists, a historian, and a magazine editor, "had no hesitation" about it.[64]

This decision opened the door to hair-thin evidence. A soldier who had seen children wearing bandages repeated what he had heard, that the Germans had cut off various body parts. A refugee testified that a woman had told her that a German had thrown her baby in the air and impaled it on his bayonet. "She was a peasant woman and I am sure she was telling the truth," the refugee said. But even self-proclaimed eyewitnesses told tales about the bayoneting of wounded prisoners or gang rapes, events that might have happened, but which these onlookers had observed from a distance of three hundred yards. A Belgian soldier said that, in mufti, he had seen the Germans gang-rape fifteen women on tables set up in the main square of Liège. He saw it all, he said, having watched for an hour and half. At Haecht, another soldier said he had seen a two- or three-year-old child nailed to a farmhouse door by its hands and feet.[65]

The 350 statements contained 155 references to mutilation, rape, deliberate murder of children, or a combination of these, but no two statements confirmed any single incident. By comparison, the more comprehensive postwar Belgian report counted thirty-six rapes and several mutilations (of men only). As for children, many died in burning buildings, from reckless gunfire, and during deportations. But as for purposeful killings, the postwar inquest charged about a dozen cases, far fewer than the Bryce testimony would suggest, and, with one exception, never in the grotesque style that the wartime atrocity tales affected.[66] The damage that this caused was incalculable, because virtually every place that appeared in the Bryce report had a legitimate complaint against the invaders, but that was not what saw print.

What was more, the British government gave the sensational findings credit by putting James Bryce's name on them. Britons knew

Bryce as a member of the House of Lords, a respected jurist, a long-time member of the House of Commons, and former chief secretary for Ireland. Americans fondly remembered his days as ambassador to Washington and a book he wrote, *The American Commonwealth.* Bryce also admired the Germans—he had studied at Heidelberg—and when war broke out had voiced understanding of encirclement fears. Perhaps most important, he had condemned British conduct during the Boer War, which suggested that he put moral concerns above what many people considered patriotic duty.[67] If any Briton was qualified to have his verdict on German crimes taken on faith, he was.

But Bryce had reasons to doubt the testimony. In late December 1914, he heard that none of the handless children nor the rape victims said to have become pregnant had been found at the addresses listed. Committee members disagreed about the taking of the testimony, with Harold Cox, who edited the prestigious *Edinburgh Review,* wanting the jurists to examine the witnesses. Bryce also went along with the proposal to release the report simultaneously in Britain and America, despite the appearance of a propaganda stunt.[68] This was a curious position, given that in September he had advised against a special atrocity campaign in the United States because "an abundant supply of facts" would speak for themselves.[69] But however worrisome the process, Bryce faced a weightier problem. Failing to support charges of gruesome crimes might, in the public mind, acquit the Germans. One historian has suggested that to avoid perpetuating this great untruth, Bryce risked telling lesser ones.[70]

None of this made the newspapers. The *New York Tribune* spoke for many: "For all who know Viscount Bryce, and no European is better known in this country, his name attached to the fatal document is as final as that of the highest court."[71] As much as the evidence, belief in Bryce pushed the American press to accept that German policy in Belgium entailed war crimes. A graphic opinion appeared in the *New York Herald,* whose drawing of a double crucifixion, titled "A Certain Frightfulness," showed a little girl's body flattened against Jesus' while a soldier wearing a spiked helmet hovered nearby.[72]

British military recruiters had a field day. One poster said, "You are wanted in bringing to justice the murderers of innocent men, women & children." As with the *Lusitania,* much Bryce propaganda targeted Ireland, exploiting Irish sympathy for Belgium. On one poster, a woman holding a rifle asked, "Will you go or must I?"

while Belgium burned symbolically in the background. Another poster asked, "Have you any women-folk worth defending? Remember the women of Belgium." The picture showed a motherly woman in a shawl. A third poster referred to German Catholics who did not protest the invasion terror and asked, "Do you think that they will spare you because you are Catholics?" But the boldest appeal was one that mentioned Bryce, described the child's crucifixion at Haecht, and called on the men of Ireland to end the "Pestilence of Prussianism."[73]

Despite the report's flaws, the Bryce committee had reached many sound conclusions, drowned out by the publicity hoopla and often dismissed since. The report summary gave a fairly accurate account of Herve, Aerschot, Andenne, and Louvain.[74] It charged the use of human shields, which critics have assumed could not have happened, but a recent study comparing German and Belgian sources has confirmed thirty-two instances.[75] Most crucial, the Bryce findings properly analyzed the character of the violence. The summary emphasized the German belief that any chance shot must have come from a civilian weapon; judged that sporadic outbursts could not account for widespread terror; and supposed that soldiers sometimes fired deliberately to cause a melee.[76] Critics have fastened on the verdict that the Germans had planned what they did, but a reasonable person could think so, given the sheer number of incidents.

Moreover, if the testimony was loaded to imply that Germans were degenerates, the summary insisted otherwise. For instance, in stating that drunkenness had aggravated the violence, the committee stressed that this did not make the Germans demons, only explained how civilized Europeans could have given themselves over to brutality. Acts of kindness had taken place, and officers had sometimes punished wrongdoers, whereas anyone who "has travelled among the German peasantry knows that they are as kindly and good-natured as any people in Europe." The authors did wonder whether mutilation might have resulted, in some cases, from a perverted sexual instinct, but they ascribed this to individuals, not the army. The report even took care to blame the terror not on the entire army but on the Prussian military caste and its notions about necessity, as laid down in *Usages of War*.[77] For an investigation that supposedly condemned a nation on flimsy evidence, this assertion was arguably too lenient, ignoring that many willing hands had made the invasion terror, and that almost no one in Germany had spoken against it.

"Murder, lust, and pillage prevailed over many parts of Belgium on a scale unparalleled in any war between civilised nations during the last three centuries," the summary remarked.[78] This statement was mocked later as an embellishment, but it may have been true according to the prevalent definition of a civilized nation. Western Europe might not have seen brutality on the scale practiced in Belgium since the Thirty Years' War (1618–48), a judgment that had occurred to several people, including Wilson, and would to others as the war progressed.[79]

Therefore, to assess the Bryce report requires separating the contents from the process of assembling them. The evidence undeniably exaggerated, but the report displayed a surer grasp of German methods—in general—than its reputation would imply. Nevertheless, the *Norddeutscher Allgemeine Zeitung* had a point: A government that constantly invoked justice and fair play should have lived by them. After the war, Britons of troubled conscience rejected the Bryce findings, the crimes against Belgium, and the Belgian insistence on them as cynical lies that had led legions of British youths to their deaths in battle.

The reaction speaks to the shame and fury at having been twisted into hating an enemy under false pretenses, and the disillusionment at the abuse of public trust. But the Bryce report reflected British views more than the Belgian case, and the attempt to exploit it for British purposes did not change a central fact: The invaders had employed illegal, systematic terror. By emphasizing rape and mutilation—and on flimsy evidence—the report obscured the murder, arson, pillage, and deportations for which Belgians, if not Britons, could hate without any manipulation necessary. The tragedy is that the Bryce report made the terror seem trivial, at least in retrospect.

The report also reinforced the impression that the invasion defined German crimes, which underlined the relative absence of the occupation in the debate on Belgium. Why the British, let alone the Belgians, made so little of the occupation is puzzling, especially when the Germans handed them fresh ammunition every week. In part, this was because no one outside Belgium could appreciate what was happening, and to do so would have required a frame of reference that they lacked. A later generation that had witnessed full-blown totalitarian regimes would have understood, but in 1914 and 1915, the occupation was hard to comprehend or credit, never mind explain.

What little information that appeared in print was seldom accurate. George B. McClellan, a Princeton professor of economic history (and son of the Civil War general) published an article in the *New York Times Sunday Magazine* in early October 1915. He reported that Brussels showed less "evidence of the war" than Paris, blamed unemployment on expatriate factory owners who refused to return, and judged that "the Germans are certainly doing their best to conciliate the Belgians." McClellan praised the occupiers for bringing order to Belgium, where, before the war, "the spirit of social unrest was constantly growing," and whose capital "was the headquarters of international anarchy." He even had the idea that the Belgians were allowed to wear the tricolor and pictures of the king in their buttonholes.[80]

But even observers who saw Belgium more clearly had trouble describing it, as Whitlock's struggles attest. On the first day of 1915, another Princeton professor named Dana Carleton Munro filed a confidential report with the Rockefeller Foundation, on whose behalf he had toured Belgium to assess the need for relief. His account revealed a keen eye for physical damage—Munro was the one who had noted how many people slept in a certain chicken coop—and, in some respects, of the emotional terrain. He described the fear the terror had inspired, the hatred of the Germans that had unified the normally fractious Belgians, the intense opposition to the occupier's will. Even so, he ascribed their failure to rebuild or even clean up largely to the wish to preserve evidence of "so-called German atrocities," and he questioned the passive strike. Rancor, not the want of resources, was the main barrier to revival. If the Belgians were willing to cooperate, the Germans would surely relax financial controls in return. Otherwise, if the population remained idle, "physical and moral decay" would blunt labor's competitive edge, and when charity ran out—as it must—the Belgians would starve.[81]

Munro's report evoked familiar themes. He accented the physical violence, as the propagandists had, over the subtler terrors starting to appear. He assumed that the Germans would make concessions, another way of saying that they had repentance in them. Finally, Munro spoke as if the Belgians' moral position were their most precious possession, perhaps forgetting that accommodations with the occupier carried moral implications. Not surprisingly, when the Rockefeller

Foundation published its findings in February 1915, Munro's criticisms did not see print, only his praise and that of other inspectors. As the *New York Times* told the story, the picture of Belgium was one of physical destruction alongside virtue under duress, which included less indulgence in alcohol or amusements. The portrayal underlined how sympathy hinged (or was thought to hinge) on Belgian purity, and how charity's guardians had concealed evidence of blemishes.[82]

But a one-dimensional portrayal of Belgium did not result only from the failure to understand or the worry that the public might take a more nuanced picture the wrong way. The mass-circulation press, which influenced as never before what people learned and how they learned it, had a product to sell. Sober accounts of economic surveillance could not compete with headlines about rape and mutilation. Even the Germans observed that Belgian reports were less lurid than British ones, whereas the Belgian Press Bureau complained to the British Foreign Office that the press either ignored or buried Belgian offerings that were not racy enough.[83] Once the Belgians had gone public with their charges in August 1914, they discovered that they no longer controlled the substance of their complaints or even the tone.

Then there was American taste. A British propaganda chief was astonished that the American appetite for atrocity stories never flagged, and that "there was no more certain appeal to the American public" than through the sensational.[84] When Whitlock visited his Ohio hometown, he wrote that a woman asked him at a dinner party, "Now Brand, did you ever see any German soldiers cutting off the hands of little children?"[85] This happened in August 1917, three years after the invasion and four months after the United States had declared war on Germany.

But newspapers were not the only information outlet. By June 1915, Wellington House guessed that it had pumped out 2.5 million copies of books, pamphlets, official reports, and speeches about "the rights and wrongs of the war," intended for opinion makers, not necessarily the general public. These publications adopted a factual, straightforward style, and the authors were respected scholars and writers.[86] Most tracts dealt with Belgium, but usually to rehash the neutrality violation and the invasion terror, not to discuss the occupation. The British needed to justify having gone to war to uphold a treaty and Belgian independence, and what had happened to the Belgians afterward did not seem to matter.

Yet the Belgians in exile themselves spent little ink on the occupation until late 1916, and then to protest a single crime, deportations for forced labor. Why they followed the British lead remains unclear, but perhaps the answer lies with how they viewed reparations. In May 1915, one Belgian author wrote, "We consider that it is a case of emergency where a debt of honor is due from the whole of humanity. Belgium has really sacrificed herself to avert from the world the domination of an unscrupulous autocracy."[87] So strong was the belief that all losses would be reimbursed that in April 1915, Albert warned the cabinet not to encourage people to think so.[88]

Consequently, expatriate Belgians may have harked back to August 1914, when their country stood alone against the invader, to recall the debt and to underscore that Belgium played a military role in the war. Outsiders, including Belgians abroad, could not readily understand that occupied Belgium was resisting too, and rumors went around that Belgians under German rule were receiving a free ride. Walter H. Page, the American ambassador in London, wrote House in late June 1915 that they were getting rich off the war. After all, the world was feeding them, their foreign investments continued to accrue capital, the Belgian government could not tax them, and German levies were not excessive.[89]

Outsiders might easily suppose that Belgium should be paid for the physical ruin of 1914, but the case for compensating people whose freedom and dignity had been robbed was abstract and harder to justify. Besides, if the Belgians in exile did not defend their honor and innocence against German accusations from 1914, skeptics could say that they had lied or exaggerated, and that Belgium deserved no reparations or sympathy.

By contrast, Belgians in occupied territory advertised their torment under German rule, publishing underground newspapers and circulating tracts or church sermons, some of which they smuggled out of Belgium. They also made their views known without words. To protest a given decree or simply the lack of free expression, crowds silently paraded the streets until they were dispersed, sometimes wearing discreet tricolor rosettes or outfits that combined the colors of the American flag. Once they demonstrated on Valentine's Day, because they thought it was American Independence Day.[90]

What the British press did say about the occupation would not have helped anyone understand it. One example appeared in February 1915, a four-part series in the *Times* titled "The Heart of Belgium."[91] The paper ascribed the articles to an anonymous American reporter and claimed that they revealed the essence of the occupation, but they reflected British views. The first installment began with the Belgian plea, "Please tell the English not to judge us by certain types of our refugees," and the last ended by noting that Belgium, unconquered, was "still a buffer for England and France against their enemies." In between, the paper showed the Belgians as dedicated, hardworking, and strict with those who expected a handout, thereby promoting the relief while answering concerns about Belgian rectitude. Further, the author admitted that he had used to think of Belgium "as a place whose nationality was created by European politics" and would not have been surprised had five months of occupation led to the Belgians "bowing to Caesar . . . for the sake of individual profit." But "nothing of the kind has happened," because "Belgian nationalism is a fact." In other words, despite popular misconceptions, occupied Belgium was fighting back.

But these stories depicted the resistance as the kind seen in a melodrama. At the mention of the Germans, the Belgians' eyes darkened or they shook their fists; even children refused to play. One article said that the Belgians were "prisoners in their own land," yet beyond references to guards on every corner—an exaggeration—or restrictions on travel and communication, no details brought home how that felt. Even more damaging, the portrayal took the existence of francs-tireurs for granted and described passive resistance as a game ("a kind of warfare more efficacious than sniping") and the Belgians as the winners. Try as they might, the Germans could not halt the display of the Belgian national colors, and "if all offenders were arrested the gaols of Germany could not hold them."

The same romantic bravado had trivialized the terror of 1914, except that here, the Germans were no longer barbarians but clumsy buffoons who would eventually topple of their own weight. By coincidence, the first article appeared on the day that Scott Hurtt Paradise saw the parents of escapees deported at Hasselt, which underlines the kind of story the *Times* might have printed. Had more outsiders understood the occupation, fewer could have put such trust in German goodwill or readiness to apologize, perhaps with less talk of necessity excusing German actions, or that every army behaved the same. Skeptics who doubted the terror might have had to admit that the Germans had the mind-set capable of inflicting it. But most important, the debate would have focused on respect for law, property, and freedom rather than whether the Belgians were saints, and the Germans, devils.

8

Hell's Premises

IN 1916, BELGIUM began to fray at the seams. Prices had more than doubled since July 1914, as witnessed by "rows of empty jars and shelves in the groceries" and the "chunks and knuckles" that had replaced carcasses in the meat markets.[1] The soil produced less, a sign that the absence of chemical fertilizers was beginning to tell. Whitlock heard that schoolchildren had trouble paying attention because of hunger, and studies debated whether they had lost or failed to gain weight compared even with 1915.[2]

No epidemics had broken out, but the incidence of tuberculosis was rising, especially among the industrial and minor commercial classes, striking adolescents hard. Even healthy industrial workers had lost weight, and one inquiry appraised the laboring man's "energy and power of production" as "considerably less" than normal. Hospitals reported lower birth weights, nursing mothers produced less milk, and the birthrate had dropped to less than half the prewar figure, despite the presence of a male population proportionally higher than in other countries.[3]

Liège pawnshops were full of sewing machines, normally the last object a thrifty Liègoise would have given up. But by summer 1916, cloth prices had risen 300 percent to 400 percent over 1915 alone, and only the wealthy were buying. After much haggling, Hoover managed to import secondhand clothes from the United States, which Belgian *ouvroirs*, or sewing workrooms, converted to new use. The mammoth Antwerp *ouvroir* employed three thousand people, mostly women who had never worked in the needle trades, and every large town had an *ouvroir*. Their handiwork was readily identifiable, wrote a CRB supervisor, for girls' dresses were cut several sizes too large and had a pretty collar or trim on the cuff to compensate. Thanks to the *ouvroirs*, he had rarely come across ragged women or children, but shoes betrayed efforts to keep up appearances because the *ouvroirs* could not patch them forever, and the Germans had taken all the leather.[4]

At Lent, Mercier observed that many young women no longer came to church because they had no shoes, only clogs. He asked wealthier women not to flaunt their fortune, which offended God, the country, and the poor, and he urged everyone to attend Mass without shame.[5] A CRB delegate who served at Hasselt and Antwerp supposed that the poor were not suffering more than in normal times, but he pitied "those in good circumstances before . . . who have lost all they had."[6]

People did not always respond with sober restraint, however. The number of movie theaters mushroomed, and for the twelve months beginning in June, occupied Belgium bought an estimated fifty million tickets. The Comité National threatened to deny relief to anyone who went to dance halls or movies, but that did not curb these passions, nor did pleas that attending censored movies was disloyal.[7] To a few visitors, especially soldiers on leave, Brussels seemed gay, bursting with plenty.[8]

Meanwhile, the occupiers continued to siphon off Belgian resources. Fifty-seven times during 1916 they decreed requisitions for commodities as varied as horses, machine tools, wool, mattresses, cocoa, tires, cloth and elastic, and the copper tubing in breweries. Factory owners had to submit lists declaring engines or pumps, machines that cut or shaped wood or metal, or tools that dredged, hauled, or excavated. Patrols held snap checks to verify the lists, and courts punished discrepancies or attempts to hide equipment, sometimes with prison terms. The occupiers printed a catalog, and industrialists sent agents to pick out the hardware they wanted for shipment to Germany.[9]

The number and thoroughness of exactions, now in their third year, might have made anyone wonder whether the Belgians had anything left to take. But as 1916 began, there was still one kind of requisition that they had not yet endured.

In February, the Germans attacked Verdun, a French fortress town on the Meuse where Charlemagne's bickering grandsons had split the Frankish Empire into kingdoms, two of which had evolved into modern France and Germany. However, the choice of target was not about a millennium-old quarrel. The German General Staff believed that

Installation des 2 moteurs soufflants de Dampremy — Avant démolition

Installation des 2 moteurs soufflants de Dampremy — Après démolitio

From the invasion period to the armistice, the occupiers took factory machinery and shipped it to Germany. Above, a factory at Dampremy, near Charleroi, with equipment intact, and below, after the pillage. Hoover Institution Archives

Verdun was indefensible, but that the French would sacrifice division after division rather than withdraw and admit defeat. Nevertheless, the strategy went awry, for though the French suffered appalling casualties to hold Verdun, the attackers bled almost as much, yet could not capture it. When neither side would abandon the struggle, the Belgians got caught in the crossfire. Weeks after the offensive began, the Germans decided to replace their losses by calling up workers whose jobs had exempted them from military service. But that would create a hole, and on 2 March, the Ministry of War told Bissing to fill it by providing four hundred thousand Belgians for German industry, forcibly if need be.[10]

The governor-general demurred. Using force, he warned, "would arouse great dissatisfaction" in the United States and other neutrals, with "highly undesirable and dangerous effects." He drew attention to the pledge in October 1914 that returning refugees need not fear forced labor, which the Dutch had cited in persuading the refugees to leave Holland. To renege would embarrass the Netherlands and make Germany look bad. Bissing added that forced labor involved "a special difficulty" in "the avoidance of a flagrant violation of the provisions of the Hague Convention," by which he meant the conscription and transportation of workers to war industries in Germany.[11]

Bissing won his point, but on condition that he supply the necessary volunteers.[12] Delivering 400,000 would be no small task, not least because the number of unemployed was uncertain. Dutch newspapers published statistics supposedly derived from the Comité National that placed the number of jobless men, women, and children at 1.4 million. A German correspondent put the total at 1.6 million, whereas Mercier said 400,000, and Vandervelde, 600,000. The real number might have been toward the low end because many people had part-time work, so that perhaps only 350,000 members of the work force were completely idle, if idleness was the criterion.[13] But however many there were, to date only about 11,000 had signed up, which suggested the size of the hurdle. Bissing's preference for going around it resulted from the premise that open confrontation would derail *Flamenpolitik*, the plan by which he hoped to court the Flemish and exploit their quarrel with the Walloons.[14]

For Bethmann, *Flamenpolitik* was insurance against Belgium's ever again allying with the Entente and, starting in January 1916, he repeatedly urged Bissing to split Belgium in two.[15] But the governor-general believed, as he wrote in a private memo in late 1915 or early 1916, that only by annexing Belgium could the Germans uphold "our influence and sphere of power." No matter how ironclad a peace treaty, an independent Belgium would "be developed and employed as a concentration area and outpost position for our enemies." Consequently, the Belgian population must "adapt itself and subordinate itself, if only gradually, to the German domination," which was where *Flamenpolitik* came in.[16]

Some Germans opposed annexation because they feared absorbing a Catholic, Latin population. Bissing contended that Belgium was Germanic, because Germanic tribes had penetrated Belgium "through and through," and "even the Walloons have been made French only by time." But he focused on the four million Flemish, for whom the occupation would pose as patron without granting the separate state that Flemish radicals dreamed of. Once the Flemish escaped "French tyranny," they would slowly rediscover their "free, although not easily controlled, Low German way of living" and acknowledge their debt to Germany. He hinted that *Flamenpolitik* would mean revising Belgian laws covering administration, language, the church, the economy, the judiciary, and the military. After the war, the Walloons would either have to declare allegiance to Germany or leave, and the property of those who left would be confiscated.[17]

Neither Bethmann nor Bissing invented *Flamenpolitik,* which derived from a popular notion of a militarily, economically, and culturally dominant Germany.[18] Friedrich von Bernhardi, who had scorned Belgian neutrality in *Germany and the Next War,* advanced his version of *Flamenpolitik* in the same book. He predicted that when the war came, the Low Countries would either conform to England's will and anger Germany, or "prefer that adhesion to the German Empire which geography dictates."[19] As an otherwise sensitive officer-novelist wrote in 1916 from Brussels, Germany's duty was to become "big brother" to "the smaller Germanic nations" in Europe, "the brother who has made good and presented them all with his . . . culture."[20] The wartime press mirrored this view.

Bissing was trying to realize these ideas, and the first battleground in his campaign was Ghent. The Flemish had always wanted the university there to be the first to adopt their language exclusively, and the school was a symbol of resistance, having remained closed since the invasion in protest. In late December 1915, he had announced that he would reopen the university as a Flemish institution, and in January 1916, he sent a representative to speak to the faculty. But nearly all the pro-Flemish professors spurned the gift, and one, Paul Fredericq, refused to meet the emissary. Only six admitted that they could lecture in Flemish, a fraction of the real number, thanks partly to lobbying by Fredericq and his friend Henri Pirenne. Outside the university community, thirty-eight noted members of the Flemish movement signed a pamphlet objecting to the policy as an unwarranted intrusion into Belgian affairs and a breach of law.

Bissing insisted, and though the professors did not yield, on 15 March he decreed that the university would reopen come autumn. Three days later, soldiers knocked on Pirenne's door and ordered him to headquarters, saying his business there would be brief. Accordingly, he left with only his hat but became suspicious when his escorts led him through deserted side streets. When they arrived, an officer said that he would be deported within the hour, on orders from Berlin, as "an extremely dangerous person" and that this was a "necessity." Unlike most dangerous people, however, Pirenne managed to persuade the officer to let his wife bring him a suitcase and to say goodbye.[21] Fredericq was deported with him. The occupiers had punished a pro-Flemish professor to advance *Flamenpolitik* and jailed two teachers in the name of academic freedom.

With one hand, Bissing had parried the Ministry of War over workers, but with the other, he took steps to see that they would volunteer. Toward the end of March, fourteen striking railwaymen were summoned to the Namur village of Jemelle—the heart of Wallonia—and offered jobs paying good salaries. All refused, believing that the work was either military (refitting cars to transport soldiers and munitions) or indirectly assisted the Germans. When days of interrogations and detention, which reportedly included rations of bread and water, did not change their minds, the Germans sentenced them to a month in prison each. Two more groups of railwaymen endured similar pressures, with mixed results—some signed contracts, some did not.[22]

To ensure that Belgian workers had no choice except to volunteer, the Germans had been delaying approval of the NOT, a proposal for which British and Belgian representatives had submitted in August 1915. By way of prompting a reply, in February 1916 the British Foreign Office published the working terms of the agreement in the

Times. The following month, Berlin responded, also through the press, to reject the plan and to end negotiations.[23] The major stated obstacle appeared to be British insistence that Britain hold Belgian revenues from export sales in escrow (though releasing funds to pay salaries in certain cases). The Germans claimed that this would deny the Belgians their rolling capital and injure their rate of exchange while aiding the pound sterling, but they may have disliked the scheme for another reason. Just as the British did not trust the Germans to keep their hands off the raw materials, the Germans may have suspected the British would use Belgian goods as credit for American arms purchases.[24] But whether the British really wanted the NOT is an open question, for they, like the Germans, may have seen opportunity in a dormant Belgian economy. After the war, with rare bitterness Pirenne blamed London for killing the NOT, saying that the British thought they had "done enough in permitting the Belgian people not to die of hunger."[25]

With that last hope gone, the net tightened around Belgian manpower, but first, in an unexpected way. In April, the occupiers ruled that young men born in Belgium of German parentage who had taken Belgian citizenship were still German nationals, subject to conscription. These Belgians were given a physical examination and released until the military authorities at Aachen decided their posting. Leading Belgians protested, citing the Fourth Convention's provisions on undue interference and military operations, and a German law from January 1914 that withdrew citizenship from any German who had accepted it from another country. But the protest went nowhere, and a senior occupation official said that if the decree had broken any law—which he contested—necessity won out.[26]

A portent for Belgium appeared in northern France. From the cities of Roubaix, Lille, and Tourcoing the Germans rounded up about twenty-five thousand civilians, whom they sent to the two departments directly south, Aisne and Ardennes, and put them to work, chiefly in the fields.[27] Because the Germans governed northern France so tightly, the news took two months to reach the foreign press, where the story assumed a typical slant. Most of the deportees were women, girls, and teenage boys because so few able-bodied men were left, but the first *Times* of London article, on 28 July, said nothing about this. Rather, the paper told how the Germans had cordoned off neighborhoods, ordered everyone into the street, chosen victims at random, and sent them, with their meager baggage, to the train station under cover of machine guns. The facts seemed to speak for themselves, and the next day, the *Times* denounced the method, which it called a "press gang," and drew attention to the victims' youth because so many were children.[28] But to evoke images of slave raids was apparently not compelling enough. Six days later, an editorial conjured up white slavery, saying that "no father and mother in Lille could go to sleep without the fear that their daughters might be hurried away, pell-mell with roughs and prostitutes."[29]

Bissing did nothing so sensational. On 2 May, he decreed that no public works could proceed without authorization, which might or might not be granted (and from then on, seldom was). On 15 May, he revised the law of August 1915, giving military courts jurisdiction over relief recipients who refused jobs. The offer of work had to come from German authorities, and international law remained a defense, but the decree allowed something new—recalcitrants could be brought to the workplace by force.[30] In a confidential circular to his subordinates, Bissing said that this meant that unemployed laborers on relief whose work for German interests in Germany or Belgium was desirable would be "compelled to do such work even against their will." But he did not advise transporting anyone older than forty, fathers of families, or farm owners, nor did he counsel ignoring "justifiable objections" under international law.[31] Finally, in June, he stopped all public works in areas where the Germans needed the labor.[32]

Hardly had these laws taken effect when the stakes rose. An Anglo-French offensive on the Somme that began on 1 July cost the British 60,000 killed and wounded on that day alone, and the two Allied armies counted 200,000 casualties after a month.[33] But the Germans lost 160,000, which, with the Verdun slaughter, cut deeply into their strength, while a perceived advantage in Allied matériel startled and concerned the German command. Something would have to give.

In early August, the German press repeated the description of a prosperous Belgium hardly touched by war. The *Norddeutscher Allgemeine Zeitung* reported on a visit that several Reichstag deputies had made, expressing their astonishment that "most industrial establishments were in full activity," and that the harvest promised a bounty. When the occupation began, 120,000 or 130,000 workers had been jobless;

now, the number had fallen to 40,000 or 50,000. The visitors had thought "constantly of the war" while in Belgium, because certain facts were inescapable. Still, as "men of honor," they "could not refrain from certifying that German organizational talent has kept the consequences of war as far as possible at bay."[34] The *Rheinisch Westfälische Zeitung* went even further, saying that to look at Belgium overall, one would scarcely know there was a war, and that the population lived better than its German counterpart.[35]

Three weeks after these articles appeared, the wind changed, and the image of a busily employed Belgium disappeared. On 31 August, the General Staff announced that weaponry had not kept pace with the enemy's and demanded steep production increases, especially in artillery and machine guns. A press campaign overstated the danger, and the government rushed to give Paul von Hindenburg, the new chief of staff, what he wanted. Whether Allied firepower at the Somme had alarmed Hindenburg, or whether slaying an imaginary dragon suited him, the result was the same. In mid-September, thirty-nine industrialists met with the General Staff and the Ministry of War to discuss the so-called Hindenburg Program's production quotas and the general situation. Manpower led the agenda. The order to raise output came as the army was drafting more workers, and Hindenburg wanted a comprehensive law to mobilize every man who could bear arms and harness every economic muscle to the war effort.[36]

To industrialists, Belgium offered a partial solution. On 14 September, Carl Duisberg, director of the Bayer chemical firm, demanded, *"Open up the great pool of Belgian labor!"* which he placed at seven hundred thousand unemployed. He feared that the ministry and Bissing would hesitate to use force.[37] That night, an industrialist who worked in raw materials procurement pleaded with Hindenburg and his second-in-command, Ludendorff, to take action. Industry could meet the quotas only if "the Belgian labor problem is solved by compulsion, which means that all questions of international prestige must be ignored." Seizing workers would wreck the CRB, but that would make little difference.[38]

The commanders did not have to be begged. Iron and steel production was less than two-thirds of the prewar figure, and textiles had dropped almost to the one-quarter mark. Lack of raw materials and fuel reduced output, but so did the drain on skilled labor. Factories had to rely on women, the young, and the rapidly trained, all overworked and undernourished. They operated machinery worn from improper use and from maintenance with substitute lubricants, the preferred ones being impossible to obtain.[39] The army had no choice but to release skilled workers from service temporarily or exempt them altogether. By mid-1916, almost two million had service deferments of some kind.[40]

In mid-September the General Staff told Bissing to prepare lists of workers to be taken at any time. Bissing objected, but more gingerly this time, because he was now dealing with the Supreme Command. In a memo he prepared before a meeting with the General Staff and War Ministry late that month, he alternated between defending his own labor policy and challenging the deportations. As before, he mentioned international law, urging that the work have a legally appropriate character. He suggested that the army claim that the deportations kept public order, which the Fourth Convention required an occupier to maintain, and that Belgian recalcitrance had forced the issue.[41]

That said, Bissing argued that neutrals would protest, and that using force would provoke unrest in Belgium, including strikes at coal mines working for Germany.[42] Besides, he knew "no means, at least no means at the disposition of a cultured State," to extract profitable labor from people determined not to give it.[43] Even after the deportations, the labor shortage would persist, and Germany would have thousands of extra mouths to feed, whereas the CRB suited German interests. But arguing with an order was inviting Hindenburg to question his fitness to command, so the governor-general noted that he had not spared the rod. He denied that Belgium was better fed than Germany or that he "treat[ed] the Belgians like his spoiled children."[44] But he did not say that deporting the Flemish would antagonize them and jeopardize *Flamenpolitik*, though he acknowledged the danger in letters to his subordinates and to Bethmann.[45] The deportations could not have come at a worse time, for only that month, Bissing had decreed that where any Flemish was spoken, civilian officials had to write all communications in that language.[46] The University of Ghent was due to reopen in several weeks.

That did not stop a decree from being posted outside his jurisdiction in the Etappengebiet on 3 October that required any able-bodied person who had sought public assistance to work if called upon, "even away from home." Further, all inhabitants must be willing, in case of accident or general peril, to lend their aid to the extent of their abilities, also away from home. The authorities could apply force to anyone who refused to work, and military tribunals could sentence them to prison for up to three years, fine them up to ten thousand marks, or both.[47]

The occupiers looked for ways to excuse the deportations. *Usages of War* had embraced "the principle that war is conducted only against States, and not against private persons," and that the "carrying away of the inhabitants into bondage or captivity" of former times was no longer acceptable.[48] Nevertheless, a congress of German jurists, convened in Brussels in September, decided that the deportations did not violate the law. One authority said that The Hague Conventions had not foreseen the relationship between Belgium and Germany, a protectorate that gave the two countries a "community of interests." Those interests, as well as necessity and the need to keep public order, permitted Germany to draft Belgian labor.[49] Another expert said that the "German conscience" would not stand for half measures in Germany's defense, and that only the German people could judge the limits of that conscience.[50]

Still, Bissing asked Bethmann to tell him how he could proceed legally, as if he did not trust his advice to Hindenburg. On 7 October, the chancellor replied that he hoped that the offer of high salaries would tempt the Belgians to volunteer. But if not, Bissing must say that the CRB and Comité National were official bodies, not private ones, so that the workers were receiving government assistance. He must also say that no jobs existed in Belgium, and that employment in Germany had no ties to war work. On those grounds, the deportations would be legal. Bethmann advised prudence, because the deportations in France had aroused opinion abroad and protests from Spain and the Vatican. Finally, the deportees must not be treated like prisoners under common law—which Bissing had proposed—so he must not invoke criminal proceedings. Threats might persuade the Belgians, but better the carrot than the stick.[51]

A week later, the German press and captive papers in Belgium briefed the public. In what became a template for apology, the *Kölnische Zeitung* of 13 October charged that "for more than a year, the Belgians in the occupied territory have abused public welfare," hence the governor-general's decrees. The longer the occupation lasted, the worse the abuse, and "unemployment is a grave threat to subsequent order and peace in the occupied territory." Conditions would not improve because England's blockade had halted imports and forced most industrial concerns to close. The most practical answer was to send workers away from where they were a public expense to employment in Germany, where many Belgians had accepted jobs and found satisfaction. "But the work-shy who preferred to live on public welfare" unlike their brother laborers "would soon be forced to undertake suitable work" that had "no connection with war production."[52]

The third week of October, disturbing rumors began to reach Robert Jackson, a CRB delegate stationed in Brabant. "We hear of Germans arresting many Belgians and sending them to work in Germany or elsewhere," he told his journal. The Germans "have demanded lists of 'chômeurs'"—the unemployed—"fr[om] all bourgomestres & the latter as such have them not."[53] For a few days, he heard nothing further, and his concern shifted to the threat by Brabant farmers to sell their wheat to the Germans, which would "create a very awkward situation a little later."[54]

But by month's end, the deportations had grabbed Jackson's attention. He had heard that the Germans "are arresting a good many Belgians . . . all the men between 18 & 30 in certain places," and had threatened to fine Brussels ten million francs unless they got the lists.[55] November first brought news "of wholesale arrests & shipment to Germany of many men in certain communes in the Hainaut."[56] A week later, the story went that women were going also, "flax workers probably. . . . Have taken 700 men in Antwerp & expect to take 2100 in all."[57] Brabant had been hit too, and he worried about the relief, but "we don't know how far these taking[s] away of Belgians are going, nor, whether we shall be able to protect our own employés."[58] He started signing CRB identity cards, hoping that would provide exemptions.

On 14 November, he went to Court-Saint-Étienne, a town sixteen miles southeast of Brussels, to "watch [the] Germans making their selection" of workers, which occurred in an empty textile mill. "In the distance the can[n]on were booming very loud, the 3rd day in succession," as a "long serpentine of men" filed into the building "to be briefly questioned by the Germans." Outside, "entirely apart & away were the mass of women & children waiting & weeping, wondering whether their men would be taken & coming as near as was permitted." If a man was told "to the left," that meant liberty—"so far as liberty exists for the inhabitants of Belgium"—and "to the right" meant Germany. "One or two so sent ran laughing & leaping. Most took their fate stolidly." Many given their freedom "were too stupified to know the way out, & tho the soldiers usually turned them back I was convinced that some went to Germany thro their own error."[59]

Like Jackson, employers and burgomasters had come to intercede for men who had jobs, but he thought that these efforts at best changed who went, not how many—about a thousand, he guessed. (The actual number at Court-Saint-Étienne was 872.)[60] The Germans were "very decent" but knowingly took "a certain number of men" regularly employed, including some of his workers.[61] Jackson supposed that they had started out intending to pick young, unmarried, jobless men, but toward the end, perhaps thinking they would not make their quota, they took whomever they wanted. When a factory owner protested that they had chosen his regular employees, the Germans told him the problem would never have arisen had the burgomaster supplied the requested list.[62] Two days later, Jackson was writing that troops had taken over every communal administrative office in greater Brussels to search for lists.[63]

His brief account omits that the selection screened men from twenty-two communes, an area representing thirty-one thousand people, of whom all males between the ages of seventeen and fifty-five were candidates for deportation.[64] Yet the whole procedure lasted only four hours. In another deportation at Nivelles, Court-Saint-Étienne's arrondissement, nineteen thousand or twenty thousand men were eligible, of whom nineteen hundred were taken, again in four hours.[65] In that time, the Germans had to check and stamp papers, handle complaints and requests, verify employment, give deportees a physical exam, offer contracts to workers they wanted, fill them out if accepted, and keep a list of those who refused. When this was finished, the Germans marched the deportees to a waiting train and loaded them.[66] They repeated this process in the Generalgouvernement daily during November and December, dispatching at least one and often several trains, each carrying from five hundred to one thousand deportees, on average.[67]

Such an immense effort required meticulous planning, as suggested in a captured dossier about Nivelles. The local commander was advised to choose a public square large enough to hold the crowd yet as far as possible from population centers, to prevent intrusion. The square must be convenient to a large building, like a factory or school, must allow for barriers to be placed inside—or else lines of troops— and preferably should be near a train station. A drawing explained how the system should work. An officer at the building's entrance should stamp the papers of men obviously unfit and send them out a separate door, whereas the rest would continue past a line of sentries to another room. There, three or four officers would confirm who was employed, directing those men out the exit. The remainder would pass by more sentries to a third room where representatives of the labor cartel were waiting. Men who signed would be allowed to leave, but all who refused would be kept under guard in a collection room, to be deported that afternoon.[68]

The instructions counseled using wire or rope barriers rather than troops, to save manpower and minimize contact with civilians. The path to the entrance should be unguarded, because the Belgians would be docile, thinking that their fate had not yet been decided. However, the route from the collection room to the train should be strictly supervised, because crowds, including men already exempted, would perhaps cause disturbances. For that reason, those not taken should be encouraged to go home and told that if they stayed, they might be swept up in error. Relatives might hand over small packages but not approach their loved ones, and better to screen the view through existing or specially erected barriers than to deploy sentries to push women and children away. "The use of cavalry to evacuate the streets and squares shows itself to be particularly useful," the author said, adding, "given the timid attitude shown by the Belgians."[69] In his final draft, he deleted the last phrase.

To the Belgians, the deportations were a baffling nightmare. Edmond Min, the burgomaster of Bolinne-Harlue, Namur province, wrote that when news that the Germans were taking workers reached his commune in mid-November, people offered wild explanations. Some had the Germans conscripting the Belgians, whereas others supposed they were trying to save money by reducing the relief rolls. Still others believed that by mistreating the Belgians, the Germans were attempting to pressure the Allies to sue for peace. Even more fantastic, some figured that the deportations presaged a retreat behind the Rhine. Other theories ventured that the Germans were trying to deny the Allies a pool of conscripts, or—shades of the invasion—to use the Belgians as shields in battle.[70]

Min wrote that 450 soldiers arrived in Bolinne-Harlue a week before the deportations, to keep order. The number seems high, especially when the selection was to occur at a nearby town, but that the soldiers arrived so long beforehand again implies careful planning. The time allotted to keep order did not correspond to that spent on selection, however, for when the day came, 140 men from Bolinne-Harlue went through the line in seven minutes.[71] He said no one spoke of unemployed workers, and that whenever he tried to intercede, he, like every Belgian authority present, was ordered to keep quiet. Despite this, he saved two or three men and was able to obtain medical exams for a few others, because he was a doctor. Even so, "the requisition was thus a real lottery," and he remarked that animals at a fair would have been chosen more carefully. The German medical examiner, "reading his newspaper or smoking his cigarette, hardly deigned to glance" at the man standing before him, though bribing the officer overseeing the entrance to the room sometimes resulted in an exemption. Near the station, a crowd of thousands applauded the deportees and booed the Germans. Some soldiers "acted like real brutes," but others offered reassurance "while taking good care" to hide their gesture from superiors. After the burgomaster left, he had gone more than two miles when he heard prolonged cries, which told him the train had pulled out.

The treatment of the men shut inside suggests that planning had gone only so far. The weather was so cold that by mid-November, Whitlock had seen hundreds of women and children in Brussels "grubbing with their fingers" for bits of coal hidden in the slag used to fill empty tram tracks where the rails had been torn up.[72] But the first deportees left in open cattle cars, and though later groups rode in coaches or boxcars, those were unheated, unlit, and so overcrowded the men could not lie down. The journey usually lasted between thirty and forty-eight hours, a span during which they received three meals at most, only one of which was the least fortifying. Some deportees fainted from hunger. Most trains lacked sanitary arrangements, and the guards often refused to let men off to relieve themselves.[73] To keep their spirits up, the workers sang "La Brabançonne" or "The Flemish Lion." People who heard the trains pass by at night said that the deportees shouted, "We haven't signed! We won't sign!" or "Long live the king! Long live Belgium!"[74]

The trains brought the deportees to less populous areas of northern Germany, where nine prison camps had been enlarged and partially evacuated. In these so-called allocation camps, the Germans had envisioned keeping the workers a matter of days, until the bourgeois propaganda that had supposedly prevented them from signing contracts wore off.[75] The inducements to sign began with the barracks, always overcrowded, sometimes unheated, where the bedding, if any, was sacks filled with wood fibers, straw, or torn-up paper. The sacks often contained vermin, but where no bedding existed, the men slept on the floors, sometimes bare earth. Windows and doors let the wind in, and many deportees had no blankets, so they slept in their clothes, soaked with rain, snow, or sweat.[76]

Then there was the food, or lack of it. Breakfast was 150 to 250 grams of bread with a liquid called tea; lunch was a half liter of watery soup made from rutabagas, beets, or kohlrabi, occasionally with fish in it; and dinner was a liter of water in which barley had been cooked. Some camps served imitation coffee, the only variation in the diet. To supplement these rations, which some men later said were thinned out over time or withheld, the Belgians ransacked the garbage for carrot or potato peels, remnants of what military prisoners ate. Deportees who would not sign were forced to stand outdoors in zero-degree weather for hours, immobile, sometimes without overcoats, hats, or gloves, and were beaten if they moved. Many men sickened; some died. Resisters were also sent on work details to woods or bogs, joined by the unskilled, the weak, or those unemployable in factories because their professions were not manual. Stubborn cases went into solitary, where they received no food except a little bread, with soup every four days.[77] The Germans also threatened to ship the headstrong to discipline camps, known familiarly as "hell's premises," where the captors did such things as hose down the barrack floors so that the inmates slept on ice.[78]

Having begged for workers, German industry had nevertheless failed to prepare for the number that arrived, a circumstance that lengthened the stay in the allocation camps even for those who signed. Such men went to farms or factories when places became available and were paid a modest salary, from which the Germans subtracted sums for food, clothes, and social benefits. The laborer received only a fraction of his pay, and his family, another fraction. But Min, the Bolinne-Harlue burgomaster, heard in mid-December that deportees from a nearby town saw so much deducted for food that they could not keep body and soul together, let alone send money home.[79] Promises of a good salary enticed relatively few, whereas the majority resisted as long as they could. For them, the few days' stay turned into a month or several months.[80] One man testified after the war that he had held out for six weeks, and that when he had signed, after two days of starvation followed by seven hours of standing in the cold, 45 men out of an original 350 remained unyielding.[81]

The world knew little or nothing of the allocation camps—never mind "hell's premises"—because no witnesses could report from them. Most information depicted deportations from the Generalgouvernement, whereas the Germans kept a tighter lid on the Etappengebiet. The silence resulted in a skewed portrait, because that less-accessible region furnished more laborers than the Generalgouvernement, who were usually shipped to northern France, where their treatment rivaled the allocation camps in harshness. In the Etappengebiet, the Germans again demanded lists under threat of punishment and summoned all males seventeen and older when the Belgians did not comply. But in places, they seized people off the street, as at Tournai and Bruges.[82] Refusing to provide lists also cost Bruges four hundred thousand marks, whereas to punish Courtrai, the Germans took four thousand deportees from the city and its environs, whose prewar population had numbered thirty-six thousand.[83]

Deportees were offered a contract, often only in German, which purported to provide a higher salary if a worker volunteered. To obtain signatures, the Germans resorted to torture, shutting the men in tight, cold places without food for several days.[84] A CRB delegate in northern France heard that more than a thousand Belgian workers had been deported to a town near him, Valenciennes, "herded together in large buildings and camps" without "blankets, extra clothing &c." One group of more than one hundred who would not work had been kept without food for sixty-three hours—"This can be proved," he said.[85] The suffering would have been even worse had French civilians not smuggled in small amounts of food past sympathetic guards.

Except for resisters, sent to Germany for softening up, Etappenge-biet deportees worked behind the battlefront. They formed Zivil Ar-beiter-Bataillonen (civilian work battalions), many of which operated along the Hindenburg Line, the defenses the chief of staff had ordered built to shorten the front. The battalions labored along the entire line, from Verdun to the Belgian coast. They laid railroad track, built bunkers, dug trenches, strung barbed wire, cut down trees, and poured concrete for heavy artillery emplacements. Around Verdun, they loaded and unloaded munitions, gravel, and cement. The Verdun battalions were the only ones to have barracks; elsewhere, the Ger-mans housed the deportees in half-bombed-out factories or schools. But everywhere, the men ate wretched food and little of it, going months without washing or changing clothes because water was lack-ing. Anyone who refused to work was made to stand for hours out-side, without food, and was beaten with sticks or rifle butts. Some-times, men too exhausted to work were beaten. Sickness did not merit treatment or excuse from work unless there was danger of an epi-demic, and some feared the beatings so much they did not admit to ill-ness. The Germans used the Belgians until they dropped.[86]

Deportations from Flanders went on even as Bissing reopened the University of Ghent on 21 October, exactly what he had wished to avoid. His inaugural speech urged the mostly Dutch and German pro-fessors who now made up the faculty to work alongside Germany "to-ward the realization of the many desiderata common to the whole Low German race."[87] To encourage this project, students who at-tended the university were exempt from forced labor, and the admin-istration gave them first crack at scholarship money. A few days later, Bissing divided the Belgian Ministry of Sciences and Arts into two sec-tions, Flemish and Walloon.[88] *Flamenpolitik* would move forward, de-portations or not.

Throughout this time, the German press continued to justify the de-portations. On 5 November, the *Kölnische Volkszeitung* said that the de-portees were "unemployed workers who do not want to work," and their "activities have become more and more a serious annoyance."[89] They were living on American aid, but the American committee did not bear the final expense "and would have to be compensated in some way." Le Havre was ignoring this, hoping for "a complete Ger-man collapse and an immense indemnity by which Germany and many others would have to assume the costs." For its own sake and Belgium's, Germany could not permit this and would deserve Belgian gratitude for not having let the populace fall into idle depravity "merely from timid shyness about these workers' 'freedom' to do nothing if that was their will."

The strongest dissent came in early December, when a few Socialist Reichstag deputies called the deportations a breach of international law. Karl Helfferich, vice-chancellor and minister of the interior, answered that what they had read in "enemy or doubtfully neutral newspapers" about "illegal recruitment of Belgian workers" operated strictly within the law. "Idleness in Belgium serves only England," he declared to brisk applause, "and English trade sees to it, [but] we will not live with it."[90]

As the lead story for 12 November, the *New York Times* ran an interview with Bissing.[91] He said that Belgian businessmen had told him they were worried about keeping their competitive edge, especially against England, and had complained of "loafing" and the effect of long idleness on their workers' skill and efficiency. Before the compulsory measure, thirty thousand Belgian workers had found happiness in Germany, but propaganda and blackballing by Belgian patriots had hindered volunteering. His administration had fostered public works, but these had burdened communities with debt to support unproductive labor. As for the deportees, they were well fed en route, no one was "compelled to participate in war enterprises," conditions had satisfied them, and German social-service organizations looked after their families.

But outside Germany, such explanations were unpersuasive. King Alfonso XIII of Spain and the Vatican protested on 10 November, and though they wielded a light hand, they renewed their objections in the following weeks.[92] Unaware of this, Albert wrote to them and to Wilson, the first time since September 1914 that he had asked for foreign help. But his requests referred only obliquely to "a rejection of the engagements solemnly contracted to" in The Hague Conventions, whereas he emphasized the effects on peacemaking, knowing that his three correspondents wished to mediate.[93] Privately, he said that "my conviction is settled on the necessity of peace to put an end to the sufferings of occupied Belgium," and he chided his cabinet's "warlike exaltation" from the safety of Le Havre.[94]

Both the government-in-exile and occupied Belgium took a more open, confrontational stance. On 19 October, Mercier began a barrage of irate letters to Bissing and Oskar von der Lancken, the occupation's chief diplomat. The cardinal also condemned the deportations from the pulpit while encouraging parish priests to do likewise.[95] The trade-union commission, workers' groups, the judiciary, scientists, and various notables were similarly vocal.[96] Whitlock wrote that the Bruxellois vented their spleen at neutral diplomats, and he received angry, anonymous letters asking why the United States had not stopped the deportations. He ascribed the letters to people who had "thought their yellow hides were safe" and had never considered trying to enlist. "Another year and I shall be as much abused in Brussels as though I were mayor of the city," he remarked.[97] Fear prompted other people to run for the border, and when the Germans redoubled their patrols, encounters resulted, with deaths on both sides.[98]

From Le Havre, Foreign Minister Beyens wrote a long article for the American press, but the presidential election of 7 November, whose outcome was in doubt for several days, kept Belgium in the background. On the thirteenth, Beyens issued a note to all nations that called the deportations "veritable slavery" and charged the Germans with having plundered the economy and left workers jobless. "The Belgian deportee has the choice between famine and treason," the note said, and denounced the "shame" perpetrated by an occupation pretending to watch over "the legitimate rights of the population" in Flanders.[99] In Washington, the Belgian minister twice approached the State Department to demand intervention, while a publicist placed stories in American newspapers.[100]

These efforts had an effect. A week after publishing the interview with Bissing, the New York Times broke ranks with Wilsonian neutrality, observing that "the passions of war do not abridge our privilege to give admonition against violation of the laws of war."[101] Even more significant, that day, the Washington Post said that nothing in the war had "so offended the world's sense of humanity" as the deportations, which also violated the Fourth Convention. The paper that had begun the war scorning treaties cited which rules the Germans had broken, commenting that "an international convention to which the United States is a party has been torn up like a scrap of paper. . . . Neutrals will not remain neutrals in the face of such a menace, but will join forces with others against the common enemy of civilization."[102]

The prediction proved accurate. On 23 November, even Switzerland spoke up—almost apologetically, reminding Germany that traditional Swiss policy avoided interceding in disputes. Still, the "sentiments of humanity" and the notion that Germany "would attach importance to public opinion of a neutral, friendly State" had inspired a remonstrance.[103] But aside from an unofficial protest that Wilson had not authorized and was furious to read of in the press, the United States had said nothing.

Critics started to badger the White House. On 27 November, the president passed on to Secretary of State Lansing a telegram signed by influential private citizens like Elihu Root and Henry L. Stimson, who had respectively held cabinet posts under Presidents Roosevelt and Taft. The telegram asked for information about the deportations in France and Belgium and called for protest.[104] Wilson, newly reelected, dismissed the cable as an attempt to embarrass his administration, whereas Lansing, who kept departmental matters private on principle, suspected that the signatories wanted to force the government to intervene. They were behind a protest movement that staged a meeting in Boston on 28 November, which two thousand people attended, and nineteen more gatherings over the next month.[105] The most impressive met in New York in mid-December, when three thousand people braved the worst snowstorm in twenty-six years to gather at Carnegie Hall.[106] Connected to this movement were petitions circulating among the faculty at more than twenty prestigious universities.[107]

Wilson acted shortly after receiving the telegram, though the timing was apparently a coincidence. On 29 November, Lansing sent the American chargé d'affaires in Berlin, Joseph C. Grew, a formal protest with instructions to keep his demarche a secret.[108] The United States, Grew was to say, was "constrained to protest in a friendly spirit, but most solemnly" against the deportations, which were "in contravention of all precedent" and "humane principles of international practice." Further, the United States was convinced that the policy, if pursued, would destroy the relief effort, "a result which would be generally deplored and . . . would seriously embarrass the German Government." But the note was not about Belgian rights or war crimes. Lansing told Grew to emphasize that the deportations had upset American opinion just when it "was more nearly approaching a balance of judgments" about the war than ever, which caused the president "serious embarrassment" concerning "steps looking toward peace." What Wilson wanted was "practical cooperation" in "creating a favourable opportunity" for a peace initiative.[109]

Among neutrals, the Dutch spoke last but most cogently. On 2 December, they quoted the Fourth Convention's prohibition against requiring war work, but, similar to the Swiss, said they would have refrained had one circumstance not compelled them. That circumstance, as Bissing had anticipated, was the promise they had made on Germany's behalf to Belgian refugees in Holland that anyone who returned to Belgium need not fear forced labor. The Dutch government "thus felt, in a certain measure, responsible for the fate of those inhabitants of Belgium" who had sought asylum in Holland and listened to Dutch assurances. Accordingly, the note requested that the deportees be repatriated.[110]

The Allies protested on 5 December, citing broken pledges not to seize native foodstuffs or interfere with the relief and repeating the indictment that requisitions had "deliberately created unemployment and misery."[111] The note also charged the occupiers with having suspended public works as an excuse to begin deportations and with organizing "man-hunts," breaching a treaty Germany had signed in 1890 to suppress the African slave trade. Finally, the Allies promised not to "desert the oppressed people of Belgium" and called on the "civilized world" to preserve the relief effort from "treachery" and "violence." This phrase tacitly backed the Spanish and Dutch protests, because both governments supported the relief diplomatically.

The Germans seemed immune to reproof. To the Spanish, who had objected that the deportations were meant to free workers to fight, Foreign Secretary Jagow replied that this argument had no basis. If it did, he observed, one could just as well criticize the employment of prisoners of war, which The Hague Conventions permitted.[112] (However, the relevant article said that "their tasks shall not be excessive and shall have nothing to do with the operations of war.")[113] The *Kölnische Zeitung* dismissed the Swiss complaint. The paper traced the "unfavorable impression" in Switzerland to French and Belgian propaganda and argued that "our military security in Belgium and the interests even of the Belgian population" took precedence in any case.[114]

Bethmann told Grew informally that he could not acknowledge that the deportations broke the law, and he insisted that the policy had been forced on Germany. The chancellor also asked whether the American public knew that the Allies had pushed Greece and Romania into the war, and that conditions in Greece were far worse than in Belgium.[115] The written German reply said that the United States had misjudged the deportations and restated Bissing's claims to the *New York Times*. The note denied that the deportations had caused hardships, blamed the Belgians for "mistakes" if the wrong people had been deported, and alleged that the Russians had shipped Germans from East Prussia to Siberia, yet no neutral had dissented.[116]

To the Netherlands, Berlin said that The Hague Conventions made the deportations legal, and that the Dutch must be misinformed about the pledges to the refugees. Those promises had guaranteed only that young men of military age could practice their professions without fear if they did not show hostility to Germany, and applied only to those who had left Antwerp. The agreement had said nothing about the unemployed. Still, to avoid misunderstanding, Germany would repatriate deportees who had fled Antwerp and its environs after the conquest, but no one else. Shortly afterward, the army relieved the military governor of Antwerp who had made the commitment to the refugees, despite his claim that his proclamation had been misinterpreted.[117]

Meanwhile, the trains carrying the deportees kept running. By the end of 1916, the occupiers had shipped almost fifty-five thousand Belgians to Germany and almost forty-seven thousand to northern France.[118] Nearly fifteen thousand others had volunteered, but at that rate, the desired four hundred thousand would not be forthcoming, and, as Bissing had warned, the measure was attracting too much criticism anyway.[119] Both arithmetic and public opinion were against the Germans, but whether that would help the Belgians any remained to be seen.

9

Taking Note of These Things

THE MOST REVEALING DISAVOWAL of the deportations arose during a conversation between Grew and Bethmann on 22 November, a week before Lansing sent the formal protest. Grew wrote that the meeting had occurred on Busstag, the national day of penitence, and supposed that Bethmann might have been meditating on the deaths of his wife and son. The chancellor had spoken of the terrible slaughter, for which "Germany's readiness for peace absolved her," repeating that "it was utter craziness to continue this useless and futile taking of human life." He had asked, "What do these difficulties in Belgium matter compared to the hecatomb of lives which have been lost on the Somme since July?"[1]

The chancellor had said more than he perhaps knew. To invoke the Somme while waving away Belgium's "difficulties" was to endorse the policy of thrusting German costs, with interest, onto a captive population because what small nations suffered did not matter. However genuine Bethmann's sorrow, he had followed the same reasoning by which he had called a treaty a scrap of paper and expressed the same undertone of contempt.

This attitude imbued the two most important occupation policies of 1916, the deportations and *Flamenpolitik*. To steal workers' livelihoods at gunpoint and force them to betray their country showed disdain for law, the Belgians, and Belgium. To claim that they, a people renowned for thrift and hard work, had brought the measure on themselves was to demean them further. Likewise, *Flamenpolitik* told the Belgians that they did not deserve to be called a nation, that Walloons had no right to their ethnicity, language, or customs, and that the law would henceforth discriminate against them. As Whitlock had said in January 1915 when he tried to summarize the occupation's character, the contempt and "the multitude of humiliations that are inflicted" were the worst aspects of German rule.[2]

Flamenpolitik lacked subtlety, but had the occupiers worked with a lighter, open hand, they might have tempted more Flemish nationalists to accept their offer. Before the war, the Belgian government's resistance to reform had inflamed the Flemish-Walloon conflict until, by 1914, some Flemish diehards wished to purge Flanders of French. Albert was the first king to swear his constitutional oath in both tongues and to address Flemish audiences in Flemish, a gesture long overdue.[3] But Belgium was governed in French, the only language on civil service examinations, and some Flemish courts held sessions in French. People who supported Flemish aims were even known by a French term, *flamingants*, whether they asked only for linguistic equality or wanted a separate Flanders.

Suzanne Lilar, a Flemish novelist of French expression who wrote a memoir of her wartime adolescence in Ghent, said that the stigma attached to Flemish was what had hurt most and redounded on the Walloons. In Lilar's family, Flemish was for angry oaths, tender nicknames, and the deathbed—her mother had spurned the language throughout her life but returned to it in her last hours. Lilar remarked that had francophone libraries contained a few Flemish volumes, the city walls might not have seen posters that read "*Weg met Franse boeken!* [No more French books].[4]

Germans who subscribed to *Flamenpolitik* misread the dispute. Just as Belgian complacency had reinforced the idea that Germany could invade unopposed, enmity toward French culture was viewed as readiness to be a German satellite. But Flemish leanings toward Germany had resulted as much from church-and-state politics as from German virtues. Even at that, Catholic and Flemish interests had not always tallied—Mercier, for one, opposed the movement[5]—and support had often come from German ultranationalists, which had disturbed some Belgians.[6] Seeing Germanic ways in Flanders was wishful thinking, not least because Flemish is Dutch by another name, and the Dutch did not consider themselves German any more than the Walloons did.[7]

Flamenpolitik provided a useful frame on which to reweave standard myths. The invasion treachery now appeared to have ethnic

Chancellor Theobald von Bethmann Hollweg wore an army uniform during this visit to Belgium in 1915. Though he opposed the military's plans to annex the country, his views represented a deep-seated German contempt for Belgium. Library of Congress, Prints and Photographs Division, LC-USZ 62-85147

roots, with the francs-tireurs coming exclusively from Walloon ranks, as Walter Bloem's *Advance from Mons*, published in 1916, tried to suggest. When he described the hard marches after crossing the frontier, he wrote that no one straggled because "the thought of falling into the hands of the Walloons was worse than sore feet." But after the men left Wallonia, the Belgian ambience changed: "That expression of hatred and suspicion on every face had gone," and the Flemish answered his questions "fearlessly and at their ease." Bloem even added a linguistic touch, saying that people laughed "whenever I attempted to make myself better understood in their own dialect." And when he asked, "Why has your little Belgium offered this senseless and useless resistance to our overwhelming superiority?" he got the desired answer. A man told him that the Belgian Army had done what self-respect demanded, but that now he hoped Albert would make peace. The response evoked another goal of *Flamenpolitik:* to divide Belgium and weaken support for the war so that the Le Havre government would have to come to terms.[8]

Scholars devised a historical context for *Flamenpolitik.* Karl Hampe, a Heidelberg medievalist, wrote that Belgium had always been an "artificial" nation. "The Flemish-Germanic majority" differed so sharply from the "Walloon-Romance minority" that "cultural unity" did not exist, and Belgium had threatened to fall apart. Flemish was like the dialect of north Germany, "homely and familiar, refreshing in its unspoiled picturesqueness and expressiveness, and in its vital force that springs from the depths of the popular soul." But within this ballad to Flanders lay a militant theme, for Hampe commented that the Belgians had benefited from German commerce, but, out of envy, had rejected Germany and put their necks in a French yoke. Now, France was dying. Echoing Bernhardi, Hampe said that the Flemish must choose a protector, looking "beyond the natural bitterness and grief of the present" to "realize the importance of this hour of destiny which has rung for them." But however they answered, Germany should not be fooled by "a temporarily unfriendly attitude" and must try to make a "Germanic bulwark" of the Flemish—an argument of which Bissing would have approved.[9]

The disdainful assault on Belgian nationality and patriotic feelings derived from the delusion that Belgium had never been independent, the logic by which Germans had explained the decision to resist and the franc-tireur war. Belgian opposition to *Flamenpolitik* was thus at best a habit to be unlearned, at worst a conspiracy. That allowed the Germans to say who was being law-abiding and who was undermining their authority, which forced the Belgians to choose between treason and obedience. The policy arguably breached the Fourth Convention articles protecting civilians from having to work against their country, and the tradition that granted the right to natural sympathies. But even if neither limit applied, the Germans could favor the Flemish only by rewriting Belgian law wholesale, which clearly exceeded an occupier's powers.

One of *Flamenpolitik*'s ironies was that the Germans did not have to go to such lengths to obtain peace talks. Albert had grown so disenchanted with the Allies that by late 1915, he could tell his diary that their diplomacy was no better than their generalship, and that their governments were useless. The Russian and British sovereigns were "nonentities," the French government lacked direction and strength, and England was "worse than a republic" and wanted "to pursue the war until the sacrifice of the last Frenchman." By mid-November 1915, he had decided that the Allies would never drive the Germans out of Belgium, and that only by bargaining with the enemy could he regain his country.[10]

He arranged for a Belgian professor named Emile Waxweiler to negotiate with Elisabeth's brother-in-law, Count Hans Törring-Jettensbach, who in turn communicated with the German Foreign Office. On the Belgian side, only Waxweiler and the monarchs knew of the talks, which happened in Zürich between November 1915 and February 1916, the envoys meeting four times.[11] Albert's messages for Törring outline his official position on German crimes against Belgium, for he edited out any reference to the invasion terror or what might have been construed as criticism for past behavior. To contest the accusation of conspiracy, he said that Belgium had always mistrusted France and Britain and had taken up arms only to defend its neutrality; as proof, he cited his refusals to join Allied attacks.[12] This apology for resistance recalled Charles Woeste's reasoning on 2 August 1914 that the Belgians could not afford to offend Germany by fighting too hard. If Albert's ministers had known, they would have been appalled.

The talks foundered largely because the Germans insisted on "real guarantees" that Belgium would detach itself from the Entente, which amounted to putting its defense in German hands and becoming a protectorate. Albert rejected this proposal, but he still believed that dealing with Germany was Belgium's only hope (which was why he later adopted a mild tone when asking neutral leaders to protest the deportations). He was unmoved when the British, who had heard of his discontent,[13] renewed their vows in February 1916 to fight until Belgium was independent, restored, and indemnified.[14] Further, he was willing to forgive the war crimes, though he knew that his people felt otherwise. He once told House during a visit to La Panne that the Belgians harbored deep hatred, but that "with time, these are things that subside especially among people who have more reason than passion," perhaps his view of himself.[15] He added that he wished to be a "good citizen," by which he would "not give vent to his own feelings or his own thoughts, but should think as the Belgian people think and feel as they feel." House, who quoted all this at face value, was taken in.[16]

But Albert's ministers, even if they did not know of his maneuvers, realized that he was carrying on a policy at odds with theirs.[17] Hymans, now minister to Britain, reported that Londoners fed up with seeing refugees out of uniform were shouting, "Bloody Belgians!" even at those too young to bear arms.[18] He himself was once upbraided, which he took as a compliment because of his age, but he thought Belgium must contribute more.[19] Similarly, Vandervelde had heard complaints that whereas the French and British were sending older men to the front, young Belgian refugees went undrafted. He suggested revising the conscription laws.[20]

The cabinet carried the motion, but Albert opposed it. The king feared that if the army became too large, he would not be able to put off Allied generals, and at least once, he falsified the number of men under his command. He dissembled so cleverly that the chief of the French mission to the Belgian Army blamed Albert's entourage and general staff for encouraging his habit of managing his resources too tightly.[21] That overlooked how those resources happened to be human beings, and with reason, Albert's troops worshiped him for his sparing way with their lives. Still, the king was taking a risk in letting the British and French think that Belgium was not sharing the load.

■

Albert might downplay the impact of war crimes, but summer 1916 witnessed a surge of feeling in Britain especially that was to have lasting consequences. On 8 July, the British Foreign Office protested the decrees requiring relief recipients to accept employment and cited past agreements not to impose war work. The note questioned how civilians would fare if they quoted The Hague Conventions to a military court and accused the occupiers of demanding a choice between sustenance on one hand or liberty and country on the other. The Germans issued a blanket denial, insisting that the decrees did not violate international law, that their military courts were renowned for fairness, and that the guarantees about war work had not been broken.[22]

But the matter did not end there. On 21 July, Belgian Independence Day, Asquith condemned the policy while standing alongside Belgian leaders. "It is to enable the German invaders to requisition Belgian labour for their own military needs. . . . In other words, they are to be treated as slaves." The crowd shouted, "Shame!" To loud cheers, Asquith continued, "We here in Great Britain are taking note of these things. We do not mean to forget them. We intend to exact reparation for them."[23] This was trotting out the April 1915 formula about British prisoners, and his words had acquired no greater incisiveness since. But he had publicly denounced a crime of the occupation.

Six days later, the mood intensified. On 27 July at Bruges, the Germans shot Charles Fryatt, a British merchant marine captain, as a "pirate" and "franc-tireur" for having tried to ram a submarine preparing to sink his ship in 1915. When the Germans captured him in June 1916, he was a hero in Britain and had been awarded two gold watches, one each from his employers and the Admiralty. The Germans thought that this aggravated the case, and they painted him as a franc-tireur who had fought on orders from above. It may have been an accident that they tried and executed him on Belgian soil, but there was no coincidence in how their leading papers cursed him as they had cursed the Belgians.[24]

The legal reasoning was familiar. By German law revised in July 1914, if an armed merchantman resisted search or seizure, the cruiser was to suppress the defense by any and all means. The crew would become prisoners of war, whereas only passengers who had resisted would be court-martialed as criminals, a rule that would seem to have protected Fryatt from execution. But as the *Kölnische Zeitung* declared, his ship was unarmed, and because he did not belong to Britain's military forces, by resisting, he had forfeited his right to be treated as a prisoner of war. The interpretation overlooked how a ship can itself be a weapon.[25]

But more important than the consistency of German argument was that other nations recognized the right of self-defense. Major American newspapers, naval officials in Washington, and a legal scholar who had represented the United States at the 1907 Hague Conference all objected.[26] The case also offended Dutch opinion—Fryatt's route had served Dutch ports for years—including the *Nieuwe Rotterdamse Courant*, usually reliable enough to be allowed into occupied Belgium. "To claim the right to kill hundreds of citizens on sight" yet label any resister a franc-tireur, the paper said, invoked a double standard that was "arbitrary and unrighteous."[27]

Of course, the angriest words came from Britain. The *Manchester Guardian* condemned the "act of murder," observing that "of all the things which it is difficult to forgive the Germans, perhaps the most difficult is their habit of treating the rest of us as cowards." Through such deeds "German militarism forces on the most reluctant the conviction that the world cannot live with it," and that "to prevail against it we must go through to the bitter end," no matter what the cost.[28] The *Times* called Fryatt's execution "a crime to be remembered like the death of Miss Cavell, and one day to be punished with it."[29] That day, irate citizens formed the League of Britons to secure trial and punishment of the kaiser and other highly placed Germans "for the murder of Captain Fryatt and other victims."[30] The league's members pledged to vote out any government that refused to make a war crimes tribunal an indispensable condition of peace, and they further insisted that those found guilty should be executed.

Asquith did not go that far, but he spoke out. On 31 July, he remarked that Fryatt's death, with the deportations in northern France, "showed that the German High Command have under stress of military defeat renewed their policy of terrorism." If Britain had any say, "When the time arrives they [the government] are determined to bring to justice the criminals, whoever they may be, and whatever their station." Asquith implied that the kaiser "may well be the most guilty of all."[31] Five days later, Minister of Trade Lord Robert Cecil repeated the vow while standing beside French and Belgian officials. "Reparation and punishment must be exacted," he said, not for "mere anger or revenge or vindictiveness," but as "a vital part of the cause" for which the Allies fought. Punishment was necessary "if we ever wished to establish among nations respect for those principles of law and justice on which international relations ought to rest."[32]

That the death of one sea captain achieved what terror throughout Belgium had not typifies public reaction to war crimes. After all, the *Lusitania* sinking stirred Americans more than Louvain, and they were more outraged over their 128 compatriots than about the thousand-plus others who had lost their lives. Still, Asquith was mistaken that the Germans had renewed their terror; they had never stopped it. As with the Cavell case, one British death could not represent what had been happening to Belgians for almost two years, and again, the individual circumstances left room for debate. Submarine sinkings and the scope of the British naval blockade were new to warfare, and the applicable laws were ambiguous.

Nevertheless, the affair served a purpose. Ascribing terror to "the stress of military defeat" was perhaps calculated to assuage the pain of losses on the Somme, particularly when the nation had recently adopted conscription for the first time. But Fryatt's execution also let Britons realize what it meant to be called a criminal for defending oneself. The Germans appeared to have said, "Stand still when we try to kill you, or we will treat you as an outlaw." They had taken that position with the ultimatum, during the invasion, and for almost two years of occupation—a stance that, as much as any scrap of paper or Hague Convention, made Germany a rogue nation. If the *Guardian* could say that crushing those who thought this way was worth any sacrifice, the gauntlet had been thrown.

Official Britain's decision to seek redress paralleled a growing body of legal opinion. Among the most outspoken advocates was Elihu Root, who, besides having served as secretary of state and in the Senate, was president of the American Society of International Law. Addressing that body in late December 1915, Root said that the "structure" of international law must be rebuilt, that "laws to be obeyed must have sanctions behind them," and that violations must bring consequences beyond the possibility of military defeat. If power were the only standard, "there would be no law as between the strong and the weak."

However, Root named three conditions without which no strong state would ever face punishment: public condemnation, judgment through a competent international court, and, most important, the adoption of the belief that lawbreaking concerned all nations. Without that change in theory, the small state had no safeguards except "the shifting currents of policy among its great neighbors," whereas powerful states would lack security "except in readiness for war."[33] This statement described prewar Europe.

In Britain, Hugh Bellot, president of the Grotius Society, agreed that an international tribunal might be the court of original jurisdiction but believed that precedent existed for individual countries to try foreign defendants. He cited statutes from several American states that allowed county courts to pursue cases regarding suspicious deaths occurring elsewhere—at sea, for instance—and Supreme Court decisions that upheld punishments of crimes against international law. Further, he contended that most Anglo-American military regulations followed common law in making members of the armed forces liable to prosecution. Bellot quoted cases in which courts had convicted despite the defense of superior orders because the acts were such that no soldier in good conscience could obey commands to commit them. (Of Fryatt, he observed that if the Germans had executed him despite—or because of—superior orders, they could not claim them as a defense in the future.) Even so, he shied away from punishments that might be impossible to carry out, preferring disgrace as a legal weapon. He suggested keeping a register at The Hague of those convicted, whom any country could then deport as an undesirable alien or deny protection under the law.[34]

But not everyone who saw German misdeeds believed that Britain could afford to throw stones. A prime example was E. D. Morel, a brilliant journalist who had, coincidentally, blown the whistle on Leopold II's Congo regime, and whose collection of wartime articles and speeches was first published in July 1916. Morel had deplored the invasion and terror, which he labeled "a high pinnacle of shame," and had joined the chorus supporting reparations for Belgium. But to pretend that the Germans owned a monopoly on wickedness was, he said, "to impair the judgment and distort the vision of our people," who would have done their duty anyway. This may have been the most lucid indictment of British propaganda ever lodged, but Morel extended the criticism to war aims. Should Britain

now offer Germany "a place in the sun"—repeating the kaiser's famous phrase—Morel believed that no German "possessed of common
sense" would ask to retain Belgium or northern France. Further, he
predicted that "tens of thousands of Germans, smitten with remorse . . . would eagerly co-operate in healing the wounds of that unhappy land."[35]

But Britain did not need to have a stainless reputation to object to the
deportations or to ask where German goodwill had figured in them.
Slavery was both illegal and repellent, and though some European
codes allowed forced labor as a punishment, the deportees had committed no crime. No article in the Fourth Convention mentioned deportations or forced labor as such, but to infer permission as the Germans did was deceitful. After all, the convention had said nothing
about cannibalism or trial by fire, but that did not make them legal,
whereas the 1907 preamble had invoked the usages of civilized nations and the laws of humanity. By treating the Belgians as movable
property that could be seized and put to military use, the Germans
had broken the Fourth Convention's rules on requisitions. The relevant article restated the ban on compelling civilians to join military
operations, saying that no requisition could imply "any obligation" to
do so.[36] Also, shipping the Belgians abroad did not serve the occupying army's immediate needs, and the deportations were particularly
flagrant because they enriched the conqueror's industries. The occupier was indeed required to "re-establish and insure . . . public order
and safety," but the Germans had done that in 1914, and since then,
the Belgians had neither disturbed the peace nor shown any sign that
they would.[37]

That careful planning had gone into the deportations aggravated
the offense. The perpetrators were not nervous Landsturmers seeing
their first battle but civilian officials and soldiers who had had the
leisure to consider their actions, and they could not even claim that
the Belgians had fired on them. The deportations involved the General
Staff, chancellor, Ministry of War, Deutsches Industriebüro, governor-
general, provincial governors, civil administrators, railway supervi-
sors, Kreischefs, military police, Meldeamt chiefs, prison camp commanders and guards, and occupation soldiers. Many, including the
policy's architects, also knew what the law said and either did not care
or pretended that it said something else. The jurist at the September

congress who had named the "German conscience" as the only arbiter had summed up the mind-set perfectly. Germans had a conscience that allowed them to defend themselves by whatever means they thought necessary, but anyone else who tried that was a criminal.

How the Germans justified the deportations was therefore important to understanding how this crime was something that the world could not live with, as the *Guardian* had said about Fryatt. A crucial point was that they—outwardly, at least—did not see why it was a crime. Calling the Belgians lazy struck a chord because Germans had sacrificed for what they believed was a fight for survival, and now their military leaders were demanding more, a national service law that would permit no shirking. The readiness to see the Belgians as idlers once more permitted the supposition that their character excused whatever the German government had chosen to do.

The German public had never been told that the occupation had crippled the Belgian economy, so it was natural to ascribe unemployment or any other misery to the blockade. However, even with the sparse information that filtered down, this made no sense. If the blockade had closed factories in Belgium, the British had made the Belgians jobless against their will, but if the real problem was Belgian laziness, the blockade was irrelevant. The contradiction appeared in black and white, for the stories about a busily employed Belgium had seen print in early August; by October, the press was saying that legions of idle Belgians were a public nuisance. Further, the assertion that the deportees would never have to do war-related work was clearly wrong, because the press noted that the national service law channeled all labor that way.[38] Workers who held jobs deemed incidental would be shifted to others or sent to the front, and easing the labor shortage in war industries would let the army conscript men who had been exempt. Where the Belgians fit into this scheme should have raised more questions than it did.

Still, the accusation of laziness held power. Both Hoover and Whitlock, who knew the occupiers from hard experience (and Dana Carleton Munro, who did not), worried that relief would corrupt the Belgians. With the deportations looming, Whitlock ranted to his diary about the "great mass of hulking young fellows playing the silly game of ball in vogue in Flanders for centuries" to be seen in public squares in Brussels and elsewhere. They were "demoralized," he thought, "and I fancy nothing will prevent the Germans from taking them to slavery temporarily."[39] Despite appearances, however, the Belgians could not get aid for the asking. At Mons, for instance, a relief applicant had to present documents that proved identity and marital status and revealed holdings in bank accounts and pensions, home ownership, possession of farm animals, and records of charitable assistance.[40] But if benevolent outsiders could fear for Belgium's immortal soul, the Belgians' enemies might draw more drastic conclusions.

Blaming the Belgians allowed the German government to focus on procedures, as if the deportations had been an ordinary measure, and that the Belgians, with typical stubbornness, had hurt themselves. The standard charge, issued in Belgium and repeated in Germany, was that no "mistakes" would have occurred had the burgomasters provided lists of unemployed. But the attempt at good faith Jackson found at Court-Saint-Étienne did not apply everywhere, and speed, if not intent, shaped the selections.[41] A CRB delegate said that when he protested the deportation of his employees at Mons, an officer replied that he had too many, and that the CRB identity cards protected nobody.[42] Elsewhere in Hainaut, the delegate said, the Germans targeted skilled laborers, employed or not, and that a glassworks at Jemappes was "practically killed" as a result.[43] After the war, the Belgians uncovered orders in Brabant to choose workers with usable skills and to keep CRB delegates—foreign eyes and ears—away from the deportation sites.[44] Also, the Germans never bothered workers in factories producing for Germany and always exempted coal miners, which may explain why they spared most of Liège province and parts of Hainaut, Namur, and Limburg.[45]

How any single deportation unfolded seems to have hinged at least partly on official whim, yet the chase after the lists was universal. Why the Germans wanted lists when every Meldeamt had names and addresses of able-bodied men remains unclear. Perhaps they wished to know who was receiving relief, because they could have threatened each recipient with loss of benefits unless he signed a contract, the legal fiction they sought. That might have enabled them to deliver workers without having to resort to naked force. But if so, that suggests that the Germans realized that the deportations violated the law.

Their press campaign said as much, for as if to head off protest abroad, they pretended that occupied Belgium had accepted the deportations. On 14 November, the *Norddeutscher Allgemeine Zeitung* emphasized the "calm and order" in Belgium, remarking with surprise that "not the least disturbance" had occurred anywhere, an observation that other newspapers echoed.[46] This was false, because apart from the crowds at deportation sites that shouted epithets, fights occasionally broke out between soldiers and civilians, and a few guards used their fists or rifle butts on women and children.[47] One burgomaster testified after the war that the populace would have stoned any official who had provided lists. He said that he had told the Germans that they could deport him, but that he had no lists and in any case "would consider myself dishonored" to comply.[48]

On 20 November the occupiers raised the war contribution to fifty million francs a month from forty million. Five provincial councils refused out of protest against the deportations, but Bissing annulled their vetoes, invoking an eighty-year-old statute that allowed the king to override council votes that "hurt the general interest." When the banks protested, Lumm declined to accept the message and sent back a circular advising that further complaints about any German law would result in fines. The banks bowed once again.[49]

. However, the protests apparently prompted Hindenburg to tell Bissing to increase the amount so heavily "that the desire for peace" became strong and that the country would be "as financially weak as possible after the war."[50] Bissing wrote back to disagree. Only by letting Belgium prosper enough to survive could the country become useful to Germany after the war, the governor-general said. Peace sentiment was strong, but if the Belgians realized that they would not recover their country after a German victory, their will to negotiate would diminish. Moreover, the notion that he was coddling Belgium came from troops passing through on leave, who assumed that the country was rich because they could buy bread and presents to bring home.

To prove that he was a stern master, Bissing tallied the requisitions, levies, forced purchases below market value, sequestrations, and coal exports his administration had assessed. He arrived at 2.5 billion francs in money and unpaid-for value transferred to Germany, with another 0.5 billion in profit received through goods. To supplement this figure, he planned to seize bank accounts belonging to enemy foreign nationals and absent Belgians, which would reap thirty million francs a month, in effect raising the war contribution to eighty million. As for postwar competition, he supposed that the loss of machinery would be crippling, as would the debt that the Le Havre government was incurring daily with foreign creditors. Add to that the cost of labor, sure to rise if skilled deported workers either stayed in Germany or returned home demanding more money, and the Belgians were unlikely to mount an economic threat.[51]

That Bissing felt compelled to write such a letter, especially then, suggests that German propaganda about the occupation's goals and methods was so potent that even Hindenburg believed it. What that says about the credulousness of people who lacked his access to privileged information may perhaps be judged from a story that the press widely reprinted from a Zürich paper in early December.[52] Britain, this tale alleged, had been forcing Belgian refugees to work in war plants, a coercion that dated from the exodus following the fall of Antwerp. British consular officials in Dutch ports and Le Havre had performed a triage on visa applicants, separating them by profession and stamping their papers with names of munitions factories where they were to work. Once in Britain, the Belgians found that conditions were akin to slavery, and if they refused to work or tried to find better jobs, they were sent to prison. From there, they could choose between internment camps or enlisting in the British or Belgian armies. Neither the British nor the Belgian press dared report this for fear of punishment, but when the war ended, "the whole truth about the fate of the Belgian slave population of England" would be told. Jackson, who clipped this article from a captive Belgian paper, wrote that to have published this claim while Germany was deporting Belgians was "interesting."[53]

No crime against Belgium, not even the invasion, aroused as much indignation in the United States. Cardinal John Murphy Farley of New York uttered a much-quoted comment: "You have to go back to the times of the Medes and the Persians to find a like example of a whole people carried into bondage."[54] The press said that Americans had not fed the Belgians so that they could be enslaved; the most outspoken editorials condemned the deportations as revolting or repugnant to modern civilization. The *New York Sun* asked whether Americans could stand by and allow slavery to be reestablished in Europe, and *The Outlook* demanded that the government break off relations with

Germany. The *Chicago Evening Post* commented that German excesses never let anyone forget the original crime against Belgium and never let anger recede.[55] But the *Chicago Tribune* accepted Berlin's justifications and deplored the protest meetings, wondering why American sympathy "exhaust[ed] itself upon distant lands."[56] The *Washington Post* barely covered the meetings while playing up (false) rumors that the Germans had begun repatriating deportees who should have been exempt.[57] This retreat from the paper's reproach of mid-November may have resulted from concern that some speakers at the meetings urged joining the war, which Belgian publicists had foreseen and wished to avoid.[58]

Wilson professed that the deportations disgusted him. To a senatorial supporter, he wrote on 5 December that they were "one of the most distressing" and "unjustifiable" incidents of the war, "and I wish I were not obliged to express judgments of this sort in private only." The protest note sent to Germany, he confided, was "very earnestly worded."[59] However, Lansing and House had prodded him to send one, and if he had followed their advice, that was because they had couched it as the means by which he could preserve his peace initiative.[60]

The president still believed that he could stop the war, and he knew that hard-liners were pressing the kaiser to permit the resumption of unrestricted submarine warfare, which had been abandoned since May. If they had their way, a break with the United States would likely result, which put Belgium's troubles in the background. The Germans had everything to gain by encouraging Wilson's diplomacy, and they suggested that Ambassador Gerard return to the United States on a long-desired vacation and talk to the president directly.[61] That left Grew in charge rather than the sometimes combative Gerard, but unlike Gerard, Grew was a career diplomat, and the Germans were mistaken if they thought they could get around him more easily.

The man they had gotten around was Wilson. The peace initiative, drafted 18 December and sent over Lansing's and House's objections, contained a thought that reflected the president's inability to discern a difference between Germany and its enemies. Wilson had framed his note as an appeal to clarify war aims, something the belligerents were reluctant to do. However, he supposed that their goals were "virtually the same, as stated in general terms. . . . Each side desires to make the rights and privileges of weak peoples and small states as secure against aggression or denial in the future as the rights and privileges of the great and powerful states now at war."[62] To equate both sides was to pretend that German crimes had no significance, and House foresaw that the note would insult the Allies (whose response focused on Belgium).[63] He wrote that he had tried to get the passage deleted, but in vain, because Wilson "seems obsessed with that thought, and he cannot write or talk on the subject of the war without voicing it."[64]

Lansing had assessed Wilson's outlook another way, in a private memo dating from September. The secretary of state had spent six months talking with Wilson about "the struggle between Autocracy and Democracy, but I do not see that I have made any great impression." He thought the president was focused on "the violation of American rights by both sides" and hardly considered what Lansing saw as the "vital interests," that "German imperialistic ambitions threaten free institutions everywhere."[65] Belgian concerns apparently meant little to Lansing except symbolically, but he may have been wondering whether the United States should join the Allies, a position he privately espoused in late January 1917.[66] Consequently, he favored protesting the deportations not to uphold international law but, more probably, to create political friction with Germany that would forestall Wilson's initiative. Nevertheless, on 22 November he wrote the president a long memo in which, with a passion he seldom expressed, he voiced his "intense feeling of abhorrence" for the deportations and his desire to find some way to end them. They were, he declared, "a direct and unjustifiable blow at the principle of individual liberty—an essential element of modern political ideas, if not of our civilization."[67]

History has been unkind to Robert Lansing, who struck several contemporaries as lacking astuteness or imagination, and whose memoranda often suggest a mind that fastened more easily onto legal pettifoggery than crucial issues. By contrast, history recalls Woodrow Wilson as an idealistic visionary, a portrayal so firmly established that the only debate is whether he was deluded or ahead of his time. Yet in autumn 1916, it was Lansing who grasped what Wilson had not: Germany, by pursuing policies like the deportations and explaining them away, had passed the point where genuine negotiation was possible. It was one thing for Wilson to uphold American neutrality (having just been reelected on the slogan, "He Kept Us Out of War"), but another to ignore what was happening. The only way he could gaze, undistracted, toward the horizon was by overlooking what lay around him.

10

Mort pour la Patrie

THE YEAR 1917 began with ill portents. The Germans announced more requisitions of metals, targeting copper and its alloys,[1] and housewives feared for their pans and kettles, "their pride, many of them heirlooms handed down from grandmothers."[2] A few unfit deportees had been released, arriving "in very bad shape fr. lack of food," Jackson heard, with "shocking" stories to tell.[3] When he protested the deportation of a railwayman who had worked nineteen months for the CRB, the Germans told him, "You see, that's just it, always the same case. He ought to be working for us."[4] On 20 January, Brussels sent off its first deportees, before a nearly silent crowd. The men bound for Germany walked rapidly, as if hurrying to catch an ordinary train, seemingly aware they were on display and determined to show no emotion.[5] Once, Jackson brought bread for departing workers, about three pounds per man, which prompted an officer to say that if they ate it en route, "they will be very fat when they reach Germany."[6]

Few Belgians ate their fill during 1917. A landmark study found that by the last quarter of 1916, the typical diet recalled that of the 1860s, and that during 1917 and 1918, food intake was so low that acute shortages resulted in deaths. A five-kilo bag of potatoes sold for ten or fifteen times the price of 1914, and the contents were likely to be stunted and black.[7] Bacon, the prewar staple of the poor, was fetching sixteen francs a kilo in Liège, eight times the prewar price,[8] whereas coal miners—the lucky, the well employed—were earning about five francs a day, 10 percent more than in 1914.[9] No wonder that the food situation was the chief topic of conversation, even in Brussels, likely the best-fed city in the Generalgouvernement.[10]

Requisitions continued, thirty-nine of them in 1917, zeroing in on mattresses, linens, bandages, medicines, chemical products, trees, and shoes, among other things.[11] Mothers had nothing with which to diaper their infants, because the Germans had taken the available cloth and rubber,[12] and no one could build anything, because the army had reserved the wood, cement, and stone.[13] The Germans were paying two francs the kilo for metals, whereas their demands for leather had driven the price of a pair of shoes past a hundred francs.[14]

Sending soldiers to collect the metals also caused tension, but burying the goods in gardens, under floors or rooflines, or behind cellar masonry only prompted the Germans to tear up floorboards, sound the walls, or ransack cabinets.[15] Even so, negotiation was sometimes possible, though not everyone tried it. One woman who had soldier sons reportedly asked what moral sense the Germans had if they believed she would give them her copper so that they could kill her children. They responded with angry thoroughness, taking every last door handle and smashing her furniture. Another time, a soldier told a man he would not enter the kitchen or search the house, but he could not leave empty-handed, so they settled on objects from the Belgian's dresser. When the Belgian asked whether the soldier was ashamed to seize personal belongings, perhaps gifts from relatives, the soldier replied that he had his orders. In another home, however, a soldier praised his host for having concealed the copper, as people did in Germany, and said that if he looked, he would surely find nothing. But if he left the house too quickly, his superiors would suspect, so he stayed five minutes, chatting.[16]

The relief's physical and psychological sustenance was therefore more vital than ever, but circumstance and German exactions impaired the CRB's ability to deliver. The occupiers were taking every available horse, leading Jackson to ask what the relief would use for local transport, when "already one sees [a] considerable number of cow & ox teams in the streets."[17] The last week of January, near-zero temperatures froze the canals, paralyzing water traffic, and the German demand on rolling stock was such that no trains were available to bring coal to Brussels or its environs.[18] Hoover persuaded the Germans to let the food travel by rail, but the worst winter in twenty-five years took its toll.[19] By February, Jackson heard that people were freezing to death in Brussels and schools were closing.[20]

Like the weather, stress left a bitter sting. A CRB supervisor wrote that near Ghent, a man shot himself to death, whereupon the Germans fined the commune for possession of a concealed weapon. The burgomaster posted a notice requesting that in the future, anyone who wished to commit suicide should do so by hanging, because using a revolver was too costly.[21] Given the tensions of daily life, it was amazing that more of them did not shoot one another. Min, the Bolinne-Harlue burgomaster, fumed that despite the deportations, some families "had so little dignity, patriotism or heart" that they gave German soldiers all they asked for—butter, eggs, flour, pork. These Belgians were "cowards and traitors." Even worse were fathers whose sons had been deported, yet who chopped down trees at the Germans' behest, which he called "revolting."[22] Whitlock said that the Belgians turned their rage against the United States for not having declared war, and that "they now detest[ed] the Americans as much as anybody."[23]

Against this background, the Germans made four pivotal decisions. The first was to announce that as of 1 February, they would resume unrestricted submarine warfare; two days later, the United States severed diplomatic relations with Germany. But Wilson did not ask Congress for war until 2 April, when he said that submarine tactics wronged the world and demanded that right, of which the United States was only one defender, be upheld. The president said that Germany's power had endangered world peace and freedom, therefore making neutrality neither feasible nor desirable. An age was beginning "in which it will be insisted that the same standards of conduct and of responsibility for wrong done shall be observed among nations and their government that are observed among the individual citizens of civilized states."[24] On 6 April, America declared war.

The return to submarine warfare also threatened the Belgian food supply. The British insisted that all CRB vessels enter a British port for inspection, but the Germans said that the only route they respected lay north of the British Isles, which would add one thousand miles to the trip. For the first time, Hoover's warning that he would fold the CRB worked no magic, and more than a dozen vessels stayed in British ports rather than risk sailing to Rotterdam. Their cargo, almost one hundred thousand tons of food, was sold so that it would not spoil.[25] More criminal than waste was that submarines began sinking CRB ships even in "safe" waters, accounting for twelve in 1917 alone.[26] Perhaps the sight of food destined for Belgium when none could reach Germany prompted retaliation, and some Germans were immovably convinced that the CRB ran weapons to Britain. But whatever the excuse, the sinkings multiplied just when courting American opinion had all but ceased to matter.

In late March, the CRB's American staff withdrew from Belgium, leaving Spanish and Dutch volunteers to carry on.[27] With an eye on *Flamenpolitik*, the Germans favored the Dutch, though both were less likely than the Americans to make trouble. But the CRB still shipped food to Rotterdam, and after the declaration of war, the United States government became the relief's sole source of funding, ending the indirect (and uncertain) subsidies from Britain and France.[28] As if fate had insisted on symmetry, the man with whom the CRB had often crossed swords, Bissing, died around the same time, from a cold that had developed into pneumonia. Oskar von der Lancken claimed in his memoirs that Bissing had caught the cold during a long, drafty train ride to Germany, undertaken to protest the deportations, but Belgians who believed in divine justice preferred another explanation.[29]

However, Bissing lived long enough to preside over the next stage of *Flamenpolitik*. On 4 February, about two hundred Flemish leaders met in Brussels under his sponsorship, calling themselves the Council of Flanders. Their manifesto demanded that the Belgian administration should be divided, and that Flanders and Wallonia should be culturally autonomous, a program that had official approval.[30] A decree requiring government communications and scientific and statistical publications to be in Flemish within territory designated as Flemish homeland was already in place, which lent apparent substance to German patronage.[31] Even so, the occupiers kept watch over the Council of Flanders, sending representatives to the meetings to assure that the Flemish radicals who dominated the council stayed within bounds. Bethmann blessed *Flamenpolitik*, saying that the kaiser "had shown himself full of sincere compassion" for the Flemish people, and that the governor-general's measures had given them the chance to realize their "free intellectual and economic development."[32]

What that meant became apparent on 21 March, when the occupation split the country into two zones. The law said that the provinces of Antwerp, Limburg, and the two Flanders and the cities of Brussels and Louvain were Flemish, whereas Wallonia comprised Hainaut, Liège, Luxembourg, and Namur provinces, and the arrondissement of Nivelles. Not only did this make the capital Flemish and shift Wallonia's administration to Namur—a calculated insult—towns found themselves changing provinces, as with Nivelles leaving Brabant and joining Hainaut.[33]

The separation's architects failed to win Belgian loyalties but succeeded in setting Belgians against one another. That the Council of Flanders had willingly served German purposes angered patriots of both ethnic groups, and its existence disproved the cherished myth that all Belgians had united in unswerving resistance. Consequently, the move to divide Belgium begot a category of Belgian collaborators, though the word was never used.[34] A sore point was that the council had not merely followed the Germans' orders but welcomed the Germans as saviors and asked them to grant self-government, quickly, before the occupation ended.[35] Only a small minority of the Flemish movement wanted this, but many Belgians considered the separatists to be traitors.

The third decision dating from early 1917 was that of 17 February, which closed all Belgian factories and businesses deemed nonessential, meaning those that either could not or would not work for Germany. The stated intent was to save fuel, but the decree also pushed factory owners to reconsider their opposition and, if they did not yield, prompted their employees to sign contracts with the Deutsches Industriebüro rather than risk deportation.[36] The occupiers spared paper factories to favor bandage manufacturers and the captive Belgian press, and glassworks because bottles and jars were useful and could be exported, notably to Scandinavia. Chemical companies also remained open, because they produced acids necessary in munitions manufacture, sometimes with German materials.[37] But of 260,000 Belgian enterprises operating in 1914, only slightly more than 3,000 functioned after the February decree, some under sequester, others under foreign administration, still others with German permission.[38] Price controls ensured that Belgian goods never undersold German ones.

The fourth, least expected action of early 1917 was the kaiser's announcement on 2 March that the deportations would end, and that employed Belgians brought to Germany by mistake would shortly go home if they had not already.[39] Nominally a response to an appeal from Belgian notables submitted in mid-February, the kaiser's clemency seemed to reward those who had protested. The leading Belgian historian of the deportations thought that the pope's complaints had borne fruit, but though Wilhelm placated the Vatican on occasion, there is no obvious reason he should have done so then.[40] However, what the kaiser intended did not matter. Hindenburg and Ludendorff were Germany's real rulers now, and the army had ordered that mass deportations from the Generalgouvernement cease as of 10 February, probably because they had created more problems than they had solved.[41] But the military leaders had not budged on the policy of requiring forced labor, and the kaiser had not promised that they would.

He had decreed that the deportations would stop "until further order," which meant that they could resume anytime. He had also mentioned only workers sent to Germany from the Generalgouvernement, the ones most visible to foreign observers, omitting those from the Etappengebiet or those shipped to northern France. In saying that only employed workers qualified for repatriation, he was referring to about twelve thousand out of some sixty thousand taken. Even at that, despite the mountain of documents the Vatican had gathered from Belgian authorities attesting to employment, extricating the lucky ones would depend largely on whether the camp commanders cared to let them go.

Which, for the most part, they did not. Rather, they redoubled their efforts to extort signatures, either through the usual tortures or by ruses. The men were told they could have a two-week stay at home if they signed a certain paper, written in German, which some were desperate enough to do, thinking—wishing—that this was a formality regarding their permanent return. But when they had spent their two weeks in Belgium and the soldiers came, the workers realized they had been deceived. Others guessed right away what they were signing and told themselves they had no intention of keeping their word, but when their brief freedom had passed, they found that they had made a bad bargain. To evade capture, they had to wander the country, in constant jeopardy from indiscretions or betrayal, and notices in post offices warned that if they did not give themselves up, their comrades would never return.[42]

Generally, however, the Germans held onto men whom they thought could be useful, previously employed or not, and released those who were either too sick to work or lacked the desired skills. Of seventeen thousand deportees returned as of 31 March, fewer than 4,300 had been employed. Thirty-three thousand others were working outside the camps, willingly or not.[43] Full repatriation of the workers covered by the kaiser's decree was supposed to occur by 1 June, and the Ministry of War—responding to an inquiry in the Reichstag—asserted that all those entitled to leave who wished to go would be gone by 15 June. But on 12 June, the ministry ordered the roughly 11,300 deportees in the camps to sign contracts, menacing recalcitrants with hell's premises. The Germans even added a twist, telling groups of the disobedient that their struggles were over, putting them on a train, and telling them that they were bound for Belgium. But the fantasy lasted only as far as Liège, from where the Germans shipped them to a discipline camp at Maubeuge.[44]

As a result, how soon a Belgian deportee left Germany depended on many things, but seldom good faith. Min wrote in late November that of the thirty-four men of his canton taken twelve months before, two were dead, twenty-eight had come back, and four remained in Germany, two of whom had never been jobless or received public assistance. None of the deportees had ever sent money home, whereas all had asked for food and clothing.[45]

Belgian medical authorities remarked with professional horror on the condition of those who returned. The worst off wore rags that flapped loosely on their emaciated bodies, and they could hardly stand, because their legs were swollen from circulatory or kidney ailments. They coughed hollowly, and their sunken eyes, "where the terror still showed itself," stared without seeing. They suffered from malnutrition, anemia, vertigo, lingering gastrointestinal ailments, rheumatism, and heart disease.[46] The 505 men who returned to Ghent between 1 January and 30 May had each lost 37 pounds, on average—and a rough average for a healthy Belgian man was 143 pounds.[47] However, German doctors' reports took a more limited view. They observed only a general lack of health, which they ascribed to conditions in Belgium or already existing problems, though they admitted that the allocation camps had not provided enough food.[48]

Further trouble awaited those who had come back. Captured German documents show that by August 1917, tens of thousands of Belgians were being made to work in their own country, most often in the Etappengebiet, but also in the Generalgouvernement. In all, the Germans employed about 230,000 workers in Belgium, and though some were foreign, as with prisoners of war, the vast majority were Belgian.[49] How many volunteered and how many the occupiers conscripted may never be known, and German claims regarding contracts are unreliable, particularly in view of an Etappengebiet decree of 11 April. Those who rejected an offer of work caused "serious military damage," the penalty for which could be death, whereas anyone who counseled resistance or failed to report the idle risked being put to forced labor.[50] Under such conditions, only the most fortunate could avoid being taken, and those who slipped through the net that gathered bodies for Belgium might still be deported to northern France.

That was perhaps the worst nightmare, returning from deportation only to be taken again. At Ghent, for example, which contributed nearly twelve thousand deportees, almost twenty-four hundred went twice, and one person went to northern France five times.[51] In the Etappengebiet, the deportations resumed twelve days after the kaiser's statement of clemency, when six hundred men left from Mons, and others subsequently from Tournai and Aalst. In May, the Le Havre government heard of deportations in Luxembourg province that included women considered strong enough to do farm work, only mothers of young children exempted.[52] To preclude flight or disturbances, the Germans began taking people at night, without warning, which caused great anxiety—people never knew, when they went to bed, whether they would still be there in the morning.[53] These conditions lasted from spring 1917 until the war ended. Even in the Generalgouvernement, the deportations did not stop altogether, for as late as summer 1917, the Germans were taking individuals and small groups, especially in the Brussels area.[54]

Belgian sources say that to staff the northern France civilian work battalions alone, the occupiers deported 62,155 people, of whom almost 12,000 were gone anywhere from three to six months, the most typical length of service. But nearly 8,000 spent between twenty-one months and two years away; how they survived may only be imagined. Of the 58,500 others sent to Germany, more than 60 percent stayed nine months or less, but as of 1 January 1918, almost 12,000 were still there. In total, then, roughly 120,000 Belgians suffered deportation, of whom the Germans took about 15,000 in 1917, and about 5,000 in 1918.[55] Consequently, though the number dropped sharply after 1916, the deportations ended only with the armistice, by which time more than 2,600 Belgians had died in exile, and tens of thousands of others had become wholly or partially disabled.[56]

These sacrifices earned admiration in Allied countries for adherence to principle, but it went unnoticed that the resistance to German demands had helped the war effort. In theory, the 400,000 workers the

Germans had wanted would have let them field almost four hundred new battalions or bring existing units up to strength. Instead, during the winter of 1916–17, the army had to release 125,000 skilled workers from the front. By mid-July, so many labor exemptions had been handed out that the average battalion had dropped from an already low 750 men to 713 in the West, and from 800 to 780 in the East.[57] What an influx of troops might have meant, especially after the submarine advocates had their way and challenged the United States, will never be known. Further, the resistance compares favorably with that during the first years of Nazi rule, when, one historian says, more than 121,000 Belgians volunteered to work in Germany before September 1941 alone, and 200,000 French people offered their services as well.[58]

Setting the Belgians to forced labor gained the occupiers of 1916–18 very little. Though the threat of deportation prompted many Belgians to sign with the Deutsches Industriebüro, the number of volunteers did not satisfy the need. For the fifteen months before the deportations, almost twenty-eight thousand had signed; in the fifteen months afterward, eighty-five thousand did. Even that increase was deceptive, because the biggest jump occurred in the second quarter of 1917, after the kaiser's announcement, which many Belgians mistook to mean that the ordeal was over.[59] The rise in signatures may have had more to do with food shortages than coercion, as a CRB delegate who had served in Hainaut wrote in a report dated June. Outside Mons, he said, the situation was so bad that German soldiers billeted in poorer homes shared their rations with the children, and Belgian workmen ate rutabagas for lunch and carried nearly empty dinner pails.[60] From the Mons area in mid-April, sixteen hundred men had signed up, and a thousand more near Charleroi followed suit—this, though not one of the province's 445 communes had provided lists of unemployed workers. The CRB delegate said that when hundreds had died or "undergone unbearable physical torture" rather than "submit for an instant . . . any one who has been a witness to these events knows the meaning of Belgium's sacrifice."[61]

The comments underlined, not for the first time, how the Germans had underestimated both the Belgian will to resist and how neutral observers would react. Karl Bittmann, an occupation official who wrote a frank assessment of the deportations from the inside, judged that the failure to anticipate these obstacles were two of the policy's defects. Others included the notion that forced laborers could or would do productive work and the negative effect on *Flamenpolitik* because of how the deportations alienated the Flemish. But the most crucial flaw was the damage from Allied publicity, "equivalent to the loss by Germany of a gigantic battle" that decided the war. As for The Hague Conventions, Bittmann concluded that violations existed only in public opinion, and whoever could "feed and direct" thinking on the matter could claim to have the law on his side.[62]

As American entry into the war looked more probable, the Belgians sought to reorient their approach to public opinion in the United States. To the American public, Belgians were still the brave, little, martyred people with nothing to eat, nothing to wear, and nowhere to live who would die without American charity. This perception opened purse strings for relief, but Belgian officials now foresaw what the accent on victimhood could cost. Once peace came, the United States would probably be the only major power to have money to spend, no losses to recoup, and no concessions to demand from Germany. Therefore, whatever funds for recovery Belgium realized from a settlement and foreign investment might depend on American resources and influence with Belgium's nominal allies. But if Americans viewed Belgium as a smoking ruin rather than a phoenix destined for rebirth, they would send their capital elsewhere. Similarly, if they imagined that Belgium's military effort had ceased with Liège or that the country merited no more than sympathy, Belgian war aims would go unheard.

A Belgian cabinet minister who had visited the United States in late 1915 had reported that in talking with any American, even "an intelligent and cultivated man," distorted notions often surfaced after "a few minutes of conversation."[63] The American would envision Belgium as a country devoid of buildings and vacant of movable goods. Americans supposed that the Belgian Army went shoeless, in rags, without food, and had no reserves except for the wounded, who of course lacked medical attention. Had the cabinet minister thought of Washington at Valley Forge, the portrayal might have made sense to him as a metaphor, particularly when newspaper editorials sometimes spoke of Lexington and Concord and Belgium in one breath. Like the thirteen American colonies, Belgium was indeed fighting for its independence, but the Belgians needed to make clear that they were struggling to regain their former position, which included their rank as an industrial power.

Accordingly, in March 1917 the propaganda director at Le Havre wrote that news stories must no longer stress atrocities or martyrdom but Belgian "vitality."[64] Pity turned hearts toward Belgium but failed to make people "appreciate what we represent in civilization" or the Belgians' "power of resurrection." Two months after America joined the war, the Belgians sent a delegation to Washington bearing a letter from Albert trying to attract American interest in postwar reconstruction and to sound out Wilson on peace terms. "The enemy brought us massacre and devastation," said Ludovic Moncheur, who led the mission, when Wilson received the Belgians at the White House, "but . . . there still remains to Belgium an industrious population of unconquerable energy."[65] In speeches to the Senate and the Washington press corps, Moncheur promoted Belgian confidence and strength under adversity while praising the Belgian Army, the royal couple, and Mercier.[66] Official Washington rose in unison to greet the Belgians, more warmly than they had Allied missions, and a far cry from the indifference of September 1914.

The administration took note and pressed the Belgians to undertake a coast-to-coast tour, hoping to drum up support for the war where it was weakest. Moncheur demurred until he realized that the more than nine hundred invitations he had received during his brief visit reflected an opportunity that could not be refused.[67] The Belgians set off on 1 July, on an itinerary that focused on the Far West and the Great Plains, twenty-one stops in twenty-four days. Moncheur and the army officers who accompanied him reported to Le Havre that their speeches duly followed the new guidelines, but that was not strictly true. At Seattle, for example, where Moncheur more or less repeated his Senate address, he mentioned the invasion atrocities, spoke of the "Holy Crusade" in which Belgium and America had joined forces, and outlined the war against the Belgian economy. He described the deportations, down to the tortures in the camps, and declared that Germany would not atone for this crime until the Hohenzollerns had been driven from the throne.[68]

The bid to exploit American sympathies was obvious. But the delegation was also advancing a political agenda in which the war crimes played a legitimate role while skirting the pitfalls of being "poor little Belgium." Though Moncheur indulged in dramatic rhetoric, he avoided exaggeration about sufferings, and much of what he said was new to his audience. Few Americans outside the Northeast had heard about the deportations in fine detail, and few Americans anywhere knew about efforts to hamstring Belgium as a postwar competitor. By talking about these subjects, he had laid the basis for reparations without using the word, and in harping on Belgian resiliency, he was planting the idea that Belgium deserved investment. In saying that a belligerent America "will deliver those of our workmen who still remain in bondage; you will restore Belgium to her own; you will put an end to military autocracy," he was stating war aims. And by emphasizing what resistance at Liège had meant to the Allies, he had cast Belgium as a worthy ally rather than a waif wanting a handout.

However, Moncheur may have at times departed from the script, because after he spoke in San Francisco, one newspaper assumed that the Belgians had come to ask for food, perhaps a sign that stereotypes died hard.[69] What was more, Belgian fund-raisers stayed with the standard line. A famous example was Suzanne Silvercruys, sister-in-law of a Louvain professor visiting at Harvard who had helped arrange the Boston protest meeting. Silvercruys toured twenty states as the "Little Belgian Girl," bringing tears to people's eyes and raising a million dollars for Belgian charities wearing an outfit tailored for the purpose.[70]

American war boosters hopped on the bandwagon. A featured cartoonist in the *Washington Post* devoted an October 1917 sketch titled "Protect Your Home" to the Belgians' plight, which he linked to the duty to aid the war effort. In the first panel, a society woman showed a Belgian wearing widow's weeds her home. "I had a pretty home like yours in Belgium but they burned it," the Belgian said, a tear on her cheek. When she saw a photo of her hostess's husband, she said, "I had a good husband but they took him in captivity and he died from brutal treatment." And so on, until the last panel, in which the society woman forsook a tango party to buy a Liberty Bond, saying, "I want to help."[71] Even less subtle was a full-page advertisement for the bond drive that appeared in the paper about two weeks later under the legend "Remember Belgium." The drawing portrayed a German firing squad wearing absurdly large spiked helmets (a design the army had abandoned in 1916), and the victim was a nurse, a stand-in for Cavell, though much younger. The lead copy: "America must never find herself with her back to the wall."[72]

With such sentiment in the air, the appetite for atrocity stories never waned, and the gruesome portrait of Belgium crowded other images out of view. Whitlock, who had different experiences to speak of if only someone would ask, was appalled during his trip home in summer 1917 when people wanted to hear about only blood and guts. He thought the "persistent morbid interest" disclosed a lack of imagination, "as though the justice of our cause depended on whether Germans killed babies in Belgium, or not."[73] As a novelist planning to write his memoirs of Belgium, Whitlock realized the power of the sensational to seduce, which he determined to resist even as publishers were rubbing their hands.[74] "The worst that happened there," he wrote, "was not the rape of women in Belgium, it was the rape of Belgium."[75]

Whitlock had used the past tense, but the violation was ongoing; Bissing's replacement as governor-general, Ludwig von Falkenhausen, kept up his predecessor's traditions. On 21 May, he demanded a new war contribution, raising the amount to sixty million francs a month from fifty million, which prompted the usual fruitless protest from the provincial councils. In November came another contribution and another protest that went nowhere.[76] By then, the occupation department overseeing commerce and industry had predicted that if the war lasted another year and a half, the country would be exhausted except for coal and phosphate deposits. Department officials foresaw rebuilding Belgium with German capital, but only as a captive market for German goods.[77]

Symbolic of Belgian exhaustion was the darkness the occupiers imposed on Brussels in late November, presumably to save fuel but doubtless also to limit human interaction. At nightfall, fixed at 4:00 P.M., stores had to lower their blinds halfway and mask with paper the single lamp they were permitted to light; cafés had to cover their windows entirely. Street lamps were kept so dim that they hardly illuminated their own bases, and at 6:00 P.M., when stores closed, people hurrying home risked colliding or stumbling in the dark. Thieves had a field day, sometimes robbing passersby of their clothes and shoes right on the street. Trams punctuated the blackness with blue-veiled lights, creating an eerie effect that recalled a theatrical extravaganza and lending "something fantastic to the sinister impression of the nocturnal appearance of the city."[78]

Ellsworth Young's classic 1918 Liberty Loan poster played to the American fascination with atrocity stories and confused the rape of Belgium with that of individual Belgians. Library of Congress, Prints and Photographs Division, LC-USZ 62-19905

Another emblem of prostrate Belgium arrived in the form of a mid-December decree that ordered large dogs delivered for slaughter—the occupiers wished to conserve the food supply. To a people who loved dogs, this was a painful blow, and a protest came quickly. On the Avenue Louise, the fanciest street in Brussels, someone left two magnificent canines dead, with a tricolor ribbon tying them together. A paper sign pinned to the ribbon read *Mort pour la Patrie* (Died for the Homeland).[79]

What that phrase might mean in the future was in doubt, for Falkenhausen had pushed *Flamenpolitik* to its conclusion and attempted to redefine homeland. An August decree made Flemish the only official language permitted in the Flemish zone and required, after an undefined grace period, organizations such as banks, local railways, and utilities to use it exclusively. The law cut only one way because French did not receive equal respect in Wallonia, where Flemish was allowed in official business.[80]

After the October Revolution in Russia, Ludendorff complained that the occupation was too soft on the Flemish, meaning that they were being promised too much freedom, and that Flemish radicals had big ideas. Lancken agreed about the radicals but said that he had never supported giving the Flemish more than token advisory power and had surely not encouraged demands for independence. The Flemish with whom the administration had dealt, Lancken said, "have never been left in doubt . . . that their aspirations can therefore only be considered in so far as they do not conflict with legitimate German interests."[81] However, he admitted that political and religious influences had worked against efforts to inspire "Germanic racial feeling," and the Flemish had a democratic outlook that made them hard to control.[82]

That attitude asserted itself on 22 December, when the Council of Flanders declared Flemish independence and, expecting that peace talks would soon begin, dissolved to prepare for elections that would provide an uncontested mandate. The Germans hastily edited the council's proclamation so that the word *independence* did not appear, only *autonomy*, but the genie they had conjured had escaped the bottle. On 20 January 1918, the council issued a manifesto asking for a full-fledged government, including a legislature, executive and judicial branches, and diplomatic representation abroad. Falkenhausen denied the request.[83]

But Belgian judicial authorities decided that the Council of Flanders had gone too far. The Court of Appeal charged the council with having disobeyed those articles of the penal code that forbade Belgian citizens to try to destroy or change the form of government and instructed the public prosecutor to bring a case.[84] On 8 February, the Belgians arrested two councilmen who happened to be in Brussels, but the Germans quickly had the pair released. The Court of Cassation, the country's highest appeals court, suspended its sessions in protest, which Falkenhausen rebuked as a "conscious political demonstration" and said he would intervene if the dissent continued. When other Belgian tribunals closed down in sympathy, three Court of Appeal justices were deported, and the occupiers barred Belgian magistrates from pursuing cases while warning that any proceeding against the council was contrary to German interests.[85]

To nail down the point, in April 1918 the occupiers substituted German criminal and civil courts for Belgian. Judges, prosecutors, and clerks would be German, the court language would be German—except in Flanders—and most of the procedures would be German. But the courts were to apply Belgian penal law, except that they suppressed jury trials, could order arrests without an inquest, and could reject any defendant's right to counsel. They could pass any sentence, including death; no defendant could examine the prosecution's charges; and introduction of defense evidence occurred at the judge's pleasure.[86]

The Fourth Convention said that an occupier could not "declare extinguished, suspended, or unenforceable in a court of law the rights and rights of action of the nationals of the adverse party."[87] Anglo-American legal texts read this clause to guarantee protection for the population's rights in court.[88] That left room for an occupier to set up military courts "where necessary" and alter the laws, especially criminal law and even legal procedure, to maintain public order or safety. But the measures the occupation had taken were a form of terror, a way of showing the Belgians that they were a subject people whose laws no longer protected them, and whose language was no longer a medium in which they could defend themselves.

That too was the intention behind *Flamenpolitik,* to demonstrate that Belgium had ceased to exist, and that Belgian laws could not prevent this. Bissing's goal of a Flemish state under German rule was *Flamenpolitik* at its extreme, but even its milder versions foresaw the crushing of what was Belgian. Had the occupiers achieved more in this direction, the Walloon minority would have approached a condition of statelessness, with no nationality to speak of and no rights before the law. Not that the Flemish would have come off much better; if the Germans had gotten their way, the dogs left on the Avenue Louise might have represented the two halves of the Belgian nation.

11

Like a Thief in the Night

MAKING BELGIUM WHOLE AGAIN figured among the topics that Wilson took up in his speech of 8 January 1918 defining Allied war aims, in which he outlined his famous Fourteen Points. True to their author, they consisted of first principles, like disarmament and freedom of the seas, and only then considered national concerns, rendered in the equivalent of shalts and shalt nots. The biblical echo was unmistakable, and the program's broad sweep captured the imagination, especially compared with Allied leaders' reluctance to commit to preventing future wars. To many people, Wilson acquired the reputation of latter-day prophet in spite of—or perhaps because of—being a junior partner in the war effort. Not only had the United States remained neutral for almost three years, it had never formally joined the Allies or signed the Pact of London and was instead, like Belgium, known as an Associated Power.

But Belgian eyes were riveted on the details of current aims rather than the tenets of future peace. What they were looking for appeared in Point Seven, which said, "Belgium, the whole world will agree, must be evacuated and restored, without any attempt to limit the sovereignty which she enjoys in common with all other free nations."[1] This spoke to Berlin's chronic unwillingness to clarify its intentions and served notice that Germany could not hope for a protectorate or trade Belgian independence for other concessions at the conference table. The next sentence cast Belgium's reestablishment as a "healing act" that, above all others, would "restore confidence in international law," without which the law's "whole structure and validity" would be "forever impaired."

But like Grey and Asquith, Wilson had not defined restoration, which could mean as much as replacing every broken window or as little as reinstating prewar boundaries. The president's vagueness contrasted with the position of British Prime Minister Lloyd George, whose government had replaced Asquith's in December 1916 and who sounded more forthright than his predecessor. Three days before Wilson's speech, the prime minister had demanded for Belgium "reparations . . . for the devastation of its towns and provinces," which would represent Germany's recognition of its crimes, necessary if the peace were to be stable.[2] But one of the attractions of the Fourteen Points was that people could read into them what they wished to see there, and the Belgians wanted to see that all their expenses would be paid.

Even so, the topic of punishment stood out by its absence, reflecting Wilson's views. In December 1915, Lansing had pressured Austria-Hungary to punish the submarine commander who had sunk the *Ancona*, an Italian passenger liner, an act that had killed more than two hundred civilians, twenty-five of them American. The Austrians indirectly refused, and the matter went no further.[3] In May 1916, the president had said that guilty submarine commanders "should have personal punishment," but he never outlined how.[4] *Literary Digest*, a magazine that surveyed American opinion, remarked that neither in the Fourteen Points nor his subsequent comments did he say much about "paying the bill," as in criminal and financial penalties.[5]

Wilson's silence did not escape the British government. Three days after the Fourteen Points address, Britain's attorney general said that deterring aggression was less a business of writing covenants than of enforcing those that existed. Speaking before the New York State Bar Association, Frederick E. Smith likened the war to a "gang of malefactors" defying the New York police, saying that the outcome would uphold either the law or the criminals. To vindicate international law, therefore, the Allies must win the war and "punish those who have broken the public laws of the world." Perhaps that would prevent strong nations from "dream[ing] of aggressive war," but even if not, he wondered whether freedom of the seas or disarmament were attainable. Regarding the League of Nations, Point Fourteen, Smith asked whether an "unpurged Germany" could be a member. And when he answered no, he concluded that every road to peacemaking always returned to the same place: "Public law disappears for ever from this world if we are proved powerless in this controversy to castigate the wrongdoer."[6]

Smith's opinions coincided with what his parliamentary constituents wanted to hear, and his viewpoint later appeared to be more flexible than his words might have suggested. Britain also had self-interest in opposing freedom of the seas and in wishing to deal a decisive blow to German power. Nevertheless, in contradicting the president—on American soil, no less—the attorney general had sketched out one difference between Wilson's vision and that of key Allied leaders, to say nothing of French and British public feeling. In this European view, international law must command respect before any limits on future war stood a chance of being realized, and that the path toward respect must involve punishing the war crimes.

Before that happened, however, the Allies must win the war, and to judge by Belgium as 1918 began, victory could not come too soon. Brussels could no longer keep its streets clean, because the animals that pulled the sanitation wagons were either dead or too weak to perform, and those that could move were being requisitioned. Diphtheria, last seen before the war, reappeared, and some of the city's children were losing their eyesight, perhaps the result of a severe vitamin A deficiency. In February, people who had not turned in their mattresses underwent household searches that always unearthed the mattresses and often more. In one wealthy home, the soldiers made forty holes in the floor hunting for treasures, and they even took the wrought-iron veranda. Yet another wave of requisitions seized window grilles, curtain rods, banisters, and pipes.[7] When the Germans ordered an inventory of church bells and organ pipes, Mercier did not bother complaining to Falkenhausen, who had assured him there was nothing to worry about. Instead, he wrote to Berlin, and the Vatican applied pressure too. The churches kept their bells.[8]

A diarist at Mons reported that by the end of April, people looked like skeletons, their bones about ready to burst through their skin. By June, cats and dogs were dying. Amid these hardships, the occupiers redoubled their measures against underground activity. The commander ordered that no object could be left outside that Allied aviators might see, such as laundry, and he apparently increased his spy network, because when people conversed on the street, they watched out for strangers who sidled up to them. Having learned since the war began that talk of cannon fire or passing trains could result in arrest, the people of Mons described these everyday events in code: "Our relatives are arriving" or "Grandpa's coughing."[9]

In May the occupiers assessed Belgium another war contribution, and when the director of the Banque Nationale protested, they deported him.[10] But that spring, the object of all conversation in Brussels was the cost of fruits and vegetables, which led to altercations between shoppers and vendors, demonstrations, and the overturning of stalls in the city's marketplaces. The vendors retaliated by going on strike, with one saying, "Ah! The Bruxellois don't want to accept our prices! Well, we'll make them eat horse dung!"[11] In a marketplace left empty over the next two days, housewives had plenty of time to repeat these words to themselves.

With most factories and workshops idle, there remained the buildings and what they contained. In July, the Germans began to dismantle the factories and their contents, whether for scrap or reassemblage in Germany. The decree nominally targeted war industries, but that could include anything. The Germans started with almost 170 factories, though captured documents suggest that they had chosen 573 companies altogether, most of which were metalworks, with others manufacturing chemicals, glass, or paper. Industrialists who had thus far refused to produce for Germany could either watch everything disappear, or give in and worry that they might be prosecuted after the war for collaboration.[12] But the large companies were not the only ones to suffer, for the law even touched craftsmen working for themselves, taking their tools and demolishing their workshops.[13]

The Germans insisted then and later that the measure had nothing to do with crippling an industrial rival, and the Belgians never found a document proving that motive.[14] However, they remarked on the German engineers and designers who made copious notes about industrial processes, and how the demolition workers zealously destroyed everything except on occasions when the plant was to be transported to Germany. If scrap metal was the object, the wrecking crews had no reason to be gentle, for they were usually employed by private firms that billed by the ton.[15] The wreckers were also supposed to write down a description of every machine they removed so that the owners could be paid, but often a machine was recorded as a certain weight of metal, nothing more.[16] Sometimes the requisition looked like vandalism, as with a Hainaut chemical plant whose two lead rooms were half stripped when one alone would have yielded the desired lead. Some of the lead was never even sent to Germany.[17] As with the deportations, the destruction occurred so quickly that German industry could not always absorb the benefit, and the machinery was sometimes found in depots, unused, after the war ended. It was as if Belgium were being smashed up and sold, yet had so little value not even competitors wanted to buy.

The war news was equally disheartening. By the Treaty of Brest-Litovsk in early March, Russia obtained peace by yielding to Germany almost a million square kilometers of land, the lion's share of its industrial and mineral output, and large amounts of food. Ending the war in the East allowed the Germans to try for that knockout blow in the West that had eluded them in 1914, except that now, they need not watch their backs. Between late March and early August, they launched several offensives, the first of which scored a major breakthrough before being checked.

The success prompted King Albert, ever wary of German power, to accept an offer from Törring to renew peace talks through the Belgian minister in Switzerland, Fernand Peltzer. Albert even thought the two sides might work out a private cease-fire. But involving Peltzer meant informing the Belgian Foreign Ministry, where Hymans was now in charge, and he told Peltzer to keep a cold but courteous demeanor and not to compromise on Belgian aims.[18] Albert seethed about ministers who cared nothing for his soldiers' lives,[19] and when the Allies agreed to place their armies under a unified command, the king, as always, declined to go along.[20] That did not stop him from urging the new generalissimo, Ferdinand Foch, to defend Flanders tooth and nail, an effort in which Belgian troops duly played their part.[21] But Albert's refusal lingered in Allied memories.

British leaders estimated that the war would last another year, by which time they expected that American manpower would end the deadlock.[22] But Albert assumed that the Allies would not break the German lines even then, hardly a vote of confidence given that 250,000 American troops arrived in France in May, as many in June, and more than that in both July and August.[23] By contrast, the German Army could not replace the losses from the spring offensives, which had cut deeply into its best remaining divisions. But if Albert's pessimism kept him from seeing the future, the present offered evidence that Germany was riding high. In May, Romania signed the Treaty of Bucharest, which echoed the terms exacted from Russia except that

Germany reserved the right, because of "military security," to detain Romanians charged with war crimes until a general settlement. This article did not say what would happen afterward, only that the amnesty clauses in the treaty did not apply to the accused lawbreakers. By implication, the Romanians were expected to prosecute.[24]

The logic followed German law, which in most cases reserved jurisdiction over war criminals to the country for which the defendants had fought.[25] But that put the Germans in a corner, for Romanian courts were unlikely to convict Romanians, especially on the charges the Germans planned to lodge. The army wanted to depose King Ferdinand and try Romanian leaders for having torn up an alliance with Germany to fight on the Allied side, and to prosecute Romanians alleged to have mistreated German prisoners. In late June, a Reichstag deputy remarked that removing a dynasty that had incited a war implied danger for the Hohenzollerns, and that trying Romanians for abusing prisoners would set an equally hazardous precedent.[26] But no one heeded his warnings, because, after all, Germany was going to win the war.

However, the situation that had looked promising in the spring collapsed on 8 August. Allied counterattacks regained the initiative, and within three weeks, the Germans had retreated almost to the Hindenburg Line, about where they had started in March. By early September, even Albert became convinced that the Allies would win, and he placed his army under Foch's authority, though he himself commanded the newly formed Army Group Flanders, which included troops from four nations.[27] However, the king did not inform his cabinet until late September, when Army Group Flanders had begun its first offensive.

With the tide turning, talk focused on peace terms the Allies should require, among them redress. On 1 September a *New York Times* editorial titled "What Restoration Means" described the occupation's ravages and tallied part of what Germany owed Belgium in compensation.[28] Eleven days later, Lloyd George said that "the first indispensable condition" of a "just and desirable peace" was a triumph so sweeping that the Germans knew they were beaten. They must be taught that "if their rulers outrage the law of nations," they would not escape punishment, and if the Allies failed to drive that lesson home, "the burdens of this war will have been in vain."[29] The next week,

Smith told his cheering Liverpool constituents that the law supplied "abundant warrant" to punish war criminals "in their persons and in their purses," and that he would not accept an escape from justice.[30]

However, the Germans did not recognize that they were beaten or that Belgium had any right to independence or indemnity. The newly appointed chancellor, Friedrich von Payer, accused Belgium of conspiring with the Entente and said that Germany would leave only if the Allies signed a satisfactory peace treaty. He said that Germany and its allies must retain their prewar boundaries, "that in Belgium no other State will be more favorably placed than we," and that the "Flemish question" must be resolved according to "the dictates of justice and wise statesmanship." Further, he rejected reparations for Belgium, saying that Germany, "as the innocent and attacked party," should be on the receiving end.[31] These terms resembled Törring's proposals to Peltzer, which Hymans had flatly rebuffed, and Törring's response to this rejection reflected the temper in Berlin. On 24 September, he accused the Belgians of telling the Allies about the peace talks and threatened Belgium with complete destruction if the German Army ever retreated across it.[32]

But this devastation was already happening, sometimes with wholesale deportations, both in Belgium and northern France. The French, believing that the Germans intended to further cripple them as an economic rival, asked Britain and the United States to warn Germany that excesses would not be tolerated. They hesitated, fearing that France meant to take reprisals if Germany were invaded, for a French patriotic committee was demanding "City for city, village for village, church for church, castle for castle."[33] Premier Georges Clemenceau denied that he had meant any such thing, but for several weeks, his allies kept silent, and the only call for action occurred behind the scenes. Smith, with Solicitor-General Gordon Hewart, urged Lloyd George to form a panel of jurists to prepare for war crimes trials.[34] But the prime minister did not act, despite the issue's importance to a general election scheduled for December.

Lansing, who liked to call the Germans "ruffians,"[35] wrote Wilson on 27 September that the United States should view the destruction "as if our own land had been occupied and our own people subjected to . . . privations and brutal treatment."[36] He reminded Wilson that the French and Belgians had been asking for a statement, but the president did nothing. However, he did tell a New York audience that there

The German retreat through Belgium left a swath of devastation twenty miles wide, with the destruction continuing up to—and sometimes past—the armistice. Here, rather than allow railroad cars full of helmets to fall into enemy hands, the German Army blew them up. Hoover Institution Archives

could be no bargained peace because the Central Powers "have convinced us that they are without honour and do not intend justice. They observe no covenants, accept no principle but force and their own interest." Further, he hinted that if the German people wanted peace, they could not have it with the governmental system then in place.[37]

Germany was not ready to dethrone Wilhelm, but pressures for change were growing. When the kaiser named yet another chancellor in Prince Max von Baden, Max drew his ministers from the Reichstag, a reform that appeared to give Germany its first true parliamentary government. This was the cabinet that the Supreme Command asked to request an armistice, "in order to avoid further bloodshed," as Max wrote to Wilson on 3 October.[38] Ludendorff wanted time to regroup, and he thought that the Allies would give it to him. Allied leaders did not take the note seriously, but just in case, their military advisers hurriedly drafted armistice conditions, which said nothing about war crimes.[39]

However, the German note gave the French an opportunity to draw attention to the wrecking of their territory, and on 5 October, they issued a warning. "Acts equally contrary to international law and to principles of human civilization will not remain unpunished. . . . The authors and organizers of these crimes will be held responsible morally, criminally and financially. . . . The account to be settled with them is open. It will be paid."[40] The communiqué cautioned that France was weighing with its allies what response to take.

The message evoked a strong reaction. A Belgian committee in London demanded reprisals, endorsed France's note, urged Lloyd George to follow suit, and adopted a slogan similar to "City for city."[41] The French Senate condemned German behavior and vowed to exact punishment.[42] In Britain, the German pretense that Max's government was democratic (and thus fulfilled Wilson's demands) aggravated the anger. The *Times* ran an editorial titled "An Old Firm Under a New Name," declaring that "the Chancellor's domestic experiments" did not matter beside "the exaction of debts to an outraged civilization," for which "the payment is not to be made in words."[43] The next day, the paper suggested that if Bruges burned, "Hamburg must pay; if Lille, then Frankfurt."[44] The *Manchester Guardian* remarked that whatever government Max had assembled, "nothing in the constitution of the German State has been altered" and warned against giving the Germans respite.[45]

American wrath went further. The kaiser took much of the heat, as he had since the declaration of war, when church sermons, movies, songs in Broadway musicals, and even a poem by Carl Sandburg had advocated a royal hanging.[46] Now, the *New York Times* spoke of destroying "the satanic Potsdam power and the Hohenzollern and Hapsburg dynasties," and said that the "imperial criminals" would receive a sentence that would bar them from a League of Nations.[47] The paper was not alone, for *Literary Digest* offered that "there seems to be considerable editorial reluctance to allow the destroyer of Belgium to enjoy a peaceful old age." The only question was what form the punishment should take.[48]

On Capitol Hill, a group of senators, most from western states that had once been staunchly isolationist, rejected talk of armistice and demanded unconditional surrender, which the Republicans were making an issue in the 1918 midterm elections. Several senators, including Henry Cabot Lodge of Massachusetts, wanted trials too and named the kaiser and "the murderers and robbers who have laid waste Belgium and France" as defendants.[49] Porter McCumber, a North Dakota Republican, sponsored a resolution to refuse an armistice until Germany agreed to reparations, which included "proper compensation" for "every crime committed by its armies contrary to the laws of warfare and humanity."[50] He read testimony about mutilations and child murders in Belgium during 1914 and recounted how the Germans had deported 7.5 million Belgians and 42 million people overall.[51]

McCumber's speech offered yet another example of how war crimes rarely received insightful public discussion; two colleagues even suggested that anyone who favored an armistice or mild terms for Germany must be disloyal.[52] But the Germans seemed bent on proving that they deserved all the criticism they got, no matter who accused them. German submarines torpedoed the passenger ferry *Leinster* in the Irish Sea, killing almost two hundred civilians, and sank a Japanese steamer, *Hirano Maru*, off Ireland. Seventeen hundred miles from the Atlantic coast, the American cargo vessel *Ticonderoga* went down too, but at least that was a military target. However, the survivors alleged that the submarine had fired on their lifeboats, a crime by any code.

The *New York Times* asked whether peace could be made "on any terms" without providing for trials that would punish such murders, the paper suggesting that the rule should apply to crimes on land.[53] The sinkings led British Foreign Secretary Arthur Balfour to say that the Germans had not changed since invading Belgium: "Brutes they were when they began the war, and as far as we can judge, brutes they remain at the present moment."[54] The *Times* of London questioned the sincerity of "a nation which sees crimes done in its name and makes no effectual protest" and repeated that Max was no different from his predecessors.[55]

The president of the United States finally joined the hue and cry. He informed Max that no armistice was possible "so long as the armed forces of Germany continue the illegal and inhumane practices which they still persist in," and he cited the sinkings and the devastation.[56] That day, 14 October, the *New York Times* reprinted commentary culled from sixty-nine newspapers coast to coast, including many from the Deep South and Far West, a sampling that filled an entire page.[57] Every single editorial either brushed aside the armistice request or demanded that Max show that his government did not represent the kaiser. Many papers said that no peace could come without justice for war crimes. The outpouring led the *Times* to remark, "Our Westerners do not like to go to war unless they are to fight to a finish, and this is their idea of a finish."[58] The paper went on to cite the precedent of Henry Wirz, the Andersonville commander, and urged that a military commission be appointed to oversee trials.

But the most impressive sign of change appeared in the *Chicago Tribune*. "Swift and certain punishment must be the sentence for Germany," the paper declared on 16 October, arguing that victory alone would not suffice. "We have been exceedingly patient with felonious German doctrine. . . . But an accounting there must be; a stern accounting. . . . Belgium was no mere local casualty of battle but the deliberate and foul handiwork of the schooled assassin." The paper noted that humanity included "those who follow us; we are not alone to be considered," and commented that "forgiveness is a virtue overdone" when it "forgives a present injury only to invite another and greater."[59]

Even so, within days, armistice discussions gathered momentum, and the prospects of an immediate peace suddenly loomed large. British opinion rallied around the call to write war crimes trials into the armistice, focusing on the mistreatment of British prisoners and vowing punishment. Leading the campaign was Lord Alfred Northcliffe, the press baron whose holdings included the *Times* and *Daily Mail*, and whom the government had named minister of propaganda. The move only made official what he had been doing since 1914, and Northcliffe's elevation did not stop him from persecuting fellow ministers he accused of failing to pressure Germany on the prisoners' behalf. But despite the vitriol, principle lay beneath the excess, and Northcliffe—whose program for prosecution was moderate—saw that the prisoners issue opened the door to trials for other crimes.[60]

The *Times*, naturally, printed myriad letters from readers who urged that Germany have no peace without surrender, and the paper accused the government of weakness.[61] But plenty of people shared that opinion. A riled House of Lords insisted on redress for the prisoners and condemned the government, which, as one speaker said, "have shown not one scintilla of courage in the matter."[62] The government finally realized the extent of the damage, and the next day, 17

October, secretly decided to form the blue-ribbon panel that Smith and Hewart had proposed.[63] But that move would have satisfied no one even had it been announced. Within a week, the ruling bodies of both major political parties had passed resolutions exhorting action, the Liberals asking that trials of defendants suspected of brutalizing British prisoners be a condition of peace.[64] Debate in the House of Commons demonstrated strong support for these resolutions.[65]

By 31 October, when Allied leaders were hashing out armistice terms, the public mood was such that Lloyd George's chief advisers counseled him to include provisions for trials. The prime minister replied that he did not want to jeopardize the armistice over this issue, seemingly content to make sure that nothing prevented later action.[66] Aside from a single, oblique reference during one meeting, no Allied representative appears to have brought up war crimes or trials, and the final draft mentioned neither.[67] Why this should have happened demands an explanation, one that the leaders responsible never gave.

Most likely, they never thought the question important enough to overshadow other interests. None of the Allies wished to govern Germany should an unconditional surrender lead to civil disorder, yet they had to make sure that Germany could not resume the war. The armistice all but crippled the German Army, which was to yield huge quantities of weapons and transport, evacuate all occupied territory (including Alsace-Lorraine) in only fifteen days, and grant bridgeheads across the Rhine. These conditions virtually amounted to a surrender without the word, and the Allies wondered whether an army that had never been forced to defend its home soil would keep fighting rather than accept such terms.[68] Germany signed, of course, but to loud howls—as one soldier wrote, "An honourable opponent ought to show regard for us rather than humiliate us by bringing us to our knees."[69] Yet Allied statesmen had not asked for trials because they thought no nation that valued its honor could consent.

This belief had colored British thinking almost from the first. On 11 October, the day Balfour spoke of "brutes," the War Cabinet, whose membership included neither Smith nor Hewart, discussed Smith's idea that an armistice should address the prisoners' issue, following the precedent in the Treaty of Bucharest. One unnamed minister averred that "it would be very difficult to fix responsibility" for the crimes, and "no nation, unless it was beaten to the dust" would submit to trials. Had the positions been reversed, a defeated England would have never allowed its officers to stand trial. The War Cabinet agreed not to press the matter and resolved instead that Germany should be told confidentially that the guilty must be punished.[70]

Still, that does not reveal why the victors agreed to an immediate peace rather than deciding to press their advantage. The answer appears to be that each leader assumed that his authority at the conference table would be greatest if the war ended right away and diminish the longer it lasted. Since 1914, British policy makers had supposed that their influence over peacemaking depended on how large an army they had when the war ended, which in turn argued for keeping the British share of fighting as small as possible.[71] But the French seemed to desire the same thing for themselves, because from summer 1918 onward, Foch consistently deployed American troops to reinforce French-held sectors rather than British ones, as if to preserve French forces at British expense.[72] By October, the British had reason to fear that the French planned to let them assume the greatest burden of the coming campaign, when British experts were already predicting a shortage of 171,000 soldiers by mid-1919.[73] This thinking assumed that the American Expeditionary Force, which senior British commanders disdained, would be of no use.

But at the rate that force was growing, American manpower would dwarf both the French and British armies if the war lasted, to say nothing of the ever-increasing power of American finance. In 1914, Britain had been the world's most important creditor. By 1919, the balance sheet would still list Britain as a net creditor, but debt to the United States alone would stand at £840 million, or almost $3.4 billion.[74] Jan Christian Smuts, South Africa's defense minister and member of the War Cabinet, put the matter squarely on 26 October. "If peace comes now, it will be a British peace," but if the war continued into 1919, "the peace which will then be imposed on an utterly exhausted Europe will be an American peace."[75] Smuts warned that the United States would replace Britain as the world's leading military, diplomatic, and financial power, and at the conference table, Britain's friends would be opponents.

Wilson adopted this reasoning in reverse. Treasury Secretary William G. McAdoo warned that the United States could not bear the strain of financing the war for another year.[76] That was one consideration, but the president seemed more concerned that too complete a victory would throw Germany into revolution and put the Bolsheviks in power, in which case he preferred the Hohenzollerns.[77] Most of all, he worried that the Allies "were getting to a point where they were reaching out for more than they should have in justice," and that their "selfish" aims must be checked.[78] As he cabled House on 28 October, "too much success or security on the part of the Allies will make a genuine peace settlement exceedingly difficult if not impossible."[79]

So it was that Germany's enemies, who had received Max's note skeptically, ended hostilities little more than a month later. As one British official wrote, peace had come "like a thief in the night," but the question of who got robbed remains controversial.[80] One view, espoused by the Germans and widely accepted, is that the Allies imposed a draconian armistice and got all they could have wanted.[81] But they omitted one item from their wish list, which soon became the subject of a dark comedy.

Nine days after the armistice, Lloyd George turned his attention to war crimes trials with a zeal that perhaps exhibited the mercurial nature for which he was famous. This quality was said to be visible in his face, which, wrote a renowned historian of prewar England, "was tragic, and sorrowful, and charming and comic by turns . . . emotions chased across it like wind across a rain puddle."[82] The consummate politician, Lloyd George had nearly resigned as chancellor of the exchequer in August 1914 to protest the declaration of war, only to stay and become known as one of the war's most vigorous supporters.

On war crimes, however, his well-tuned flair for drama may have misled him, for he focused on the most difficult, sensational case. On 20 November, he told the Imperial War Cabinet (the War Cabinet plus leaders from the empire) that he wanted to try the kaiser, and when he sensed disagreement, got his blood up. He launched into a speech about the man who had "put to death hundreds of thousands of prime young fellows from this country and did it very recklessly. . . . I think rulers who plunge the world into all this misery ought to be warned for all time that they must pay the penalty sooner or later."[83]

His words failed to convince. Making war was not a crime, the ministers said, but even if it were, Wilhelm's guilt would be hard to separate from his advisers', and a court might acquit him. Wilhelm had fled to Holland, which might refuse extradition, but even if the Allies got him, his trial might rally nationalist elements in Germany.

Annoyed, Lloyd George began to argue as if he were in a courtroom, which prompted the cabinet to put up a mock defense. The skeptics guessed that Wilhelm would say that Russia, not Germany, had started the war, and they worried that this gambit would throw the trial off track. The prime minister, seeing that the politicians would not yield, did the only thing he could: He said he would refer the case to Smith's lawyers.[84]

By a four-three vote, the jurists supplied the desired indictment, which listed fifteen categories of potential charges, including unrestricted submarine warfare, the mistreatment of prisoners, the execution of hostages, and—despite objections—waging aggressive war.[85] Smith now had to plead this brief before the Imperial War Cabinet on 28 November, a task for which he possessed two advantages over Lloyd George. Not only was the tall, dark, slender attorney-general the crown's highest-ranking legal official, he had a lower-key eloquence than the prime minister. He spoke in a "beautiful drawl" and projected the "airs of a fox-hunting man who could swear elegantly in Greek," a style that had served him (and befit his title of Lord Birkenhead).[86] But he also argued from reason rather than spirit, saying that the legal and moral case would suffer if the Allies pursued lesser criminals and let the greatest one escape. He proposed either punishing Wilhelm without trial, as Napoleon had been treated, or trying the kaiser before an international tribunal, preferably one whose judges came from Allied countries alone.[87]

Smith recognized the problem of appearing to have meted out victor's justice. But he said that the Allies must take "our stand upon the universally admitted principles of the moral law, take our own standards of right and commit the trial of them to our own tribunals."[88] As the Imperial War Cabinet had, he predicted that an indictment for aggression would lead to a "meticulous examination of the history of European politics for the past twenty years" and sidetrack the case. Rather, he recommended charges of violating Belgian neutrality and the criminal acts that followed, on which "I do not think that any honest tribunal could hesitate." Finally, he said that unrestricted submarine warfare must be punished, to uphold the law and secure future British interests.[89]

When Smith finished, no one argued with the decision to prosecute. But the proceedings had a whiff of politicking, because two naysayers from the previous meeting were absent, and because Smith asked Lloyd George privately whether he might tell his constituents what the cabinet had decided.[90] Lloyd George replied that he planned to do so himself the next day. At Newcastle-on-Tyne, he thrilled a crowd with Smith's reasoning, delivered in his own, rousing manner, and promised "just, fearless, and relentless" action. However, he restored one element that the attorney general had dropped—trying the kaiser for "the great crime against humanity involved in deliberately planning and plotting a great war."[91] That idea took hold, for when Allied leaders convened in London in early December, they issued a joint announcement calling for Wilhelm's extradition and trial "for his crimes against humanity."[92]

But, like the Imperial War Cabinet, they were less committed than they appeared. The Italians had reservations, and the Allies had not yet consulted the United States (House had been too ill to attend the meeting). Nonetheless, when Wilson arrived in Paris in December 1918 for the upcoming peace conference, his remarks over lunch with Poincaré at the Elysée Palace did not betray that he disapproved of war crimes trials. Rather, he said that like Poincaré, he appreciated that the final settlement must "not only rebuke . . . terror and spolia-tion, but make men everywhere aware that they cannot be ventured upon without the certainty of just punishment."[93]

During the armistice discussions, some Belgians felt elation as the tide of liberation crept toward the heels of the German retreat. On 21 October the king and queen led a triumphant procession on horseback into Bruges, Albert wearing the infantryman's helmet in which he had posed for the photographs that so many Belgian homes possessed. Now, incredibly, the people of Bruges saw him wearing it in the flesh. Carton de Wiart, who came along as part of a government delegation, wrote that shopkeepers proudly displayed in their windows the copper objects and woolen goods that they had hidden from requisition, the symbols of their resistance. When he bought a tricolor rosette and paid for it in coin, the shopkeeper exclaimed for joy. Less happy were women who had consorted with Germans, whose heads had been shaved, a practice that the minister of justice seemed not to mind and which he said "did not lack for picturesqueness."[94]

But most of Belgium still lived under terror. Outside Antwerp, a roundup of five hundred or six hundred men for forced labor resulted in perhaps six deaths, because the lieutenant in charge did not feed the Belgians and for days threatened to shoot anyone who tried.[95] The German Army was busy destroying railways and canals in a zone twenty miles wide across the country,[96] and factory demolition went ahead so energetically that Allied soldiers surprised one crew at work.[97] In early November, German soldiers put explosive charges in the Hainaut coal mines, despite army promises to leave them intact, and only diplomatic pressure from neutral and Allied nations prevented disaster. Around Mons, troops removed equipment without which the mines could not function, and they deported able-bodied men at gunpoint, taking hay, straw, coal, oils, and the mining horses.[98]

A Liège province diarist (who had penned his entries on the backs of Comité National ration forms) anticipated being free: "We were going to be able to drive, move, think, speak, write according to our whim."[99] But following the armistice, retreating soldiers stole every conceivable commodity from grain to vegetables to liquor to clothes, curtains, and kitchen utensils, while breaking furniture and windows. Troops from one regiment even set fire to houses they had pillaged—it was like summer 1914 all over again.[100] Such scenes were not unusual.[101]

But a Limburg priest said that beside a few pillagers, the soldiers behaved themselves, and that the officers, stripped of their insignia, were not obeyed—and lowered their eyes when a Belgian looked them in the face. With "hundreds of carts, cars, trucks and vehicles of all kinds" piled with all they could carry, including chickens, rabbits, and pigeons, the column looked like a "horde of Gypsies rather than an army on the march."[102] Some Belgians bought stolen goods and German weapons for fantastic prices. A more popular item—at Mons, anyway—was a calendar showing the Manneken Pis, the Brussels statue of a urinating boy, dousing the retreating army.[103] An irreverent sense of humor was one thing the Germans had not been able to take away.

Léon Delacroix, about to become prime minister (the first to hold that title), reportedly asked to borrow undergarments "in order to cut an honorable figure"—or so wrote Carton de Wiart, who said he lent them.[104] A British officer among the soldiers liberating a Flemish mining village said that a woman rushed out of her house "to give me a lump of bread, thinking that we must all be as hungry as she and her neighbours."[105] Not all the celebrations were as meager, of course. Whitlock told of an officer cousin whose detachment of doughboys entered a village just as the Germans were leaving from the other end of town. No sooner had the newcomers arrived than flags appeared, a piano played American songs, and the townspeople rushed out to kiss the soldiers and give them apples, cakes, and wine.[106] When the king came to Brussels on 22 November, after solemn speeches and the prayers at Sainte-Gudule Cathedral, "enthusiasm erupted, overflowed, and did not stop."[107] Crowds sang "La Brabançonne" over and over—the anthem had never sounded so beautiful, wrote Carton de Wiart—and a farandole snaked through the streets, sweeping up visiting Allied officers whether they wished to join the dance or not.

Shortly afterward in the capital, two British officers went walking late one night. Despite the hour, the main boulevard was "densely crowded with radiant citizens," enjoying their freedom to be out after dark for the first time in more than fifty months. One of the officers had a wooden leg and walked with difficulty, and it seemed that almost at once everyone noticed this "khaki-clad man, maimed in the discharge of an Allied obligation to Belgium." The crowd "fell silent and opened out spontaneously along the whole length of a long avenue of bare-headed men and bowing women."[108] The war was over.

12

It Is Impossible
That We Will Be Abandoned

BELGIAN INDUSTRY LAY IN RUINS in 1919. Of the sixty blast furnaces operating in 1913, only nine had survived intact, and steel production had fallen to 10 percent of prewar figures.[1] At one Charleroi
blastworks, the Germans had removed rivets and sawed trusses so
that if the furnace were loaded, the whole structure would collapse.[2]
From textile mills, they had taken spindles, motors, belts, and metal
fittings, often targeting the newest technology. Belgian looms were
silent until spring 1919, and by June, only 30 percent were producing.[3]
A similar timetable applied to the chemical and glass industries, sometimes for want of raw materials.[4] Quarries lay idle while engineers
tried to reverse wartime ravages.[5] Overall, seven-eighths of the industrial work force was jobless, and the CRB, back in American hands,
was feeding the country.[6] Hoover estimated in December 1918 that
two million Belgians were on relief, though he expected that number
soon to drop by half.[7] By January 1919, the Brussels price index had
risen to 639 percent of its prewar level.[8]

Coal mines had escaped demolition, but equipment requisitions
and poor nutrition among the miners had sent output tumbling. Also,
some industries needed high-grade coal, of which Belgium mined little, having always depended on British and German imports, now un-
obtainable.[9] One such industry was brick manufacture, whose inability to produce to capacity was critical when more than eighty thousand buildings had been wholly or partly destroyed, and another two
hundred thousand damaged.[10] But even if the mines could have provided coal in quantity and of superior grade, the Germans had
wrecked the railways needed to ship it. Some eleven hundred kilometers of track would have to be replaced, about a third of the national
network; of thirty-five hundred locomotives in prewar service, eighty-
one were left, and the surviving rolling stock had been run into the

ground. This damage did not include local networks, which had lost half their rails and rolling stock.[11]

Compared with the swath of northern France rendered unfit for agriculture, Belgian land had escaped damage, but few farmers possessed the fertilizer, plows, or machinery with which to plant or harvest. Despite this, in spring 1919 farmers sowed 92 percent of the acreage normally under cultivation, but Belgian yields, the envy of prewar Europe, were low and remained so in 1920. The Germans had seized more than half the cattle, two million fowl, two-thirds of the horses, and nearly half the pigs, many confiscations taking place during the retreat, which violated the armistice.[12] Before the war, breeding stock for draft horses had been a prized export. However, the occupiers had taken these animals, breaking promises not to,[13] and now, the Germans foresaw displacing Belgian breeders in the world market.[14]

As the victors gathered at the Paris Peace Conference to negotiate peace—the Germans would be invited only to receive the terms—the Belgians looked forward to vindication. They were confident that the guarantees of restoration would be fulfilled, and that compensation would be swift and ample. They further anticipated that they would be a leading participant in action against war criminals, and that the major powers recognized and shared Belgium's interest in this and wished to see justice done.

But Belgium's reputation for nobility was slipping. Whitlock remarked on 1 January that people were used to being idle and would rather "live on three francs a day and doing nothing to living on ten francs a day and having to work for it." The occupation had reduced the Belgians physically and morally and rewarded skill at lies and subterfuge.[15] Carton de Wiart reported that to escape charges of collaboration, some Belgians had sought asylum in Holland, where they wore out their welcome.[16] The tension came at an inopportune time, because the Belgian government was hoping to get Dutch consent to reverse the territorial clauses in the Treaty of 1839 and because Belgium owed Holland for expenses incurred in harboring Belgian refugees.

Vance C. McCormick, a member of the American delegation, wondered why the French and Belgian governments had delayed reconstruction, and he thought "the people are being spoiled and riding for a fall."[17] He seemed to be saying that the refusal to rebuild was a ploy to make the case for reparations. But that was a less harmful judgment than that of a *Chicago Tribune* correspondent who, said Whitlock, after having spent just two days in Brussels, was "indignant" because people were "carousing by night in the cabarets."[18] Whitlock soothed him, trying to forestall a series of articles about the sham of Belgian suffering. He succeeded only in that the reporter quoted him briefly before detailing the lavish dining and dancing going on into the small hours.[19]

Many people saw France as the war-torn country and Belgium as a pretender. Belgium had counted 40,000 killed and 77,500 wounded in about four years of combat,[20] but France had lost more in a single four-day stretch just before Louvain burned. Flanders fields aside, France *was* the Western Front. "The traveler by motor can pass through and from end to end of the devastated area of Belgium almost before he knows it," wrote the British economist John Maynard Keynes, "whereas the destruction in France is on a different kind of scale altogether."[21]

Belgium's reputation worsened the closer one got to the center of power. As plenipotentiaries to Paris, Belgium had sent Hymans (as foreign minister), Jules van den Heuvel, and Emile Vandervelde, obeying the rule that a triumvirate required a Liberal, a Catholic, and a Socialist. But when the conference opened on 18 January, Hymans found that Belgium had been allotted two seats, whereas Brazil had been given three.[22] Clemenceau, who presided over the conference like a guardian superintending an unruly orphan, took offense at Hymans's protest, and though the Belgian prevailed, he had raised Clemenceau's hackles.

The seventy-seven-year-old premier was not a man to cross, for, as House described him, "He was afraid of nothing, present or to come, and least of all mere men." With a large head and penetrating eyes set wide apart, and a skullcap and suede gloves worn to conceal eczema, he projected a "gnome-like appearance," perhaps a hint of the sinister.[23] In substance, he supported Belgian claims when they paralleled French ones, as they sometimes did. But his main goal was gaining security against a future German attack, and, like most French politicians, he saw Belgium as a French satellite.

The British believed implicitly that the French would have their way, which partly explains why they saw no reason to do Belgium any favors. Meeting in the so-called Council of Four—Lloyd George, Clemenceau, Wilson, and Premier Vittorio Orlando of Italy—the leaders of the great powers treated Belgium like any small nation that deserved no special consideration. They blocked access to deliberations or denied membership on committees whose workings directly affected Belgian interests, such as the Armistice Commission and discussions concerning the postwar occupation of the Rhineland, to which Belgium was expected to contribute troops. Committees overseeing the International Labor Organization and the League of Nations had no Belgian delegates, though Hymans and Vandervelde had belonged to councils that had created both agencies. Later, when German emissaries presented their observations about the treaty, the Belgians were not consulted before the Allies wrote their reply.

Hymans repeatedly objected that Belgium deserved a voice, but that seldom changed anything and confirmed Allied leaders in their opinion that he was a troublemaker. He did manage to obtain a seat for Belgium on the committee dealing with war crimes, but that he had to fight for this suggests what he was up against.[24] By the end of January, he was venting his spleen to Whitlock about the Allies and the United States, Lansing in particular, who was siding with the Dutch on the territorial questions.[25]

Henri Davignon, the former foreign minister's son, wrote later that de Broqueville or Beyens should have gone to Paris instead, though neither were in the government.[26] Beyens was Belgium's most capable diplomat, and de Broqueville was a gifted horse trader, whereas Hymans thought that he needed only to insist long enough, and the Allies would fulfill their promises, especially the British, whom he trusted. But though Hymans's prickly self-righteousness served him poorly with the world's sharpest statesmen, he was fighting a losing battle. His chief antagonist was Lloyd George, who had been grumbling even before the conference convened that Belgium had suffered fewer casualties than Australia, Canada, or New Zealand.[27] This was his tune throughout. The disdain went deep, because the British delegation never asked Hymans to any social functions, none but Keynes accepted Belgian invitations, and Lloyd George answered only one of Hymans's many letters, not acknowledging the rest.[28] The Belgians sensed, perhaps rightly, that the prime minister disliked Catholic countries, but he may also have blamed Belgium for dragging Britain into the war.[29]

Still, Lloyd George was a political animal, and his hostility served a purpose. His government had ridden to victory in the December elections partly by telling the voters that Germany would pay for the war. First Lord of the Admiralty Sir Eric Geddes had said that "we will get everything out of her that you can squeeze out of a lemon, and a bit more. . . . I would strip Germany as she has stripped Belgium."[30] This uncannily echoed Bissing's June 1915 remark comparing Belgium to a squeezed lemon, but the other implications were more important. If Germany were stripped to pay Britain, another country would have to take less, and that country could not be France.

One item on the Belgian wish list that Lloyd George opposed was the right to be first in line for reparations. The Belgians thought the victors owed them this priority, which would help relieve their immense debt burden and hasten their recovery, but the Allied governments had never promised it.[31] The demand nevertheless reflected how most people had recognized Belgium's primary claim as far back as August 1914. Hoover lobbied for Belgian priority, and so did other Americans, especially House, though Wilson himself remained aloof, as he did regarding most problems for which the Belgians sought American help.[32]

His inattention marked a turnabout. In late October 1918, Hoover had proposed a plan by which American aid would rebuild Belgium, an effort he expected would take twelve to eighteen months. Wilson had liked the idea, but the 1918 elections left the Republicans controlling Congress, and they favored commercial loans at conventional interest rates. However, the news that Britain had used borrowed American capital to lend to Belgium, undercutting American bankers, pushed even the outgoing Democratic Congress to act. In mid-February 1919, it decided that the United States government should not lend to Europe; by May, Hoover was scrambling to keep relief funds from being withheld.[33]

The preference to withdraw from Europe found expression among the American delegation. One member wrote in late February that the Europeans were readying themselves for another war, wanted to fight it on American money, and that only Germany was sincere about disarming. If the United States were to announce that the only help would come either through charitable food deliveries or loans based on sound credit, "it would be the most humane thing . . . for the peoples of Europe."[34] McCormick helped draft a scheme to float international bonds, backed by American credit, because he thought "our great rich nation, practically untouched by the war" must "do something to help our bankrupt Allies."[35] But he decided against the bonds, because the Europeans were playing "the same old game they have been working on all through the conference, to get the United States to underwrite their debts."[36]

Like the rest of Europe, the Belgians had debts, and they had expected Germany to assume them. The Le Havre government, having lacked an industrial base or tax receipts, had borrowed to meet every expense, and until the economy revived, Premier Delacroix's government could only do likewise. He told his cabinet in May 1919 that debt had totaled four billion francs before the war and seventeen billion since, most of which ensued from the war contributions.[37] During the conference, Germany reimbursed the forced levies—fines exacted from various cities—but the Belgians argued that the rest resulted from an illegal invasion, which entitled them to payment.[38] House had adopted their logic in his official reading of the Fourteen Points during the armistice talks, which the Allies had presumably accepted.[39] But in effect, this was granting Belgium its war costs, which Lloyd George knew he could not ask for Britain despite his administration's pledges, and at the conference, he resisted the claim.[40] Once, he said that Scotland had a smaller population than Belgium, had suffered more battle deaths to liberate Belgian soil, and would emerge with heavy debts, yet the Belgians wanted theirs paid.[41] McCormick, who challenged him twice over this issue, wrote, "I never saw him so excited."[42]

That excitement derived partly from the obvious, that Belgium had borrowed heavily from Britain, and that transferring the debt to a former enemy made its repayment less probable. But the references to casualties imply more than that. After all, Belgian refugees had left a bad taste in British mouths, and Albert had preserved his army while Britons bled in Flanders. Perhaps Lloyd George personally regretted Britain's intervention, a decision in which he had acquiesced despite his stated doubts and to which he had later lent his celebrated eloquence. In September 1914, a London audience had applauded his statement that Belgium, being weak, "could not have compelled us" to fight, "but the man who declines to discharge his duty because his creditor is too poor to enforce it is a blackguard."[43] Lloyd George had gone on to say that he was sorry he was too old to enlist, and that "I envy you young people your opportunity . . . an opportunity that only comes once in many centuries to the children of men."[44]

If he recalled these words in 1919, they would have sounded different from when he had said them. But whatever the case, when he published his six-volume war memoirs in the 1930s, he hardly found space to mention Belgium, and when he did, his resentment showed. Of the ultimatum, he wrote that "Belgian ministers hesitated" but "Belgium's heroic king" had answered for them—which, among other things, was a subtle dig at Hymans.[45]

A third Belgian aim that Britain opposed concerned the six billion paper marks the Germans had introduced in Belgium, whose value against the franc had fallen by more than half. Wishing to make a generous gesture, Delacroix's predecessor, Gerard Cooreman, had authorized the Banque Nationale to convert each mark on demand to 1.25 francs—the occupiers' artificial rate—which greatly favored the holder. However, the news had leaked before the armistice was signed, and because the Belgians could not seal the border, marks flowed in from Germany, the Grand Duchy, and Holland that the Banque Nationale had to honor. The Belgians had assumed that Germany would take back the paper and pay gold in exchange, but they were wrong, and the redemption cost 7.5 billion francs, aggravating their debt. France had faced a similar problem in Alsace-Lorraine but had taken steps to protect its currency at the Alsatians' expense. Like Britain, therefore, France was not about to bail the Belgians out.[46]

The German stance on the marks foreshadowed the victors' difficulties with the nation they had supposedly defeated. On 2 January, the Reich Ministry of Finance disputed the Belgian figure of 6.0 billion marks in circulation, citing a ministry estimate dated September of 1.3 billion. Even the "very extensive purchases" during the withdrawal could not have accounted for the difference, the ministry said, and asked for proof. To show that the victors were asking too much, an appendix noted that the German iron industry was crippled by "excessive wage demands and strikes," which had driven up the cost of production, leaving it unable to compete.[47]

Ellis Dresel, an American diplomat in Germany who wrote up his observations for the United States delegation, heard variations on the theme. On 10 January, Dresel reported complaints about the armistice, chiefly the loss of rolling stock, which stopped coal shipments to many places and led to factory closures and unemployment.[48] Many Germans said that an immediate supply of raw materials was essential, and that lack of these and of food would lead to bolshevism's spreading throughout Germany and, later, the world. They asked for "energetic relief measures," though Dresel believed famine was not imminent, despite signs of "under-nutrition."[49] He also heard that Germany would survive only if the Allies were lenient about reparations, and the Germans hoped that "the events of the war will be overlooked and condoned."[50]

During the war, the Allies had waxed indignant over German attempts to wave away the war crimes. Yet in 1919, Belgian claims were called exaggerated, and Germany's recovery meant more to its trading partners, especially Britain, than Belgium's did. The victors viewed dire German predictions with jaded eyes, but what a discontented Germany might do troubled everyone, whereas nobody worried about unhappy Belgians. Even so, Clemenceau had no illusions about German repentance, and Lloyd George was wary too; it was Wilson who dismissed their dread as selfish. This held a grain of truth, because the Europeans put their countries first, whereas Wilson had an international agenda. They were "mad men," he once told McCormick, particularly Clemenceau, with "such fear of the Germans and such great self pity."[51]

But whereas Allied leaders disputed the definition of justice, the Germans mostly agreed among themselves. On 4 February, an American observer reported that the German press, "instead of treating the pressing economic and political problems confronting Germany, indulges in bitter recrimination against the Entente and in tearful complaints of its brutality."[52] Only *Vorwärts*, he said, "has kept some dignity." Later that month, twenty-two respected intellectuals drafted a resolution in Heidelberg rejecting German war guilt and calling for a neutral commission to investigate. "We do not deny the responsibility of those in power," they said, but other nations were culpable too, and the Allies had "no right to pronounce judgment in a case in which they themselves are involved."[53]

However, the victors had pronounced nothing. The treaty's infamous war-guilt clause had not yet been written, nor had a committee examining the causes of the war reported its findings. The victors' intent was obvious, but the Heidelberg intellectuals were voicing outrage before anything was on paper, and they were known as moderates. Further, by pinpointing former leaders, they were exonerating their current government and the people at large, including themselves. They made this specific, saying that during the war, they had challenged a policy that "disregarded the rights of other nations," Belgium in particular, though they had "differed as to which form of opposition . . . could be reconciled with Germany's security."[54] The resolution did not mention redress or regrets.

Around that time, Foreign Minister Ulrich von Brockdorff-Rantzau told the new National Assembly at Weimar that Germany denied sole blame for aggression or war crimes and invited "unprejudiced men" to study these issues. He also rejected paying Entente war costs, though "we are duty bound and willing to make good the damages incurred through our attack by the civil population in the regions occupied by us."[55] To emphasize the point, he said, "Certainly Germany will have heavy damages to pay both within and without, especially to Belgium, and on that we have no inclination to speak haughtily."[56]

But Brockdorff-Rantzau did not mention France. The omission took on greater meaning when, in mid-March, the General Staff denied that German troops had "systematically destroyed French industry" to cripple a rival. Rather, the British blockade had forced the army "to utilize the auxiliary resources of Northern France," a policy that "no sensible person" could reproach.[57] Consequently, Germany would not stand accused before "the law of nations," but her opponents would, "for the destruction they have worked to German economic life, which was pursuing only peaceful ends."[58] The General Staff was unlikely to apologize, and its views did not necessarily represent the government's. But Matthias Erzberger, minister without portfolio and head of Germany's Armistice Commission, declared that his country had no moral obligation to anyone but Belgium, and no responsibility for acts after the December 1916 peace feeler.[59] Perhaps most significant, Brockdorff-Rantzau's speech had referred to "damages incurred through our attack," which left open whether Germany should pay for those dating from the occupation or the retreat.

This question arose at a cabinet meeting on 21 March, when the government considered ways to forestall reparations, chiefly by proving that Germany had not started the war. At least several ministers did not realize that the Allies would want compensation for more than

Belgium and northern France, and nearly all spoke of restoration in the sense of repairing combat damage only.[60] One minister worried about having to pay for "damage by enemy artillery in occupied areas"; two others brought up Entente air attacks on Belgian cities. Germany had to protect its standard of living and might be able to scare the Allies with the bolshevism menace. Even then, the cabinet was still arguing about whether the invasion was justified, and one minister invoked necessity.[61]

Official Belgian claims, submitted in 1921, totaled $2.22 billion for damage, about $1.5 billion in war debt, and $500 million for pensions and other costs. These figures may have exaggerated but were within reason, especially as the calculations involved guesswork about future rates of exchange and inflation.[62] However, before the conference, the Germans had placed property damage in Belgium and northern France together at 9.3 billion gold marks, or about $2.3 billion by 1921 exchange rates, barely enough to cover Belgium alone.[63] *Vorwärts*, more mindful of foreign perspectives, supposed in mid-February 1919 that the bill would run to 50 billion marks, but even that was less than half of what the Allies wound up asking for.[64]

The conflict among the victors carried over into the discussion of war crimes, but at first, the drama played out in the wings. At center stage, all seemed in agreement. On 17 January, when the powers were preparing the conference agenda, Lloyd George made sure that trials figured on it.[65] The next day, when Clemenceau opened the first plenary session, he urged punishment and ordered that all delegations receive a pamphlet by two French jurists that expressed the essence of the European brief on war crimes.[66]

The pamphlet followed reasoning more than 150 years old but still revolutionary. Fernand Larnaude and Albert de Lapradelle cited an eighteenth-century thinker, Emmer de Vattel, who had said that the nations could unite to suppress one that showed itself "anxious and harmful," "always ready to injure others."[67] Those who had waged the unjust war, including the prince who had ordered it, would be liable for damages and punishment, "for the security of the injured party, and for that of human society."[68] Larnaude and de Lapradelle argued that Germany was such a violator, having wreaked destruction beyond military purpose, and Wilhelm such a prince, as supreme commander. His crimes were violating Belgium and the Grand Duchy and breaching The Hague Conventions. "Modern law no longer recognizes irresponsible authority, even at the head of hierarchies," Larnaude and Lapradelle said. "The State must be taken down from its pedestal while making it subject to the judge's rule."[69]

Making recommendations on this and other arguments fell to the fifteen-member Commission on the Responsibility for the Authors of the War and the Enforcement of Penalties, which met in secret for two months. The commission consisted of three subcommittees, which were to study who was responsible for the war; whether aggression was a crime, and whether national leaders could be tried for it; and how to proceed against accused war criminals. To sort out issues of jurisdiction, which defendants to prosecute, and under what principles was a tall order, particularly when war crimes trials existed mostly in theory. The task was even harder because so many reports had been written (more by the Belgians than anyone) that the commission could not have read them all, especially in the time allotted. The jurists were so conscious of the pressure that they knew they could address only the most flagrant violations, but they disliked the weeding out and had trouble deciding what limits to apply.[70]

Nevertheless, they would have gotten further had Lansing not been put in charge. Someone who believed that no sovereign nation should answer to any other was the wrong choice to lead a war crimes commission, yet the Europeans did not object. Lansing not only opposed prosecution, he worried that provoking Germany would spread bolshevism,[71] and he made his resistance to trials felt at the commission's first meeting. When British and French delegates suggested writing a clause into the armistice, up for renewal, to compel the handing over of accused criminals, Lansing immediately changed the subject. When the Europeans introduced the motion at the next meeting, he ruled them out of order and refused to bring it to the Supreme War Council, as they wanted. When the British forced a vote, only Lansing and James Brown Scott, the other American member, opposed the motion, but the British sidestepped them anyway by asking Balfour to take it to the war council.[72] He did so on 10 February, but with no enthusiasm, professing to see both sides and calling himself "profoundly perplexed."[73] Wilson called the plan "futile," and the Allies did not adopt it.

One Saturday in mid-March, Lansing astonished his colleagues by saying that American judges would reserve the right to withdraw from any international tribunal. Then, by prior arrangement, he had himself called away to let the Europeans stew until the next session, on Monday.[74] Not surprisingly, Scott later recalled that on the commission, "feeling ran about as high as feeling can run," especially among the British and French delegations, so much so "that relations were somewhat suspended."[75] But coming from Scott, the comment held a certain irony, because when Larnaude explained why he thought the kaiser should face trial, Scott lectured the University of Paris law dean on the proper way to interpret international law.[76]

Lansing's opposition was partly political because, as he told the American delegation, he supposed that the British "were not very sincere" about trying the kaiser, and that they and the French were simply out for revenge.[77] To the commission, he said that trying a head of state had no precedent, and that leaders were responsible only to their countries' laws. He presumed Wilhelm's moral guilt, which he denounced, but moral crimes did not belong in court. The Europeans retorted that Wilhelm was no longer a head of state, had no immunity, and was not even living in his own country. They also pointed out that the American government had called the *Lusitania* sinking an illegal, immoral act, which forced Lansing to admit that the United States could conceivably take Germany to court for it.[78]

Nevertheless, when the commission drafted its final report at the end of March, at Wilson's request, Lansing and Scott repeated their objections, which the Japanese delegates joined on the matter of trying the kaiser. Allied leaders, said Scott and Lansing, might level political sanctions for the neutrality violations, but that would be a political decision. As for war crimes, only military authorities from the offended nation or nations could prosecute, and only if an international statute outlawed the crime. This "no crime without law, no penalty without crime" condition made prosecution almost moot, because The Hague Conventions were notably vague. Even at that, Lansing and Scott recognized necessity as a defense. Crimes against humanity did not exist because war was contrary to humanity, and perceptions of inhuman behavior were bound to differ.[79]

By contrast, the commission majority named thirty-two kinds of war crimes and asserted that rank would protect no lawbreaker, even the kaiser. If a head of state evaded justice, that would fail to uphold the law and would compromise trials of other offenders, who could plead superior orders. Moreover, there was "little doubt" that high authorities knew what had gone on, and that "a word from them would have brought about a different method in the action of their subordinates."[80] Accordingly, the commission proposed an international tribunal to try the kaiser for war crimes, and that a treaty article should gain Germany's consent. For other defendants, each belligerent could hold trials under civil or military law, except when no unique national jurisdiction applied, as with prison camps whose inmates had belonged to various countries. A tribunal of judges from the Allied and Associated Powers would hear these cases, determining its own procedure and passing sentence according to the laws of the convicted party or any country on the court. The enemy governments were to recognize the victors' jurisdiction, provide relevant documents about campaigns on land and sea, names of prison camp commanders, and the persons accused of crimes.[81]

Regarding Belgian neutrality, the commission majority agreed that Germany's violation must be strongly criticized yet could not be tried.[82] On the surface, this made no sense, for the Treaty of 1839 and the Fifth Convention put the violation beyond doubt, and officially, the Germans did not argue. Trying the case would have provided a chance to discredit the rule of necessity without getting bogged down in issues like war guilt. Lloyd George saw the possibilities when he said on 8 April that he wanted to charge Wilhelm for the treaty violation alone, though he included the invasion terror in that arraignment.[83]

But this argument had its weaknesses. If tearing up a treaty was a crime, the Germans would want to know why Italy and Romania could disregard their prewar obligations to the Central Powers. Further, the Belgians said that because their country was a monarchy, they "could not take the lead in prosecuting a monarch," so if Wilhelm were involved, a key witness might be reluctant to testify.[84] Then too, as Wilson noted, no law named a penalty. Lloyd George and Clemenceau were willing to invent one to establish a principle, but Wilson argued that trying Wilhelm before a high tribunal would glorify him, and that public opinion would be the strictest punishment.[85] Clemenceau answered, "Don't count on it," but the commission took the president's view.[86] Its report cited many offenses within the neutrality violation, including the pretense of peril and "the guise of tempter" under which Germany tried to buy "the sacrifice of honour."

Still, "these gross outrages upon the law of nations and international good faith" could not be prosecuted in court.[87]

As the Commission on Responsibility was issuing its findings, the leaders debated what justice meant and what Belgium was entitled to. On 27 March, Clemenceau agreed with Wilson that "we must do everything we can to be just towards the Germans," but convincing them that they were being treated justly was another matter.[88] They had, he said, a different idea of justice and were "a servile people who need force to support an argument," an opinion shaped by years of study and observation. The Allies were right to tread lightly regarding bolshevism but should not invite it amongst themselves by losing sight of just claims for France and Britain.[89] The next day, he added, "Don't believe [the Germans] will ever forgive us," because they only wanted revenge and were furious that their attempt at world conquest had failed.[90]

If reports out of Germany were accurate, Clemenceau had grounds for suspicion, which Lloyd George shared to a degree, as he did the outrage over German crimes. But when Hymans was admitted before the Council of Four on 31 March, consideration for Belgium seemed absent and, as usual, Hymans's style did not help.[91] He charged that the Allies were planning to occupy the left bank of the Rhine with Belgian participation but without consulting him, and that they were assigning reparations in the same fashion. When Lloyd George said that England was also in poor shape, Hymans countered, "Excuse me! You have raw materials, you have machines, your industries are working, you can sell and buy." Wilson remarked that reparations would be decided by a commission on which Belgium had a seat, but Hymans brushed that aside. He asked about the territorial questions, which he had raised before but about which the Allies had said nothing. "This silence and the way we are treated are creating a distressing impression in Belgium, which could turn against the Allies."

Lloyd George exploded. "You don't have any right to speak thus of France and Great Britain. English soldiers died by the hundreds of thousands for the liberation of Belgium," and Australia lost four times as many men as Belgium.

"If we didn't have more soldiers," Hymans retorted, "that was because our country was occupied. You don't know what an invasion is.

You haven't seen your country under the boot of a conqueror for several years. We are waiting for the help which you promised us."

"It seems to me that we gave Belgium a promise which cost us the lives of 900,000 men," Lloyd George said. "If you speak to us in this way, we won't listen to you any longer."

"I simply ask you to listen to me when it is a matter of my country's interests," Hymans replied, but the harm was done. His memoirs emphasized the prime minister's disdainful gestures and suggested that Lloyd George had misheard Hymans to say that Britain had not helped Belgium during the war.[92] But whether his version reveals what the published transcript does not show, to have spent a rare chance to speak by launching recriminations, however deserved, was an error. Moreover, rather than charge headlong into Lloyd George, he might have pleaded with Clemenceau as the representative of another invaded nation—and Clemenceau had kept silent during the whole exchange.

For the moment, Belgium vanished from sight, but the issue of justice remained, as Wilson tried to dissuade his colleagues from taking the Germans to court. On 2 April, he deplored victor's justice, saying that to permit an injured party to judge its attacker would set an alarming precedent.[93] Lloyd George replied that all the powers would judge, not just France and Belgium, and that the League of Nations should oversee this process in the future. But Wilson did not want to involve the league, having defeated in committee Larnaude's proposals that the league accept jurisdiction, charge Germany with war guilt, and pledge to further "the work begun by The Hague Conference."[94] So the president avoided resuming this debate by saying that the victors could not make war crimes a matter of personal responsibility when the law had never specified this. Such a claim would "give retroactive force to the principles we pose."[95]

His objection paired the axiom that no law could make an act criminal after the fact and Lansing's "no crime without law, no penalty without crime" rule. "No crime without law" has been cited against the "crimes against humanity" classification (and the Nuremberg trials), which Wilson probably did not recognize.[96] But the president was talking about something else. He was saying that the Fourth Convention was too ambiguous, whereas national laws defined crimes and punishments. Consequently, if Germany promised to try the criminals, he would withdraw his objections. He wished to avoid "leaving to historians any sympathy whatsoever for Germany," giving that country over "to the execration of history" while making sure that the victors did not overreach.[97]

The recommendation skirted several pitfalls. The Commission on Responsibility majority report had called for extradition, civil judges, and international tribunals, none of which had any precedent. (After the Boer War, the British had demanded the surrender of accused criminals, but the Boers had known who they were before signing the Treaty of Vereeniging. The treaty also granted an amnesty and made the defendants British subjects, so technically, they would be tried in their own courts.)[98] Returning the cases to Germany would avoid extradition or other radical steps and remove any confusion about jurisdiction or the choice of code. Left unspoken was the political advantage, as Wilson saw it, of having placated Germany and assured that no one could say that the victors had acted out of vindictiveness.

But the president also voiced his fear that "the judgment will be passed in an atmosphere of passion." Whenever he read atrocity reports, he "saw red, and I was very careful not to take a decision in such moments," so as not to lose his reason. Lloyd George responded that war crimes had made the victors almost too numb to feel indignation, and he supposed that in fifty years, people would judge Germany more harshly. But Wilson insisted, "I struggle constantly against emotion, and I am compelled to put pressure on myself to keep my judgment sound." To that, Clemenceau, who had said nothing until then, remarked, "Nothing is done without emotion. Was not Jesus Christ driven by passion on the day when he drove the merchants from the temple?"[99]

The comment illustrated his annoyance with Wilson as a self-styled prophet; in October, he had quipped, "God was satisfied with Ten Commandments. Wilson gives us fourteen."[100] But a political context lay beneath the flippancy. For several months, Wilson had declined to visit devastated areas in France, and when he went, he chose places where Americans had fought, not where the ruin was remarkable. A Wilson biographer has written that the president believed that he did not need to see what he had weighed in his mind and that having said that he felt for France and Belgium was enough.[101] McCormick, less bound by such constraints, made two trips to ruined France, the second of which convinced him that the

French merited sympathy, especially because of the scorched earth during the retreat.[102] But Wilson considered himself knowledgeable nevertheless. He recalled his early boyhood in Civil War Virginia, saying that having been born in "a conquered and devastated country . . . has helped me, believe me, to understand the questions which are raised here."[103] However, Clemenceau had not only lived in the United States immediately after the Civil War, he had seen France invaded twice.

Wilson did not visit Belgium until ten days before the treaty was signed, a snub that the Belgians interpreted as contempt, said Whitlock.[104] During the two-day trip, the king and queen showed Wilson the Charleroi blast furnaces and the library at Louvain, whose destruction impressed him. Amid the roofless rubble, the university conferred on him an honorary doctorate of law. There and before the Belgian Parliament, he made eloquent speeches that the Belgians applauded with fervor.[105] But it was House who had pushed on their behalf at Paris and was primarily responsible for Belgium's getting any reparations at all.[106]

Rumor went that Wilson had avoided seeing what the Germans had done because he did not want to "hate the enemy too much." The *London Morning Post* commented, "We are willing to recognize that to love your enemies is a Christian precept, but it becomes less admirable when acted upon at the expense of your friends."[107] Clemenceau stated the issue more diplomatically: "Believe me; amongst the peoples who have suffered for these five years, nothing would sow so many real seeds of hatred as an amnesty granted to all the criminals."[108]

The Belgians worried that their chances for reparation were slipping away. Three days after Lloyd George's row with Hymans, the prime minister announced that King Albert would visit the following day's session, "accompanied by M. Hymans who, like well-bred children, will be seen but not heard."[109] The news was extraordinary, for no other king attended the conference, and Albert created a stir by flying to Paris.[110] His appearance before the Council of Four was low-key but determined as he went methodically through the Belgian wish list, emphasizing the economic pillage to justify the demands. Lloyd George tried to chip away at his position with subtle questions seemingly designed to show that conditions were better than the Belgians

The Council of Four during an informal moment: left to right, Lloyd George, Vittorio Orlando of Italy, Clemenceau, and Wilson. Orlando had the least impact on Belgian interests because he missed certain negotiating sessions, but when Italy withdrew from the conference, for a time, that made the Belgian threat to walk out seem more serious. Library of Congress, Prints and Photographs Division, LC-USZ 62-7483

admitted, but Albert had his facts and figures ready.[111] Hymans wrote later that Lloyd George seemed curious about the damage, whose extent he seemed not to have grasped.[112]

Perhaps the prime minister had not understood. He was known not "to read anything if he could avoid it," preferring to pick people's brains instead, and he had refused to talk to the Belgians.[113] But if Albert had enlightened him, that made little difference. The next day, Lloyd George said that he would not make an exception to cover Belgian war costs, and he dismissed McCormick's reminder that Belgium had the right to them. During the following days, he repeated his position, though he said that Hymans and Vandervelde seemed "satisfied" with the arrangement.[114]

How satisfied they were may be judged by the Belgian delegation's protest before the Council of Four on 29 April, when Hymans recited Allied pledges and asked whether they would be kept.[115] Lloyd George said he was willing to grant reparations priority but not debt privilege, which, he said, would open the door to Serbia, Romania, and France claiming the same thing. Van den Heuvel said that you could not compare the way Serbia and Belgium had entered the war, and that Belgium had "served as a standard for all the nations" that had fought.[116] Vandervelde added that eight hundred thousand unemployed Belgians had shown forbearance in not turning Bolshevist and stressed the great service that Belgium had done the Allies in resisting Germany.[117]

The Allied leaders consulted with their financial experts and offered Belgium a $500 million priority on the first sums that Germany paid and agreed to make the food relief, which Van den Heuvel had mentioned, a reimbursable expense. But Hymans said that was not enough.[118] Clemenceau replied that Belgium would not be less well off than any other country, and that its "moral standing remains very high."[119] He called the Belgian position "intransigent" and said that he could have broken up the negotiations several times had he done what Hymans was doing. Further, he alluded to Belgium's unwillingness to place its troops under a unified command and cautioned, "It would be a pity to see you leave here slamming the doors." But Hymans did not promise to sign the draft terms, which the Germans were to receive in a week—and with that, the Belgians left the room. Not once had Wilson spoken, perhaps because he had suffered a mild stroke the day before and could not follow the conversation.[120]

The Belgian threat to bolt put the Allies in a bind because of Belgium's value in public relations, and because Italy had left and Japan was thinking of doing so. The Allies rushed to accord a $500 million priority and pass Belgian debts to Germany, so that when Hymans traveled to Brussels to consult his government, he had these concessions in hand.[121] McCormick wrote that the Belgians had "a good case and a popular one," and that their demarche had "struck the Big Three like a bomb shell."[122] Lloyd George said that he feared Belgian "blackmail."[123]

This was no idle apprehension, for the Belgians were furious. Whitlock wrote House, "In all the years of the war, I have never seen Belgium quite so depressed and discouraged."[124] He reportedly told

Hymans that he could not venture out in Brussels, and that he had gotten letters of reproaches and insults.[125] The press violently objected to the thought that Belgium would get less than it deserved; the Senate voted unanimously to reject any treaty that did not pay for the paper marks within three years.[126]

When Hymans told the cabinet of the terms, a spirited debate ensued. Delacroix remarked that between the war contributions and the paper marks redemptions alone, Belgium had taken on huge debts and could not afford to come away empty-handed. He agreed that the treaty had caused "profound disillusionment" and that the Allies had not kept their word, but he feared the risks of refusing to sign. The world would not lift a finger, and the Belgian public would demand an accounting. "Our responsibility would be great if we lacked the courage to enlighten public opinion and if we led the country toward ruin," he warned.[127]

But Jules Renkin, minister of railroads, said, "It is impossible that we will be abandoned," and "world opinion" would not admit that Belgium "should be sacrificed by three men."[128] Henri Jaspar, minister of economics, insisted that the conference could not make peace without Belgium, which should hold out to the last.[129] The next day, Renkin argued that by Delacroix's own arithmetic, the $500 million priority covered only about half the restoration costs—and Renkin did not know that Belgium's total share would pay for no more than 35 percent of reconstruction.[130] Nevertheless, Delacroix's view gained ground, especially when Hymans said that Belgium could not hope for a better deal. The cabinet decided to sign but to note reservations.[131]

Gaining Belgium's agreement solved a minor problem for the Allies, but a larger one remained, how to explain the grounds for German liability. Lloyd George and Clemenceau knew that Germany could not pay for everything, but they could not afford to concede that they had misled their publics, nor did they wish to let Germany off the hook. Consequently, they wanted to appear to ask for war costs, but without naming a sum, leaving the details to a commission that would report later.

Wilson countered that the treaty must restrict liability consistent with his note of 5 November, sent just before the Allies had presented the armistice. By this text, "invaded territories must be restored," which omitted Britain, except that damage to civilians and their property caused "by the aggression of Germany" on land, sea, and air must be compensated.[132] That seemed to put Britain back in, for the U-boat war and the shelling of coastal towns, if nothing else. But resolving this ambiguity to British and American satisfaction would have been hard enough without having to make Germany appear responsible for damages that would likely never be paid. In late April, McCormick noted that Allied leaders were hoping "to work out a treaty clause which postpones the evil day and conceals temporarily the whole situation. I wish we could blow up the whole plan, but the governments would fall and only Germany would benefit."[133]

He did not know half of it. As the German peace delegation prepared to go to Versailles to receive the treaty, on 21 April Brockdorff-Rantzau issued his instructions. The foreign minister read the 5 November note to refer only to occupied areas, only to damage caused by German troops, and only to civilian property. Reconstruction would occur in kind, without cash payments, because those would increase German debt. No reparations were payable until German exports revived, and German entrepreneurs would oversee the rebuilding projects. (This would protect foreign exchange while favoring German businesses and workers at French and Belgian expense.) Where the damage resulted from an alleged breach of international law, only an international court of arbitration could decide whether Germany must make amends. But no reparations were due Italy or Romania because these countries had broken treaties with Germany.[134]

These guidelines denied the meaning of restitution, not least in the apparent attempt to make the process unpleasant for the victims. Such reparations could not achieve the "healing act" of Point Seven or redress the damage by land, sea, and air stated in the 5 November note. But the Allies played right into German hands through the compromise clause that McCormick had written of. It appeared in the Treaty of Versailles as Article 231, which ascribed the war to "the aggression of Germany and her allies," which bore responsibility for all the victors' injuries.[135] This was the war-guilt clause, around which a crusade formed to accuse the Allies of vindictive greed and redeem German honor.

Dresel reported that when the treaty terms became known in Germany, "the shock" was "all the more terrific" because people were unprepared.[136] He said that they had not grasped the "true feeling of the

Allied countries toward Germany" and had thought that peace based on the Fourteen Points would not have required admitting guilt or making atonement or reparation. They had assumed that Wilson would "see to it that the peace terms would not greatly inconvenience Germany." Most people, Dresel said, had embraced "the entirely insincere belief" that Germany had agreed to the armistice only on condition that the Wilsonian agenda, "as interpreted for the benefit of Germany, would be enforced." He interviewed the leader of the Independent Socialist Party, who said that Germany "simply cannot pay indemnities" and warned of catastrophe if the Allies insisted on them.[137] Marriage would become an economic impossibility, free cohabitation would "assume unheard of proportions," and the birth rate would drop, whereas the incidence of abortion and venereal disease would rise.

The treaty's criminal articles roused resentment too. Under Article 227, the "Allied and Associated Powers publicly arraign[ed]" Wilhelm "for a supreme offence against international morality and the sanctity of treaties."[138] The powers would ask the Netherlands to yield him up, after which he would face a tribunal of five judges, one each from the United States, Great Britain, France, Italy, and Japan. The tribunal would "be guided by the highest motives of international policy, with a view to vindicating the solemn obligations of international undertakings and the validity of international morality," and would fix the penalty.

Article 227 thus ignored the Commission on Responsibility's finding that the neutrality violation could not be prosecuted, and Lansing's brief that moral offenses did not belong in court. Further, the article had named two powers to the tribunal, Japan and the United States, whose jurists had formally objected to trying the kaiser. (Orlando was none too sure either, which risked putting France and Britain in a minority.) Equally critical was that extradition treaties the Netherlands had signed with the United States, France, and Britain required definite criminal charges, with specific penalties—no law, no crime—as the Dutch constitution demanded.[139]

How the victors could have disregarded their own lawyers to craft such an article, which had the disadvantage of legal flabbiness while provoking the Germans, has never been explained. It has been supposed that Lloyd George and Wilson had not read the commission findings with care, and that a compromise wording resulted from bargaining that concerned other matters.[140] Wilson may have gone along because he thought the trial would never take place, and Lloyd George did not seem to mind how Wilhelm was punished as long as it happened. If nothing else, Article 227 revealed how difficult it was for the victors to state their aims in a coherent, unified fashion.

By the other criminal articles, numbered 228 to 230, Germany would recognize the right of the Allied and Associated Powers to try "persons accused of having committed acts in violation of the laws and customs of war."[141] They would, "if found guilty, be sentenced to punishments laid down by law." Each power's military tribunals would bring charges whenever the victims were that country's nationals, acting together only when the same crime offended more than one power. The victors reserved the right to prosecute cases that Germany or its allies had already tried. Germany agreed to hand over any person named as a defendant, along with information "considered necessary to ensure the full knowledge of the incriminating acts, the discovery of offenders, and the just appreciation of responsibility."

When Brockdorff-Rantzau received the treaty on 7 May, he exploited these articles. "The demand is made that we shall acknowledge that we alone are guilty of having caused the war," he said. "Such a confession in my mouth would be a lie."[142] Of war crimes, he said that "they may not be excusable, but they are committed in the struggle for victory, when we think only of maintaining our national existence, and are in such passion as makes the conscience of peoples blunt." He accused the Allies of having killed hundreds of thousands of civilians through starvation since the armistice (a charge that belied what Dresel had written and set off a controversy that persists to this day). "Remember that, when you speak of guilt and atonement."

The criminal articles and the war-guilt clause soon became known in Germany as the "points of honor," the rallying cry against the Treaty of Versailles.[143] The German delegation contested each article, and when that availed nothing, offered at the eleventh hour to accept the treaty, minus the offending clauses.[144] Bethmann even suggested substituting himself for the kaiser, writing Clemenceau that "in accordance with the constitutional laws of Germany, it is I who . . . bear the exclusive responsibility for political acts of the Emperor during my tenure of office."[145] The victors rebuffed these proposals, and the Germans relented because they thought their country needed peace more than anything else.

McCormick, in describing the signing ceremony of 28 June, wrote, "It was a solemn moment when the two lone German delegates walked in. You could have heard a pin drop." The pair were "pale and ghastly looking" in their "black frock coats of old style," and they approached the vacant seats at the table "with straight backs and heads held high in the air, but looking like death." The rest of the ceremony lasted about a half hour, McCormick said. "We all left the Hall of Mirrors and strolled out on the terraces and watched the crowds cheer the big fellows when they came out. It was impressive and yet did not have the thrill you might have expected."[146]

13

A Trifle

GETTING GERMANY'S CONSENT to war crimes trials was a victory only on paper. Barely more than a month later, Matthias Erzberger, the German minister of finance, asked for a delay in extradition because conservatives and Independent Socialists were agitating against the criminal articles. Without the support of the military and former officers, who were also holding protest rallies, the government would fall, he said.[1]

The Allies realized that this might be a smokescreen, but they did not know what to do. The treaty laid down many requirements but few means of enforcement, and though the political leaders asked Foch whether military action was feasible, no one wanted to resume the war and march on Berlin.[2] Besides, insisting on prosecutions was difficult, said a Belgian legal expert, when everyone spoke of "a state of economic and perhaps social appeasement," and when so many months had elapsed since the armistice.[3] Had the Allies acted decisively, they might have concealed their weaknesses, but their slowness gave Erzberger the delay he wanted, even as they rejected his request.

Germany's chief weapon was public opinion, an explosive that the government pretended was beyond control while trying to light the fuse. The Allies saw the complicity, but they knew that street fighting and political murders were common in Germany. The chief of the British military mission in Berlin wrote that Erzberger had exaggerated, and that resistance to extradition came almost entirely from the army and rightist or centrist parties. However, all parties opposed the kaiser's trial as "an insult to the nation," as they would an attempt to prosecute Hindenburg, whereas "subordinates accused of definite crimes would arouse very little sympathy"—submarine captains or prison camp commanders, for example.[4] Should a neutral court hold the trials, and should the Allies publish the charges now, that would help to persuade the Germans that justice, not revenge, was the object.

242

On reading this report, Balfour agreed on 8 August that the Germans perceived vengeance and wondered whether "means could not be found to explain . . . the real facts" about the war crimes, "of which they are evidently ignorant."[5]

Perhaps Balfour knew how late it was to decide that the Germans had no grasp of "the real facts," or that an explanation would give them one. But that was only the beginning. Handing the cases to a neutral court would have violated the treaty and gone against the Commission on Responsibility's unanimous opinion that neutrals should have no say in the prosecutions.[6] The reluctance to try Hindenburg, though understandable, also negated the commission's findings and breached the treaty's spirit if not its letter.

The contradictions multiplied. In early September, Lloyd George proposed to limit the number of trials to accommodate the German government, which he preferred to its Bolshevist or militarist alternatives. Clemenceau agreed that the trials "should merely be a symbol,"[7] but even then, the victors were preparing lists of defendants that ran to three thousand names.[8] Belgium alone supplied more than eleven hundred.[9] Compiling them took time, and Belgium, which had been working on war crimes for five years, did not submit its paperwork until late October.

November marked a year since the armistice, half a year since the Allies had presented the treaty. The Germans chose this juncture to suggest that they conduct the trials at their highest court, the Reichsgericht (Supreme Court) at Leipzig, guaranteeing that "this procedure will be followed with all desired strictness and impartiality."[10] They would remove jurisdictional hurdles and offered any injured country the chance to participate, virtually ceding the right to plead the cases. They further proposed that if, despite this involvement, the Allies did not recognize the proceedings as just, they could appeal to an international tribunal or other body supervised by the League of Nations.

The Allies did not bite. Outwardly, they seemed ready to fulfill the treaty, as when they created a commission to oversee the Mixed Tribunals that included judges from more than one country.[11] The French also acted on their own, pursuing trials against defendants whom their occupying forces had captured on German territory.[12] But cracks in Allied unity became more visible. On 19 November, the United States Senate rejected the Treaty of Versailles, and though another vote would come up the following session, it was now less likely that

America would join the League of Nations or help enforce the treaty. Moreover, the Europeans fell to arguing about whether the Germans would find extradition more palatable if fewer defendants were involved. Over the next three months, the three thousand names became one thousand; in January 1920, the British pressed for deeper cuts, over French and Belgian objections.

Lloyd George took the lead, but Smith, now lord chancellor, seconded him. The former attorney general admitted that he had lobbied for prosecutions in 1918 but insisted that given the turmoil in Germany, demanding a thousand names was unwise.[13] The French and Belgian representatives agreed but contended that halving the number was pointless when the Germans were determined not to hand over anybody.[14] One remark of Lloyd George's summed up the mood in those weeks. He said that if "even twenty were shot it would set an example," as if he had been tired of the war crimes problem and wanted it out of the way.[15]

Then there was the kaiser, who remained lord of his castle in the Netherlands. Having tried once to extradite him, the Allies sent another note in mid-January, averring that the Dutch would never wish to cover "violations of the essential principles of the solidarity of nations" by protecting the man most responsible.[16] When this approach failed, Lloyd George considered stronger medicine, such as severing relations with Holland or blocking its entry into the League of Nations. But British diplomats in Holland let it be known that the threat was a bluff, and the Dutch again refused.[17] The British ambassador reported that they did not necessarily like their uninvited guest, but yielding him up "would be totally incompatible with their ideas of liberty and law."[18] Some people wished that the waters flooding Wilhelm's cellar might rise, but that short of "some act of Providence," he would be free to live his life in the Netherlands.[19]

Meanwhile, the Germans seized the initiative. Erzberger began negotiations regarding the paper marks with Emile Francqui, director of the Société Générale and former head of the Comité National. However, Erzberger had not consulted the Reichsbank, and when the talks came to light, the German government disavowed them. An embarrassed Erzberger claimed that in return for reimbursement, he had obtained Francqui's promise that the Belgians would cease to ask for accused war criminals. The Belgians denied this and said that Francqui had lacked the authority to make that deal. Whether Francqui had indeed offered to drop the trials or Erzberger was merely covering himself, the German press accused the Belgians of going back on their word.[20]

On 20 January, Chancellor Gustav Bauer hinted to André de Kerchove de Denterghem, the Belgian minister in Berlin, that even if Francqui had gone beyond his instructions, Germany hoped the Belgians would not repudiate him. Bauer said he disapproved of the invasion, which, reported de Kerchove, was "the first time a German statesman had expressed regrets to me on the subject of the infamy committed on 4 August 1914."[21] But the chancellor stressed that with food supplies low and the Bolsheviks making trouble, handing over anyone was impossible. When de Kerchove said that Belgian opinion was as indignant as in 1914, Bauer agreed that the perpetrators of Termonde and Louvain must be punished, but by German courts. The German people would never stand for extradition, and though the treaty required it, he hoped the Belgians would not insist. But de Kerchove did not take these statements at face value. When the press kept attacking the Belgians over the next three weeks, he wrote that the government was partly to blame but had not yet "managed to provoke the popular agitation that would help it resist Allied demands."

Like the French, the Belgians made arrests in occupied territory, after a Ministry of Justice decree of January 1919 allowed the seizure of any person suspected of committing war crimes in Belgium. Most of the ensuing trials involved property, usually the purchase of requisitioned Belgian machinery by German industrialists, but a few cases concerned violence. A Belgian soldier guarding a mine recognized a miner named Bockstegen as a suspect in murders of Belgian villagers in summer 1916. When a Belgian court convicted Bockstegen, he appealed, claiming that only a military court could prosecute him, that he had gone before a German tribunal already, and that the Belgians lacked jurisdiction. The appeal was heard in Brussels in early winter 1920, just as extradition was coming to a head. The court upheld the conviction, ruling that Belgium had an original right to prosecute, and cited Article 229, which allowed the Allies to try anyone no matter what verdict a German tribunal had rendered.[22]

But Berlin kept pushing. Gustav Noske, minister of defense, told Lord Kilmarnock, the British ambassador, that extradition would bring about chaos "leading to civil war and dangers of Bolshevism."[23] If the Allies would only accept the German proposal to hold the trials on German soil, they could still supervise. Kurt von Lersner, who led the German delegation at Paris, wrote Clemenceau that German opposition was unanimous and repeated the offer to hold rigorous, exacting trials. He said the proposal proved "that the German Government has no intention of shielding the guilty persons from their penalties."[24] The Vatican joined in, cautioning Britain that trials would "keep alive international hatreds," that Germany should not "be obliged to hand over her own children," and that a "militarist-Bolshevik" revolution would "react on the whole of Europe."[25]

Kilmarnock warned of "harm to our interests," chiefly reparations, "which may accrue if our demands are pressed to the full limit."[26] On 31 January, he resumed the theme. "As the price of defeat and in expiation for their past crimes, the German people may be forced to make bricks without straw—they cannot make them without clay."[27] The remark implied that reparations were equally vengeful and just while likening the Germans to the Children of Israel enslaved in Egypt, a summation that underlines the confusion among British officials. Kilmarnock thought the despairing Germans would try to fulfill their obligations only if they anticipated "the slightest chance of success." But he saw strain, exhaustion, "the ever-present menace of anarchic violence," spendthrift war profiteers and people living recklessly on their capital, and "in the background . . . temporarily quiescent . . . sinister, resentful—the devotees of reaction" who hoped for chaos. A compromise on trials would help ease the tension.

Such beliefs had their effect. In mid-January, Italian Premier Francesco Nitti endorsed trials held by the Germans.[28] By month's end—but before Kilmarnock's long dispatch—Lloyd George let the British ambassador in Paris know that he "would not be indisposed" to consider trials held on German soil.[29] But he wanted them in occupied territory, and though the judges would be German, the Allies would prosecute the cases. The "fundamental essential" was that "the criminals should be strictly and sternly tried" and given suitable punishments for "proven crimes."

Still, on 3 February, the Allies gave Lersner the roster of accused criminals, now numbering 854 (though some had been indicted by more than one country).[30] Belgium and France had each designated 334, and the next-highest total was Britain's, at 95. The Belgians named Bethmann for the neutrality violation and the deportations; Hindenburg, for the deportations; and Falkenhausen, for deportations of Belgian notables, attacks on sovereignty, and industrial damage. Regarding the invasion terror, the Belgians charged officers from generals down to lieutenants, paying particular attention to the massacres at Louvain and Andenne.

But Lersner returned the Allies' roster, saying that they would never find a German official to share this shameful undertaking.[31] He explained that had he accepted the list, protests by German diplomats abroad would no longer have been taken seriously, but that does not say why he leaked the names to the press. *Vorwärts* criticized Lersner's appeal to nationalist feeling, saying that the masses did not share it.[32] The paper thought the list unjust but noted that Germany had signed the treaty, and that breaking it could provoke sanctions, such as further territorial occupation.[33] Throughout Germany, the inclusion of Hindenburg and other generals caused a "great sensation" and was "viewed with consternation by persons of all political complexions" who wanted a stable regime, wrote Kilmarnock on 5 February.[34] Two days later, he reported protests by the Bavarian Landtag, the president of East Prussia, and the Berlin Chamber of Commerce, among others.[35] But Independent Socialist leaders told him that most people were indifferent, though they might not stay that way if the press goaded them. "If Germany can be said to possess a soul, that soul has been touched," the ambassador said.[36]

Army officers and Socialists alike believed that the Allies wanted only to make an impossible demand as a pretext to impose sanctions.[37] But whether most Germans cared enough to face down the Allies remains unclear. Kilmarnock predicted either a right-wing revolution or passive resistance—"the difference can be only one of degree."[38] But a *Times* of London correspondent told him the Allies were being misled and referred to confidences from German journalists that "though they are forced to write in a strain of defiance," they would rather the Allies took the criminals away.[39] Kilmarnock said these journalists wanted to provoke Germany's breaking apart, but he observed that the Germans "may weld themselves into a nation which may again prove formidable to the world. It is more than doubtful whether they have learnt the lesson which the war should have inculcated."

He judged that "the choice is one of extreme difficulty, but we stand now at the parting of the ways"—the Allies could crush the German menace, but only at cost to everyone, including the loss of reparations.[40] He again counseled compromise, which Lloyd George took up at an Allied conference on 12 February. He professed surprise that Hindenburg, Bethmann, and Ludendorff figured on the list and rebuked Hindenburg's indictment as "a political mistake of the first magnitude."[41] He must have known the top leaders would be named, and he had hunted Wilhelm's head more aggressively than anyone, but the prime minister's zigzags were beside the point. Hindenburg had ordered the occupation's signature crime, and if he went free, subordinates could claim superior orders for that or any other offense. Even so, Lloyd George wanted the lists reduced to those who had "carried out direct outrages," particularly against women. British opinion about the war crimes had changed, he contended, "and there was a general desire to return to the ordinary business of life."[42]

The conference debated trying the criminals in absentia, but Delacroix objected that this would "be a parody of justice and we should have the Germans laughing at us."[43] Besides, the prosecutors would be unable to fix responsibility between subordinates and superiors, and crucial evidence would be lacking, resulting in acquittals. He preferred to have the Mixed Tribunals present indictments and turn them over to the Germans—what Northcliffe had suggested in November 1918. Lord George Curzon, the British foreign secretary, added that the Germans were making a "counterlist" of Allied criminals, whom they might try in absentia, which would make everything absurd.[44] He proposed testing the Germans' sincerity by letting them hold trials in occupied territory. But Alexandre Millerand, the president of France, thought the German offer was trickery, a plan to "engage us in a discussion which would be drawn out interminably."[45] Millerand saw troubles with extradition, but punishment was less the aim than that the world know the truth. If the Allies gave way, that would lead to further compromises, and he feared "a breakdown of the whole treaty."

Nevertheless, on 13 February the Allies consented to the Leipzig plan, even as the German government had alerted the army should they insist on extradition.[46] Curzon lectured the German chargé in London about keeping press and public from acclaiming the defendants.[47] De Kerchove, more skeptical, wrote that what the Belgians called crimes, German law recognized as "necessities of war."[48] He predicted that the Reichsgericht would acquit anyone the Belgians accused.

■

The German government greeted the deal with relief and realized that the Allies had made a huge concession, for the Reichsgericht would be able to acquit or pardon any defendant without interference.[49] But the hardliners resented yielding to the enemy, and to gain the Reichstag's approval, Minister of Justice Eugen Schiffer said that only through a sacrifice that abided by German law and maintained German honor could Germany avoid a greater evil.[50] After some debate, the Reichstag approved, and the government communicated formal acceptance on 7 March.[51]

But before that happened, the Germans protested Allied arrests in occupied territory, which they called illegal and contrary to the Leipzig arrangement. They also pressed for an amnesty covering cases not slated for Leipzig, because "the re-establishment of normal relations between the nationals of either party is hardly possible" unless the Allies limited their power to prosecute.[52] A refusal would "make it necessary for the German government . . . to take measures with regard to indictable acts" committed during the war against Germany. The Allies did not agree to an amnesty, which would have curtailed their rights under the criminal articles, but they did order the arrests to cease, displeasing the Belgians.[53]

In early May 1920, the Allies submitted forty-six cases, sixteen of them Belgian, for what the victors warily presumed to be the first round of prosecutions.[54] Two months later, when they asked why no trials had taken place, the Germans claimed that some cases "were still in a state of preliminary investigation, but no further action could be taken for want of sufficient evidence."[55] But the Allies did not hurry them, and in October, the British ambassador in Berlin drew "earnest attention" to the delay.[56] Only in March 1921, a year after Germany agreed to prosecute, did the Allies threaten sanctions, and even then, they listed other complaints too, concerning reparations and German disarmament.[57] The Germans balked at fulfilling the treaty, the Allies occupied the Ruhr, the German cabinet fell, and its successor agreed to comply. As a consequence, in late April, German witnesses went to a London court to give depositions relating to charges of mistreating British prisoners. When the witnesses emerged from the courthouse during a lunchtime adjournment, an angry crowd nearly caused a riot.[58]

That may have been the last time the Germans did what their enemies wanted. When the trials began in May, the Reichsgericht charged three men with having robbed a Belgian at gunpoint in late October 1918, a crime absent from Allied lists. When the court sentenced the accused to prison, the left-wing press objected that three "proletarians"—a carpenter, mechanic, and a sailor—had faced justice, whereas officers who had done worse went free.[59] But the Berlin right-wing press, said the *Times* of London, daily accused the Allies of various crimes; party newspapers were also "exciting venom"; and tempers were rising.[60] In Leipzig, which the *Times* called "one of the most serene" of German cities, a "handsome city full of open places, red tiled roofs, and columned facades," the atmosphere was testy.[61] The local citizens' council asked those who had no direct connection to the trials to stay away, advice that was largely ignored.

The Reichsgericht, formally known as the Criminal Senate of the Imperial Court of Justice, occupied one of Leipzig's "stateliest and perhaps most august" buildings, an imposing structure whose cupola supported a colossal statue of Truth.[62] In the great hall lay a courtroom whose oak-paneled walls held portraits of Saxon kings and coats of arms from the German states.[63] Dominating the room was a horseshoe-shaped table covered in green baize that opened toward the spectators and seated seven judges who wore crimson robes, crimson velvet birettas, and white ties. The presiding judge, or president, commanded the bend of the horseshoe, and witnesses faced him to testify, with the prosecution and defense on either side, and the German press behind. The arrangement did nothing to compensate for the poor acoustics, which everyone criticized, and which most affected the spectators, who sat behind the German press and in the galleries.[64]

But the layout reflected a presiding judge's powers under German law. Before a trial, he read every deposition, decided who would be called as a witness, and which testimony was relevant. He opened the trial by examining the defendant, asking, among other questions, whether the accused had ever been punished. Then the president called witnesses in any order he liked and rejected whatever they said that he thought immaterial or that made a point he considered established. Only after he had questioned a witness could attorneys for either side do so, and he could order that they speak through him. Whenever testimony conflicted, the president instantly demanded an explanation, whether from the defendant or a previous witness. Both the prosecution and the defense admitted hearsay without a murmur.[65]

Claud Mullins, a lawyer who served the British mission to Leipzig chiefly as an interpreter, wrote that cross-examination was "almost unknown," and that he never saw witnesses pressed hard.[66] "It was obvious" that many testified reluctantly and "were saying a good deal less than they in fact knew." Therefore, Mullins said, if the president were biased against a defendant, an acquittal was impossible. Yet he came away impressed with Karl Schmidt, the Reichsgericht's president, before whom "I should be willing to be tried . . . on any charge, even on one which involved my word against that of a German."[67] Both Mullins and Sir Ernest M. Pollock, the solicitor-general who led the British mission, said that Schmidt had handled their cases fairly and conscientiously despite intense political pressure.

During a twelve-day stretch that began 23 May, the Reichsgericht heard four cases from the British list. The first three had to do with prison camps. The defendants were a former corporal, captain, and private, respectively, and the charges ranged from verbal abuse to blows to torture to negligence that led to deaths from disease.[68] Dozens of former prisoners testified, and Schmidt earned British regard for how he cut short efforts by the defense to exploit minor discrepancies.[69] At one point, he remarked that whether the defendant had struck a man at the top of a ladder or the bottom made no difference, so long as he had struck him, and Schmidt believed he had. He also deplored that same defendant's treatment of "defenceless prisoners," which undermined "the good reputation of the German Army" and respect for Germany "as a nation of culture."[70]

But Schmidt let defense lawyers and expert witnesses make speeches about military necessity, how the prisoners had not understood it, their hostility and bias, the crucial importance of preventing mutiny, and the effects of the blockade.[71] The court took these circumstances into consideration, admitting that certain acts might be illegal but refusing to condemn or even examine the philosophy behind the method. The negligence charges fell away because conditions were judged to lie beyond any person's control, and the need for obedience excused the means by which the defendants had obtained it. What remained were instances of gratuitous violence, which the court viewed as "an exaggerated conception of military necessity and discipline."[72] But even that, as one ruling said, tempered the severity of the act. In another category, one defendant was shown to have called the prisoners *Schweinhund* (swine; bastard) several times.[73]

The court handed down convictions and prison sentences of ten months, six months, and six months. The German nationalist press and the *Times* of London said that justice had miscarried, though for opposite reasons, and wondered what political constraints had been brought to bear.[74] The *Berliner Tageblatt,* more liberal than most German papers, rebuked criticism of the Reichsgericht but commented that the German people had cause to wish that criminals who had brought the country into disrepute should be tried.[75] *Vorwärts* remarked that war criminals came in retail and wholesale varieties, that the corporal sentenced to ten months was retail, and that the general who had spoken about necessity in his defense was the wholesale kind.[76]

The Reichsgericht kept the fourth trial at the retail level too. A former submarine captain, Lieutenant-Commander Karl Neumann, stood accused of sinking a British hospital ship, *Dover Castle,* an act that had killed six crewmen.[77] Neumann admitted the facts but cited a general order to sink hospital ships in certain waters, a policy arising from the navy's belief that the British were using these vessels for military purposes. To try Neumann was to question this aspect of submarine warfare, and his acknowledgment that he had had no reason to suspect *Dover Castle* of carrying munitions or otherwise abusing her immunity might have aggravated the case.

But the court heard no testimony, only comments by defense counsel about British hospital ships. The trial consisted of a conversation between Neumann and Schmidt, after which the court acquitted the defendant: He had followed orders.[78] The verdict explained that he could have been convicted only had he exceeded them or known that they ran contrary to military or civil law, but neither condition applied. Neumann had read navy memoranda on hospital ships, heard what comrades had said about British practices, and had even given a certificate to a captive British officer confessing the sinking. It was as if the court were saying that because Neumann's conscience was clear, he must be innocent. "It was an edifying spectacle," an angry *Times* said on 6 June, to see Neumann "wearing a smart swallow-tailed suit and fancy vest, his Iron Cross displayed at the waist," a hero "lionized throughout the proceedings. To-day he is lionized throughout the country."[79]

The meaning of German crimes to postwar relations surfaced in the next case, that of Max Ramdohr, a civil servant who had worked for the occupation in Belgium. Attached to the secret police in Grammont, East Flanders, in 1917 and 1918, Ramdohr was charged with imprisoning and torturing boys between the ages of twelve and fourteen to extort confessions.[80] He had placed these confessions before a military tribunal, which, in April 1918, condemned fourteen boys and two adults said to have encouraged them to prison terms of several years each. Supported by medical testimony, the boys claimed that Ramdohr and an associate had beaten them and denied them food until they admitted to destroying railway signals, a crime of which they had known nothing, and that the tribunal had been stacked against them. The Belgians also alleged that the affair had resulted from a feud between neighborhood boys and a railwayman who had worked for the Germans, and that Ramdohr had invented the sabotage story.

The case evoked the petty vindictiveness, judicial misconduct, and suspicion that had marked the occupation. But Schmidt appeared to reject any testimony that led that way; the Belgian observers believed that he was willing to convict Ramdohr so long as the charge was trivial.[81] They reported that Schmidt let the children describe punches or kicks they had received, but that he interrupted as soon as they mentioned weapons or more violent abuse. Why did one witness say his captor had beaten him with a wooden ruler, when another boy had spoken of a metal one? the president asked. Why did one witness say his head had been thrust into a bowl of water, when someone else had talked about a basin? As for the wartime tribunal that had convicted the children, no German officer could have testified before a court and said anything that did not conform to reality. The children, however, were impressionable and had, consciously or not, repeated impossible tales heard from one another.

The Belgian observers failed to say that, in German eyes, the children had created a poor impression.[82] They seemed to have been coached, reciting their evidence flawlessly until an unexpected question from Schmidt made them freeze. The defense lawyers may have coached their witnesses too—so alleged the *Times* about one of the prison camp trials—but the problem was more complex.[83] Unless the charges had been fabricated, the children were facing their tormentor, a confrontation that would have unsettled many an adult. They were in a hostile environment and spoke no language but Flemish—and the court translator, a Flemish radical who had fled Belgium, addressed asides and personal remarks to them.[84] The court might have tried to learn whether the children had faltered out of nervousness or for some other reason, but Schmidt made no allowances, and two of his colleagues allegedly showed their disdain through gestures and comments. French observers noted that the children contradicted one another in small details but were convincing overall, and from reading the court judgment, Mullins thought the same.[85]

Ramdohr's acquittal on 12 June met with jubilation in the Berlin press. The Belgian minister wrote Brussels that the papers asked why the case had even come up and praised the court for vindicating a man who had only done his duty. He paraphrased the reaction as "One can almost qualify as a scandal the fact that our highest tribunal must waste its time with such a trifle, a trifle in which no tribunal in the world would see anything punishable."[86] But the Belgians were stunned. The day before the verdict, Le Soir's Leipzig correspondent had written about a German industrialist-politician's recent call for "minds to disarm" and for Europeans to acquire a "mentality of peace." Reason told the journalist to accept, but he confessed that because of what he had heard in court, "I felt a shiver of indignation, not to say hatred" that he could not master.[87] Now, hearing of the acquittal, "I gave a start," and he remarked that the verdict reflected not only a "caricature of justice" but the "Prussian conception" against which the Allies had fought.[88]

The government agreed. Minister of Justice Vandervelde told Parliament that Belgium would ask for sanctions, and that he was sure a vigorous protest would express the "deep and unanimous sentiment" of the Belgian people.[89] The chamber answered with long, loud applause, which implied that for Belgium, Leipzig was a dead letter. One deputy said, "Brigands judging other brigands must no longer be allowed!"

France's turn came in early July, when the Reichsgericht tried Lieutenant General Karl Stenger for having allegedly ordered his men to kill French prisoners. Stenger wore the Pour le Mérite, Germany's highest medal, and he walked with crutches because he had lost a leg to a French artillery shell. That the French had dared prosecute a hero of his rank and stature incensed German nationalists, but the witnesses who testified against him were German. The court ruled "no opinion," which amounted to an acquittal, but convicted a major who had served under him of negligence, sentencing him to three years and stripping him of his uniform. After the verdicts came in, a crowd tried to spit at the French delegates, and Stenger received so many congratulatory letters that he placed a notice in a newspaper by way of thanks.[90] A Dutch observer thought the trial had been fair, but the American press widely condemned the verdict, as did some German opinion.[91]

A few days later, the court shifted again to take up another British case. The charges said that in June 1918 off Ireland, a submarine had torpedoed the hospital ship *Llandovery Castle,* after which the U-boat had surfaced and used a deck gun to shell the lifeboats trying to escape. The court accepted this and decided that the commander had known that *Llandovery Castle* was sailing waters in which the navy had forbidden hospital sinkings, yet had gone ahead, convinced (wrongly) that the ship was carrying munitions and American airmen. Worse, having sunk at least two lifeboats, he had falsified his log books and sworn his two officers of the watch to secrecy.[92] The court ruled that he had committed homicide and that "the firing on the boats was an offence against the law of nations," a code that, despite its general ambiguities, clearly forbade the act.[93]

What made the case more remarkable was that the commander, Helmut Patzig, never appeared in court, because the German legal authorities said they could not find him. Instead, they tried the two officers of the watch, Ludwig Dithmar and John Boldt, whom the British had not named, and who insisted that they had done nothing wrong. In rejecting the defendants' plea of superior orders, the court decided that they must have known that Patzig was directing them to break the law—the facts were ironclad—and should have disobeyed. Such a supposition applied "only in rare and exceptional cases," the court said, but this was one.[94] For the rule to apply, the prosecution had to prove (a) that the order was intended to commit a crime, and (b) that the defendant knew this. Thus, in the *Dover Castle* case, Neumann would have gone free even had he believed that the order to sink hospital ships was illegal, because he could not have guessed his superiors' motives.[95] Dithmar and Boldt, however, knew that sinking lifeboats was inexcusable and that Patzig knew this too.

However, the verdict sidestepped whether sinking hospital ships was a crime, and whether necessity was to blame. Rather, as in the Stenger case, the court pursued a lesser charge for which subordinates had to answer. The Reichsgericht sentenced Dithmar and Boldt to four years in prison, dismissed Dithmar from the navy, and stripped Boldt of the right to wear his officer's uniform, the heaviest penalties exacted at Leipzig. The navy assailed the verdict as an attack on its honor, and Dithmar and Boldt became heroes.[96] But the German press was more cautious than usual, and even the nationalist *Kreuz Zeitung* admitted, "It is possible they [the defendants] overshot the mark and did wrong." Still, the paper said, Germany's enemies had done much worse.[97]

Once again, the Allies found themselves in a weak position. The French had recalled their observers from Leipzig, but otherwise, they were stymied. Premier Aristide Briand told an Allied conference in early August that the French public wanted to enforce the criminal articles, but he doubted the Allies could do that, and he suggested that a legal committee study the trials.[98] The Allies agreed, but five days later, Solicitor-General Pollock told the House of Commons that "for the first time in the history of the world, we have made the vanquished country try some of its own criminals."[99] Britons might think the sentences inadequate, but in Germany they "carry a severe stigma," and the highest German court had decided that Germans had "committed atrocities" for which they "deserve and are to receive punishment." Therefore, Pollock said, the Leipzig trials "mark a new milestone in the course of international justice," and he expected them to realize notable "moral effects."

The German press published these remarks, which jilted the French and Belgians and bound Britain to the Leipzig process, for better or for worse.[100] With little enthusiasm, the British joined the Germans in a preliminary hearing regarding another hospital ship case, but both governments wanted the prosecutions to lapse, and no more foreign observers went to Leipzig.[101] On 7 January 1922, the commission reported that the trials had resulted in too few convictions and imposed punishments that were too light, and that the Allies should invoke their rights to prosecute under the criminal articles.[102] The French voiced interest, but the British resolutely opposed any extraditions, and the effort went nowhere.

Instead, the French and Belgians began holding trials in absentia. The French put their original lists of criminals on the docket—two thousand names, minus a few, like Hindenburg and Ludendorff—and by December 1924 had convicted more than twelve hundred of them.[103] They had also instructed their consuls not to grant visas to known criminals, but neither policy achieved much except to annoy

Germany. The Belgians prosecuted far fewer cases, perhaps no more than eighty, and by mid-1925 were wishing the whole matter would go away for the sake of foreign relations.[104] They were getting criticism abroad and pressure from a Germany indignant that "leading German personalities . . . continued to run the risk, if they set foot on French or Belgian soil, of being arrested and sentenced."[105] When the Belgians asked the French their opinion, the French replied that they could not end their trials but would wind them down.[106] They had had to make exceptions anyway in their visa policy to accommodate trade, and they were willing to follow the Belgian lead and ease international tensions. Both countries let the trials fade, and in December 1925, they signed the Treaties of Locarno, which guaranteed the boundaries of Germany, Belgium, and France as an aid to peace. Conciliation was the policy of the day.

But though the Belgians had not embraced trials in absentia, during the early 1920s they had considered making more arrests in occupied territory. One person they particularly wanted was a former Colonel von Thessmar, who had allegedly ordered 122 civilians shot at Arlon, Luxembourg province, in August 1914.[107] He had reportedly approved the executions by telephone after having decided not to send for railway cars to deport the captives, because, he was quoted as saying, they were only francs-tireurs. In July 1921, Thessmar was living in Trier, occupied territory about a hundred kilometers from Arlon, but when the victims' relatives signed a petition, the Allies expelled him, despite repeated German protests. The Belgians never apprehended Thessmar, though, and in April 1923 decided that it was useless to arrest anyone, however tempting the opportunity. Pursuing a handful of cases was not worth the adverse publicity throughout Europe and rekindling "hatreds and nationalist passions in Germany," especially when so many other criminals had escaped justice.[108]

The Mixed Tribunal heard one meaningful war crimes case, however, when an organization of former deported workers sued the German government for damages. The plaintiffs argued that violent constraint constituted a violation of human rights and was therefore grounds for restitution, and that the deportees had suffered undeniable losses, whether through death, disability, or injury to health. They also contended that the losses occurred in civil law, under the category of work contracts, and therefore lay outside the reparations specified in the Treaty of Versailles. As evidence of a private, civil connection between government and deportees, the Belgians pointed to a payment Germany had made in 1919 of money withheld from forty thousand salaries.[109] The Mixed Tribunal sided with the plaintiffs, and in July 1925, the German government agreed to pay twenty-four million francs, which amounted to about $1.1 million because of the franc's fall on the open market.[110]

Meanwhile, though, the Germans had been busy erasing the traces of Leipzig. In early 1922, nationalists sympathetic to Dithmar and Boldt arranged their escape from prison with little difficulty. Two other convicted defendants had been released early, one because his family needed his support, and the other because of ill health.[111] Britain protested,[112] but to no avail, and at a rally in Germany to support Dithmar and Boldt, Hitler met Goering for the first time.[113] During the next several years, the Reichsgericht went through the 854 accused criminals and cleared them so that the French and Belgians did not have the last word. To see who had been convicted, German diplomats in Paris and Brussels read the daily newspapers, relaying the names back to Berlin.[114] (Thessmar's turn came in April 1926.)[115] In 1925, the Reichsgericht overturned the convictions of Dithmar and Boldt in secret session, and six years later, publicly ruled that political motives alone had resulted in the charge of shelling lifeboats.[116] When the Nazis came to power, they had the court reverse all the convictions, including those of the three defendants sentenced for armed robbery. A judge who had sat at Leipzig wrote in 1939 that having to try his countrymen for war crimes marked the "most painful and saddest" chapter in his career.[117] He added that making this concession to the Allies went against German honor.

14

A Popular Delusion

SIX MONTHS AFTER THE TREATY WAS SIGNED, a thirty-six-year-old genius gave it a thrashing that ruined its reputation forever. In *The Economic Consequences of the Peace*, John Maynard Keynes charged that the victors had fought "a war ostensibly waged in defense of the sanctity of international engagements," only to abandon this ideal at the conference table.[1] "There are few episodes in history which posterity will have less reason to condone," he predicted. He did not mean the criminal articles, which he never mentioned, or the war-guilt clause, which was "a matter of words" that did no harm and would soon be forgotten.[2]

Rather, Keynes meant the reparations articles, which to him constituted a breach of international law and morality comparable to the invasion of Belgium.[3] He accused the victors of having exaggerated German wrongdoing to take the moral high ground and to justify inflated reparations, and he cited Belgium to support his case. Belgian claims were "simply irresponsible" and totaled more than the country's estimated prewar wealth. Belgian industry was paralyzed, but only temporarily, and a "few tens of millions" would have paid for every machine that Belgium had ever possessed, let alone any the Germans had taken.[4]

Belgian industrial damage mattered little anyway. Most of the land, "which is Belgium's chief wealth, is nearly as well cultivated as before," and most of the fighting had occurred in West Flanders, "backward, poor, and sleepy" to begin with. The Belgians had an "unusually well developed" gift for "individual self-protection," revealed in the stockpiling of paper marks, and in how "certain classes" had profited despite "the severities and barbarities of German rule."[5] Belgium's "relative sacrifices, apart from those sufferings from invasion which cannot be measured in money," lagged behind Australia's, so that thinking of Belgium as the war's primary victim was "a popular delusion," based on a remembrance of 1914.[6]

Keynes pleaded that the treaty must be revised. He blamed the peacemakers for "reducing Germany to servitude for a generation," "degrading the lives of millions," and "depriving a whole nation of happiness," an "abhorrent and detestable" procedure that would "sow the decay of the whole civilized life of Europe."[7] But he never referred to the deprivations the Germans had visited on Belgium after 1914; whether German methods or philosophy were abhorrent or threatened Europe never entered the picture. Germany thus appeared to be the victim, and the Allies, with Belgium riding their coattails, the persecutors.

This analysis was especially damaging because few commentators possessed the authority or firsthand knowledge that Keynes did. He had attended the peace conference representing the British Treasury and had been the chancellor of the exchequer's deputy on the Supreme Economic Council, but he had resigned both posts three weeks before the treaty signing in protest. *The Economic Consequences of the Peace* took Britain by storm in December 1919 and sold seventy thousand copies in the United States by spring, before the Senate rejected the treaty for good. By 1924, Keynes's treatise had appeared in eleven languages, and a colleague estimated that at least a half-million people who had never read a book on economics had read this one.[8]

The impact was enormous; the echoes resound even today. As Martin Gilbert has written, "Keynes destroyed British faith in Versailles" and for twenty years lent credence to the opinion that the treaty was unworthy of Britain's signature. "A feeling of guilt came to pervade all discussion. . . . Keynes made appeasement public property."[9]

The outcry over injured Germany neglected the treaty's inequities toward Belgium. Replacing the missing machines was more complex than Keynes made out, for the treaty effectively forced the Belgians to trace and retrieve them rather than buy new ones at German expense. The machines proved hard to find, and those the Belgians located had often been ruined from overuse or carelessness in transit and were not worth the cost of shipment home.[10] As for livestock, the German peace delegation offered to return only blood stallions, and only those that could be positively identified as Belgian property.[11] The treaty did grant the Belgians a 10 percent levy on German herds over three years—at American insistence, over British opposition—but what they collected amounted to about 2 percent in nearly all cases. Yet German herds had stood at two-thirds their prewar size in 1919, not counting what the army had taken during the retreat. By 1920, German livestock had largely recovered, whereas Belgian herds did not regain their 1913 levels until 1930.[12]

In May 1921, the Reparations Commission devised a settlement requiring Germany to pay 132 billion gold marks, about $33 billion. Several historians have challenged Keynes and said that Germany could have complied had the Weimar government followed "a politically courageous fiscal policy."[13] Others disagree,[14] but the bottom line is that Germany did not pay. Over thirteen years, the Germans handed over about 22 billion marks, slightly more than what was due in May 1921 alone, and less than a third of the total payment was in cash.[15] In 1924, the Dawes Plan lent Germany funds to pay much-reduced reparations, and in 1930, the Young Plan lowered German debt yet again. One historian has argued that Germany disbursed no net reparations, using American commercial loans to meet the obligation and finance recovery, only to default on the debt in the 1930s.[16] Moreover, despite the worries that Dresel had reported hearing from German leaders, Germany did not become a desert where no one would marry or procreate. In fact, Germany witnessed strong gains in birth and marriage rates in 1919—higher than Belgium's.[17]

But Belgium's postwar struggles received little help or heed. Most of Belgium's share of the first billion marks that Germany paid in 1921, 350 million, went to repay loans from American and British commercial banks.[18] During the following years, while Germany was paying 2.5 percent and 5 percent interest on reparations bonds, France and Belgium were borrowing from American banks at 8.5 percent.[19] When the Senate rejected the Treaty of Versailles and the bargain that absolved Belgium of prearmistice debt—which Wilson had concealed from Congress until February 1921—the Belgians had to pay up.[20] They reached an agreement with American negotiators in August 1925, the year they finally received their $500 million priority. They were lucky to get it, because the Allies tried to take it, but even so, the country was deeply in debt, and the priority did not fulfill its purpose of immediate help.[21] The franc, weakened by continued borrowing, crashed in 1926. Belgium never regained its stature as a commercial and industrial power.

Meanwhile, the crimes against the invaded nations were fading from American and British memories. In March 1920, after Germany had agreed to hold the Leipzig trials, a Boston magazine commented that France and Belgium were the only countries where enforcing the criminal articles had broad public support. Had specific charges against Germany "been widely published in Great Britain and America," the editorial said, "it might have revived the sympathy for such a policy that undoubtedly existed during and immediately after the war."[22] Even at that, the magazine was probably talking about the invasion terror, not the occupation.

The Belgians were partly responsible for the lack of public awareness. Their postwar inquiry, which covered every terror imposed during fifty-two months of war, did not appear until 1922 and 1923, and was published in a multivolume format more suitable for historians than the general public. Of the sixteen defendants Belgium listed for trial at Leipzig, only two, Ramdohr and an associate, Ernst Zahn, had been occupation officials, and low-level ones, to boot. They were charged not with deporting thousands of workers or pillaging factories but with police brutality and extortion committed against a handful of victims.

The Belgians had reason to limit the scope of prosecution given the tension over the trials and the doubtful chances of winning convictions. Nevertheless, of the forty-six defendants on the Leipzig list, only one besides Ramdohr and Zahn was accused of a crime of occupation, and Italy was the country that named him.[23] Every other case involved the abuse or death of prisoners, the invasion terror, or submarine warfare, nearly all of which concerned random violence during combat or near the battlefront. As a result, France and Belgium had almost entirely forgone the attempt to prosecute crimes in which the victims were civilians, the perpetrators had planned their offenses in detail, and whose motives implied a policy of political and economic subjugation.

By failing to make that case, the victors strengthened the impression that German terror had ended in 1914, and that in the main, talk of war crimes meant assessing how the armies had behaved in battle. Such judgments were hard to draw because, for instance, soldiers of both sides had killed prisoners of war on occasion. As an editorialist for the conservative Socialist weekly *Die Glöcke* wrote during the Leipzig trials, "There were only too many Huns and barbarians under both banners."[24] What made this admission more remarkable was that the author favored the trials and cited the Belgian deportations, the scorched-earth policy of 1918, and the *Lusitania* as evidence of criminal thinking.[25] Still, if an open-minded observer could weigh those crimes against Allied actions, the victors would not meet their burden of proof by focusing on 1914 or the battlefield alone.

The editorialist also suggested that war criminals from all armies deserved to face trial, and no doubt, the Allies would have demonstrated good faith by cleaning their own houses. But Belgium was a unique test case. Belgium had entered the war because of invasion, and, unlike France, had harbored no wishes to recapture lost provinces. Nothing that Belgium or the Entente had done remotely resembled the fifty-two months of Belgian torture, and though France had undergone the same or worse afflictions, Belgian neutrality aggravated the case. Some Germans seemed to sense that a reckoning was due. C. E. Montague, a British officer who participated in the postwar occupation of Cologne, wrote that "German civilians clearly expected some kind of maltreatment, such perhaps as their own scum had given to the Belgians. They strove with desperate care to be correct in their bearing, neither to jostle us accidentally in the streets nor to shrink away from us pointedly." To their surprise and shame, Montague said, they found that the English behaved better than they had.[26]

But above all, Belgium had represented Britain's stake in the war and the victors' claim to have fought for justice. Proving the facts of the occupation would have restated the case, perhaps more eloquently than anything else could have done. In February 1920, a French writer asked for this pledge to be renewed, and though he concerned himself mostly with the crimes against France and the kaiser's role in them, his remarks fit Belgium too. People had fought for justice, he said, not to destroy imperial rivals, and "for our soldiers and common people even more than for our statesmen, this was a war essentially different from any other." He wanted the Germans' "peculiar law of war" to be discredited and to show that ideals of justice had meant "something more than oratorical phrases."[27]

Instead, Allied silence gave the skeptics room to challenge the prosecutions, and the fixation with the invasion terror that had served wartime propagandists now aided their critics. During the Leipzig trials, the *Manchester Guardian* ran an editorial about the *White Book,* just published in English for the first time, an oddity that the paper found suspicious. Wondering why the wartime government had forbidden its translation, the *Guardian* found the answer in the text, which allegedly revealed that "there seems to have been little murder or arson by troops simply out on the loose." The paper conceded that "the old Germany's early record in Belgium was bad" but said that Britain had no right to complain, because German behavior in Belgium compared favorably with British brutalities in India and Ireland.[28]

To ascribe permissiveness toward criminal behavior to the "old Germany" was ironic; the day that this comment appeared, the Reichsgericht acquitted Karl Neumann of sinking a hospital ship. Moreover, to reproach Germany's "early record" evoked the typical misperception of Belgium, and the paper further downplayed the invasion terror by accepting that francs-tireurs had provoked the invaders. Holding Britain responsible for oppressing the occupied peoples of India and Ireland was a worthy point, but even if Britain had no right to bring charges, Belgium surely did.

Even Claud Mullins, who said he had "no reason to be tender towards Germany" and "no patience with those who fail to realise the reality of hatred," struggled with the morality of trials.[29] He surmised that the Reichsgericht had admitted more British evidence than French or Belgian because the British witnesses, "however great their sufferings . . . showed no sign of malice or bias."[30] He had not seen the other trials, but he guessed that anger had emerged because of "national temperament" and because France and Belgium had suffered more directly than Britain. Outrage was natural but might have insulted the court, whereas the British had succeeded because of "their ability to get free from any idea of revenge."[31] Consequently, despite the light sentences, the trials had taught the lesson from which "nations learn best the road back to civilisation and true progress," lessening the chances "that history should repeat itself."[32]

We know now what Mullins did not, that history did repeat itself, and that Belgium presaged a later, more rapacious, occupation. Even so, from the information he possessed, he might have asked whether Leipzig had taught anything. He had watched the Reichsgericht embrace necessity while avoiding discussion of wartime policies, and he had seen the German public react when their heroes were accused. How strange too that Mullins could accept legal proceedings that allowed judges to vent their prejudices but denied that privilege to witnesses. The German reaction might have been expected, but not the way in which much British and American opinion deplored the trials and worried that the desire to punish would redound on the victors.

Six months after Leipzig, an American jurist thought it better that "the monstrous war crimes of Germany should go unpunished" than "that further seeds of hatred between the nations should be sown."[33] A British author who disputed the *White Book* and the translator's favorable assessment of it nevertheless remarked, "No good purpose is served by deliberately dragging to the front hideous memories that are receding into the background of our minds." He hoped that the Germans were learning to examine the terror "in which, at the outset of the war, they openly gloried."[34]

An American jurist called the treaty's criminal articles "a reprisal pure and simple," an "act of political hate" comparable to those of the medieval era.[35] "Far better to let a guilty man escape through national sentiment than that an enemy should be unfairly tried by a court with mind perverted by patriotic war-time propaganda," he wrote.[36] In a later article, he said that trials discriminated against the individual soldier, "whose nerves were on edge, who was in the midst of excitement, who scarcely knew what he was doing," or thought that superior orders justified him, or that he must obey.[37] Evidence of routine, premeditated crimes would have answered such arguments.

With the worry about German hatred, the Belgians were supposed to swallow theirs. A school textbook published in Brussels in 1919 described German crimes, particularly the invasion terror and the deportations, and urged, "Never forget, children, never forget what you have seen, what you have heard recounted."[38] The book advised waiting to see whether Germany was deemed fit to join the League of Nations, and whether Germans chose leaders who kept their promises. Only then, "*without ever forgetting,* you can cease hating, because hate is a sad thing. When the German people have become sincere, they will detest their crime, and they may be pardoned."[39]

The essence of this brutally frank statement was not new. In 1915, Mercier had written, "How do you think that we could obtain a sincere word of [Belgian] resignation and of pardon . . . as long as those, who have made them suffer, refuse to admit it, or to utter a word of regret, or a promise of reparation?"[40]

The Germans showed that they were not about to regret or admit anything. In late June 1921, a Reichstag committee looking into war guilt reassessed *Usages of War* and acknowledged that the author, one Major (later Lieutenant General) von Friedrich, had displayed "virtually complete ignorance" of The Hague Conventions. The committee ruled that he had never heard of them, an assertion that failed to account for his having referred to them.[41] *Usages of War* was not an official service publication, having been intended only to create "a stimulating effect on the officer corps." But because Germany's enemies had used it to make "false judgments" that had "rabble-rousing" implications, Friedrich might have taken care to avoid this injury to army and country.

Six years later, the Reichstag committee published reports on the outbreak and conduct of the war. One, titled *The Belgian People's War,* reaffirmed the *White Book* and quoted the British translator's observations about the psychological frailties of people who credited atrocity stories.[42] The study also cited Reichsgericht hearings that confirmed the official version that francs-tireurs were entirely responsible for Aerschot, Andenne, Dinant, and Louvain[43] and repeated several of the *White Book*'s more outlandish assertions.[44] "Belgium was a victim of its geographical situation and its deficient organization, not German cruelty," the report decided.[45] Some Germans, notably Social Democrats, did not entirely go along. Having read Belgian pamphlets about Louvain and Dinant—which the German postal ministry tried to ban— they accepted that the army had suffered from a "collective hallucination" at those two places.[46] But in the main, *The Belgian People's War* held sway in Germany.

Another report, delicately titled *The Forced Transport of Belgian Workers to Germany,* echoed the wartime claims about the deportations.[47] For the first and only time, however, a minority on the panel filed a dissent. The brief charged that the Supreme Command, urged by industrialists, had devised the deportations not to keep order but to obtain labor for military purposes. These authorities had known that they risked violating international law; Bissing had told them so. Further, where the majority opinion ascribed the deportees' agonies to Belgian stubbornness or difficulties beyond German control, the dissenters blamed poor planning and said that the policy could not justify the practices.[48] To have said this in print took some courage because Hindenburg was now president of the Weimar Republic, and his complicity could not be denied. But the minority stopped short of calling the deportations a war crime, admitting neither the illegality nor the brutal coercion.

These two reports, and a third that discussed the neutrality violation, upset the Belgian government, which replied with sharp protests and its own, shorter, parliamentary papers.[49] However, the Germans had also proposed to submit the franc-tireur controversy to an international inquiry, and, though most of the Belgian cabinet opposed this, Vandervelde, now minister of foreign affairs, accepted without consulting anyone.[50] The naysayers, led by Premier Henri Jaspar and Hymans, minister of justice, warned that permitting the investigation would reopen feuds better left to die out in the spirit of Locarno.[51] Hymans also predicted that a neutral commission would bow to German influence, and that the Germans would dig up witnesses who would swear they had seen Belgian francs-tireurs.[52]

When the Belgian government declined to cooperate, critics like C. Hartley Grattan, an American who wrote a book titled *Why We Fought*, asked why the Belgians would refuse an "impartial investigation" and implied that they had something to hide.[53] But when informal word reached Brussels that in the United States, publications sympathetic to Germany had made people wonder whether the Belgians had exaggerated the crimes, Vandervelde rejected the idea of a pamphlet campaign. "Are we going to continue ten years after the war to direct Belgian propaganda toward German 'atrocities,'" he asked, "whereas since then we have signed the Locarno accords?"[54]

The controversy brought propaganda to the fore, and critics, often to argue for treaty revision, asserted that war crimes accusations libeled Germany. A main figure in this effort was a small unit of the German Foreign Office, the Kriegsschuldreferat (War Guilt Department), which monitored German publications about the causes and conduct of the war. The department successfully lobbied the Reichstag committee to alter its reports, tried to prevent the release of compromising diplomatic documents, and attempted to suppress the work of an author who analyzed Germany's responsibility for the war.[55] During the 1920s, the Kriegsschuldreferat also subsidized German and foreign authors who included war crimes in their brief to discredit the treaty on various grounds. They, and others who published without German help, created a large, growing body of protest writings.

The invasion terror came in for scrutiny, and deservedly so, but the appraisals could have been more forthright. One popular American author, for instance, dismissed the fables about handless babies and crucifixions without mentioning the real terrors that had taken place.[56] A British writer implied that the Entente had provoked "Belgian resistance which prevented Germany from behaving in a more exemplary way."[57] She added that "if the Belgian atrocities had not happened it would have been necessary to invent them."[58] A French author discounted all talk of terror because whereas "no one had ever proven that the Germans had cut off Belgian children's hands," Leopold II's colonial officials had cut off the hands of their Congolese subjects.[59] Arthur Ponsonby, a former member of Parliament, wrote that anyone would "deeply resent having his passions roused, his indignation inflamed, his patriotism exploited, and his highest ideals desecrated" by lies and trickery.[60] But Ponsonby himself skirted the truth. To ridicule propaganda about Louvain, he said that only one-eighth of the city had burned, but he did not explain how the fires started.[61] Other writers insisted that the facts remained too obscure to permit a verdict, like Grattan, who said that "any candid student must admit that no final judgment can be given" about Louvain.[62] Similarly, he said that though the deportations were a "tactical blunder," whether they were "legally and morally wrong is debatable."[63]

The carping over how much of Louvain had burned illustrated how far the debate had strayed from the legal and moral issues that Belgium represented. Few critics emulated Montague, whose memoir, *Disenchantment*, recognized both the crimes and the way governments had used them to manipulate the public. Yes, Montague said, the Germans had done terrible things and offered lame excuses that had made their enemies despise them even more. But the propagandists had gone too far, trying "to make out that the average German soldier . . . was one of the monsters who hang about the gates of Vergil's Hell."[64] Montague told an anecdote about an infamous British lie of 1917, that the Germans had built a factory near Liège to make soap from soldiers' corpses. In 1918, his unit had stumbled on the alleged "factory," and when his men saw nothing to corroborate the story, one said, "Can't believe a word you read, sir, can you?"[65]

■

The invasion terror plagued Belgian politics into the 1930s. In 1927, the government asked Dinant not to refer to "German barbarism" and "Teutonic fury" in memorials the city was designing, because German nationalist veterans' associations were demanding that Berlin protest. The Dinantais agreed to choose a different inscription. But later, they changed their minds, and in 1933, pressure from Germany made Albert and de Broqueville (back in power), try to get them to relent. Instead, they denounced the government, and the quarrel grew to such a pitch that fund-raising fell off, so that the monument, dedicated in August 1936, was smaller than first planned.[66] That was not all: In 1932, Dinant and Aerschot sued Baedeker's, the Leipzig-based tourist-guide publisher, whose then-current edition blamed Belgian civilians for the massacres there. A Brussels court ruled for the plaintiffs in 1934, but the Belgian government, mindful of German sensibilities, pushed for compromise. The two towns accepted wording that would say the events were under dispute; Baedeker's revised its guidebook and promised to be more careful; and the German government paid the legal costs.[67]

At Louvain in 1928, an inscription similar to Dinant's caused another dispute. When a balustrade went up without the offending quote, a Belgian foreman who had been wounded and deported by the Germans as a fifteen-year-old smashed it. On his arrest, he said, "We aren't all Boches in Louvain yet," implying that he stood out from his fellow townspeople in his refusal to adhere to German wishes.[68] After the structure was rebuilt, another worker destroyed it, saying, "It's Hitler's balustrade."[69] Hitler was unmoved. He said that "the honor of the German Army cannot be soiled by our enemies' attacks. Nor can provocative monuments and inscriptions undermine it."[70]

By the time Europe went to war again, the assumption that nobody should believe atrocity reports had taken hold. In October 1939, seven weeks after Hitler invaded Poland, the American Institute of Public Opinion asked, "Why do you think we entered the last war?" The most popular answer, with 37 percent of the total responses, was "America was the victim of propaganda and selfish interests." Only 26 percent believed that "America had a just and unselfish cause."[71] Also in October 1939, a book alleging that British propaganda had dragged the United States into war had just gone into its third printing in five months. The author maintained that Britain had fabricated or grossly exaggerated the crimes against Belgium, particularly in the

Bryce report, which had fobbed off "the usual barbarous aspects of war" as atrocities.[72] Even the CRB "served to spread the propaganda of the Allies" while making money for American merchants and "enlist[ed] the sympathies of all those Americans who contributed."[73]

"One of the most successful of the propaganda attacks" concerned the deportations, which were "not unprecedented" and which, the author suggested, were reasonable given the German mistrust of a hostile population.[74] He said that the policy counteracted food shortages worsened by the blockade, but he did not mention the tortures the Belgians endured or the kind of work they were forced to do. Likewise, another book that appeared in 1941 could say that the deportations were "exaggerated in propagandistic exploitation." The author wrote that the Belgian workers suffered in the "forcible ejection . . . from their homes," but that the deportations amounted to an atrocity "only by a very loose and almost metaphorical use of the term."[75]

Shortly after the United States entered the war, American journalists temporarily interned in Germany discussed how they would treat German attitudes and the direction that Allied propaganda should take. One correspondent wanted evidence of atrocities to be so convincing that no one would question them, and added, "I believe it would be better to ignore the atrocity idea" because of how "it became quite discredited" during the previous war.[76]

The general public shared his skepticism, for people remembered stories about the invasion terror, which fueled doubts about the Holocaust.[77] Paul Fussell has written, "No one can calculate the number of Jews who died . . . because of the ridicule during the twenties and thirties of Allied propaganda about Belgian nuns violated and children sadistically used."[78] Propaganda Minister Joseph Goebbels waved away accusations of mass murder by reminding Germans how their enemies had lied during the First World War.[79] Helmuth von Moltke of the German resistance (and the former chief of staff's son) wrote that he could not have persuaded 90 percent of the German populace that the extermination was real. He said people would reply, "You are just a victim of British propaganda, remember what ridiculous things they said about our behaviour in Belgium in 1914/18."[80] The Liège "corpse factory" had a notable legacy, leading even a senior British intelligence official, who conceded that Germany was annihilating Jews, to dismiss accounts of gas chambers.[81] The connection between Belgium and the Holocaust came full circle during the invasion of Lithuania in June 1941, when, as death squads murdered Jews by the thousands, German propaganda accused "Jewish delinquents" of sniping at German troops.[82]

The questions remain whether the victors of 1919 could have handled the crimes against Belgium astutely and decisively, and whether they could have realized why they should bother, given the information they possessed. Allied leaders at the peace conference thought of Belgium as a pretentious nuisance, but Allied self-interest and the moral principles that Belgium stood for ran along parallel lines. The Allies had said ever since 1914 that Germany had threatened the world order, but the war's survivors wanted proof, and Belgium offered it. Had the Belgians been shrewder diplomats, they would have pointed this out rather than count on Allied sympathy and honor.

The reparations settlement was an opportunity for the Allies to show that they remembered their ideals. For instance, Keynes suggested that Britain should have ceded cash reparations in favor of Belgium, France, and Serbia, estimating that $7.5 billion would cover "material injury" from actual invasion.[83] The figure may have been low, and, oddly, he ranked Belgium third in merit behind Serbia, which had a poor reputation in the West. Even so, Keynes's idea is intriguing. Setting a modest, fixed sum would have announced that aggression would be punished but avoided provocative talk of war guilt. Moreover, rewarding the Belgians for having resisted invasion was only practical if Germany attacked again, as Clemenceau assumed it would.

Lloyd George said that the voters would turn him out of office if he disappointed them on reparations, but it is not clear they would have wanted the money at Belgium's expense. Still, forbearance was politically risky, and anyhow, the Germans might not have accepted even a modest bill for reparations. Brockdorff-Rantzau's instructions to the German peace delegation read more like a conqueror's dictation to a beaten opponent than contrition or an honest attempt to arrive at a just bargain. Dresel reported the widespread belief that peace should cause Germany no pain, and in keeping with this, the postwar government made only token efforts to raise revenue through tax reform and left loopholes that permitted evasion.[84]

But if the Germans had refused to pay even for invasion damage, that would have undermined their campaign to portray themselves as victims. Their unwillingness to cooperate would have belied their insistence that they would meet any reasonable demands, which would have made Germany, not the Allies, look like a selfish hypocrite. German intransigence would have underlined Allied charges of bad faith, suggesting that Germany was indeed a rogue nation, and that the treaty need not be revised.

Alternatively, the victors might have had less trouble exacting reparations had they invaded in 1918 rather than tender an armistice. After all, when the Germans occupied a swath of France in 1871 to guarantee their indemnity under the Treaty of Frankfurt, the French rushed to pay, and public loans for that purpose were oversubscribed.[85] The Treaty of Versailles worked in reverse, using the threat of further occupation as collateral, and as the French learned in the Ruhr, this tactic carried political drawbacks. But aside from an invasion's impact on reparations, the Germans did not appreciate the extent of their military defeat, and carrying the war to German soil would have made that explicit. Carton de Wiart wrote that in December 1918, Albert told him that the armistice had come too quickly for Germany to know the feeling of being beaten—this, from a man who had tried for years to negotiate peace.[86] Further, when the Allies offered an armistice, neither they nor the Germans realized that the German military was near collapse, and that a final campaign would likely have lasted only weeks.[87]

Invading Germany would have also smoothed the way for war crimes trials, by displaying the victors' commanding power and permitting them to arrest the criminals themselves, right away, before German opposition gathered and extradition became a sore point. But the problems with prosecution began in August 1914. Belgium should never have hurried to publish dubious atrocity reports, Britain should never have embroidered them, and both should have abandoned them to concentrate on the occupation's danger to democratic ideals. Calling the Germans barbarians camouflaged their barbarities and shifted emphasis from what they had done to who they were, which inevitably rang hollow later. To stress rape and mutilation compounded the error and changed what should have been a legal debate into a question of whether the invaders had respected women and children, as if manliness had been the issue, not justice.

The victors could have overcome these blunders had they tried to prove German crimes in court, but the governments resisted the clamor for trials until 1916, and then failed to act resolutely or in concert. Once the Fryatt case had pushed Asquith to declare himself, he let the matter drop, and Lloyd George's government did likewise. Since 1914, jurists had been saying that trials required thought and preparation, and the French and Belgians had at least gathered evidence. Yet only in October 1918 did Lloyd George form his committee. Only on 7 November, the day before the German delegation crossed Allied lines to receive the armistice, did Smith announce what his panel was doing.

All the victors share blame for failing to press the issue, but Wilson's attitude toward the war—not just war crimes—is particularly suspect. His war message of 2 April 1917 condemned German force but said nothing about its use except to criticize submarine warfare. Not a word did he utter about Belgian neutrality or the occupation; he did not mention Belgium except in the context of U-boats sinking CRB ships. Nor did he speak of the Allies or suggest that they had been fighting for nearly three years to uphold the principles he was talking about.

The president had little wiggle room with the isolationists, but he had done nothing to prepare them or the public for the prospect of war. His neutrality policy had tried to forestall talk about individual belligerents, a dialogue that might have served his purposes while leading opinion toward the idea of having to intervene if necessary. As a result, less than four months after his December 1916 peace initiative said that Germany and the Allies were fighting for the same goals, Wilson had to go before the nation and say otherwise. Having always construed the German menace as a question of American interests, he now had to weave submarine sinkings into a brief for global freedom, which was stretching a point. If the United States stood for making the world safe for democracy, declaring war in autumn 1916 would have shown more moral sense. The deportations had been an urgent call to arms, and Wilson bears much responsibility for the country's deafness to it, as a political and moral theorist and as a chief executive.

Not that the Allied approach to trials was sound. Charging the kaiser with having started the war was equivalent to writing Germany's guilt into the treaty, and further, nothing could be proved against him without cross-examining hostile witnesses formerly from his inner circle. The other criminal articles should perhaps be judged more leniently as the first attempt to institute war crimes trials en masse, but the procedures were flawed. Separating prosecutions by nationality undermined the plea that the community of nations was determined to uphold the law because an injury to one was an injury to all. To allow each nation to proceed alone implied that the trials were more political than judicial, which invited the Germans to play one former enemy against another.

In the end, the Allies pursued contradictory goals—to punish an aggressive enemy while trying to placate it—and achieved neither. Expediency was understandable, but, as Millerand said during the discussions over the Leipzig plan, more than anything, the Allies had to verify the truth. By debunking the German claim to innocence, they would have redeemed their word and kept faith with those who had sacrificed. Neither side could pretend to righteousness at Ypres, Verdun, or the Somme, but the victors did not have to prove that they were better than the Germans or without sin. They had to prove only that German warmaking had ventured into a realm in which a suspicious, irresponsible arrogance could sweep aside any known law or custom, of which Belgium supplied the plainest example. Instead, there was Leipzig.

Armed with the truth, the world could have reacted differently to Nazi crimes and moved more quickly to stop them. Occupied Europe, if not Nazi Germany before 1939, would have seemed like the re-creation of known terrors on a grander scale instead of something entirely new or too fantastic to believe. With proper knowledge about Belgium, the most an honest skeptic could have said in 1941 or 1942 was that some German crimes of 1914–18 had been exaggerated, but that many had not, and that perhaps the rule applied again. Either way, more eyes would have been opened sooner, strengthening the motive to act.

Whether arraigning German officers in 1919 would have itself deterred future crimes is hard to say because generals usually expect to win their wars, which makes prosecution moot, and when their methods turn criminal, they seldom admit it. But if establishing a standard saves just one town from being razed, that is worthwhile. Even Leipzig set a precedent, because in 1945, at least one legal writer rebutted the defense of superior orders by citing the conviction in the *Llandovery Castle* case.[88]

But the number of criminals the victors could have punished in 1919 was less important than challenging necessity, a pernicious doctrine that the German Army had cited since 1871 and that had survived the war intact. The world had to know the truth in case Germany rode to battle again because if she did, necessity was likely to ride with her. And the truth mattered because it was the truth, the only antidote to the delusions that the German Army had held about itself, and which had led to the charge that the Belgians were the deluded ones. The Belgians deserved to have the record set straight, to bear witness, to be heard. That is the least the powers could have provided after they had failed to prevent a war in which Belgium was sure to be invaded, then arrived almost too late to repel the attack.

For its part, America was guilty of silence if not worse, despite the Commission for Relief in Belgium. Wilson, Lansing, and Scott had worked to deny the victims their day in court, and ever since, the United States has repeatedly hesitated to use its power or influence against violators, even to support an international tribunal. It is as if Americans believe that lawlessness cannot cross the oceans that protect the United States. Perhaps 11 September will persuade us otherwise.

After the peace conference, the desire to resume friendly relations prompted calls to forgive Germany's wrongs, or at least to cease dwelling on them. Concerning crimes against Belgium, this judgment was the Belgians' to make. Yet since 1920, Britain had been pushing France and Belgium to forsake the criminal articles, and at Leipzig, behaved as if the only verdicts that counted involved British cases. In effect, Britain had decided for everyone that war crimes must be forgotten, a symptom of how a great power sees a world war as a contest between itself and a single antagonist. Treaty revisionists in Germany made the same mistake. Max Montgelas, who had signed the Heidelberg intellectuals' resolution and represented Germany at Versailles, wrote in 1925 that though Germany did wrong by invading Belgium, that did "not give the other Powers any right to sit in judgment on her."[89] But he had overlooked Belgium, which had that right.

The pressure to forgive puts an injured nation in a bind. Chaim Herzog addressed this dilemma in 1987 when he became the first president of Israel to visit Germany, a gesture of goodwill. His itinerary included Bergen-Belsen, the site of a concentration camp he had seen as a British Army officer in 1945, shortly after its liberation. Forty-two years later, he said, "I do not bring forgiveness with me, nor forgetfulness. The only ones who can forgive are dead; the living have no right to forget."[90]

Notes

NOTES TO CHAPTER 1: YOUR NEIGHBOR'S ROOF

1. *Le Soir,* 30 July 1914, 3.

2. *XXe Siècle,* 1 Aug. 1914, 3.

3. *L'Étoile Belge,* 1 Aug. 1914, 3.

4. Pirenne, *Belgique,* 46; *Le Soir,* 1 Aug. 1914, 3.

5. Schmitz and Nieuwland, *L'Histoire de l'invasion* 1:4, 6.

6. Davis, *With the Allies,* 9.

7. Georges Rency, *La Belgique et la guerre* (Brussels, 1920), 1:17. Vierset, *Mes souvenirs,* 2.

8. Lichtervelde, *Avant l'orage,* 150.

9. Ponchelet, 1–3 Aug. 1914, Archives Privées (hereafter AP), no. 37:4.

10. Rency, *Belgique et la guerre,* 15.

11. Godenne journal, 1 Aug. 1914, AP, no. 1:1.

12. For a genealogy, see Jacques Willequet, *Albert Ier, roi des belges: un portrait politique et humain* (Paris, 1979), 8.

13. Thielemans and Vandewoude, *Roi Albert,* 503.

14. Quoted in (hereafter Q.) Cammaerts, *Albert of Belgium,* 405–6.

15. Gibson to mother, 26 Oct. 1914, Gibson Papers, box 32.

16. Marks, *Innocent Abroad,* 6–9; Alberic Rolin, *Le droit moderne de la guerre* (Brussels, 1921), 3:30–32.

17. Q. David Hunter Miller, *My Diary at the Conference of Paris, with Documents* (New York, 1925), 10:254.

18. Albert Duchesnes, "L'Armée et la politique militaire belges de 1871 à 1879, jugées par les attachés militaires de France à Bruxelles," *Revue belge de philologie et d'histoire* 39, no. 4 (1961): 1121.

19. Bitsch, *Entre la France et l'Allemagne,* 392, 406–8. See Miller, *My Diary,* 246–82, for a mid-1880s memo about future war.

20. Davignon, *Souvenirs d'un écrivain,* 212.

21. Poncelet, *In Years Gone By,* 26.

22. Crokaert, "L'Ultimatum allemand," 319; Raymond Recouly, "Les heures tragiques de l'avant-guerre," *Revue de France* 1, no. 4 (Sep.–Oct. 1921): 37; Vierset, *Mes souvenirs,* 4.

23. *Le Soir,* 3 Aug. 1914, 1. Below-Saleske's remarks were reprinted the day after.

24. Recouly, "Heures tragiques," 34.

25. Marks, *Innocent Abroad*, 31.

26. Lichtervelde, *Avant l'orage*, 152.

27. Crokaert, "L'Ultimatum allemand," 308; Hymans, *Mémoires* 1:84–85.

28. Rency, *Belgique et la guerre*, 21.

29. Crokaert, "L'Ultimatum allemand," 325.

30. Ibid., 309.

31. Davignon, *Souvenirs d'un écrivain*, 217.

32. Gibson, *Journal from Our Legation*, 9.

33. Recouly, "Heures tragiques," 35.

34. Crokaert, "L'Ultimatum allemand," 313.

35. Gibson to mother, 27 Aug. 1914, Gibson Papers, box 31.

36. De Bassompierre, *Night of August 2–3*, 26.

37. Great Britain, *Collected Diplomatic Documents Relating to the Outbreak of the European War: The Belgian Grey Book* (London, 1915), 309–11.

38. Lichtervelde, *Avant l'orage*, 167.

39. Crokaert, "L'Ultimatum allemand," 316.

40. Except as noted, this account comes from Papiers Schollaert-Helleputte, 124. For a different reading of them, see Marie-Rose Thielemans and Emile Vandewoude, "Les conseils des ministres et de la Couronne du 2 août 1914," *Acta Historica Bruxellensia 4, Histoire et Méthode* (1981): 417–44.

41. Luigi Albertini, *The Origins of the War of 1914*, trans., ed., Isabella M. Massey (London, 1957), 3:439; Thielemans and Vandewoude, *Roi Albert*, 495.

42. Hymans, *Mémoires* 1:80.

43. Ibid., 84.

44. Carton de Wiart, *Souvenirs politiques* 1:207.

45. See Higgins, *Hague Peace Conferences*, 282, for the Fifth Hague Convention, Article 10.

46. Great Britain, *Belgian Grey Book*, 312.

47. Lichtervelde, *Avant l'orage*, 169.

48. Q. Thielemans and Vandewoude, *Roi Albert*, 67.

49. Lichtervelde, *Avant l'orage*, 169.

50. De Bassompierre, *Night of 2–3 August*, 33; see also Lichtervelde, *Avant l'orage*, 170.

51. Vierset, *Mes souvenirs*, 5.

52. Q. Cammaerts, *Albert of Belgium*, 19.

53. *Times* of London, 4 Aug. 1914, 6.

54. Napoléon Eugène Beyens, *Deux années à Berlin* (Paris, 1931), 2:272.

55. *Le Soir*, 4 Aug. 1914, 1.

56. Lichtervelde, *Avant l'orage*, 196; Vierset, *Mes souvenirs*, 7.

57. Davignon, *Souvenirs d'un écrivain*, 225.

58. Whitlock, *Belgium*, 59–61; Whitlock, *Journal*, 10–11.

59. Lichtervelde, *Avant l'orage*, 197; Vierset, *Mes souvenirs*, 7.

60. Gibson, *Journal from Our Legation*, 22.

61. Jarausch, *Enigmatic Chancellor*, 179; Luckau, *German Delegation*, 282.

62. Jarausch, *Enigmatic Chancellor*, 176.

63. Whitlock, *Journal*, 14.

NOTES TO CHAPTER 2: MARCHING THROUGH HELL

1. Belgium, *Rapports et documents* 1, t. 1:17–18, 317, 329.

2. Q. *New York American*, 22 Sep. 1914, 3; *New York Times*, 7 Aug. 1914, 2; *San Francisco Chronicle*, 6 Aug. 1914, 2; *Times* of London, 6 Aug. 1914, 6.

3. Horne and Kramer, *German Atrocities*, 13, 77.

4. German Ministry of War, *The German Army in Belgium*, 58–59 (hereafter *White Book*).

5. De Thier and Gilbart, *Liège* 2:92, Belgium, *Rapports et documents* 1, t. 1:52; Belgium, *Réponse au livre blanc*, 123.

6. Lemaire journal, 7 Aug. 1914, AP, no. 27, 1:19.

7. Gibson to mother, 5 Aug. 1914, Gibson Papers, box 31.

8. Ibid., 7 Aug. 1914.

9. Ibid.

10. Diederich to Bryan, 26 Aug. 1914, U.S. Department of State, *Foreign Relations, 1914 Supplement*, 793 (hereafter *Foreign Relations*).

11. Mokveld, *German Fury*, 34, 36.

12. Bloem, *Advance from Mons*, 27.

13. Ibid., 29.

14. Whitlock, *Journal*, 23.

15. *Le Soir*, 7 Aug. 1914, 1.

16. *L'Étoile Belge*, 8 Aug. 1914, 1; *Le Soir*, 9 Aug. 1914, 1.

17. *Le Soir*, 8 Aug. 1914, 1.

18. Horne and Kramer, *German Atrocities*, 13.

19. *Le Soir*, 10 Aug. 1914, 1; Davignon, *Souvenirs d'un écrivain*, 226.

20. Vierset, *Mes souvenirs*, 15.

21. Barbara Tuchman, *The Guns of August* (New York, 1962), 219.

22. Michel Vanderschaeghe, *Stavelot*, 36.

23. Schmitz and Nieuwland, *L'Histoire de l'invasion* 1:25.

24. Davis, *With the Allies*, 42–44.

25. *Kölnische Volkszeitung*, 15 Aug. 1914, 1.

26. Höcker, *An der Spitze*, 34–35.

27. Belgium, *Rapports et documents* 1, t. 1:18.

28. Edmonds, *Military Operations* 1:34, 35n.

29. Davis, *With the Allies*, 17.

30. Ibid., 18–20; Gibson to mother, 20 Aug. 1914, Gibson Papers, box 31.

31. Davis, *With the Allies*, 23–24, 27–29.

32. Gibson to mother, 20 Aug. 1914, Gibson Papers, box 31.

33. Belgium, *Rapports et documents*, 4:96.

34. Riezler, *Tagebücher*, 199.

35. Belgium, *Rapports et documents*, 4:143.

36. Horne and Kramer, *German Atrocities*, 77.

37. Belgium, *Rapports et documents*, 1, t. 2:37–49.

38. Ibid., t. 1:97–109.

39. Ibid., 143–45.

40. Ibid., 151–53.

41. Davis, *With the Allies*, 87–88; Theodore Wesley Koch, *The University of Louvain and Its Library* (London 1917), 15, 17, 18; *New York Times*, 4 Oct. 1914, sec. 4:9

42. Mayence, *Legend*, 36; Belgium, *Rapports et documents* 1, t. 2:396.

43. L. H. Grondys, *The Germans in Belgium, Experiences of a Neutral* (London, 1915), 6.

44. *White Book*, 207.

45. Edmonds, *Military Operations* 1:132–33.

46. Belgium, *Rapports et documents* 1, t. 2:62–118; 393–518.

47. Davis, *With the Allies*, 87.

48. Belgium, *Rapports et documents* 1, t. 2:70.

49. Ibid., 75.

50. Ibid., 418–21.

51. Ibid., 103.

52. Ibid., 422.

53. Ibid., 398, 500.

54. Ibid., 444, 478.

55. Gibson to mother, 29 Aug. 1914, Gibson Papers, box 31.

56. Ibid.

57. Belgium, *Rapports et documents* 1, t. 2:398, 402.

58. *White Book*, 193.

59. Ibid., 193–94.

60. Ibid., 197.

61. Ibid., 197, 202.

62. Ibid., 194, 196.

63. Ibid., 195.

64. Ibid., 196.

65. Ibid., 195, 232.

66. Ibid., 196.

67. Ibid., 223, 255.

68. Ibid., 274.

69. Ibid., 215, 223, 226, 227, 228, 229.

70. Ibid., 200, 207, 225, 227, 281.
71. Ibid., 212.
72. Ibid., 201, 206, 223, 230, 236, 240, 250, 275.
73. Ibid., 206, 232, 253.
74. Ibid., 275–76.
75. Ibid., 201, 203, 260.
76. Ibid., 203.
77. Ibid., 248.
78. Ibid., 244, 261, 267, 273.
79. Belgium, *Rapports et documents* 1, t. 2: 103; Marc Derez, "The Flames of Louvain: The War Experience of an Academic Community," in Hugh Cecil and Peter Liddle, eds., *Facing Armageddon: The First World War Experienced* (London, 1996), 618.
80. Belgium, *Rapports et documents* 1, t. 2: 464, 465, 506, 517.
81. Gibson to mother, 29 Aug. 1914, Gibson Papers, box 31.
82. Gille, Ooms, and Delandsheere, *Cinquante mois* 1:30.
83. Belgium, *Rapports et documents* 1, t. 2, 118.
84. In assessing Louvain's impact, Wolfgang Schivelbusch has disputed the traditional belief that Arab soldiers burned the library at Alexandria in 641. He writes that a Christian army did so in 391, almost two centuries before Muhammad's birth. Wolfgang Schivelbusch, *Die Bibliothek von Löwen* (Munich, 1988), 9–10.
85. Belgium, *Rapports et documents* 1, t. 2:118, 473, 490.
86. Gille, Ooms, and Delandsheere, *Cinquante mois* 1:30–31.
87. Whitlock, *Belgium,* 159–60.

NOTES TO CHAPTER 3: THE GHOST OF 1870

1. Ritter, *Schlieffen Plan,* 19–22.
2. Ibid., 46–48.
3. Bucholz, *Moltke, Schlieffen,* 120, 122, 131.
4. Ibid., 146.
5. Ritter, *Schlieffen Plan,* 136, 146.
6. O'Brien, "Military Necessity," 116.
7. Best, *Humanity in Warfare,* 172.
8. U.S. War Department, *Land Warfare,* 14 (hereafter *Land Warfare*).
9. Westlake, *International Law,* 117.
10. Q. Best, *Humanity in Warfare,* 175.
11. Jarausch, *Enigmatic Chancellor,* 175.
12. Ibid., 179; Luckau, *German Delegation,* 282.
13. Bitsch, *Entre la France et l'Allemagne,* 458, 461, 462.
14. Thielemans, *Albert Ier,* 52.

15. Q. Ritter, *Schlieffen Plan*, 173.

16. Hall, *Treatise*, 586–87.

17. Ibid., 594; see also Phillipson, *Wheaton's*, 640.

18. Hall, *Treatise*, 620–21.

19. Higgins, *Hague Peace Conferences*, 281–82.

20. German Ministry of War, *War Book*, 196–97 (hereafter *Usages of War*).

21. Jean Stengers, "Belgium," in Keith Wilson, ed., *Decisions for War, 1914* (New York, 1995), 159–60.

22. Bernhardi, *Germany and the Next War*, 32, 111.

23. Fischer, *World Power or Decline: The Controversy Over "Germany's Aims in the First World War,"* trans. Lancelot Farrar, Robert Kimber, and Rita Kimber (New York, 1974), 4.

24. Poster Collection, UK nos. 243, 244.

25. Theobald von Bethmann-Hollweg, *Reflections on the World War*, trans. George Young (London, 1920), 158n.

26. Michael Howard, *The Franco-Prussian War: The German Invasion of France, 1870–71* (New York, 1962), 252.

27. Q. ibid., 380.

28. Marks, *Innocent Abroad*, 31.

29. Pirenne, *Belgique*, 26.

30. Bitsch, *Entre la France et l'Allemagne*, 407.

31. *XXe Siècle*, 1 Aug. 1914, 1.

32. Bucholz, *Moltke, Schlieffen*, 211.

33. Bitsch, *Entre la France et l'Allemagne*, 87, 119; De Kerchove, *L'Industrie belge*, 20; Gay, *Public Relations* 2:316; Marks, *Innocent Abroad*, 12; Passelecq, *Déportation et travail*, 63; Pirenne, *Belgique*, 29; Thielemans, *Albert Ier*, 19.

34. Bitsch, *Entre la France et l'Allemagne*, 105.

35. B. R. Mitchell, *International Historical Statistics, Europe, 1750–1993*, 4th ed. (New York, 1998), 14.

36. Hymans, *Mémoires* 1:78.

37. Q. Theodor Wolff, *The Eve of 1914*, trans. E. W. Dickes (London, 1935), 469.

38. Whitlock, *Journal*, 494.

39. Pirenne, *Belgique*, 39.

40. See, e.g., Höcker, *An der Spitze*, 38.

41. *Le Soir*, 6 Aug. 1914, 2; Van Langenhove, *Growth of a Legend*, 128–29.

42. Horne and Kramer, *German Atrocities*, 149–51.

43. Q. ibid., 161–62.

44. *Usages of War*, 69, 70–72, 84.

45. Ibid., 149, 157.

46. Ibid., 77–78.

47. Ibid., 157.

48. Ibid., 158.

49. Ibid., 182.

50. Ibid., 152.

51. Ibid., 156.

52. O'Brien, "Military Necessity," 130; Westlake, *International Law,* 57. See Higgins, *Hague Peace Conferences,* 219, 221, 235, 237, 245, 247, 249.

53. Higgins, *Hague Peace Conferences,* 209, 211.

54. *Land Warfare,* 14.

55. Higgins, *Hague Peace Conferences,* 247.

56. Oppenheim, *International Law* 2:304.

57. *Land Warfare,* 23, 123–24.

58. Higgins, *Hague Peace Conferences,* 219.

59. Ibid., 245, 247, 249.

60. Bordwell, *Law of War,* 94; Graber, *Belligerent Occupation,* 211–212.

61. James W. Garner, *International Law and the World War* (London, 1920), 1:6–8; Horne and Kramer, *German Atrocities,* 149.

62. Estimates vary because the Germans deployed seven armies, the first four forming the right wing. But part of Fifth Army invaded southeastern Belgium, though the army as a whole belonged to the center. Reichsarchiv, *Der Weltkrieg* 1:229, Map 3.

63. Ritter, *Schlieffen Plan,* 136–46, 187–91.

64. Bucholz, *Moltke, Schlieffen,* 278.

65. Ibid., 158.

66. Pirenne, *Belgique,* 15.

67. Bucholz, *Moltke, Schlieffen,* 165.

68. Erich Ludendorff, *Ludendorff's Own Story: August 1914–November 1918* [n. trans.] (New York, 1919), 1:38–39.

69. Bucholz, *Moltke, Schlieffen,* 266.

70. Hew Strachan, *The First World War,* vol. 1, *To Arms* (London, 2001), 178.

71. Q. Van Langenhove, *Growth of a Legend,* 216.

72. *Kölnische Volkszeitung,* 7 Aug. 1914, 2; 8 Aug., 1; 9 Aug., 1; 10 Aug., 1; 14 Aug., 2.

73. *New York Times,* 20 Aug. 1914, 2.

74. Bloem, *Advance from Mons,* 20.

75. William Archer, "The Germans in Belgium," *Quarterly Review* 236, no. 468 (1921): 198.

76. Walter Bloem, *Volk wider Volk* (Leipzig, 1912), 327.

77. Bloem, *Advance from Mons,* 25.

78. Van Swygenhoven memoir, AP, no. 29:12; Belgium, *Rapports et documents* 1, t. 2:34; Whitlock, *Journal,* 264.

79. Schmitz and Nieuwland, *L'Histoire de l'invasion* 1:18, 4a:17–18.

80. Min journal, 21 Aug. 1914, AP, no. 34, 1:24.

81. Mokveld, *German Fury,* 93.

82. Fernand Heusghem, *Jeunesse 1914–1918: Souvenirs de l'Occupation* (Paris, 1938), 18.

83. Van Swygenhoven memoir, AP, no. 29:11; Belgium, *Rapports et documents* 1, t. 1:443; *White Book,* 43.

84. Belgium, *Rapports et documents* 1, t. 1:3, 4, 7.

85. Ibid., 432.

86. "The Belgians Under the German Occupation," Dec. 1918, 18, Angell Papers, box 3 (hereafter "The Belgians").

87. Höcker, *An der Spitze,* 30–31.

88. Van Langenhove, *Growth of a Legend,* 198.

89. *Hamburger Nachrichten,* reprinted *Täglicher Rundschau,* 15 Sep. 1914, "Vom Franktireurkrieg in Belgien," clipping in Marawske Collection, box 23, unnumbered folder.

90. Van Langenhove, *Growth of a Legend,* 201.

91. Horne and Kramer, *German Atrocities,* 123–24.

92. I have derived these figures from the *White Book* and from Belgium, *Rapports et documents* 1, t. 1:605–23; t. 2:679–704.

93. Horne and Kramer, *German Atrocities,* 75.

94. Pirenne, *Belgique,* 61.

95. Van Swygenhoven memoir, AP, no. 29:10.

96. Generalstab des Heeres, ed., *Der Handstreich gegen Lüttich vom 3. bis 7.* August 1914 (Berlin, 1939), 12.

97. See Schmitz and Nieuwland, *L'Histoire de l'invasion* 1: 42–47, for cases in Luxembourg that the Germans investigated.

98. Gibson, *Journal from Our Legation,* 196.

99. Whitlock, *Journal,* 51–52.

100. Van Swygenhoven memoir, AP, no. 29:11.

101. Petri and Schöller, "Franktireurproblems," q. 248; Belgium, *Rapports et documents* 1, t. 1:88–89.

102. Belgium, *Rapports et documents* 1, t. 2, 33.

103. Schöller, *Louvain et le Livre Blanc,* 38–40.

104. Mayence, *Legend,* 38.

105. Ibid., 30; Schöller, *Louvain et le Livre Blanc,* 20.

106. Mayence, *Legend,* 30.

107. *White Book,* 78, 90.

108. Mayence, *Legend,* 38.

109. Van Langenhove, *Growth of a Legend,* 11–12, 269; Belgium, *Réponse au livre blanc,* 76.

110. *White Book,* 83, 86, 89, 100; Reichsarchiv, *Der Weltkrieg,* 96.

111. Fernand Mayence, "The Blame for the Sack of Louvain," *Current History* (July 1928): 569.

112. *White Book,* 79, 87.

113. Schöller, *Louvain et le Livre Blanc,* 79.

114. Horne and Kramer, *German Atrocities,* 74; Schöller, *Louvain et le Livre Blanc,* 79.

115. *White Book,* 84.

116. Mayence, *Legend,* 29.

117. Passelecq, *Déportation et travail,* 5.

118. Schöller, *Louvain et le Livre Blanc,* 108–9.

119. See, e.g., Belgium, *Rapports et documents* 1, t. 2:467.

120. Ibid., 516.

121. *White Book,* 258.

122. Horne and Kramer, *German Atrocities,* 171–72.

123. Q. *Chicago Tribune,* 1 Sep. 1914, 1.

124. Blücher, *English Wife,* 117; Hans Peter Hanssen, *Diary of a Dying Empire,* trans. Oscar Osburn Winther, ed. Ralph H. Lutz, Mary Schofield, and O. O. Winther (Port Washington, NY, 1973), 55; Georg Alexander von Müller, *The Kaiser and His Court: The Diaries, Note Books and Letters of Admiral Georg Alexander von Müller, Chief of the Naval Cabinet, 1914–1918,* ed. Walter Görlitz (New York, 1964), 36.

125. Blücher, *English Wife,* 25; Hunt, *War Bread,* 167; Mokveld, *German Fury,* 47, 60–61; *New York Times* 16 Sep. 1914, 5; Pirenne, *Belgique,* 56; Paradise, 9 Dec. 1914, folder 5:3, Paradise Papers.

126. *White Book,* 192.

127. Schöller, *Louvain et le Livre Blanc,* 69.

128. Belgium, *Rapports et documents* 1, t. 2:456.

129. Gustave Somville, *The Road to Liège: The Path of Crime, August 1914,* trans. Bernard Miall (London, 1916), 78, 162, 193, 200, 205.

130. *White Book,* 245.

131. Petri and Schöller, "Franktireurproblems," 245–47; Schöller, *Louvain et le Livre Blanc,* 45–48.

132. Gibson to mother, 29 Aug. 1914, Gibson Papers, box 31.

133. Schöller, *Louvain et le Livre Blanc,* 98–99.

134. Min journal, 21 Aug., 5 Nov. 1914, AP, no. 34, 1:24, 36; Belgium, *Rapports et documents,* 1, t. 2:475.

135. Höcker, *An der Spitze,* 38.

136. Ibid., 31.

137. *White Book,* 276; "Das Strafgericht in Löwen," *Berliner Tageblatt,* 28 Aug. 1914, Marawske Collection, folder 2, box 23.

138. "Das Strafgericht"; see also Höcker, *An der Spitze,* 26.

139. Höcker, *An der Spitze,* 38, 52.

140. Helmut Otto and Karl Schmiedel, *Der Erste Weltkrieg: Dokumente* (Berlin, 1977), 84.

141. Horne and Kramer, *German Atrocities*, 44, 134.

142. Höcker, *An der Spitze*, 22.

143. Gibson to mother, 3 Sep. 1914, Gibson Papers, box 32.

144. Q. Gille, Ooms, and Delandsheere, *Cinquante mois* 1:452.

145. Montague, *Disenchantment*, 95.

NOTES TO CHAPTER 4: BELGIUM DOES NOT ASK FOR PITY

1. Belgian Delegates, *Case of Belgium*, 21–24; Gibson to mother, 27 Aug. 1914, Gibson Papers, box 31.

2. Q. Cammaerts, *Albert of Belgium*, 170.

3. *New York Times*, 22 Aug. 1914, 1; Tassier, *L'Entrée en guerre*, 54.

4. Gibson to mother, 27 Aug. 1914, Gibson Papers, box 31.

5. Tassier, *L'Entrée en guerre*, 42.

6. Thielemans and Vandewoude, *Roi Albert*, 521.

7. Q. *New York American*, 2 Sep. 1914, 2.

8. Carton de Wiart, *Souvenirs politiques* 1:230.

9. *New York Times*, 1 Sep. 1914, 2.

10. Tassier, *L'Entrée en guerre*, 53–54.

11. See *American Review of Reviews* 50, no. 4 (Oct. 1914): 397–98.

12. *Chicago Tribune*, 31 Aug. 1914, 2; *San Francisco Chronicle*, 31 Aug. 1914, 34; *Washington Post*, 1 Sep. 1914, 5.

13. Link, *Papers of Woodrow Wilson*, 30:332 (hereafter *Wilson Papers*).

14. Ibid., 342.

15. *New York American*, 22 Sep. 1914, 16.

16. *Washington Post*, 19 Aug. 1914, 3.

17. *Wilson Papers* 30:432.

18. *Washington Post*, 19 Aug. 1914, 6.

19. *Chicago Tribune*, 20 Aug. 1914, 6.

20. *Christian Science Monitor*, 26 Aug. 1914, 18.

21. *Wall Street Journal*, 31 Aug. 1914, 1.

22. *Washington Post*, 14 Aug. 1914, 6; 29 Aug., 1.

23. *New York Times*, 29 Aug. 1914, 8.

24. *Chicago Tribune*, 31 Aug. 1914, 1.

25. "Das Strafgericht in Löwen," *Berliner Tageblatt*, 28 Aug. 1914; untitled, *Vossische Zeitung*, 28 Aug. 1914; "Organisierter Bandenkrieg in Belgien: Die Stadt Löwen vernichtet," *Deutsche Tageszeitung*, 28 Aug. 1914, reprinted, *Das Echo*, 3 Sep. 1914; all in folder 2, Marawske Collection, box 23.

26. House, *Intimate Papers*, 1:293.

27. Bernstorff to Bryan, 3 Sep. 1914, *Foreign Relations, 1914 Supplement*, 793.

28. Gerard to Bryan, 7 Sep. 1914, ibid., 794.

29. The *Kölnische Volkszeitung* disputed the charges against priests and was

briefly suspended. *Kölnische Volkszeitung,* "Geistliche und Guerillakrieg in Belgien," 10 Sep. 1914, 2; Van Langenhove, *Growth of a Legend,* 271.

30. *Washington Post,* 6 Sep. 1914, 4.

31. Lewis et al., to New York, 3 Sept. 1914, *Foreign Relations, 1914 Supplement,* 801.

32. *Chicago Tribune,* 8 Sep. 1914, 6.

33. Carton de Wiart, *Souvenirs politiques* 1:236; Hymans, *Mémoires* 1:112; Tassier, *L'Entrée en guerre,* 160.

34. *New York Tribune,* 12 Sep. 1914, 7; compare *New York Herald,* 12 Sep., 12.

35. Hymans, *Mémoires* 1:128.

36. Carton de Wiart, *Souvenirs politiques* 1:236.

37. *Chicago Tribune,* 13 Sep. 1914, 3.

38. *Wilson Papers* 31:16.

39. Tassier, *L'Entrée en guerre,* 47.

40. Belgian Delegates, *Case of Belgium,* vii.

41. Remarks of the President to the Belgian Commission at the White House, 16 Sep. 1914, *Foreign Relations, 1914 Supplement,* 796–97.

42. Bryan to Gerard, 16 Sep. 1914, ibid., 797.

43. Hymans, *Mémoires* 1:116.

44. *New York American,* 17 Sep. 1914, 2; *San Francisco Chronicle,* 17 Sep. 1914, 1.

45. *Chicago Tribune,* 17 Sep. 1, 4.

46. Belgium, *Rapports et documents* 1, t. 2:146–47, 181, 197, 215, 222, 223.

47. *Chicago Tribune,* 18 Sep. 1914, 6.

48. Tassier, *L'Entrée en guerre,* 49–50.

49. Ibid., 53–54.

50. Roosevelt, *Letters,* 8:831, 831n.

51. *Wilson Papers* 31:121–22.

52. Wilson to Bryan, 4 Sep. 1914, U.S. Department of State, *Lansing Papers* 1:33 (hereafter *Lansing Papers*).

53. *Wilson Papers* 31:181.

54. *New York Times,* 28 Nov. 1914, 1.

55. Belgian Delegates, *Case of Belgium,* 31–48. The first two reports are also in Belgium, *Reports on the Violation* 1:1–10.

56. *Wilson Papers* 30:459–60.

57. Ibid.

58. Belgium, *Rapports et documents* 1, t. 2:31–36; also in Belgium, *Reports on the Violation* 1:16–20.

59. *New York Times,* 13 Nov. 1914, 4.

60. Belgian Delegates, *Case of Belgium,* 33–43.

61. Belgium, *Rapports et documents* 1, t. 2:16–17.

62. Ibid., 111.

63. Belgian Delegates, *Case of Belgium*, xvii.

64. Q. Amara, "Propagande belge," 179.

65. Q. Thomas J. Knock, *To End All Wars: Woodrow Wilson and the Quest for a New World Order* (New York, 1992), 20.

66. Maurice Tschoffen, *Le sac du Dinant et les légendes du Livre blanc allemand du 10 mai 1915* (Leyden, 1917); extracts in Belgium, *Rapports et documents* 1, t. 1:153–65; Van Langenhove, *Growth of a Legend*.

67. *New York Times*, 16 Sep. 1914, 10.

68. Powell, *Fighting in Flanders*, 89–90.

69. *New York American*, 17 Sep. 1914, 4; 24 Sep. 1914, 3.

70. *Wilson Papers* 31:85.

71. *Times* of London, 23 Aug. 1914, 2.

72. Belgium, *Rapports et documents* 1, t. 1:xiii.

73. Van Langenhove, *Growth of a Legend*, 307–8.

74. *Everyman, Special Belgian Relief Number* (Nov. 1914), 6.

NOTES TO CHAPTER 5: A VAGUE AND MISTY UNREALITY

1. Belgium, *Rapports et documents* 3, t. 2:9–10.

2. Fischer, *Germany's Aims*, 112.

3. For two views of *Flamenpolitik*, see Bissing, *Testament*; and Karl Hampe, "Belgium and the Great Powers," in *Modern Germany in Relation to the Great War: By Various German Authors*, trans. William Wallace Whitelock (New York, 1916), 340–80.

4. Fischer, *Germany's Aims*, 104.

5. Graber, *Belligerent Occupation*, 153.

6. *Usages of War*, 180–81.

7. Higgins, *Hague Peace Conferences*, 245.

8. Gibson to mother, Gibson Papers, 16 Sep. 1914, box 32.

9. Ibid., 22 Sep. 1914.

10. Pirenne and Vauthier, *Législation*, 7–8; Belgium, *Rapports et documents* 4:144.

11. De Kerchove, *L'Industrie belge*, 31.

12. Fischer, *Germany's Aims*, 221, 265, 267, 593.

13. Q. Étienne Mantoux, *The Carthaginian Peace, or the Economic Consequences of Mr. Keynes* (Pittsburgh, 1964), 43.

14. Albert Henry, *Le Ravitaillement de la Belgique pendant l'occupation allemande* (Paris, 1924), 20–22, 31.

15. Marion C. Siney, *The Allied Blockade of Germany 1914–1916*, University of Michigan Publications, History and Political Science, vol. 23 (Ann Arbor, 1957), 22.

16. Best, *Humanity in Warfare*, 251–56, compares the legality of the block-

ade with that of submarine warfare. See also William Beveridge, *Blockade and the Civilian Population*, Oxford Pamphlets on World Affairs, no. 24 (Oxford, 1939), 6–7.

17. Siney, *Allied Blockade*, 22–23.

18. *Correspondence and Documents Respecting the International Naval Conference Held in London, December 1908–February 1909*, Cmd. 4544, Misc., no. 4:8, 82.

19. Best, *Humanity in Warfare*, 254, 256.

20. Beveridge, *Blockade*, 27.

21. V. H. Rothwell, *British War Aims and Peace Diplomacy, 1914–1918* (Oxford, 1971), 18.

22. Gibson, *Journal from Our Legation*, 272.

23. Nash, *Hoover*, 71; Whitlock, *Journal*, 77.

24. Belgium, *Rapports et documents* 1, t. 2:243–50.

25. Horne and Kramer, *German Atrocities*, 73.

26. Van Swygenhoven memoir, AP, no. 29:11–12.

27. Edmonds, *Military Operations* 2:32–33.

28. Asquith, *Letters*, 258.

29. Ibid., 268.

30. Hunt, *War Bread*, 90–91.

31. Powell, *Fighting in Flanders*, 193–95, 197.

32. Hunt, *War Bread*, 107, 112, 125.

33. Suzanne Lilar, *Une enfance gantoise* (Paris, 1976), 98.

34. Emile Vandervelde, *Souvenirs d'un militant socialiste* (Paris, 1939), 190.

35. Edmonds, *Military Operations* 2:300.

36. Q. Cammaerts, *Albert of Belgium*, 209.

37. Pirenne, *Belgium*, 277–78; De Schaepdrijver, "Occupation," 270.

38. Passelecq, *Déportation et travail*, 14–15.

39. Bitsch, *Entre la France et l'Allemagne*, 454; Marks, *Innocent Abroad*, 14; Bernhard Schwertfeger, *Amtliche Aktenstücke zur Geschichte der Europäischen Politik, 1885–1914 (Die Belgischen Dokumente zur Vorgeschichte des Weltkrieges)* (Berlin, 1925), suppl., 2:181, 193.

40. Schwertfeger, *Amtliche Aktenstücke*, suppl., 2:193.

41. *New York Times*, 16 Oct. 1914, 5.

42. *Chicago Tribune*, 15 Nov. 1914, 6.

43. Gille, Ooms, and Delandsheere, *Cinquante mois* 1:98–99.

44. Edmonds, *Military Operations* 1:29.

45. Gibson to mother, 13 Sep. 1914, Gibson Papers, box 32.

46. Thielemans and Vandewoude, *Roi Albert*, 100.

47. Gibson to mother, 26 Oct. 1914, Gibson Papers, box 32.

48. Willequet, *Albert Ier*, 121.

49. Belgium, *Reports on the Violation* 1:xxxiii.

50. Willequet, *Albert Ier*, 122.

51. Thielemans, *Albert Ier*, 46.

52. *Wilson Papers* 31:458–59.

53. *New York Times*, 2 Oct. 1914, 2.

54. "Report of the War Relief Commission," 1 Jan. 1915, 17, Munro Papers.

55. Whitlock, *Journal*, 52.

56. Gibson to mother, 6 Dec. 1914, Gibson Papers, box 32.

57. "Report of the War Relief Commission," 1 Jan. 1915, 17, Munro Papers.

58. "The Belgians," 70, Angell Papers.

59. *New York Times*, 1 Oct. 1914, 4.

60. Paradise, 9 Dec. 1914, folder 5:4, Paradise Papers.

61. *New York Times*, 1 Oct. 1914, 4.

62. Riezler, *Tagebücher*, 218.

63. Hunt, *War Bread*, 158.

64. Rudolf Binding, *Fatalist at War*, 19.

65. Q. Gay, *Public Relations* 1:481.

66. Min journal, 24 Oct. 1914, AP, no. 34, 1:35.

67. Pirenne, *Belgique*, 16.

68. Q. Gay, *Public Relations* 1:481.

69. *New York Times*, 13 Oct. 1914, 2.

70. Bisschop, "War Legislation," 110, 123; Köhler, *Occupied Territories*, 22; Passelecq, *Déportation et travail*, 11.

71. Belgium, *Rapports et documents* 4:139.

72. Vierset, *Mes souvenirs*, 365.

73. Feldman, *Army, Industry, and Labor*, 52; Jarausch, *Enigmatic Chancellor*, 235.

74. De Thier and Gilbart, *Liège*, 3:40; Belgium, *Rapports et documents* 3, t. 1:30.

75. James W. Garner, "Punishment of Offenders Against the Laws and Customs of War," *American Journal of International Law* 14 (Jan. 1920): 79–80.

76. De Kerchove, *L'Industrie belge*, 21–22.

77. Pirenne and Vauthier, *Législation*, 42.

78. De Kerchove, *L'Industrie belge*, 30; Belgium, *Rapports et documents* 3, t. 2:124, 126.

79. De Kerchove, *L'Industrie belge*, 37.

80. Belgium, *Rapports et documents* 3, t. 1:139.

81. Ibid., 184.

82. Pirenne and Vauthier, *Législation*, 7; Belgium, *Rapports et documents* 3, t. 1:86; t. 2:127–29.

83. Whitlock, *Journal*, 143–44.

84. Q. Nash, *Hoover*, 112.

85. Bisschop, "War Legislation," 142; Gay, *Public Relations* 1:228.

86. Bordwell, *Law of War*, 96; Graber, *Belligerent Occupation*, 254; *Usages of War*, 178; Westlake, *International Law*, 95.

87. Belgium, *Rapports et documents* 4:150.

88. Ibid., 126.

89. Ibid., 3, t. 2:129–30.

90. Lemaire journal, AP, no. 27, 9:4.

91. Binding, *Fatalist at War*, 31.

92. *New York Times*, 27 Oct. 1914, 1; Whitlock, *Letters*, 181.

93. Nash, *Hoover*, 35.

94. *New York Times*, 14 Nov. 1914, 2.

95. Gay, *Public Relations* 1:233; Nash, *Hoover*, 28, 74.

96. Q. Nash, *Hoover*, 69.

97. Whitlock, *Journal*, 107.

98. "The Belgians," 19, Angell Papers.

99. Hunt, *War Bread*, 265.

100. Paradise, 13 Jan. 1915, folder 5:14, Paradise Papers.

101. "Reports 1915," Paradise, folder 8:2, Commission for Relief in Belgium (hereafter CRB), box 126; Hunt, *War Bread*, 331.

102. Hunt, *War Bread*, 225.

103. Pirenne, *Belgique*, 81.

104. Henri Pirenne, *Journal de guerre*, 7.

105. Gille, Ooms, and Delandsheere, *Cinquante mois* 1:101; Pirenne and Vauthier, *Législation*, 25.

106. Collège Echevinal, *L'Occupation allemande à Bruges: Court aperçu* (Bruges, 1919), 3; Duchesne, "Jodoigne," 29.

107. Bruyr memoir, AP, no. 33:17; Van Swygenhoven memoir, AP, no. 29:18.

108. Min journal, 23 Dec. 1914, AP, no. 34, 1:40.

109. Gille, Ooms, and Delandsheere, *Cinquante mois* 1:476; "German Pettiness," 23 Jan. 1917, folder 4, Green Papers, box 20.

110. Feldman, *Army, Industry, and Labor*, 31–32; Albrecht Mendelssohn-Bartholdy, *The War and German Society: Testament of a Liberal* (New Haven, 1937), 108–9.

111. Paradise, 19 Jan. 1915, folder 6:51, Paradise Papers.

112. Hunt, *War Bread*, 168.

113. Nelson letter, 14 Dec. 1914, Nelson Papers.

114. "War Relief Commission," 1 Jan. 1915, 18–19, Munro Papers.

115. Mercier, *Voice of Belgium*, 5–29.

116. Pirenne, *Belgique*, 75.

117. Robert Dunn, *Five Fronts* (New York, 1915), 209, 210; Grondys, *Germans in Belgium*, 84; Hunt, *War Bread*, 165; Vernon Kellogg, *Headquarters Nights* (Boston, 1917), 79.

118. Gille, Ooms, and Delandsheere, *Cinquante mois* 1:103.

119. Hunt, *War Bread*, 241.

120. Pirenne, *Belgique*, 75.

121. De Schaepdrijver, "Occupation," 277.

122. Paradise, 31 Jan. 1915, folder 5:19, 20, Paradise Papers.

123. Hunt, *War Bread*, 216.

124. Bordwell, *Law of War*, 300.

125. Gibson to mother, 16 Nov. 1914, Gibson Papers, box 32.

126. Gille, Ooms, and Delandsheere, *Cinquante mois*, 1:222, 290.

127. Graber, *Belligerent Occupation*, 153.

128. Westlake, *International Law*, 90.

129. Hunt, *War Bread*, 243.

NOTES TO CHAPTER 6: THIS POISONED ATMOSPHERE

1. Whitlock, *Journal*, 84–85.

2. Pirenne, *Belgique*, 277.

3. Gibson to mother, 6 Jan. 1915, Gibson Papers, box 32.

4. Firmin Bonhomme, *Mes souvenirs de la Guerre 1914–1918* (Aywaille, Liège, 1980), 5–13.

5. Pirenne and Vauthier, *Législation*, 27.

6. Bordwell, *Law of War*, 304.

7. Paradise, 10 Feb. 1915, folder 5:22, Paradise Papers.

8. Lemaire journal, AP, no. 27, 9:1; Pirenne and Vauthier, *Législation*, 28–29.

9. De Thier and Gilbart, *Liège* 3:85.

10. Francis Bertie, *The Diary of Lord Bertie of Thame, 1914–1918*, ed. Lady Algernon Gordon Lennox (New York, n.d.), 1:160; Whitlock, *Journal*, 120.

11. *L'Indépendance Belge*, 5 Nov. 1914, 1; *Manchester Guardian*, 7 May 1915, 10; *New York Times*, 11 Jan. 1915, 5.

12. Passelecq, *Déportation et travail*, 16; Pirenne and Vauthier, *Législation*, 28.

13. "Sondersteuer für landflüchtige Belgier," 28 Jan. 1915, n.p., folder 1, Marawske Collection, box 23; Köhler, *Occupied Territories*, 72.

14. Passelecq, *Déportation et travail*, 16.

15. Lemaire journal, AP, no. 27, 11:1; Min journal, 19 Jan. 1915, AP, no. 34, 2:5; Duchesne, "Jodoigne," 30; Gille, Ooms, and Delandsheere, *Cinquante mois* 1:223, 234; Belgium, *Rapports et documents* 3, t. 2:131, 134–35.

16. Gibson to mother, 11 Jan. 1915, Gibson Papers, box 32.

17. Paradise, 15 Apr. 1915, folder 5:35, Paradise Papers.

18. Whitlock, *Journal*, 85.

19. Nash, *Hoover*, 115.

20. Belgium, *Rapports et documents* 3, t. 1: 87, 88, 90.

21. Ibid., 2:134; De Kerchove, *L'Industrie belge*, 44.

22. Belgium, *Rapports et documents* 3, t. 1:71–72.

23. Ibid., 54.

24. Q. Passelecq, *Déportations belges*, 164n; *Das Echo*, 18 Mar. 1915, 428–30.

25. Q. Fischer, *Germany's Aims*, 261.

26. Pirenne and Vauthier, *Législation*, 64; Belgium, *Rapports et documents* 4:24–25.

27. Pirenne and Vauthier, *Législation*, 65–66; Belgium, *Rapports et documents* 4:26.

28. Pirenne and Vauthier, *Législation*, 67.

29. Min journal, 12 Mar. 1915, AP, no. 34, 2:15.

30. Pirenne and Vauthier, *Législation*, 19.

31. Whitlock, *Journal*, 147.

32. Ibid., 126.

33. Paradise, 9 Dec. 1914, 31 Jan. 1915, folder 5:3, 18, Paradise Papers; "Reports 1915," Paradise, folder 8:1, CRB, box 126.

34. "Reports 1915," Gardner Richardson, folder 8:3, CRB, box 126.

35. Paradise, 13 Apr. 1915, folder 5:32, Paradise Papers.

36. Köhler, *Occupied Territories*, 14–15.

37. Pirenne, *Journal de Guerre*, 9.

38. "The Belgians," 177, Angell Papers.

39. Paradise, 19 Jan. 1915, folder 6:29, Paradise Papers.

40. Min journal, 23 Apr. 1915, AP, no. 34, 2:22.

41. Passelecq, *Déportation et travail*, 51–52, 70.

42. De Kerchove, *L'Industrie belge*, 59.

43. "The Belgians," 73, Angell Papers.

44. Henry, *Ravitaillement*, 53–54.

45. Köhler, *Occupied Territories*, 85.

46. Gay, *Public Relations* 1:59; "Memorandum on Mr. Hoover's Trip to Havre and Paris, March 1915," folder 5, CRB, box 21.

47. Passelecq, *Déportation et travail*, 17.

48. Ibid., 18–19.

49. Belgium, *Rapports et documents* 3, t. 2:47, 49.

50. Ibid., 56.

51. Ibid., 56, 68–69, 87, 97–100, 101–8, 109–11, 115.

52. De Kerchove, *L'Industrie belge*, 48–49; Pirenne, *Belgique*, 174.

53. Gay, *Public Relations* 1:56.

54. Min journal, 2 Aug. 1915, AP, no. 34, 3:4.

55. Pirenne and Vauthier, *Législation*, 23–24.

56. Belgium, *Rapports et documents* 3, t. 1:353–54; Passelecq, *Déportation et travail*, 19.

57. Belgium, *Rapports et documents* 4:101.

58. Whitlock, *Journal*, 205.

59. Belgium, *Rapports et documents* 2:35–37.

60. Passelecq, *Déportation et travail*, 87–88.

61. Gay, *Public Relations* 1:64.

62. De Kerchove, *L'Industrie belge*, 85; Belgium, *Rapports et documents* 2:256–57.

63. Gay, *Public Relations* 2:37–38.

64. Gille, Ooms, and Delandsheere, *Cinquante mois* 1:485; Pirenne and Vauthier, *Législation*, 30, 75.

65. Passelecq, *Déportation et travail*, 20–21.

66. Min journal, 31 Dec. 1915, AP, no. 34, 4:12; Van Swygenhoven memoir, AP, no. 29:19–20.

67. De Kerchove, *L'Industrie belge*, 40; Belgium, *Rapports et documents* 3, t. 2:12.

68. Bisschop, "War Legislation," 142; Belgium, *Rapports et documents* 4:127.

69. Blücher, *English Wife*, 85; Herman Sulzbach, *With the German Guns: Four Years on the Western Front, 1914–1918*, trans. Richard Thonger (London, 1973), 132.

70. Q. Gibson, *Journal from Our Legation*, 360.

71. Archives Générales du Royaume, *La Belgique occupée, 1914–1918*, Service Éducatif, Dossiers, Première Série, no. 20 (Brussels, 1998), 63.

72. Garner, *International Law and the World War* 2:96.

73. Belgium, *Rapports et documents* 4:28.

NOTES TO CHAPTER 7: AT LEAST THEY ONLY *DROWN* YOUR WOMEN

1. *Times* of London, 24 Aug. 1914, 7.

2. Ibid., 29 Aug. 1914, 9.

3. *Manchester Guardian*, 4 Aug. 1914, 6; 29 Aug., 6.

4. Asquith, *Letters*, 195.

5. *Times* of London, 9 Nov. 1914, 10.

6. *Speech Delivered by the Rt. Hon. Sir Edward Grey, K.G., British Secretary of State for Foreign Affairs, Bechstein Hall, London, 22 March 1915* (London, 1915), 9.

7. Q. Louis Renault, "L'Application du droit pénal aux faits de guerre," *Revue générale de droit international public* 25 (1918): 26.

8. Higgins, *Hague Peace Conferences*, 213.

9. Renault, "L'Application du droit pénal," 25.

10. *Land Warfare*, 129; Bellot, "War Crimes: Their Prevention," 46.

11. *Chicago Tribune*, 25 Aug. 1914, 6.

12. Ibid., 12 Sep. 1914, 6.

13. Randall Kennedy, *Race, Crime, and the Law* (New York, 1997), 42.

14. *Times* of London, 31 Aug. 1914, 9; 16 Sep., 9.

15. Ibid., 17 Sep. 1914, 9.

16. Alexandre G. J. A. Mérignhac, "De la sanction des infractions au droit des gens commises au cours de la guerre européene, par les empires du centre," *Revue générale du droit international public* 24 (1917): 35–36; Schwengler, *Völkerrecht*, 63; Willis, *Prologue to Nuremberg*, 13.

17. Louis Renault, untitled, *Revue pénitentiaire et de droit pénal* 39 (1915): 425–29.

18. Q. *New York American*, 15 Sep. 1914, 3.

19. *Literary Digest*, 49, no. 11 (12 Sep. 1914): 458, 460.

20. Schivelbusch, *Löwen*, 23, 36.

21. Q. *New York Times*, 27 Sep. 1914, 3.

22. *Chicago Tribune*, 12 Sep. 1914, 6.

23. Belgium, *Rapports et documents* 1, t. 2:414.

24. Ibid., 4:162.

25. Müller, *The Kaiser*, 36.

26. Ibid.

27. Q. *New York Times*, 22 Sep. 1914, 4.

28. Q. ibid., 4 Oct. 1914, sec. 2:14.

29. Q. ibid., 8 Oct. 1914, 3.

30. Horne and Kramer, *German Atrocities*, 282.

31. Q. *Everyman, Special Belgian Relief Number* (Nov. 1914), 30.

32. *L'Indépendance Belge*, 27 Oct. 1914, 1.

33. Ibid., 2 Nov. 1914, 1; 6 Nov., 1; 11 Nov., 1.

34. Q. *New York Times*, 1 Oct. 1914, 1.

35. "The Belgians," 78, Angell Papers; Lichtervelde, *Avant l'orage*, 138.

36. Hunt, *War Bread*, 237.

37. Q. *New York Times*, 11 Sep. 1914, 3.

38. Roosevelt, *Letters* 7:795.

39. Tassier, *L'Entrée en guerre*, 53.

40. Roosevelt, *Letters* 8:821.

41. *New York Times*, 8 Nov. 1914, sec. 5:1.

42. Ibid., sec. 2:2.

43. Lansing to Bryan, 23 Jan. 1915, *Lansing Papers* 1:192–94.

44. Lansing memo, 9 Feb. 1915, ibid., 202, 203, 209.

45. See Lansing's *Notes on Sovereignty: From the Standpoint of the State and of the World* (Washington, 1921).

46. Willis, *Prologue to Nuremberg*, 17.

47. *Times* of London, 10 Mar. 1915, 11; 16 Mar., 7.

48. Speech of 27 Apr. 1915, q. *Times* of London, 29 July 1916, 9.

49. Ibid., 28 Apr. 1915, 9.

50. *New Statesman* 5, no. 108 (1 May 1915): 77. The article did not mention Armenia. On 24 May, London, Paris, and St. Petersburg accused Turkey of

massacring the Armenians and warned that Turkish leaders and "their agents who are implicated" would be held responsible. Willis, *Prologue to Nuremberg*, 26.

51. *Irish Times*, 8 May 1915, 4.

52. *Chicago Tribune*, 8 May 1915, 8; *Washington Post*, 9 May, 4; Tassier, *L'Entrée en guerre*, 91.

53. *New York Tribune*, 9 May 1915, 12.

54. *Wilson Papers* 33:149.

55. *New York Tribune*, 12 May 1915, 8.

56. *Irish Times*, 13 May 1915, 4; *Manchester Guardian*, 13 May 1915, 6.

57. *New York Tribune*, 13 May 1915, 1.

58. *Literary Digest*, 50, no. 22 (29 May 1915): 1257; Trevor Wilson, "Lord Bryce's Investigation into Alleged German Atrocities in Belgium, 1914–15," *Journal of Contemporary History* 14, no. 3 (July 1979): 381.

59. *New York Herald*, 13 May 1915, 10.

60. *Literary Digest*, 50, no. 22 (29 May 1915), 1259.

61. *Norddeutscher Allgemeine Zeitung*, 20 May 1915, 1.

62. Gullace, "Sexual Violence," 717; Messinger, *British Propaganda*, 75.

63. Great Britain, *Report of the Committee on Alleged German Outrages*, 3–6 (hereafter Bryce report).

64. Ibid., 6n.

65. Great Britain, *Committee on the Alleged German Outrages: Evidence and Documents*, 5, 10, 18, 120, 123.

66. For a numerical roster, see Belgium, *Rapports et documents* 1, t. 1, 605–23; t. 2:679–704. For crimes against children, see, e.g., t. 1:120, 138; t. 2:205, 206, 239–41.

67. Messinger, *British Propaganda*, 72–73.

68. Ibid., 77–79.

69. Horne and Kramer, *German Atrocities*, 254.

70. Trevor Wilson, "Lord Bryce's Investigation," 381.

71. *New York Tribune*, 13 May 1915, 8. See also: *Manchester Guardian*, 13 May, 6; *Times* of London, 13 May, 9; *New York Herald*, 13 May, 10; *Literary Digest* 50, no. 22 (29 May 1915): 1259.

72. *New York Herald*, 14 May 1915, 12.

73. Poster Collection, UK nos. 520, 528, 548, 588, 625.

74. Bryce report, 10, 14–16, 22–24, 29.

75. Ibid., 61. For examples, see Horne and Kramer, *German Atrocities*, 445–49. For critics, see, e.g., Messinger, *British Propaganda*, 73.

76. Bryce report, 41, 44, 55.

77. Ibid., 40, 42, 44, 49.

78. Ibid., 61.

79. *Belgian Independence Day: Addresses Delivered at the Royal Albert Hall*, 21

July 1916 (London, 1916), 32; Bellot, "War Crimes: Their Prevention," 32; House, *Intimate Papers* 1:293; Root, "Opening Address," 10; *Times* of London, 1 Sep. 1914, 12.

80. *New York Times,* 10 Oct. 1915, sec. 4:1–3.

81. "War Relief Commission," 17, 20, 77, 78, Munro Papers.

82. *New York Times,* 15 Feb. 1915, 4.

83. Gullace, "Sexual Violence," 725.

84. Q. ibid., 741.

85. Whitlock, *Letters,* 234.

86. Gullace, "Sexual Violence," 717.

87. Q. *American Review of Reviews* 51, 6 (June 1915): 743.

88. Thielemans, *Albert Ier,* 186.

89. *Wilson Papers* 33:524.

90. Paradise, 31 Jan., 10 Feb. 1915, folder 5:15, 21, Paradise Papers.

91. *Times* of London, 10 Feb. 1915, 9–10; 11 Feb., 9–10; 12 Feb., 7; 13 Feb., 6.

NOTES TO CHAPTER 8: HELL'S PREMISES

1. "The Belgians," 53, Angell Papers; Baudhuin, *Histoire économique* 1:36.

2. Unpaginated report, 18 Sep. 1916, "Reports 1916," folder 10, CRB, box 126; Whitlock, *Journal,* 239.

3. Undated William Palmer Lucas report, "Reports 1916," folder 12:3, 5, 9–11, CRB, box 126.

4. "The Belgians," 54–56, 65, 67–69, Angell Papers.

5. Mercier, *Voice of Belgium,* 251.

6. Withington to family, 31 May 1916, Withington Papers.

7. De Schaepdrijver, "Occupation," 276–77.

8. Dunn, *Five Fronts,* 207; Emily Hobhouse, *Emily Hobhouse: A Memoir,* comp. A. Ruth Fry (London, 1929), 274; Green diary, 13 Oct. 1915, 12, unnumbered folder, Green Papers, box 20; ibid., "Curfew Regulations," 1 Feb. 1917, folder 4; *New York Times,* 10 Oct. 1915, sec. 4:1–3; Sulzbach, *With the German Guns,* 90.

9. Gille, Ooms, and Delandsheere, *Cinquante mois* 2:50–51, 100, 246, 337; De Kerchove, *L'Industrie belge,* 114–18; De Thier and Gilbart, *Liège* 3:197.

10. Belgium, *Rapports et documents* 2:45; Passelecq, *Déportation et travail,* 70.

11. Q. Köhler, *Occupied Territories,* 195.

12. Passelecq, *Déportation et travail,* 73.

13. Passelecq, *Déportations belges,* 107–8.

14. Passelecq, *Déportation et travail,* 72.

15. Riezler, *Tagebücher,* 340n.

16. Bissing, *Testament,* 16, 19.

17. Ibid., 20, 24, 28.

18. Fritz Fischer, *World Power*, 14.

19. Bernhardi, *Germany and the Next War*, 158.

20. Q. de Schaepdrijver, "Occupation," 281.

21. Pirenne, *Journal de guerre*, 12. Pirenne spent nearly the rest of the war in Germany. For a while, though, he was allowed to teach, and even his captors attended his lectures.

22. C. M. Torrey to Hoover, 29 Mar. 1916, folder 1, Green Papers, box 6; published in Gay, *Public Relations* 2:42–43.

23. Passelecq, *Déportation et travail*, 61.

24. De Kerchove, *L'Industrie belge*, 49.

25. Pirenne, *Belgique*, 174.

26. Belgium, *Rapports et documents* 4:101, 103–4.

27. Passelecq, *Déportation et travail*, 6n.

28. *Times* of London, 28 July 1916, 7; 29 July, 9.

29. Ibid., 3 Aug. 1916, 7.

30. Passelecq, *Déportation et travail*, 73–75; Belgium, *Rapports et documents* 2:39.

31. Passelecq, *Déportation et travail*, 83; Belgium, *Rapports et documents* 2:42.

32. Passelecq, *Déportation et travail*, 88.

33. John Keegan, *The First World War* (New York, 1999), 297.

34. *Norddeutscher Allgemeine Zeitung*, 7 Aug. 1916, 2.

35. Q. Passelecq, *Déportations belges*, 121.

36. Feldman, *Army, Industry, and Labor*, 152–53, 161.

37. Germany, *Zwangsüberführung*, 387.

38. Q. Robert B. Armeson, *Total Warfare and Compulsory Labor: A Study of the Military-Industrial Complex in Germany during World War I* (The Hague, 1964), 32.

39. Jürgen Kocka, *Facing Total War: German Society, 1914–1918*, trans. Barbara Weinberger (Leamington Spa, Warwickshire, 1984), 27.

40. Ibid., 187n; Feldman, *Army, Industry, and Labor*, 301.

41. Q. Passelecq, *Déportation et travail*, 439.

42. Q. ibid., 440–41.

43. Q. ibid., 441.

44. Q. ibid., 444.

45. Germany, *Zwangsüberführung*, 359, 363.

46. Gille, Ooms, and Delandsheere, *Cinquante mois* 2:302; Belgium, *Rapports et documents* 4:77.

47. Belgium, *Rapports et documents* 2:47.

48. *Usages of War*, 147–48, 177.

49. Pirenne and Vauthier, *Législation*, 52.

50. Ibid.

51. Germany, *Zwangsüberführung*, 366–70.

52. *Kölnische Zeitung*, 13 Oct. 1916, 2.

53. Jackson diary, 19 Oct. 1916, Jackson Papers.

54. Ibid., 24 Oct. 1916.

55. Ibid., 30 Oct. 1916.

56. Ibid., 1 Nov. 1916.

57. Ibid., 8 Nov. 1916.

58. Ibid., 9 Nov. 1916.

59. Ibid., 14 and 15 Nov. 1916.

60. Passelecq, *Déportation et travail*, 210.

61. Jackson diary, 14 Nov. 1916, Jackson Papers.

62. Jackson to Hoover, 15 Nov. 1916, folder 1, Green Papers, box 6; published in Gay, *Public Relations* 2:53–54.

63. Jackson diary, 17 Nov. 1916, Jackson Papers.

64. Passelecq, *Déportation et travail*, 139.

65. Ibid., 140.

66. Ibid., 140–41.

67. Belgium, *Rapports et documents* 2:139.

68. Passelecq, *Déportation et travail*, 128–29.

69. Ibid., 144.

70. Min journal, 17 Nov. 1916, AP, no. 34, 6:3; Whitlock, *Journal*, 319.

71. Min journal, 30 Nov. 1916, AP, no. 34, 7:8–9; published in Belgium, *Rapports et documents* 2:179.

72. Whitlock, *Journal*, 322.

73. Passelecq, *Déportation et travail*, 106, 204, 208; Belgium, *Rapports et documents* 2:122–23.

74. Passelecq, *Déportation et travail*, 200.

75. Ibid., 387.

76. Ibid., 263.

77. Ibid., 264.

78. Belgium, *Rapports et documents* 2:275.

79. Min journal, 10 Dec. 1916, AP, no. 34, 7:21.

80. Belgium, *Rapports et documents* 2:266–67.

81. Ibid., 270.

82. Passelecq, *Déportation et travail*, 105, 119.

83. Ibid., 110, 111.

84. Ibid., 106.

85. Philip N. Potter to Gregory, 27 Nov. 1916, folder 1, Green Papers, box 6.

86. Pirenne and Vauthier, *Législation*, 55; Passelecq, *Déportation et travail*, 333–34.

87. Pirenne and Vauthier, *Législation*, 89–90.

88. Belgium, *Rapports et documents* 4:78.

89. *Kölnische Volkszeitung*, 5 Nov. 1916, 1.

90. *Norddeutscher Allgemeine Zeitung*, 3 Dec. 1916, 3.

91. *New York Times,* 12 Nov. 1916, 1–2.

92. Passelecq, *Déportation et travail,* 292, 297.

93. Thielemans, *Albert Ier,* 94, 369–70.

94. Ibid., 373–74.

95. Passelecq, *Déportation et travail,* 188–92.

96. Commission syndicale, 14 Nov. 1916, folder 1, Green Papers, box 6; Passelecq, *Déportations belges,* 67–69.

97. Whitlock, *Journal,* 322, 324.

98. Gille, Ooms, and Delandsheere, *Cinquante mois* 2:390.

99. Q. Passelecq, *Déportation et travail,* 287–88.

100. Amara, "Propagande belge," 186–87.

101. *New York Times,* 19 Nov. 1916, sec. 7:2.

102. *Washington Post,* 19 Nov. 1916, 4.

103. Passelecq, *Déportation et travail,* 292.

104. *Wilson Papers* 40:88.

105. Amara, "Propagande belge," 188, 189.

106. *New York Times,* 16 Dec. 1916, 1, 5.

107. Amara, "Propagande belge," 189.

108. Lansing to Grew, 29 Nov. 1916, *Foreign Relations, Supplement 1916,* 71.

109. *Wilson Papers* 40:94.

110. Passelecq, *Déportation et travail,* 299–300.

111. Gay, *Public Relations* 2:61–62.

112. Passelecq, *Déportation et travail,* 305.

113. Higgins, *Hague Peace Conferences,* 223.

114. *Kölnische Zeitung,* 29 Nov. 1916, 1.

115. Grew to Lansing, 5 Dec. 1916, *Foreign Relations, 1916 Supplement,* 868.

116. Grew to Lansing, 11 Dec. 1916, ibid., 869. The Russian Army treated German civilians fairly well in 1914, but in 1915, deported more than 1.5 million Russian minorities, many of them Jews, to the hinterland. Horne and Kramer, *German Atrocities,* 79, 80, 84.

117. Passelecq, *Déportation et travail,* 301, 302–03.

118. Ibid., 398.

119. Ibid., 390.

NOTES TO CHAPTER 9: TAKING NOTE OF THESE THINGS

1. *Wilson Papers* 40:428–29.

2. Whitlock, *Journal,* 84.

3. Cammaerts, *Albert of Belgium,* 71.

4. Lilar, *Enfance gantoise,* 41, 45.

5. Strikwerda, *House Divided,* 279.

6. Bitsch, *Entre la France et l'Allemagne,* 321.

7. But perceptions changed with the beholder. According to Whitlock, by 1917 the French were gibing that Belgian refugees were "more Boche than the Boches." Whitlock, *Journal*, 443.

8. Bloem, *Advance from Mons*, 32, 34, 49.

9. Hampe, "Belgium and the Great Powers," 340, 342, 375.

10. Thielemans, *Albert Ier*, 228, 230, 231.

11. Fischer, *Germany's Aims*, 216–21; Thielemans, *Albert Ier*, 60–61.

12. Thielemans, *Albert Ier*, 52.

13. Ibid., 58, 59; Thielemans and Vandewoude, *Lettres*, 647.

14. Osborne to Lansing, 17 Feb. 1916, *Foreign Relations, Supplement 1916*, 18.

15. Thielemans, *Albert Ier*, 253.

16. House, *Intimate Papers* 2:168.

17. Thielemans, *Albert Ier*, 64.

18. Ibid., 78.

19. Hymans, *Mémoires* 1:142.

20. Thielemans, *Albert Ier*, 77–78.

21. Ibid., 78, 80.

22. Passelecq, *Déportation et travail*, 76–78, 78–80.

23. *Belgian Independence Day: Addresses Delivered at the Royal Albert Hall, 21 July 1916* (London, 1916), 33–34.

24. See, e.g., *Kölnische Zeitung*, 5 Aug. 1916, 1.

25. Ibid. Another merchant captain, captured in December 1916 after trying to ram a U-boat, never faced trial, perhaps because his ship was armed. My thanks to Capt. G. F. Boxall, MN (Ret'd.), who told me about this case in October 2001.

26. *New York Times*, 29 July 1916, 2; see also *Chicago Tribune*, 29 July, 4, and *Washington Post*, 29 July, 3; James Brown Scott, "The Execution of Captain Fryatt," *American Journal of International Law* 10 (Oct. 1916): 877.

27. Q. *New York Times*, 29 July 1916, 3.

28. *Manchester Guardian*, 29 July 1916, 6.

29. *Times* of London, 29 July 1916, 9.

30. *New York Times*, 30 July 1916, 3.

31. *Times* of London, 1 Aug. 1916, 10.

32. Ibid., 6 Aug. 1916, 8.

33. Root, "Opening Address," 2, 3, 5, 6, 8, 9.

34. Bellot, "War Crimes: Their Prevention," 30, 32, 44, 47, 50, 55; Bellot, "War Crimes and War Criminals," 37, no. 1:14, 21.

35. E. D. Morel, *Truth and the War*, 3d ed. (London, 1918), 3, 5, 121–22.

36. Higgins, *Hague Peace Conferences*, 249.

37. Ibid., 245.

38. Passelecq, *Déportations belges*, 229, 230.

39. Whitlock, *Journal*, 306.

40. "Reports 1915," Angell, folder 8:9, CRB, box 126.

41. See, e.g., Bruyr memoir, AP, no. 33:17.

42. Gade to Brussels, 17 Nov. 1916, folder 1, Green Papers, box 6; published in Gay, *Public Relations* 2:64.

43. Gade to Green, 28 Nov. 1916, folder 1, Green Papers, box 6. See also ibid., Richardson letters, 22 and 30 Nov. 1916.

44. Belgium, *Rapports et documents* 2:109–110.

45. Passelecq, *Déportation et travail*, 377.

46. *Norddeutscher Allgemeine Zeitung*, 14 Nov. 1916, 2. See also Passelecq, *Déportations belges*, 20–21.

47. Min journal, 30 Nov. 1916, AP, no. 33, 7:9; Virton memo, 6 Dec. 1916, folder 2, Green Papers, box 6.

48. Belgium, *Rapports et documents* 2:160.

49. Bisschop, "War Legislation," 142; Belgium, *Rapports et documents* 4:128.

50. Q. Passelecq, *Déportation et travail*, 446.

51. Ibid., 445–52.

52. *La Belgique*, 12 Dec. 1916, n.p., clipping in Jackson Papers.

53. Ibid., diary, 12 Dec. 1916.

54. Q. Matthias Erzberger, *Souvenirs de guerre de Matthias Erzberger*, n. trans. (Paris, 1921), 24; James W. Gerard, *My Four Years in Germany* (New York, 1917), 351.

55. Tassier, *L'Entrée en guerre*, 120, 125, 126, 129.

56. *Chicago Tribune*, 30 Dec. 1916, 6; 17 Dec., 5.

57. *Washington Post*, 16 Dec. 1916, 2; 17 Dec., 6.

58. Amara, "Propagande belge," 188.

59. *Wilson Papers* 40:168.

60. Ibid., 38:650–52, 656–658.

61. Gerard, *My Four Years*, 351.

62. *Wilson Papers* 40:273.

63. Allied Powers, 30 December 1916, *Foreign Relations, Supplement 1916*, 125.

64. House, *Intimate Papers* 2:405.

65. Q. Daniel Smith, "Robert Lansing and American Neutrality," *University of California Publications in History* 59 (1958): 146.

66. Ibid., 154.

67. Lansing to Wilson, 21 Nov. 1916, *Lansing Papers* 1:43–44.

NOTES TO CHAPTER 10: *MORT POUR LA PATRIE*

1. Min journal, 3 Jan. 1917, AP, no. 34, 7:31.

2. Whitlock, *Journal*, 339.

3. Jackson diary, 4 Jan. 1917, Jackson Papers.

4. Ibid., 6 Jan. 1917.

5. Gille, Ooms, and Delandsheere, *Cinquante mois* 3:33.

6. Jackson diary, 20 Jan. 1917, Jackson Papers.

7. Peter Scholliers and Frank Daelemens, "Standards of Living and Standards of Health in Wartime Belgium," in Richard Wall and Jay Winter, eds., *The Upheaval of War: Family, Work and Welfare in Europe, 1914–1918* (Cambridge, 1988), 144, 153.

8. Lemaire journal, AP, no. 27, 6:4.

9. Baudhuin, *Histore économique* 1:36.

10. "General Impressions," 1 Feb. 1917, Green Papers, box 20.

11. Gille, Ooms, and Delandsheere, *Cinquante mois* 3:261, 267, 287, 327, 473, 546.

12. Ibid., 287.

13. Belgium, *Rapports et documents* 3, t. 1:97.

14. Lemaire journal, AP, no. 27, 11:1; Gille, Ooms, and Delandsheere, *Cinquante mois* 3:473.

15. Pirenne, *Belgique,* 177.

16. Gille, Ooms, and Delandsheere, *Cinquante mois* 3:154.

17. Jackson diary, 9 Jan. 1917, Jackson Papers.

18. Ibid., 24, 25, 26 Jan. 1917.

19. Nash, *Hoover,* 314.

20. Jackson diary, 8 Feb. 1917, Jackson Papers; Gille, Ooms, and Delandsheere, *Cinquante mois* 3:61, 80.

21. "Affiches," 23 Jan. 1917, Green Papers, box 20.

22. Min journal, 31 Dec. 1916, AP, no. 34, 7:30.

23. Whitlock, *Journal,* 345.

24. *Wilson Papers* 41:523; for whole address, see 519–27.

25. Nash, *Hoover,* 314–15.

26. Scholliers and Daelemens, "Standards of Living," 142.

27. Nash, *Hoover,* 337, 338.

28. Ibid., 358.

29. James Morgan Read, *Atrocity Propaganda 1914–1919* (New Haven, 1941), 173n. As it happens, Mercier had written Bissing on 31 January invoking "the inescapable judgment of the God of Justice" to avenge the deportations. Q. Passelecq, *Déportation et travail,* 256–58.

30. Fischer, *Germany's Aims,* 445.

31. Belgium, *Rapports et documents* 4:78.

32. Pirenne and Vauthier, *Législation,* 93.

33. Ibid., 107; Belgium, *Rapports et documents* 4:78.

34. Sophie de Schaepdrijver describes the tension in "Idealism Remembered, Idealism Dismembered: Contested Memories of the German Occupation of Belgium" (Paper delivered at "Demobilizing the Mind: Culture, Politics, and

the Legacy of the Great War, 1918–1933," Trinity College, Dublin, 26–28 Sep. 2001).

35. Fischer, *Germany's Aims*, 446–47.

36. De Kerchove, *L'Industrie belge*, 120; Belgium, *Rapports et documents* 3, t. 1:125.

37. De Kerchove, *L'Industrie belge*, 128, 129, 135, 138, 139.

38. Pirenne and Vauthier, *Législation*, 48.

39. Belgium, *Rapports et documents* 2:53.

40. Passelecq, *Déportation et travail*, 313. See also Erzberger, *Souvenirs de guerre*, 23–24.

41. Passelecq, *Déportation et travail*, 317.

42. Ibid., 320.

43. Germany, *Zwangsüberführung*, 375.

44. Passelecq, *Déportation et travail*, 321.

45. Min journal, 30 Nov. 1917, AP, no. 34, 10:35.

46. Passelecq, *Déportation et travail*, 274, 339, 342.

47. Ibid., 342.

48. Germany, *Zwangsüberführung*, 376–80.

49. Passelecq, *Déportation et travail*, 349.

50. Pirenne and Vauthier, *Législation*, 61.

51. Passelecq, *Déportation et travail*, 338.

52. Ibid., 326–27.

53. Ibid., 329–30.

54. Ibid., 347–48.

55. Ibid., 349.

56. Ibid., 399.

57. Feldman, *Army, Industry, and Labor*, 301.

58. Philippe Burrin, *France Under the Germans: Collaboration and Compromise*, trans. Janet Lloyd (New York, 1993), 284.

59. Passelecq, *Déportation et travail*, 389, 390.

60. "Reports, 1917," Maurice Pate, folder 14:3–4, CRB, box 126.

61. Ibid., 10.

62. Q. Passelecq, *Déportation et travail*, 391–92.

63. Q. Amara, "Propagande belge," 178.

64. Q. ibid., 191–92.

65. *New York Times*, 19 June 1917, 1.

66. Ibid., 21 June 1917, 7; 23 June, 8.

67. Amara, "Propagande belge," 205.

68. *Seattle Times*, 9 July 1917, 1, 7.

69. Amara, "Propagande belge," 207.

70. Ibid., 211.

71. *Washington Post*, 11 Oct. 1917, 10.

72. Ibid., 24 Oct. 1917, 11.

73. Whitlock, *Journal*, 440.

74. Whitlock, *Letters*, 234, 240.

75. Ibid., 237.

76. Bisschop, "War Legislation," 142; Belgium, *Rapports et documents* 4:128.

77. Belgium, *Rapports et documents* 3, t. 1:119, 128, 129.

78. Gille, Ooms, and Delandsheere, *Cinquante mois* 3:547–48.

79. Ibid., 552.

80. Belgium, *Rapports et documents* 4:79, 80.

81. Fischer, *Germany's Aims*, 449.

82. Q. ibid., 450.

83. Ibid.

84. Bisschop, "War Legislation," 135; Belgium, *Rapports et documents* 4:50.

85. Pirenne and Vauthier, *Législation*, 110.

86. Ibid., 115–17; Belgium, *Rapports et documents* 4:9, 10, 61.

87. Higgins, *Hague Peace Conferences*, 235.

88. Oppenheim, *International Law* 2:306–7.

NOTES TO CHAPTER 11: LIKE A THIEF IN THE NIGHT

1. Luckau, *German Delegation*, 137.

2. *British War Aims: Statement by the Prime Minister, the Right Honourable David Lloyd George, on January 5, 1918* (London, 1918), 7.

3. Lansing to Penfield, 6 Dec. 1915, *Foreign Relations, 1915 Supplement*, 624.

4. House, *Intimate Papers* 2:239.

5. *Literary Digest* 59, no. 4 (26 Oct. 1918): 15.

6. F[rederick] E[dwin] Smith, *Speeches of Lord Birkenhead* (London, 1929), 99, 109, 110–12.

7. Gille, Ooms, and Delandsheere, *Cinquante mois* 4:15–16, 30, 31, 152.

8. Fernand Mayence, ed., *La Correspondance de S. E. le cardinal Mercier avec le gouvernement général allemand pendant l'occupation* (Louvain, 1918), 396–403; Bruyr memoir, AP, no. 33: 32.

9. Oudou journal, 14 and 22 Apr. 1918, 18 May 1918, 10 June 1918, AP, no. 24:3, 5, 8, 11.

10. Belgium, *Rapports et documents* 4:129.

11. Gille, Ooms, and Delandsheere, *Cinquante mois* 4:239–40.

12. De Kerchove, *L'Industrie belge*, 162; Belgium, *Rapports et documents* 3, t. 1:113.

13. Belgium, *Rapports et documents* 3, t. 1:165.

14. Köhler, *Occupied Territories*, 170; Belgium, *Rapports et documents* 3, t. 1:212.

15. De Kerchove, *L'Industrie belge*, 167; Belgium, *Rapports et documents* 3, t. 1:213.

16. De Kerchove, *L'Industrie belge*, 166.

17. Ibid., 170.

18. Thielemans, *Albert Ier*, 145.

19. Thielemans and Vandewoude, *Lettres*, 454–55.

20. Thielemans, *Albert Ier*, 153.

21. Thielemans and Vandewoude, *Lettres*, 464, 473.

22. French, *Strategy*, 235.

23. *Wilson Papers* 51:404.

24. Clive Parry, ed., *The Consolidated Treaty Series*, vol. 223: *1917–18* (Dobbs Ferry, NY, 1981), 311.

25. Schwengler, *Völkerrecht*, 61–62.

26. Q. A. Joseph Berlau, *The German Social Democratic Party, 1914–1921,* Studies in History, Economics and Public Law, no. 577 (New York, 1949), 152–53.

27. Thielemans, *Albert Ier*, 158–59.

28. *New York Times,* 1 Sep. 1918, sec. 4:1.

29. *Times* of London, 13 Sep. 1918, 8.

30. Ibid., 19 Sep. 1918, 3.

31. Carnegie Endowment for International Peace, Division of International Law, *Official Statements of War Aims and Peace Proposals,* James Brown Scott, ed., pamphlet no. 31 (Washington, 1921), 384–85.

32. Thielemans, *Albert Ier*, 151.

33. *Journal du droit international* 45 (1918): 1620.

34. Willis, *Prologue to Nuremberg*, 51.

35. House, *Intimate Papers* 4:15; Lansing to Wilson, 4 Oct. 1918, *Lansing Papers* 2:159.

36. Lansing to Wilson, 27 Sep. 1918, *Lansing Papers* 2:156.

37. *Wilson Papers* 51:129.

38. Ibid., 253.

39. Lowry, *Armistice 1918*, 12.

40. *Journal du droit international* 45 (1918): 1618.

41. Ibid., 1621.

42. Ibid., 1624–30.

43. *Times* of London, 8 Oct. 1918, 9.

44. Ibid., Oct. 1918, 7.

45. *Manchester Guardian,* 7 Oct. 1918, 4.

46. Willis, *Prologue to Nuremberg*, 40–41.

47. *New York Times,* 7 Oct. 1918, 12.

48. *Literary Digest* 59, no. 4 (26 Oct. 1918): 14.

49. *Cong. Rec., Senate,* 65th Cong., 2d sess., vol. 56, pt. 11:11157, 11160.

50. Ibid., 11162.

51. Ibid., 11224–25.

52. Ibid., 11156, 11163.

53. *New York Times,* 12 Oct. 1918, 12.

54. *Times* of London, 12 Oct. 1918, 2.

55. Ibid., 7.

56. *Wilson Papers* 51:333.

57. *New York Times,* 14 Oct. 1918, 3.

58. Ibid., 16 Oct. 1918, 14.

59. *Chicago Tribune,* 16 Oct. 1918, 6.

60. Northcliffe said that special tribunals should weigh evidence against defendants from all belligerents, who, if indicted, would be prosecuted in their own countries. *Spectator,* no. 4716 (16 Nov. 1918): 642.

61. *Times* of London, 14 Oct. 1918, 6, 9.

62. *Parliamentary Debates,* 5th ser., Lords, vol. 31 (16 Oct. 1918): 720. For the whole debate, see 709–29.

63. Willis, *Prologue to Nuremberg,* 53.

64. *Times* of London, 23 Oct. 1918, 6.

65. *Parliamentary Debates,* 5th ser., Commons, vol. 110 (29 Oct. 1918): 1311–90.

66. Willis, *Prologue to Nuremberg,* 54.

67. Ibid.

68. Lowry, *Armistice 1918,* 120.

69. Sulzbach, *With the German Guns,* 231.

70. Bass, *Stay the Hand of Vengeance,* 64.

71. French, *Strategy,* 272.

72. Ibid., 271–72.

73. Lowry, *Armistice 1918,* 190, note 8.

74. French, *Strategy,* 292.

75. Q. ibid., 276–77.

76. *Wilson Papers* 51:412, 414.

77. Ibid., 415.

78. Ibid., 415, 504.

79. Ibid., 473.

80. Q. French, *Strategy,* 12.

81. See, e.g., Lowry, *Armistice 1918,* 168.

82. George Dangerfield, *The Strange Death of Liberal England, 1910–1914* (New York, 1961), 22.

83. Q. Bass, *Stay the Hand of Vengeance,* 66.

84. Ibid., 66–68.

85. Willis, *Prologue to Nuremberg,* 58.

86. Dangerfield, *Strange Death,* 54.

87. Bass, 70–71.

88. Q. ibid., 71.

89. Q. ibid., 72.

90. Ibid., 73.

91. *Times* of London, 30 Nov. 1918, 6.

92. Ibid., 4 Dec. 1918, 9.

93. Close to Lansing, 11 Dec. 1918, *Foreign Relations, Paris Peace Conference, 1919,* 1:147 (hereafter *Foreign Relations, PPC*).

94. Carton de Wiart, *Souvenirs politiques* 1:377–78.

95. Belgium, *Rapports et documents* 2:247.

96. Hoover to Rickard, 18 Dec. 1918, folder 18:3, American Relief Administration, European Unit, box 339.

97. De Kerchove, *L'Industrie belge,* 173.

98. Ibid., 176–77.

99. Lemaire journal, AP, no. 27, 13:8.

100. Ibid., 9:7, 15:10.

101. Min journal, 11 and 19 Nov. 1918, AP, no. 34, 13:26, 28; Vanderschaege, *Stavelot,* 153.

102. Van Swygenhoven memoir, AP, no. 29, 28.

103. Oudou journal, 26 Nov. 1918, Ap, no. 24, 36.

104. Carton de Wiart, *Souvenirs politiques* 2:10.

105. Montague, *Disenchantment,* 177–78.

106. Whitlock, *Letters,* 277.

107. Carton de Wiart, *Souvenirs politiques* 2:17.

108. Montague, *Disenchantment,* 178.

NOTES TO CHAPTER 12: IT IS IMPOSSIBLE THAT WE WILL BE ABANDONED

1. Marks, *Innocent Abroad,* 173.

2. Belgium Articles, 25 May 1919, folder 18:2, American Relief Administration, European Unit, box 339.

3. Ibid., Hoover to Rickard, 18 Dec. 1918, folder 3:4, box 436; Charles P. Wood, *Industrial Machinery in France and Belgium,* U.S. Department of Commerce, Bureau of Foreign and Domestic Commerce, Special Agents Series, no. 204 (Washington, 1920), 29.

4. Marks, *Innocent Abroad,* 173.

5. De Kerchove, *L'Industrie belge,* 63.

6. Marks, *Innocent Abroad,* 173.

7. Hoover to Rickard, 18 Dec. 1918, folder 18:3, American Relief Administration, European Unit, box 339.

8. Marks, *Innocent Abroad,* 176.

9. De Kerchove, *L'Industrie belge,* 264.

10. Ibid., 269; Baudhuin, *Histoire économique* 1:64.

11. De Kerchove, *L'Industrie belge*, 264; Marks, *Innocent Abroad*, 174.

12. Marks, *Innocent Abroad*, 175.

13. Jackson diary, 16 Nov. 1916, Jackson Papers.

14. 2 Feb. 1919, Waldmann article, folder 18, American Relief Administration, European Unit, box 339.

15. Whitlock, *Journal*, 544.

16. Carton de Wiart, *Souvenirs politiques* 2:27.

17. McCormick diary, 24 Jan. 1919, 33, McCormick Papers.

18. Whitlock, *Journal*, 550.

19. *Chicago Tribune*, 8 Feb. 1919, 3.

20. Patrick Lefèvre, *La Belgique et la première guerre mondiale: bibliographie* (Brussels, 1987), 118n, 120n.

21. Keynes, *Economic Consequences*, 122; see also Luckau, *German Delegation*, 115.

22. Hymans, *Mémoires* 1:309.

23. House, *Intimate Papers* 4:191.

24. Marks, *Innocent Abroad*, 128–30.

25. Whitlock, *Journal*, 583.

26. Davignon, *Souvenirs d'un écrivain*, 308.

27. Marks, *Innocent Abroad*, 97.

28. Ibid., 323.

29. Ibid., 56, 113.

30. *Manchester Guardian*, 10 Dec. 1918, 8.

31. See, e.g., Carton de Wiart, *Souvenirs politiques* 2:29.

32. House, *Intimate Papers* 4:353; McCormick diary, 11 Feb. 1919, 40, McCormick Papers.

33. Marks, *Innocent Abroad*, 325.

34. Bliss to American Peace Commission, 26 Feb. 1919, 3, Bliss Papers.

35. McCormick diary, 24 Apr. 1919, 74, McCormick Papers.

36. Ibid., 25 Apr. 1919, 75.

37. Conseil des Ministres, 3 May 1919, 144, 147.

38. Marks, *Innocent Abroad*, 177.

39. *Wilson Papers* 51:500.

40. Mantoux, *Deliberations* 1:154, 173.

41. Ibid., 456.

42. McCormick diary, 2 May 1919, 80, McCormick Papers.

43. *Speech Delivered by the Right Honourable David Lloyd George, M.P. (Chancellor of the Exchequer), at the Queen's Hall, London, on September 19th, 1914* (London, n.d.), 2.

44. Ibid., 13.

45. David Lloyd George, *War Memoirs* (Boston 1935), 1:68.

46. Marks, *Innocent Abroad*, 179.

47. Luckau, *German Delegation*, 151.

48. Dresel to Grew, 10 Jan. 1919, *Foreign Relations, PPC* 2:139.

49. Ibid., 142.

50. Ibid., 138.

51. McCormick diary, 15 May 1919, 86, McCormick Papers.

52. R. Gherardi to Commission to Negotiate Peace, 4 Feb. 1919, *Foreign Relations, PPC* 12:5.

53. Luckau, *German Delegation*, 47.

54. Ibid.

55. Brockdorff-Rantzau to National Assembly, 14 Feb. 1919, *Foreign Relations, PPC* 12:17.

56. Ibid., 26.

57. Luckau, *German Delegation*, 178.

58. Ibid., 181.

59. *New York Times*, 18 Mar. 1919, 2.

60. Hagen Schulze, ed., *Das Kabinett Scheidemann 13. Februar bis 20. Juni 1919*, Akten der Reichskanzlei, Weimarer Republik (Boppard am Rhein, 1971), 78, 80.

61. Ibid., 78, 79.

62. Marks, *Innocent Abroad*, 180.

63. Schwengler, *Völkerrecht*, 152.

64. *Vorwärts*, 18 Feb. 1919 (P.M. edition), 1.

65. Council of Ten, 17 Jan. 1919, *Foreign Relations, PPC* 3:606.

66. Ibid., Clemenceau to conference, 18 Jan. 1919, 3:161.

67. Fernand Larnaude and Albert de Lapradelle, "Examen de la responsabilité pénale de l'empereur Guillaume II d'Allemagne," *Journal du droit international* 46 (1919): 145n.

68. Ibid., 151.

69. Ibid., 150.

70. Albert de Lapradelle, ed., *La paix de Versailles* (Paris, 1929–39), 3:237, 245, 248.

71. Robert Lansing, "Some Legal Questions of the Peace Conference," *American Journal of International Law* 12 (1919): 632ff.; Willis, *Prologue to Nuremberg*, 41.

72. Willis, *Prologue to Nuremberg*, 70.

73. Council of Ten, 10 Feb. 1919, *Foreign Relations, PPC* 3:953–54.

74. Willis, *Prologue to Nuremberg*, 74–75.

75. Edward Mandell House and Charles Seymour, eds., *What Really Happened at Paris* (New York, 1921), 480.

76. Willis, *Prologue to Nuremberg*, 73.

77. American plenipotentiaries meeting, 4 Mar. 1919, *Foreign Relations, PPC* 11:92.

78. Bass, *Stay the Hand of Vengeance*, 102; *Times* of London, 1 May 1919, 11.

79. Garner, "Punishment of Offenders," 135, 141, 143, 144, 145, 146, 150, 151.

80. Carnegie Endowment for International Peace, Division of International Law, *Violation of the Laws and Customs of War: Reports of Majority and Dissenting Reports of American and Japanese Members of the Commission of Responsibilities, Conference of Paris, 1919,* pamphlet no. 32 (Oxford, 1919), 20.

81. Ibid., 23–26.

82. Ibid., 22.

83. Mantoux, *Deliberations* 1:189.

84. Council of Ten, 16 Apr. 1919, *Foreign Relations, PPC* 4:482.

85. Mantoux, *Deliberations* 1:190, 193.

86. Ibid., 190.

87. Carnegie Endowment, *Violation of the Laws,* 22.

88. Mantoux, *Deliberations* 1:33.

89. Ibid., 35.

90. Ibid., 63

91. Ibid., 90–92.

92. Hymans, *Mémoires* 1:436–37.

93. Mantoux, *Deliberations* 1:120.

94. David Hunter Miller, *The Drafting of the Covenant* (New York, 1928), 2:298–99.

95. Mantoux, *Deliberations* 1:121.

96. Aryeh Neier, *War Crimes: Brutality, Genocide, Terror, and the Struggle for Justice* (New York, 1998), 16.

97. Mantoux, *Deliberations* 1:121.

98. Gordon Wallace Bailey, *Dry Run for the Hangman: The Versailles-Leipzig Fiasco, 1919–1921* (College Park, MD, 1971), 81–82.

99. Mantoux, *Deliberations* 1:123.

100. Reginald Esher, *Journals and Letters of Reginald Viscount Esher* (London, 1938), 4:215; see also *New York Times,* 2 Nov. 1918, 14. My thanks to Robert Hanks for giving me the sources for this remark.

101. August Heckscher, *Woodrow Wilson* (New York, 1991), 501–2.

102. McCormick diary, 30 Mar. and 27 Apr. 1919, 60, 76, McCormick Papers.

103. Mantoux, *Deliberations* 1:230.

104. Whitlock, *Journal,* 559.

105. McCormick diary, 18 and 19 June 1919, 104–8, McCormick Papers.

106. House, *Intimate Papers* 4:353, 354, 357; Hymans, *Mémoires* 1:397; Marks, *Innocent Abroad,* 182.

107. Q. *New York Times,* 14 Feb. 1919, 2.

108. Mantoux, *Deliberations* 1:194.

109. Ibid., 129.

110. Marks, *Innocent Abroad,* 120.

111. Mantoux, *Deliberations* 1:135–44.

112. Hymans, *Mémoires* 1:445.

113. French, *Strategy,* 14.

114. Mantoux, *Deliberations* 1:154, 173, 177, 239.

115. Ibid., 411–12.

116. Ibid., 414.

117. Ibid.

118. Ibid., 417.

119. Ibid., 418.

120. Ibid., 419.

121. Marks, *Innocent Abroad,* 196.

122. McCormick diary, 29 Apr. 1919, 78, McCormick Papers.

123. Mantoux, *Deliberations* 1:461.

124. Q. Marks, *Innocent Abroad,* 199.

125. Hymans, *Mémoires* 1:411.

126. Marks, *Innocent Abroad,* 196.

127. Conseil des Ministres, 3 May 1919, 144, 146, 147.

128. Ibid., 145.

129. Ibid., 148.

130. Ibid., 155; Marks, *Innocent Abroad,* 368–69.

131. Conseil des Ministres, 3 May 1919, 153, 155.

132. Luckau, *German Delegation,* 147.

133. McCormick diary, 2 Apr. 1919, 63, McCormick Papers.

134. Schulze, *Das Kabinett Scheidemann,* 187, 200.

135. Philip Mason Burnett, *Reparation at the Paris Peace Conference: From the Standpoint of the American Delegation* (New York, 1940), 1:69, 149.

136. Dresel to Commission to Negotiate Peace, 10 May 1919, *Foreign Relations, PPC* 12:119.

137. Ibid., 121.

138. Carnegie Endowment, *Violation of the Laws,* vii.

139. Bailey, *Dry Run for the Hangman,* 202.

140. Willis, *Prologue to Nuremberg,* 81.

141. Carnegie Endowment, *Violation of the Laws,* vii–viii.

142. Luckau, *German Delegation,* 220.

143. Ibid., 106; Herman Joseph Wittgens, "The German Foreign Office Campaign Against the Versailles Treaty" (Ph.D. diss., University of Washington, 1970), 14.

144. German Delegation to Clemenceau, June 1919, *Foreign Relations, PPC* 6:875–76.

145. Bethmann to Clemenceau, 25 June 1919, *Foreign Relations, PPC*, 6:757.

146. McCormick diary, 28 June 1919, 116, McCormick Papers.

NOTES TO CHAPTER 13: A TRIFLE

1. Heads of delegations meeting, 1 Aug. 1919, Great Britain, *Documents on British Foreign Policy* 1:271 (hereafter *DBFP*).

2. Heads of delegations meeting, 6 Aug. 1919, ibid., 1:336.

3. Commission on the Organization of Mixed Tribunals, 9 Jan. 1920, *DBFP* 6:975.

4. Malcolm to Balfour, 5 Aug. 1919, *DBFP* 6:124.

5. Balfour to Curzon, 8 Aug. 1919, ibid., 137.

6. Statement by Pollock et al., 7 June 1919, *Foreign Relations, PPC* 6:369.

7. Heads of delegations meeting, 9 Sep. 1919, *DBFP* 1:699.

8. Conference of 15 Jan. 1920, ibid., 2:886.

9. Conseil des Ministres, 27 Oct. 1919, 2.

10. Crowe to Curzon, 6 Nov. 1919, *DBFP* 6:332; ibid., Crowe to Curzon, 7 Nov. 1919, 353.

11. Heads of delegations meeting, 11 Nov. 1919, ibid., 2:279.

12. *Times* of London, 22 Nov. 1919, 12.

13. Commission on the Organization of Mixed Tribunals, 9 Jan. 1920, *DBFP* 5:968–76.

14. Ibid., 972, 975.

15. Heads of delegations, 15 Jan. 1920, ibid., 2:887.

16. Note to the Queen of Holland [*sic*] Demanding the Delivery of the Kaiser for Trial, ibid., 913.

17. Willis, *Prologue to Nuremberg,* 108.

18. Graham to Curzon, 30 Jan. 1920, *DBFP* 9:623.

19. Ibid., 624.

20. De Kerchove to Hymans, 9 Feb., 13 Feb. 1920, Belgian Ministry of Foreign Affairs (hereafter MFA), 324, XIII, "Manoeuvres de Erzberger pour la non-livraison des coupables."

21. De Kerchove to Hymans, 20 Jan. 1920, ibid.

22. Ernst Fraenkel, *Military Occupation and the Rule of Law: Occupation Government in the Rhineland, 1918–1923* (New York, 1944), 56–57; *Pasicrisie Belge* (1920) 1:104.

23. Kilmarnock to Curzon, 23 Jan. 1920, *DBFP* 10:2.

24. Lersner to Clemenceau, 25 Jan. 1920, Great Britain, *Protocols and Correspondence between the Supreme Council and the Conference of Ambassadors and the*

German Government and the German Peace Delegation between January 10, 1920, and July 17, 1920, respecting the Execution of the Treaty of Versailles of June 28, 1919, Cmd. 1325 (1921), 21.

25. De Salis to Curzon, 26 Jan. 1920, *DBFP* 9:619.

26. Kilmarnock to Curzon, 26 Jan. 1920, ibid., 616.

27. Kilmarnock to Curzon, 31 Jan. 1920, ibid., 27.

28. Schwengler, *Völkerrecht*, 333.

29. Hardinge to Derby, 30 Jan. 1920, *DBFP* 9:621.

30. Meeting at the Quai d'Orsay, 20 Jan. 1920, ibid., 2:928.

31. Lersner to Millerand, 3 Feb. 1920, *Protocols* 32.

32. *Vorwärts*, 4 Feb. 1920, 1 (A.M. ed.).

33. Ibid., 8 Feb. 1920, 1 (Sun. ed.).

34. Kilmarnock to Curzon, 5 Feb. 1920, *DBFP* 9:651.

35. Kilmarnock to Curzon, 7 Feb. 1920, ibid., 673.

36. Ibid., 675.

37. Michel report, 16 Feb. 1920, MFA, 324, XIV.

38. Kilmarnock to Curzon, 10 Feb. 1920, *DBFP* 9:57.

39. Ibid.

40. Ibid., 58.

41. Allied conference, 12 Feb. 1920, ibid., 7:9.

42. Ibid., 17.

43. Ibid., 16.

44. Ibid., 13–14.

45. Ibid., 14–15.

46. Schwengler, *Völkerrecht*, 316.

47. Curzon to Kilmarnock, 21 Feb. 1920, *DBFP* 9:85.

48. De Kerchove to Hymans, 22 Feb. 1920, MFA, 324, II.

49. Schwengler, *Völkerrecht*, 319.

50. Ibid., 320.

51. Ibid., 321.

52. Müller to Clemenceau, 7 Mar. 1920, *Protocols,* 51.

53. Minute of 6 May 1920, MFA, 324, XV.

54. Première liste des personnes désignées par les Puissances alliées pour être jugées par la Cour suprême de Leipzig, *DBFP* 8:238.

55. International conference, 9 July 1920, ibid., 498.

56. D'Abernon to Curzon, 24 Oct. 1920, ibid., 10:322.

57. Allied conference, 3 Mar. 1921, ibid., 15:264.

58. *New York Times,* 27 Apr. 1921, 1.

59. Schwengler, *Völkerrecht*, 345.

60. *Times* of London, 21 May 1921, 10.

61. Ibid., 24 May 1921, 10.

62. Ibid.

63. *New York Times*, 24 May 1921, 19.

64. Ibid.; *Times* of London, 24 May 1921, 10; *Washington Post*, 24 May 1921, 5; Mullins, *Leipzig Trials*, 40–41.

65. Mullins, *Leipzig Trials*, 37, 38.

66. Ibid., 39.

67. Claud Mullins, "The War Criminals' Trials," *Fortnightly Review* 116, no. 657 (1921): 420.

68. Great Britain, *German War Trials*, 8–9, 29–30, 37; also Prèmiere liste, *DBFP* 8:239.

69. Mullins, *Leipzig Trials*, 12.

70. *German War Trials*, 9.

71. *Manchester Guardian*, 30 May 1921, 7; *Times* of London, 30 May 1921, 10; *Vorwärts*, 25 May 1921, 7 (A.M. ed.).

72. *German War Trials*, 35, 37; Mullins, *Leipzig Trials*, 66.

73. Mullins, *Leipzig Trials*, 67.

74. *Times* of London, 27 May 1921, 11; 31 May, 10; q. 2 June, 9.

75. Q. Mullins, *Leipzig Trials*, 227.

76. *Vorwärts*, 26 May 1921, 1 (P.M. ed.).

77. *German War Trials*, 43–45; Mullins, *Leipzig Trials*, 101, 107.

78. *German War Trials*, 44–45, *Times* of London, 6 June 1921, 10.

79. *Times* of London, 6 June 1921, 10.

80. Belgium, *Rapports et documents* 1, t. 2:271.

81. Report of 15 June 1921, MFA, 324, VI; published in Belgium, *Rapports et documents* 1, t. 2:294, 298.

82. Della Faille to Jaspar, 14 June 1921, MFA, 324, V.

83. *Times* of London, 31 May 1921, 10.

84. Della Faille to Jaspar, 29 July 1921, MFA, 324, XVI; see also Belgium, *Rapports et documents* 1, t. 2:289–90.

85. Report of 16 June 1921, MFA, 324, VI; Mullins, *Leipzig Trials*, 150.

86. Della Faille to Jaspar, 14 June 1921, MFA, 324, V.

87. *Le Soir*, 11 June 1921, 2.

88. Ibid., 13 June 1921, 2.

89. Vandervelde speech of 16 June 1921, MFA, 324, V; MFA to Gaiffier d'Hestroy, ibid., 24 June 1921.

90. Allied conference, 13 Aug. 1921, *DBFP* 15:709; Glueck, *War Criminals*, 32.

91. Willis, *Prologue to Nuremberg*, 137; *Literary Digest* 70, no. 1631 (23 July 1921): 11; *New York Times*, 9 July 1921, 8; *San Francisco Chronicle*, 5 July 1921, 24; 15 July, 22; q. *Nation* (New York), 3693 (12 Oct.): 397.

92. *German War Trials*, 47, 51, 53, 54.

93. Ibid., 55.

94. Ibid., 56.

95. Glueck, *War Criminals,* 153, 154.

96. Schwengler, *Völkerrecht,* 355.

97. Q. *Manchester Guardian,* 18 July 1921, 7.

98. Allied conference, 12 Aug. 1921, *DBFP* 15:708.

99. *Parliamentary Debates,* 5th ser., Commons 146 (17 Aug. 1921): 1535–36.

100. Della Faille to Jaspar, 20 Aug. 1921, MFA, 324, VI.

101. Willis, *Prologue to Nuremberg,* 139–40.

102. Commission on Leipzig Trials, 7 Jan. 1922, MFA, 324, VIII.

103. Horne and Kramer, *German Atrocities,* 353.

104. Willis, *Prologue to Nuremberg,* 142.

105. Q. Glueck, *War Criminals,* 33.

106. Berthelot to Vandervelde, 28 July 1925, MFA, 324, XII.

107. Horne and Kramer, *German Atrocities,* 57–58; Belgium, *Rapports et documents* 1, t. 1:259.

108. MFA minute, 25 Apr. 1923, MFA, 324, XIII, "Coupables de guerre: cas divers."

109. J. Pirenne, "Le procès des déportés belges contre le Reich allemand," *Revue de droit international et de législation comparée,* 3d ser., 5 (1924): 102, 106, 114.

110. *Times* of London, 14 July 1925, 13.

111. Schwengler, *Völkerrecht,* 355.

112. Conversation between Crowe and the German ambassador, 3 Feb. 1922, *DBFP* 20:375.

113. Willis, *Prologue to Nuremberg,* 141.

114. Horne and Kramer, *German Atrocities,* 353.

115. Adelmann to MFA, 30 Apr. 1926, MFA, 324, XIII, "Coupables de guerre: cas divers."

116. Schwengler, *Völkerrecht,* 358.

117. Q. ibid., 356–57.

NOTES TO CHAPTER 14: A POPULAR DELUSION

1. Keynes, *Economic Consequences,* 145.

2. Ibid., 153.

3. Ibid., 64.

4. Ibid., 122, 123.

5. Ibid.

6. Ibid., 125, 126.

7. Ibid., 225.

8. William R. Keylor, "Versailles and International Diplomacy," in Boemeke, Feldman, and Glaser, *Treaty of Versailles,* 486n; Étienne Mantoux, *Carthaginian Peace,* 6.

9. Martin Gilbert, *The Roots of Appeasement* (New York, 1966), 64–65.

10. Wood, *Industrial Machinery*, 22.

11. Luckau, *German Delegation*, 357.

12. Sally Marks, "Smoke and Mirrors: In Smoke-Filled Rooms and the *Galerie des Glaces*," in Boemeke, Feldman, and Glaser, *Treaty of Versailles*, 363; Marks, *Innocent Abroad*, 175, 176.

13. See, e.g., Keylor, "Versailles and International Diplomacy," 502; Ferguson, *Pity of War*, 410–415.

14. See, e.g., Gerald D. Feldman, "A Comment," in Boemeke, Feldman, and Glaser, *Treaty of Versailles*, 446–47.

15. Marks, "Smoke and Mirrors," 367; "Notes to Part VIII, Articles 231 to 247," *Foreign Relations, PPC* 13:408–9.

16. Keylor, "Versailles and International Diplomacy," 502, citing Stephen A. Schuker.

17. B. R. Mitchell, *European Historical Statistics, 1750–1975*, 2d rev. ed. (New York, 1980), 124, 126.

18. Marks, *Innocent Abroad*, 326–27.

19. Marks, "Smoke and Mirrors," 362.

20. Marks, *Innocent Abroad*, 325, 326–27.

21. Ibid., 203.

22. *Living Age* 304 (27 Mar. 1920): 745.

23. *DBFP* 8:238–52.

24. Q. *Living Age* 311 (July 1921): 36.

25. Ibid.

26. Montague, *Disenchantment*, 181.

27. Q. *Living Age* 304 (27 Mar. 1920): 756, 757, 759, 760.

28. *Manchester Guardian*, 4 June 1921, 8.

29. Mullins, *Leipzig Trials*, 18.

30. Ibid., 192.

31. Ibid., 194.

32. Ibid., 234.

33. George Gordon Battle, "The Trials Before the Leipsic Supreme Court of Germans Accused of War Crimes," *Virginia Law Review* 8, no. 1 (Nov. 1921): 17.

34. William Archer, "The Germans in Belgium," *Quarterly Review* 236, no. 468 (1921): 190.

35. Elbridge Colby, "War Crimes and Their Punishment," *Minnesota Law Review* 8, 1 (Dec. 1923): 44.

36. Ibid., 45.

37. Elbridge Colby, "War Crimes," *Michigan Law Review* 23, no. 5 (March 1925): 496.

38. C. Perlès, *Histoire de la Grande Guerre racontée aux enfants belges* (Brussels, 1919), 170.

39. Ibid. Italics original.

40. Mercier, *Voice of Belgium*, 174.

41. Schwengler, *Völkerrecht*, 48n.

42. Germany, *Der Belgische Volkskrieg*, 143, 206.

43. Ibid., 227–39.

44. Ibid., 242, 244.

45. Ibid., 206.

46. Horne and Kramer, *German Atrocities*, 391–93.

47. Germany, *Die Zwangsüberführung*, 193–97.

48. Ibid., 197, 198.

49. Conseil des Ministres, 23 May 1927, 427; 20 June, 506–7.

50. Ibid., 2 Sep. 1927, 634–35.

51. Ibid., 30 Aug. 1927, 618–19.

52. Unsigned, unaddressed memo, "Violation du droit des gens pendant la guerre 1914–1918," Jan. 1928, MFA, 298 VI.

53. C. Harley Grattan, *Why We Fought* (New York, 1929), 70.

54. Vandervelde to de Broqueville, 13 Oct. 1927, MFA, 298, V.

55. Wittgens, *German Foreign Office Campaign*, v, 99, 148.

56. Harry Elmer Barnes, *In Quest of Truth and Justice* (Chicago, 1928), 94–95.

57. Irene Cooper Willis, *England's Holy War: A Study of English Liberal Idealism During the Great War* (New York, 1928), 5.

58. Ibid., 186.

59. Georges Demartial, *La guerre de 1914: Comment on mobilisa les consciences* (Paris, 1922), 16.

60. Arthur Ponsonby, *Falsehood in War-Time: Containing an Assortment of Lies Circulated Throughout the Nations During the Great War* (New York, 1928), 29.

61. Ibid., 21. For a similar rhetorical device, see George Sylvester Viereck, *Spreading Germs of Hate* (New York, 1930).

62. Grattan, *Why We Fought*, 69.

63. Ibid., 383.

64. Montague, *Disenchantment*, 95.

65. Ibid., 98.

66. Horne and Kramer, *German Atrocities*, 384, 398; *Revue belge des livres, documents et archives de la guerre 1914–1918*, no. 2 (Feb.–Apr. 1937): 306–7.

67. Horne and Kramer, *German Atrocities*, 391; *Revue belge*, no. 2 (Feb.–Apr. 1937): 307–8.

68. Horne and Kramer, *German Atrocities*, 387.

69. *Revue belge*, no. 2 (Feb.–Apr. 1937): 306.

70. Ibid., 307.

71. Wittgens, *German Foreign Office Campaign*, 261.

72. H. C. Peterson, *Propaganda for War: The Campaign Against American Neutrality, 1914–1917* (Norman, OK, 1939), 38.

73. Ibid., 65.

74. Ibid., 244.

75. Read, *Atrocity Propaganda,* 286.

76. Q. Richard Breitman, *Official Secrets: What the Nazis Planned, What the British and Americans Knew* (New York, 1998), 125.

77. Walter Laqueur, *The Terrible Secret: Suppression of the Truth about Hitler's "Final Solution"* (Boston, 1980), 8–9.

78. Paul Fussell, *The Great War and Modern Memory* (New York, 2000), 316.

79. Breitman, *Official Secrets,* 104.

80. Q. Laqueur, *Terrible Secret,* 32.

81. Breitman, *Official Secrets,* 119.

82. Q. Konrad Kwiet, "Rehearsing for Murder: The Beginning of the Final Solution in Lithuania in 1941," *Holocaust and Genocide Studies* 12, no. 1 (Spring 1998): 5–6.

83. Keynes, *Economic Consequences,* 269–70.

84. Ferguson, *Pity of War,* 410–11.

85. Marks, "Smoke and Mirrors," 349.

86. Carton de Wiart, *Souvenirs politiques* 2:26.

87. David French, "'Had We Known How Bad Things Were in Germany, We Might Have Got Stiffer Terms': Great Britain and the German Armistice," in Boemeke, Feldman, and Glaser, *Treaty of Versailles,* 81, 85.

88. Willard B. Cowles, "Universality of Jurisdiction over War Crimes," *California Law Review* 33, no. 2 (June 1945): 198.

89. Max Montgelas, *The Case for the Central Powers: An Impeachment of the Versailles Verdict,* trans. Constance Vesey (New York, 1925), 225.

90. Q. *New York Times,* 7 Apr. 1987, 12.

Bibliography

ARCHIVAL SOURCES

ARCHIVES GÉNÉRALES DU ROYAUME/ALGEMEEN RIJKSARCHIEF, BRUSSELS

Papiers des Conseils des Ministres, 1919, 1927.
Papiers Schollaert-Helleputte, 124. Unofficial notes of ministerial deliberations, 2 August 1914.
Archives Privées, Mémoires de Guerre, 1914–1918, B94:
    Nos. 1–6, folder 1. Journal of Dr. J. Godenne, Malines. August 1914.
    No. 24. Journal of D. Oudou, Mons. April–November 1918.
    No. 27. Journal of Charles Lemaire, Sart-le-Spa (Liège). July 1914–November 1918.
    No. 29. Memoir of Charles Van Swygenhoven, curate, Beeringen (Limburg). August 1914–November 1918.
    No. 33. Memoir of Jean Bruyr, curate, Sosoye-Maredret (Namur). August 1914–November 1918.
    No. 34. Journal of Dr. Edmond Min, burgomaster, Bolinne-Harlue (Namur). August 1914–November 1918.
    No. 37. Extracts of letters of René Ponchelet, army enlistee, Ghent, to his parents. August 1914.

BELGIAN MINISTRY OF FOREIGN AFFAIRS, BRUSSELS

298, V Atrocités allemandes—francs-tireurs—projet enquête internationale 1927.
298, VI Atrocités allemandes, Francs-Tireurs XI.
324, II Livraison des coupables, correspondance.
324, V Livraison des coupables, correspondance.
324, VI Livraison des coupables, Article 228 du Traité de Versailles.
324, VIII Procès Leipzig.
324, XII Liste des jugements rendus à charge d'allemands coupables de guerre.
324, XIII Cas particuliers: Allemands qui protestent contre leur inscription sur la liste des coupables.
324, XIII Manoeuvres de Erzberger pour la non-livraison des coupables.

324, XIII Coupables de guerre: cas divers.
324, XIV Coupables de guerre.
324, XV Coupables de guerre.
324, XVI Affaire Ramdohr, pièces principales.

HOOVER INSTITUTION ARCHIVES, STANFORD UNIVERSITY

American Relief Administration, European Unit, Box 339. Folder 18, Paris Office Countries File, Belgium Articles, 1919.

Frank Angell Papers. Box 3, "The Belgians Under the German Occupation," December 1918.

Tasker H. Bliss Papers. Letter to the American Peace Commission, 26 Feb. 1919.

Commission for Relief in Belgium. London Office General File. Box 126, folders 8, 10, and 14. Belgium field reports, 1915–17. Box 21, folder 5. "Memorandum on Mr. Hoover's Trip to Havre and Paris, March 1915."

Hugh Gibson Papers. Boxes 31–32, letters to Gibson's mother, July 1914–Jan. 1915.

Joseph Coy Green Papers. Box 20, diary selections, 1915–17. Folder 4, essays about occupied Belgium. Folder 6, letters.

Robert A. Jackson Papers. Box 1, diaries, 1915–17.

Max Marawske Collection. Subject File, Box 23, three unnumbered folders of German press clippings about Belgium, 1914–18.

Vance C. McCormick Papers. Diary of the Paris Peace Conference, Jan.–June 1919.

Dana Carleton Munro Papers. Box 1, Belgium folder. Report of the War Relief Commission to the Rockefeller Foundation, 1 Jan. 1915.

David Theodore Nelson Papers. Box 1, letters and diaries of David T. Nelson, 1914–1919. Edited by John P. Nelson.

Scott Hurtt Paradise Papers. Box 1, folders 1–6. Reports from Belgium, Dec. 1914–Apr. 1915.

Eugene F. Poncelet. *In Years Gone By*. Printed memoir of a Belgian-American engineer. 1978.

Poster Collection. BE, GE, UK series, 1914–18.

Robert Withington Letters. Folder of letters home, 1916.

PRINCIPAL NEWSPAPERS AND MAGAZINES

Chicago Tribune
L'Étoile Belge
L'Indépendance Belge
Kölnische Volkszeitung
Kölnische Zeitung

Literary Digest
Manchester Guardian
New York American
New York Herald
New York Times
New York Tribune
Norddeutscher Allegemeine Zeitung
San Francisco Chronicle
Le Soir
Times of London
Vingtième Siècle
Vorwärts
Washington Post

BOOKS, PAMPHLETS, REPORTS, AND JOURNAL ARTICLES

Amara, Michaël. "La propagande belge et l'image de la Belgique aux États-Unis pendant la Première Guerre mondiale." *Revue belge d'histoire contemporaine* 30, nos. 1–2:173–226.

Asquith, H[erbert] H[enry]. *Letters to Venetia Stanley.* Edited by Michael Brock and Eleanor Brock. Oxford, 1982.

Bass, Gary Jonathan. *Stay the Hand of Vengeance: The Politics of War Crimes Tribunals.* Princeton, 2000.

Bassompierre, Albert de. *The Night of August 2–3, 1914, at the Belgian Foreign Office.* London, 1916.

Baudhuin, Fernand. *Histoire économique de la Belgique, 1914–1939.* 2d ed. vol. 1. Brussels, 1946.

Belgian Delegates to the United States. *The Case of Belgium in the Present War: An Account of the Violation of the Neutrality of Belgium and the Laws of War on Belgian Territory.* New York, 1914.

Belgium. Ministry of Justice, Ministry of Foreign Affairs. *Réponse au Livre Blanc allemand du 10 Mai 1915.* Paris, 1916.

Belgium. Ministry of Justice. Commission d'Enquête sur les Violations des Règles du Droit des Gens, des Lois et des Coutûmes de la Guerre. *Reports on the Violation of the Rights of Nations and of the Laws and Customs of War in Belgium.* 2 vols. London, 1915, 1916.

———. *Rapports et documents d'enquête.* Vol. 1, *Rapports sur les attentats commis par les troupes allemandes pendant l'invasion et l'occupation de la Belgique.* Tome 1, Brussels, 1922. Tome 2, Brussels, 1923.

———. Vol. 2. *Rapports sur les déportations des ouvriers belge et sur les traitements infligés aux prisonniers de guerre et aux prisonniers civils belges.* Brussels, 1923.

———. Vol. 3. *Rapport sur les mesures prises par les allemands à l'égard de l'industrie belge pendant l'occupation.* Tomes 1, 2, Brussels, 1921.

———. Vol. 4. *Rapports sur les mesures législatives, judiciaires, administratives et politiques prises par les Allemands pendant l'occupation. Rapport d'ensemble et conclusions.* Brussels, 1923.

Bellot, Hugh H. L. "War Crimes and War Criminals." *Canadian Law Times* 36, no. 10 (Oct. 1916): 754–68; 11:876–86; 37, no. 1:9–22.

———. "War Crimes: Their Prevention and Punishment." *Transactions of the Grotius Society* (Mar. 1916): 31–55.

Bernhardi, Friedrich Adam Julius von. *Germany and the Next War.* Translated by Allen H. Powles. New York, 1914.

Best, Geoffrey. *Humanity in Warfare: The Modern History of the International Law of Armed Conflicts.* London, 1980.

Binding, Rudolf. *A Fatalist at War.* Translated by Ian F. D. Morrow. Boston, 1929.

Bisschop, W. R. "German War Legislation in the Occupied Territory of Belgium." *Transactions of the Grotius Society* 4 (1919): 110–68.

Bissing, Moritz von. *General von Bissing's Testament: A Study in German Ideals.* [no trans.] London, 1917.

Bitsch, Marie-Thérèse. *La Belgique entre la France et l'Allemagne, 1905–1914.* Paris, 1994.

Bloem, Walter. *The Advance from Mons.* Translated by G. C. Wynne. London, 1930.

Blücher, Evelyn. *An English Wife in Berlin.* New York, 1920.

Boemeke, Manfred F., Gerald D. Feldman, and Elisabeth Glaser, eds. *The Treaty of Versailles: A Reassessment after 75 Years.* Washington, 1998.

Bordwell, Percy. *The Law of War Between Belligerents: A History and Commentary.* Chicago, 1908.

Bucholz, Arden. *Moltke, Schlieffen and Prussian War Planning.* New York, 1991.

Cammaerts, Emile. *Albert of Belgium, Defender of Right.* [no trs.] New York, 1935.

Carton de Wiart, Henry. *Souvenirs politiques.* 2 vols. Brussels, 1981.

Crokaert, Jacques. "L'Ultimatum allemand du 2 août 1914." *Le Flambeau* 5, no. 3 (March 1922): 307–330.

Davignon, Henri. *Souvenirs d'un écrivain belge (1879–1945).* Paris, 1954.

Davis, Richard Harding. *With the Allies.* New York, 1917.

De Thier, Jules, and Olympe Gilbart. *Liège pendant la grande guerre.* 4 vols. Liège, 1919.

Duchesne, Oscar. "Jodoigne pendant l'occupation allemande 1914–1918." *Service de recherches historiques et folkloriques du Brabant* 9 (1930): 9–77.

Edmonds, J. E. *Military Operations: France and Belgium, 1914.* 2 vols. London, 1926.

Feldman, Gerald D. *Army, Industry, and Labor in Germany, 1914–1918.* Princeton, 1966.

Ferguson, Niall. *The Pity of War: Explaining World War I.* New York, 1999.

Fischer, Fritz. *Germany's Aims in the First World War.* [no trs.] New York, 1967.

French, David. *The Strategy of the Lloyd George Coalition, 1916–1918.* Oxford, 1995.

Gay, George I. *Public Relations of the Commission for Relief in Belgium: Documents.* 2 vols. Stanford, 1929.

Germany. Ministry of War. *The German Army in Belgium: The White Book of May 1915.* Translated by E. N. Bennett. New York, 1921.

———. *The War Book of the German General Staff: Being "The Usages of War on Land" Issued by the Great General Staff of the German Army.* Translated by J. H. Morgan. New York, 1915.

Germany. Nationalversammlung, Untersuchungsausschuss. *Das Werk des Untersuchungsausschusses der Verfassunggebenden Deutschen Nationalversammlung und des Deutschen Reichstages, 1919–1928. Völkerrecht im Weltkrieg.* Dritte Reihe im Werk des Untersuchungsausschusses. Vol. 2, *Der Belgische Volkskrieg.* Eugen Fischer, Berthold Widmann, and Johannes Bell, eds. Berlin, 1927.

———. Vol. 3, *Die Zwangsüberführung belgischer Arbeiter nach Deutschland.*

Germany. Reichsarchiv. *Der Weltkrieg 1914 bis 1918: Die militärischen Operationen zu Lande.* vol. 1. Berlin, 1925.

Gibson, Hugh. *A Journal from Our Legation in Belgium.* New York, 1917.

Gille, Louis, Alphonse Ooms, and Paul Delandsheere. *Cinquante mois d'occupation allemande.* 4 vols. Brussels, 1919.

Glueck, Sheldon. *War Criminals: Their Prosecution and Punishment.* New York, 1944.

Graber, Doris Appel. *The Development of the Law of Belligerent Occupation, 1863–1914: A Historical Survey.* New York, 1949.

Great Britain. Committee on Alleged German Outrages. *Report of the Committee on Alleged German Outrages Appointed by His Britannic Majesty's Government and Presided Over by the Right Hon. Viscount Bryce.* New York, 1915.

———. *Evidence and Documents Laid Before the Committee on Alleged German Outrages: Being an Appendix to the Report of the Committee Appointed by His Britannic Majesty's Government and Presided Over by the Right Hon. Viscount Bryce, O.M.* New York, 1915.

Great Britain. Foreign Office. *Documents on British Foreign Policy.* 1st ser., 1919–1929. London, 1946–.

Great Britain. Parliament. *German War Trials: Report of Proceedings Before the Supreme Court in Leipzig.* House of Commons Sessional Papers. *Reports from Commissioners,* 11–12. vol 2. Command Paper 1422. London, 1922.

Gullace, Nicoletta F. "Sexual Violence and Family Honor: British Propaganda and International Law during the First World War." *American Historical Review* 102, no. 3 (1997): 714–47.

Hall, William Edward. *A Treatise on International Law.* 6th ed. New York, 1909.

Higgins, A. Pearce. *The Hague Peace Conferences and Other International Conferences Concerning the Laws and Usages of War: Texts of Conventions with Commentaries.* Cambridge, 1909.

Höcker, Paul Oskar. *An der Spitze meiner Kompagnie.* New York, 1914.

Horne, John, and Alan Kramer. *German Atrocities, 1914: A History of Denial.* New Haven, 2001.

House, E. M. *The Intimate Papers of Colonel House.* Edited by Charles Seymour. 4 vols. Boston, 1926.

Hunt, Edward Eyre. *War Bread: A Personal Narrative of the War and Relief in Belgium.* New York, 1916.

Hymans, Paul. *Mémoires.* 2 vols. Brussels, 1958.

Jarausch, Konrad H. *The Enigmatic Chancellor: Bethmann Hollweg and the Hubris of Imperial Germany.* New Haven, 1973.

Kerchove de Denterghem, Charles de. *L'Industrie belge pendant l'occupation allemande, 1914–1918.* Histoire économique et sociale de la guerre mondiale, série Belge. Paris, n.d.

Keynes, John Maynard. *The Economic Consequences of the Peace.* New York, 1920.

Köhler, Ludwig von. *The Administration of the Occupied Territories.* Vol. 1, *Belgium.* Translated by W. R. Dittmer. Washington, 1942.

Lichtervelde, Louis de. *Avant l'orage (1911–1914).* Brussels, 1938.

Link, Arthur S., ed. *The Papers of Woodrow Wilson.* vols. 30–51. Princeton, 1979–.

Lowry, Bullitt. *Armistice 1918.* Kent, OH, 1996.

Luckau, Alma Maria. *The German Delegation at the Paris Peace Conference.* 1941. Reprint. Ann Arbor, 1987.

Mantoux, Paul. *The Deliberations of the Council of Four (March 24–June 28, 1919): Notes of the Official Interpreter.* Translated and edited by Arthur S. Link, with Manfred F. Boemeke. 2 vols. Princeton, 1992.

Marks, Sally. *Innocent Abroad: Belgium at the Paris Peace Conference of 1919.* Chapel Hill, 1981.

Mayence, Fernand. *The Legend of the "Francs-Tireurs" of Louvain: A Reply to the Report of Dr. Meurer, Professor at the University of Würzburg.* Translated by E. Louisa Thompson. Louvain, 1928.

Mercier, Cardinal Desiré. *The Voice of Belgium: Being the War Utterances of Cardinal Mercier.* [no trans.] London, n.d.

Messinger, Gary S. *British Propaganda and the State in the First World War.* New York, 1992.

Mokveld, L. *The German Fury in Belgium: Experiences of a Netherland Journalist During Four Months with the German Army in Belgium.* Translated by C. Thieme. New York, 1917.

Montague, C. E. *Disenchantment.* London, 1922.

Mullins, Claud. *The Leipzig Trials: An Account of the War Criminals' Trials and a Study of German Mentality.* London, 1921.

Nash, George H. *The Life of Herbert Hoover.* Vol 2, *The Humanitarian, 1914–1917.* New York, 1988.

O'Brien, William V. "The Meaning of `Military Necessity' in International Law." *World Polity* 1 (1957): 109–76.

Oppenheim, Lassa. *International Law: A Treatise.* 4th ed. Vol. 2, *War.* Edited by Arnold D. McNair. London, 1926.

Passelecq, Fernand. *Déportation et travail forcé des ouvriers et de la population civile de la Belgique occupée (1916–1918).* Histoire économique et sociale de la guerre mondiale, série Belge. Paris, 1927.

———. *Les déportations belges à la lumière des documents allemands.* Paris, 1917.

Petri, Franz, and Peter Schöller. "Zur Bereinigung des Franktireurproblems vom August 1914." *Vierteljahrshefte für Zeitgeschichte* 9, no. 3 (July 1961): 234–48.

Phillipson, Coleman. *Wheaton's Elements of International Law.* 5th English ed. New York, 1916.

Pirenne, Henri. *The "Journal de guerre" of Henri Pirenne.* Edited by Bryce Lyon and Mary Lyon. Amsterdam, 1976.

———. *La Belgique et la guerre mondiale.* Histoire économique et sociale de la guerre mondiale, série Belge. Paris, 1928.

Pirenne, J[acques], and M[aurice] Vauthier. *La Législation et l'administration allemandes en Belgique.* Histoire économique et sociale de la guerre mondiale, série Belge. Paris, 1925.

Powell, E. Alexander. *Fighting in Flanders.* New York, 1914.

Renault, Louis. "L'Application du droit pénal aux faits de guerre." *Revue générale de droit international public* 25 (1918): 5–29.

Riezler, Kurt. *Kurt Riezler: Tagebücher, Aufsätsze, Dokumente.* Edited by Karl Dietrich Erdmann. Deutsche Geschichtsquellen des 19. und 20. Jahrhunderts, vol. 48. Göttingen, 1972.

Ritter, Gerhard. *The Schlieffen Plan: Critique of a Myth.* Translated by Andrew Wilson and Eva Wilson. New York, 1958.

Roosevelt, Theodore. *The Letters of Theodore Roosevelt.* Vols. 7, 8. Edited by Elting E. Morison. Cambridge, MA, 1954.

Root, Elihu. "Opening Address." *Proceedings of the American Society of International Law at Its Ninth Annual Meeting.* Washington, 1916.

Schaepdrijver, Sophie de. "Occupation, Propaganda, and the Idea of Belgium." In Aviel Roshwald and Richard Stites, eds. *European Culture in the Great War: The Arts, Entertainment, and Propaganda, 1914–1918.* Cambridge, 1999.

Schmitz, J., and Norbert Nieuwland. *Documents pour servir à l'histoire de l'invasion allemande dans les provinces de Namur et de Luxembourg.* Vols. 1, 4. Brussels, 1919.

Schöller, Peter. *Le cas de Louvain et le Livre Blanc allemand: Étude critique de la documentation allemande relative aux événements qui se sont déroulés à Louvain du 25 au 28 août 1914.* Translated by E. Nieuwborg. Louvain, 1958.

Schwengler, Walter. *Völkerrecht, Versailler Vertrag und Auslieferungsfrage: Die Strafverfolgung wegen Kriegsverbrechen als Problem des Friedensschlusses 1919/20.* Stüttgart, 1982.

Strikwerda, Carl. *A House Divided: Catholics, Socialists, and Flemish Nationalists in Nineteenth-Century Belgium.* Lanham, MD, 1997.

Tassier, Suzanne. *La Belgique et l'entrée en guerre des Etats-Unis (1914–1917).* Brussels, 1951.

Thielemans, Marie-Rose. *Albert Ier: Carnets et correspondance de guerre, 1914–1918.* Paris, 1991.

Thielemans, Marie-Rose, and Emile Vandewoude. *Le Roi Albert au travers de ses lettres inédites, 1882–1916.* Brussels, 1982.

U.S. Department of State. *Papers Relating to the Foreign Relations of the United States.* Washington, 1925–.

———. *The Lansing Papers, 1914–1920.* 2 vols. Washington, 1939.

———. *Paris Peace Conference, 1919.* Washington, 1930.

U.S. War Department. Office of the Chief of Staff. *Rules of Land Warfare, 1914.* New York, 1914.

Vanderschaege, Michel. *La vie quotidienne à Stavelot pendant la guerre 1914–1918.* Stavelot, 1982.

Van Langenhove, Fernand. *The Growth of a Legend: A Study Based Upon the German Accounts of Francs-Tireurs and `Atrocities' in Belgium.* New York, 1916.

Vierset, Auguste. *Mes souvenirs sur l'occupation allemande en Belgique.* Paris, 1932.

Westlake, John. *International Law. Part II: War.* Cambridge, England, 1907.

Whitlock, Brand. *Belgium: A Personal Narrative.* 2 vols. New York, 1919.

———. *The Letters and Journal of Brand Whitlock.* Edited by Allan Nevins. 2 vols. New York, 1936.

Willis, James. F. *Prologue to Nuremberg: The Politics and Diplomacy of Punishing War Criminals of the First World War.* Westport, CT, 1982.

Index

absentia trials, 248, 256–57

Aerschot, massacre at: 29, 82; Belgian inquiry into, 72–74; in Bryce report, 135; in foreign press, 76, 129; German charges concerning, 55, 56; postwar controversy about, 266, 269

Albert I, king of the Belgians: and Belgian government, 14–16, 18–20, 86–87, 166, 169–70; character of, 7; diplomacy of, 6–7, 19, 68–69, 160, 169–70, 193, 204, 234–35; generalship of, 27, 55, 73, 84, 170, 204, 205; and German crimes, 62, 87, 169, 170, 269; mistrusts Allies, 87–88, 139, 169–70 204, 223; popularity of, 63, 100, 131, 170, 215; views of Germany, 16, 19, 40, 87–88, 169–70, 204, 272

Allies: Albert's mistrust of, 87–88, 139, 169–70, 204, 223; and Antwerp, 82–83, 86; and Belgium, 8–9, 19, 59, 62, 81–82, 117, 124, 168, 169, 268, 269–70, 271; and deportations, 156, 163; and peace terms, 205–7, 208–13, 221–40, 260, 262, 271–74; and U.S., 180–81, 193–94, 200, 222–23, 273; and war crimes, 122–23, 125, 172–73, 201–2, 205, 213–15, 227–31, 232–34, 239–40, 242–49, 251–58, 262–64, 273–74. See also Britain; France; Leipzig trials

Andenne, massacre at: 29, 82; alleged perpetrators accused, 247; in Bryce report, 135; German charges concerning, 53, 55, 56, 58, 82; postwar controversy about, 266

Antwerp (city): 18, 24, 27, 29, 30, 34, 51, 59, 71, 76, 85, 88, 89, 90, 93, 179; and deportations, 153, 163, 164, 215; importance of, 8–10, 14, 15, 17, 44–45, 78, 83; military operations at, 27, 30–31, 55, 62, 73, 82–83, 84; under occupation, 90, 102, 110, 142, 153

Antwerp (province), 90, 117, 186

armistice: 190, 207, 212–13, 215–16, 219, 221, 222, 223, 224, 226, 228, 237, 239, 240, 242, 243, 261, 272, 273; German

objections to, 211, 224–25, 239; public opposition elsewhere, 206–10; and war crimes, 210–11

Asquith, H. H., 81, 82, 95–96; and war crimes, 131, 171, 172, 200, 273

atrocity stories: American taste for, 138, 194–95; Belgians reconsider, 193; and Bryce report, 131–32, 133, 134; charges against Belgians, 22–23, 27, 29–30, 34–36, 51, 59, 65–66, 68; charges against Germans, 20, 70–71, 73–75, 77; discounted, 67, 121–22, 124, 132, 233, 265, 266–67, 268; mentioned, 44; and Nazis, 269–71. See also press; war crimes

Austria, 5, 8, 41, 201

Baden, Max von, 207, 208, 209, 213

Balfour, Arthur, 209, 211, 228, 243

Banque Nationale, 5, 29, 63, 117, 203, 224

Belgium: and Allied cause, 85, 87, 95–96, 169–70, 190–91, 217, 219–20, 222, 225, 230, 231–32, 233–34, 259–63, 268–71, 274–75; American opinion of, 63–72, 75–76, 121–22, 123, 128–30, 131–32, 134, 137–38, 161–63, 179–82, 192–95, 205–10, 219–20, 265, 267, 268, 269–70; attitude toward occupiers of, 109–10, 137, 139, 262; British blockade and, 80–82, 95–96, 160; British views of, 118–21, 131–32, 134–35, 138–41, 172–73, 208, 259–60, 262–64, 268; creation of, 8–10, 45; decision to resist Germany of, 14–19, 46–47, 61, 77; domestic politics of, 10, 14, 44–45, 62–63, 67, 68, 184–85, 198, 219, 236–37, 254; and Fleming-Walloon dispute, 8, 78, 145–47, 165–69, 197–98; and Franco-Prussian War, 7, 44; geography of, 9–10; German contempt for, 42–43, 45–47, 59–60, 165–66; liberation of, 215–17; military operations in, 22–27, 29–31, 53–61, 73, 82–85, 86–87, 204, 205, 215–17; mobilization of, 5–6, 12; neutrality of, 5, 7–8, 11, 16–18, 19–20, 38–43, 85–88, 138–39, 229,

Belgium (*Continued*)
230, 263, 273; postwar trials and, 243–45, 248, 252–54, 256–58; relations with Britain, 85–88, 147–48, 170–71, 221–22, 223–24, 231–32, 234–36; relations with Germany, 11–13, 19, 24–26, 42- 43, 51, 169–70, 204, 206, 244–45, 267, 269; relations with U.S., 62–63, 66–69, 71–72, 192–93, 222, 234; reluctance to arm of, 10, 16, 18, 44–46; statistics relating to, 5, 44–45, 80, 85, 90, 111, 118, 142, 145, 164, 183, 187–90, 218–19, 261. *See also* atrocity stories; deportations; *Flamenpolitik*; food shortages; occupation; Schlieffen, Alfred von; Treaty of 1839; war crimes

Below-Saleske, Karl-Konrad von, 11–12, 14, 19, 42

Bernhardi, Friedrich von, 42–43, 146, 168

Bernstorff, Johann von, 66, 86

Bethmann Hollweg, Theobald von: contempt for Belgium, 40, 43; deportations and, 152, 163–65; *Flamenpolitik* and, 78, 145–46, 151, 186; mentioned, 20, 89, 91, 124; and Treaty of Versailles, 240, 246, 248

Beyens, Napoléon Eugène, 19, 46, 161, 221

Bissing, Moritz von: character of, 93; death of, 186, 195; and deportations, 149, 150, 151, 159, 160, 163, 266; economic policies of, 106–7, 222; and *Flamenpolitik*, 145–47, 151, 159, 186–87; labor policies of, 111–16, 145, 147–49; and political surveillance, 116–17; views on Belgium, 97, 108, 112–13, 145–46; and war contributions, 93–94, 117, 178

Bloem, Walter Julius, 25, 51, 58, 60–61, 168

Boer War, 49, 82, 127, 134, 233

Boldt, John, 255–56, 258

bolshevism, fears of, 213, 225, 228, 231, 243; Germans invoke, 227, 245

Brabant, 27, 29, 30, 49, 187; and deportations, 153–55, 177; and war contributions, 117

Brest-Litovsk, Treaty of, 204

Britain: Albert mistrusts, 86–88, 169–70; and armistice, 208, 210–12; and Belgian refugees, 85, 106, 170, 179, 223; and Belgian relief, 81, 95–96, 147–48, 171, 185–86; as Belgium's guardian, 8–9, 19, 40, 43–44; Belgium's moral value to, 19, 77, 81, 95–96, 118–19, 140–41, 263–64; blindness to Belgium, 82–83, 118–19, 136–38, 140–41, 173, 273–75; blockade and, 80–82, 92, 97, 113, 130, 147–48, 171, 185–86; Boer War and, 49, 82, 127, 134, 233; and Bryce report, 131–36; and Cavell case, 117–19, 172; and Ducarne-Bernardiston affair, 85–86; and Fryatt case, 171–73; German accusations of, 66, 80–81, 85–86, 160, 171, 176, 179, 224, 225, 240; legal interpretations of, 48–49, 80–81, 101, 120; and *Lusitania*, 131; military operations of, 27, 30–31, 34, 62, 72, 77, 89, 149; as naval power, 10, 45, 202, 214; and reparations for Belgium, 120–21, 170, 172–73, 200–201, 219, 222–24, 231–32, 234–37, 259–62, 271; and resentment toward Belgium, 170, 220–22, 231–32; and sympathy for Belgium, 43, 88–89, 131–32, 136, 140, 171, 205, 208, 260; view of in U.S., 64, 66, 95–96, 269–70; and war crimes, 120, 122, 123, 130–32, 134–36, 171–73, 201–2, 205–6, 208–15, 227, 230, 232–33, 242–44; and war crimes, postwar doubts about, 136, 259–60, 264–65, 268; and war crimes, postwar trials of, 239–40, 242–49, 251–52, 255–56, 263–65, 272–73, 275. *See also* Asquith, H. H.; atrocity stories; Lloyd George, David; Paris Peace Conference; press

Brockdorff-Rantzau, Ulrich von, 226, 238, 240, 271

Broqueville, Charles de: and German ultimatum, 12–13, 14, 18, 20; mentioned, 45, 62, 67, 86, 128, 221, 269

Brussels: conditions in, 90, 95, 114, 137, 143, 153, 176, 183, 195, 197, 203, 217; congresses at, 112–14, 152, 186; deportations in, 183, 190; on eve of war, 5–6, 10–13, 19–20; fall of, 27- 29, 80; food shortages in, 80, 95, 183; in 1919, 237; under occupation, 161, 190, 195, 197, 203; resistance in, 99–100, 101, 106, 114, 117, 153, 154; in war's early days, 24, 26, 37

Bryce, James, 132, 133–35

Bryce report, 131–36, 270
Bucharest, Treaty of, 204–5, 211

Carton de Wiart, Henry, 18, 87, 215, 216, 217, 219, 272; and mission to U.S., 62–63, 67, 68, 71, 76
Case of Belgium, The, 70–71, 73–75
Catholic Party, 10, 16, 67, 220
Cavell, Edith, 117–19, 172, 194
Charleroi, 89, 191, 218, 234
Chicago Tribune, 65, 86, 131, 180, 210, 220; doubts Belgian claims, 65, 67, 69–70, 72, 121–22, 124, 220
Churchill, Winston, 83, 95, 130
Clemenceau, Georges: description of, 220; at Paris Peace Conference, 220, 221, 225, 227, 230–34, 236, 237, 240, 271; and war crimes, 206, 225, 230, 231, 233, 234, 243, 246
Comité National de Secours de l'Alimentation, 111–12, 113, 115, 143, 145, 216, 244; and Belgian resistance, 112, 113, 115, 143, 152
Commission for Relief in Belgium (CRB): activities of, 95, 97, 107, 111, 112, 142, 183, 184, 218; and belligerents, 95–97, 107, 150, 151, 177, 179, 183, 185, 273; and Herbert Hoover, 95–96, 99, 107, 112, 142, 176, 184, 185, 218, 222; postwar reputation of, 270; witness to occupation, 99–100, 109–11, 142–43, 153–54, 158, 177, 183, 184
Commission on the Responsibility for the Authors of the War and the Enforcement of Penalties, 228–31, 233, 239, 243
Curzon, George, 248

Davignon, Henri, 12, 221
Davignon, Julien, 12, 14, 16, 72
Davis, Richard Harding, 6, 26, 27, 28, 30, 31
Delacroix, Léon, 216, 223, 224, 237, 248
deportations: defenses of, 150, 152–53, 163–65, 171, 175–79, 266–67, 270; during invasion, 30, 32, 36, 57, 58, 59, 133, 136; during 1918 retreat, 206, 215–16; and *Flamenpolitik*, 145, 151, 192; for forced labor, 139, 150–65, 175–83, 185, 187–92, 194, 204, 215–16, 257–58, 263, 270; in France, 148–49, 152, 162, 172,

206; as political punishment, 97, 104–5, 109, 112, 116, 140, 147, 198, 203; postwar views of, 246–47, 262, 265, 266–67, 270; protests against, 160–63, 171, 179–82, 183, 186, 187–88, 194, 273; statistics on, 164, 188–91, 209
Deutsches Industriebüro (Office of German Industry), 111–13, 155, 175, 187, 191
Dinant, massacre at, 30, 56, 57, 58, 60, 62, 75, 131; and German charges regarding, 56, 266; postwar controversy concerning, 266, 269
Dithmar, Ludwig, 255–56, 258
Dresel, Ellis, 224–25, 238–39, 240, 261, 271
Ducarne-Bernardiston conversations, 85–87

East Flanders, 49, 82, 90, 114, 253
Elisabeth, queen of the Belgians, 6–7, 63, 87, 100, 169
Emmich, Otto von, 46, 54
Erzberger, Matthias, 226, 242, 244–45
Etappengebiet: decrees in, 112, 114, 116–17; defined, 151–52; deportations in, 158–59, 188, 189–90. *See also* occupation

Falkenhausen, Ludwig von, 195, 197–98, 202, 246–47
Flamenpolitik: definition of, 78; and deportations, 145, 151, 159, 192; purpose and workings of, 145–47, 165–66, 168–69, 186–87, 197–99
Foch, Ferdinand, 204, 205, 212, 242
food shortages, 75, 80, 82, 94–95, 107, 110, 117, 183, 185, 191, 197; and British blockade, 80–82, 95–97, 270. *See also* Comité National de Secours de l'Alimentation; Commission for Relief in Belgium (CRB)
France: Belgian mistrust of, 8, 16, 86–88, 166, 204; and Belgian relief, 186; compared with Belgium, 45, 220, 263; damage to, 219, 220, 233–34, 263; as danger to Belgium, 5, 8, 10, 11, 15, 16, 40–41, 44, 63, 145; deportations in, 148–49, 152, 162, 172, 206; deportations to, 158–59, 164, 188, 190; and expatriate Belgians, 85, 105–6; and Franco-Prussian War, 38,

France (*Continued*)
44, 47, 120, 272; Germans suspect influence over Belgium, 25, 40, 46–47, 51, 78, 110 166, 168–70; home of Belgian government-in-exile, 85; postwar trials of, 254–55, 256–57; relations with Britain, 19, 220–21, 222, 231, 275; and reparations, 220, 222–24, 226–27, 231, 234, 236–38, 261, 272; and Schlieffen plan, 38–39, 41, 49–50, 77; ties to Belgium, 8–9, 140; and U.S., 204, 206, 208–10, 261; and war crimes, 49, 123, 206, 208, 230–34, 239–40, 243–44, 246–48, 254–55, 256–58, 262–64, 275. See also *Flamenpolitik*; Paris Peace Conference

francs-tireurs, 25, 27, 29–30, 55–56, 57, 75; and Louvain, 31–36, 55–57, 65–66, 266; and anti-Catholic feeling, 32, 34, 36–37, 51, 56, 77; in foreign press, 65–66, 69, 140, 264; and Franco-Prussian War, 38, 44, 47–48; and Fryatt case, 171–72; German hatred for, 22–23, 25, 27, 30, 51–53, 54, 58, 59–61, 65–66, 68, 77, 125; in German writings, 25, 47, 51, 57–61, 65–66, 125, 132, 168, 266; and Holocaust, 270–71; lack of evidence for, 53–57, 76–77; postwar controversy regarding, 257, 265–69. See also Hague Conventions, The

Fryatt, Charles, 171–73, 174, 176, 273

Garde Civique, 19, 24, 30, 36, 105

Generalgouvernement: conditions in, 91, 97, 183; defined, 90–91; deportations in, 153–58, 187–90. See also occupation

Gerard, James W., 71, 180

Germany: and Allies, 19, 59, 63, 145, 149, 150, 155, 204–5, 207–8; accuses Belgium, 22–23, 27, 34–36, 46–47, 51, 55–57, 58–59, 65–66, 69, 85–86, 139, 152–53, 176–77, 266–67; Albert's connections to, 6–7; and British blockade, 80–81, 92, 96–97, 130–31, 176, 185–86, 240, 270; contempt for Belgium, 42–43, 45–47, 51, 59–60, 146, 165–66, 168–69, 175–77; danger to Belgium, 5, 10, 11, 16, 17, 42–43, 78–79, 206; dissent in, 57, 126, 160, 205, 247, 256, 263, 266–67; economy of, 44–45, 80, 107–8, 111, 113,

145, 150–51, 176, 179, 187, 203–4, 224–25, 261, 271; fears encirclement, 13, 23, 25, 40–41, 42, 46–47, 49, 50–51, 59, 61, 76, 102, 145–46, 168–69, 240; and Franco-Prussian War, 38, 44, 47, 104–5; and international law, 39–42, 43, 47–49, 65–66, 69, 80–82, 100–102, 104–5, 113–14, 115–16, 117–18, 124–26, 132, 145, 149, 151, 152–53, 160, 163–64, 165, 169, 171–72, 175, 192, 198, 205, 226, 238, 240, 249, 251–52, 255–56, 258, 263, 266–67; invasion by, 20, 22–24, 25–37, 49–62, 82–85; military control in, 40, 99, 150, 188, 207; negotiates with Albert, 169–70, 204; objects to peace terms, 211, 224–27, 238–40, 242–47, 249, 257; press in, 51, 65–66, 108, 132, 148, 149–50, 152–53, 159–60, 171, 176, 178, 179, 225, 245, 247, 250, 252, 254; and ultimatum (of 2 August 1914) to Belgium, 12–20, 38, 40, 41–43, 46, 76, 77, 173, 224; and U.S., 66–67, 71, 86, 131, 162–63, 164–65, 180, 185, 200–202, 204–5, 206–210, 267, 270, 273, and war planning of, 38–51. See also atrocity stories; deportations; *Flamenpolitik*; Leipzig trials; occupation; war crimes

Ghent: and deportations, 189, 190; and *Flamenpolitik*, 146–47, 151, 159; mentioned, 6, 9–10, 83–84, 90, 109, 118, 166, 184–85

Gibson, Hugh, 24, 28–29, 55, 60, 79, 82, 101, 104; and Belgian leaders, 62, 87; at Louvain, 33–34, 36, 58–59

Goltz, Colmar von der, 78, 80, 90–91, 92–93, 96–97, 99, 101

Grattan, C. Hartley, 267, 268

Grey, Edward, 19, 86, 95, 120–21, 200

Hague Conferences, The, 122, 128, 172, 232

Hague Conventions, The: absence of penalties in, 121, 229; and civilians, 48; and deportations, 145, 152, 160, 161, 163, 164, 175, 192; drafting of, 48; "family honour" clause, 49, 105; Fifth Convention, on neutrality, 41, 81, 85, 129, 230; and *Flamenpolitik*, 169; Fourth Convention, on land war, 39, 48, 66, 71, 82, 228; German views of, 39–40,

47–49, 66, 112, 113–14, 171–72, 266; and occupiers' duties, 79, 100–102, 113, 151, 169, 198; and private property, 49, 79, 92, 117, 175; and sovereignty, 79, 148, 169; use in court, 121, 228, 229, 232–33; and war work, 49, 105, 112, 114, 115, 148, 160, 171. *See also* francs-tireurs; invasion terror; war crimes

Hainaut, 27, 90, 115–16, 186, 203; conditions under occupation, 153, 177, 191, 202, 216

hatred: Belgian for Germans, 110–11, 126–27, 136, 137, 170, 265–66; and forgiveness, 118, 124, 126–27, 233–34, 254, 257; German for Belgians, 37, 46–47, 121–22; seen in trials, 265

Hauptmann, Gerhart, 125–26

Heidelberg resolution, 225–26, 274

Herve, 23–24, 25, 26, 135

Herzog, Chaim, 275–76

Hindenburg, Paul von: and arms program, 150; and Bissing, 151, 152, 178–79; and deportations, 151–52, 188, 266–67; prosecution of, 242, 246–48, 256

Höcker, Paul Oskar, 27, 53, 58, 59, 60

Holland: as asylum for Belgians, 85, 97, 103–6, 219; and Belgium's creation, 8–10; and British blockade, 81, 95, 113; and Commission for Relief in Belgium, 95, 185; and deportations, 145, 163–64; and Fryatt case, 172; and Kaiser Wilhelm, 213, 239, 244; and paper marks, 224; trade with Germany, 81, 108, 113; and reversing Treaty of 1839, 219, 221; and Schlieffen plan, 39, 50

Hoover, Herbert. *See under* Commission for Relief in Belgium (CRB)

House, Edward M.: comments on Wilson, 66, 181; correspondence with, 64, 139, 213, 236; describes Clemenceau, 220; lobbies for Belgium, 222, 223, 234; visits Albert, 170; and war crimes, 180, 215. *See also* Paris Peace Conference; Wilson, Woodrow

Hunt, Edward Eyre, 83, 90, 97, 99, 100

Hymans, Paul: and Albert's peace feelers, 204, 206; character, 15, 221; as envoy to U.S., 63, 67–70; and German ultimatum, 15–18, 41, 224; as minister to Britain, 170; and 1913 army bill, 45; at

Paris Peace Conference, 220–21, 231–32, 234–37; and postwar franctireur controversy, 267; and Treaty of 1839, 87

invasion terror: affects Belgian government, 62–63; Albert's views on, 169–70; and Antwerp bombing, 62, 71; and banks, 29, 58; and Battice, 25, 26, 51; explanations for, 53–61; German beliefs about, 51–53, 57–61, 102; and German strategy, 47–49, 50–51, 60; and Hague Conventions, 48–49; and Lloyd George, 230, overshadows occupation, 136–41, 262–66; perceived abroad, 64–77, 88, 120–32, 134–36, 267–68; prosecution of, 245, 247; unplanned, 60–61; statistics on, 22–23, 53–54, 56. *See also* Aerschot, massacre at; Andenne, massacre at; atrocity stories; Bryce report; Dinant, massacre at; Herve; Louvain; Tamines; Visé

Jackson, Robert, 153–54, 177, 179, 183, 184

Jagow, Gottlieb von, 19, 46, 124–25, 163

Japan, 229, 236, 239

Jaspar, Henri, 237, 267

Kerchove de Denterghem, André de, 245, 248

Keynes, John Maynard, 220, 221, 259–61, 271

Kilmarnock, Lord (British ambassador), 245–48

Kitchener, H. H., 82, 95, 97

Kölnische Volkszeitung, 51, 159–60, 286–87n. 29

Kölnische Zeitung, 60, 152–53, 163, 171–72

Kriegsraison, 39–40

Kriegsschuldreferat (War Guilt Department), 267–68

Lancken, Oskar von der, 161, 186, 197

Lansing, Robert: and deportations, 162–63, 165, 180–82; opposes protest over Belgium, 130; at Paris Peace Conference, 221, 228–29, 275; and submarine cases, 201, 229; urges warning to Germany, 206; and war crimes, 130, 228–29, 232, 239

Lapradelle, Albert de, 227–28

Larnaude, Fernand, 227–29, 232

laws of war: and blockade, 80–81; and escapes, 105; and *Kriegsraison*, 39–40; and levies, 94; and neutrality, 41, 64; and occupation, 79, 94, 100–102, 113–14; and *Usages of War*, 47–48. *See also* Hague Conventions, The

League of Nations, 129, 201, 208, 244, 265; and Paris Peace Conference, 221, 232

Leipzig trials: cases heard, 250, 251–56; cases submitted, 249, 262; diplomacy surrounding, 243, 245–48, 262, 275; Germans annul, 258; procedures of, 250–51, 252; reactions to verdicts, 252, 254, 255, 256, 262–65

Leopold II, king of the Belgians, 6, 45–46, 174, 268

Lersner, Kurt von, 246–47

Lessines quarries, 115–16

Liberal Party (Belgium), 10, 15, 67, 220

Lichtervelde, Louis de, 18, 67

Liège (city): and Bryce report, 133; and "corpse factory," 268, 270; and deportations, 189; forts at, 10, 13, 14, 26; geographical importance of, 9; German annexation and, 78; German suspicions and, 53, 76–77; military operations near, 22, 23, 25–27, 29, 53, 54, 62, 82; and Schlieffen plan, 40, 50; under occupation, 90, 92, 99, 183

Liège (province): 9, 49, 58, 104, 177, 186; conditions in, 94, 105, 216

Limburg, 9, 49; under occupation, 54–55, 82, 95, 105, 117, 177, 186, 216

Literary Digest, 201, 208

Lloyd George, David: and armistice negotiations, 211; and Belgian relief, 95; and hostility to Belgium, 221–22; and Hymans, 231–32; at Paris Peace Conference, 221–25, 227–37, 239–40; and reparations, 200–201, 222–24, 231–32, 234–36, 237, 271; and war crimes trials, 205, 213–15, 227, 230–31, 232, 233, 239–40, 243–44, 246, 247–48, 273

Locarno, Treaties of, 257, 267

Louvain: and Belgian innocence at, 55–61; and Bryce report, 135; description of, 30; and *Flamenpolitik*, 186; German beliefs regarding massacre at, 34–36,

55–61, 65–66, 125–26, 245, 266; postwar controversy regarding, 266, 268–69; prosecution of massacre, 247; sack of, 30–37, 55–62, 220, 234; as symbol, 120, 122–26, 129, 131, 281n. 84; under occupation, 73, 89, 93. *See also* invasion terror

Ludendorff, Erich, 25, 50, 150, 188; and armistice, 207; and *Flamenpolitik*, 197; and postwar trials, 248, 256

Lumm, von (Reichsbank director), 79, 94, 107, 117, 178

Lusitania, 61, 131–32, 134, 173, 229, 263; and Bryce report, 131–32

Luxembourg (Belgian province), 44, 90, 115, 116, 186, 190, 257; strategic importance of, 9, 49

Luxembourg, Grand Duchy of, 9, 11, 20, 39, 49, 224, 227

Maeterlinck, Maurice, 126, 128

Manchester Guardian, 120, 131–32, 172, 173, 176, 208, 264

Marne, battle of the, 72–73, 79

Meldeamt (registration office), 105, 175, 177

Mercier, Desiré Cardinal, 143, 145, 166, 193, 303n. 29; and deportations, 161; preaches resistance, 99–100, 101; and war crimes, 127–28, 265–66

Millerand, Alexandre, 248, 274

Min, Edmond, 155–56, 158, 185, 189

Mixed Tribunals, 243, 248, 257–58

Mons, 30–31; under occupation, 177, 190, 191, 202, 216

Montague, C. E., 263, 268

Mullins, Claud, 251, 254, 264–65

Munro, Dana Carleton, 137–38, 176

Namur (city), 9, 10, 14, 29, 40; fall of, 62, 82

Namur (province), 9, 27, 29, 49, 85, 147, 186; conditions in, 90, 92, 95, 98, 109 117, 155–56, 177, 185

naval blockade: and Belgian economy, 92, 107–8, 113; and Belgian food supply, 80–82; and deportations, 153, 176, 270; and Fryatt case, 171; and Leipzig trials, 251; legality of, 80–81; and submarines, 130; and war crimes debate, 226, 240.

See also Commission for Relief in Belgium (CRB)

Nazi era, 191, 258; Belgium affects perceptions of, 269–71; foreshadowed by Belgium, 103, 274

necessity: and British blockade, 81; and Bryce report, 135–36; and deportations, 152; as doctrine, 39–40, 41, 47, 48; Lansing embraces, 130, 229; and Leipzig trials, 251, 255, 264; and postwar German government, 227; and Theodore Roosevelt, 128; and war treason, 48, 101–2. See also *Kriegsraison*

Netherlands, the. *See* Holland

Neumann, Karl, 252, 255, 264

neutrality, law of, 16, 17, 41, 64

neutrality, U.S.: angers Belgians, 161; and deportations, 145, 150, 161–63, 179–82; Lansing's views on, 130, 181–82; public support for, 64–65, 68, 71–72, 121–22; Roosevelt challenges, 128–29; Wilson's policy of, 64, 71, 180–81, 185, 200, 273; Wilson's private views on, 66, 88, 180

New York American, 64, 76

New York Times: on deportations, 160, 161, 164; on German crimes, 65, 76, 123; mentioned, 51, 63, 95, 205; on occupation, 90, 137; on peace terms, 208–10; on "posse comitatus," 129

New York Tribune, 67, 123, 131, 132, 134

Norddeutscher Allgemeine Zeitung, 132, 136, 149–50, 178

Northcliffe, Alfred, 210, 248, 307n. 60

NOT (Nederlanse Overzeetrust), 113, 147–48

occupation: administration of, 90–91; censorship under, 79, 97–98, 100–102, 103, 139, 143, 178, 202; damage to Belgium from, 218–19, 223, 224, 227, 260–62; and disarray of first months, 79, 80, 89–90; economic measures of, 79–80, 91–94, 106–8, 111–16, 117, 143, 147–49, 176–77, 178–79, 195, 202–4, 206, 216; German press on, 108, 149–50, 152–53, 159–60, 176, 178, 179; liberation from, 215, 216–17; passive resistance to, 98, 99–100, 110–12, 113, 115–16, 140, 190–91; perceptions of, 88–89, 118–19, 136–41, 158, 192–95, 219–20, 231–32,

259–60, 262–64, 273; political measures of, 91, 97–98, 100–106, 108–9, 114–19, 198–99; recovery from, 261–62; tone of, 78–79, 88, 90–91, 97–103, 109–11, 114, 117, 118, 142–43, 184–85, 195, 197; and war crimes trials, 252–54, 257–58. *See also* deportations; *Flamenpolitik*; food shortages; Hague Conventions, The; laws of war

Pact of London, 87, 200

Paradise, Scott Hurtt, 99, 100, 105, 109–11, 140

Paris Peace Conference, 215, 219–41, 259–60, 271–75; Albert at, 234–35; American disillusionment with, 219–20, 222–23, 238; and Belgian aims, 219, 222–23, 234–37; German views of, 224–27, 238–40; and Lansing, 228–29; and opposition to Belgian aims, 219–24, 231–32, 233–37; and war crimes, 227–31, 232–34, 239–40, 273–74, 275; and Wilson's views, 222, 225, 228–31, 232–34, 237, 239, 240, 275. *See also* Versailles, Treaty of

Pirenne, Henri, 97–98, 100, 110, 147, 148, 298n. 21

Poincaré, Raymond, 40, 42, 215

Pollock, Ernest M., 251, 256

press: and armistice negotiations, 208–11; and Belgian image in U.S., 137–41, 192–95, 219–20; and Bryce report, 131–32, 134; and deportations, 149–50, 152–53, 159–62, 176, 179–80; and disbelief of war crimes, 267–68, 270–71; and foreign views of occupation, 136–40; and franc-tireur charges, 22–23, 51, 57, 76–77; and Fryatt case, 171–73; and *Lusitania*, 131–32; in postwar Germany, 225, 242, 245, 247, 250, 252, 254, 256; and rape and mutilation stories, 76–77

Ramdohr, Max, 252–54, 262

refugees, 25, 28, 83, 85, 88, 89, 95, 219; German pledge to, 85, 145, 163–64, 179; number of, 85; reputation abroad, 105–6, 140, 170, 219, 223, 301n. 7; as witnesses to terror, 132–33

Reichsgericht (Criminal Senate of the Imperial Court of Justice), 243, 248,

Reichsgericht (*Continued*)
249–50, 258, 264, 266, 274–75; cases before, 251–56; court described, 250–51
Reichstag: and Bethmann, 20, 40; and deportations, 160, 188; and Leipzig plan, 249; mentioned, 80, 94, 149, 205, 207, 226; postwar reports of, 266–67
reparations: and focus on invasion terror, 139; Germany opposes, 159–60, 206, 224–27, 238–39, 249, 261, 271; payment of, 261; settlement criticized, 259–60; and suspicions of Belgium, 137, 219–20; wartime demands for, 87, 120–21, 131, 139, 170, 171, 172, 174, 192, 194, 201, 205–6, 209. *See also* Paris Peace Conference
Rolland, Romain, 124–25
Romania, 164, 204–5, 230, 236, 238
Roosevelt, Theodore, 63, 70, 72, 73, 162; and violation of Belgium, 128–30
Russia, 8, 103, 169, 197, 214; and Schlieffen plan, 38, 41 and Treaty of Brest-Litovsk, 204; and war crimes, 125, 164, 295–96n. 50, 300n. 116

Sadeleer, Louis de, 17, 67, 71
Schlieffen, Alfred von, 38–39, 40, 41, 43; beliefs about Belgium, 39, 40, 45; invasion plan of, 41, 49–51
Schmidt, Karl, 251–54
Scott, James Brown, 228–29, 275
"scrap of paper," 20, 66, 103, 165, 173; allusions to, 65, 86, 103, 161; effect of, 43
Serbia, 5, 41, 236, 271
Smith, Frederick E. (Lord Birkenhead), 201–2, 206, 211, 214–15, 244, 273
Smuts, Jan Christian, 212
Socialists: in Belgium, 10, 15, 67, 75, 80, 220; in Germany, 57, 80, 160, 239, 242, 247, 263
Soir, Le (Brussels), 11, 19, 26, 254
statistics on Belgium: deportations, 57, 188, 189, 190–91; escapes and arrests, 103–4, 118; invasion terror, 54, 56; prices, 142, 183; prewar economy, 44–45; postwar economy, 218–19, 261–62; refugees, 85; unemployment, 145, 218; war criminals, 243–44, 246–47, 249

Stenger, Karl, 254–55
Switzerland, 106, 108, 162, 163, 204

Tamines, 29–30, 57, 58
Times (London), 79, 140, 148–49, 208, 247; on Leipzig trials, 250, 252, 253; on punishing Germany, 120, 122, 130–31, 172, 208, 209, 210
Törring-Jettensbach, Hans, 169, 204, 206
Treaty of 1839: Belgian trust in, 8, 44, 72, 81; and Bethmann, 20, 43, 165; as grounds for prosecution, 121, 230; importance to Britain, 19, 43, 95–96; mentioned, 9, 16–17, 23, 41, 66, 128–30, 230; in propaganda, 43, 71, 86; reversal of, 87, 219, 221; terms of, 9, 121
Triple Entente. *See* Allies

ultimatum of 2 August 1914. *See under* Germany
United States: armistice and, 208–210, 212–13; and Belgian mission of 1914, 62–78; atrocity stories and, 75–76, 138, 195; and break with Germany, 180–82, 185, 191; and Bryce report, 131–32, 134; legal positions of, 39, 48, 101, 121, 130, 172; and *Lusitania*, 131–32, 173, 229; mentioned, 45, 200–201, 206, 212–13, 215, 221, 234, 239, 270, 275; protest over Belgium, 64, 66–69, 71–72, 128–30, 145, 160, 161–65, 179–82, 208–10; and Treaty of Versailles, 239, 244, 260, 261. *See also under* Belgium, American opinion of; Commission for Relief in Belgium (CRB); Lansing, Robert; neutrality, U.S.; Paris Peace Conference; Wilson, Woodrow
Usages of War on Land, 79, 91, 94, 135, 152, 266; and Hague Conventions, 41, 47–49, 114, 266
U.S. Congress, 185, 193, 208–9, 222, 243, 260, 261

Van den Heuvel, Jules, 17–18, 222, 236
Vandervelde, Émile, 15, 84, 145, 170, 254; as envoy to U.S., 67, 70, 75; at Paris Peace Conference, 220, 221, 236; and postwar franc-tireur controversy, 267
Vatican, 152, 160, 187, 202, 246

Versailles, Treaty of, 238–44, 247–48, 257, 259–61, 265, 267–68, 271–72, 273–74; Article 227 of (indicting Kaiser Wilhelm), 239–40, 273; Articles 228–30 of (concerning war crimes trials), 240, 245, 256–57, 265, 273–74; Article 231 of (charging war guilt), 238, 259; Germans object to criminal articles, 240, 242–49, 258, 266–68; and Keynes, 259–60, 271; reparations clauses in; 237–38, 259–62; weaknesses in, 271–74. *See also* Paris Peace Conference

Visé, 22, 25, 26, 27, 29, 53, 58, 89, 104; destruction of, 27, 29, 58

Vorwärts (Berlin), 57, 225, 227, 247, 252

war contributions, 29, 93–94, 95, 117, 178–79, 195, 203; debt from, 93–94, 223, 237

war crimes: and Albert, 87, 169–70; deportations as, 171, 175–77, 179–82, 270; Fryatt case and, 172–73; mentioned, 44, 69–70, 102, 114, 117–18, 138–39, 161; and Paris Peace Conference, 224–31, 232–34, 239–40, 273–74, 275; postwar German views of, 225–27, 238–40, 242–49, 250, 266–69; trials of, 123, 251–58; wartime debate on, 120–41, 171–75, 177–82, 200–202, 205–12, 213–15; Wilson and, 88, 136, 201, 209, 212–13, 215, 228, 229, 230, 232–34, 273. *See also* atrocity stories; deportations; *Flamenpolitik*; invasion terror; Leipzig trials; Louvain; occupation

Washington Post, 64, 65, 131, 161–62, 180, 194

West Flanders, 55, 82, 84–85, 89, 91, 92, 114, 259

Westlake, John, 39–40, 94, 101–2

White Book, 56, 58–59, 61, 264, 265, 266. *See also* atrocity stories; invasion terror

Whitlock, Brand: on atrocity stories, 20, 138, 195; and Belgian relief, 94–95, 96, 107; on Bissing, 93; mentioned, 37, 55, 113, 115, 137, 216–17, 221; on occupation, 103, 109, 114, 117, 142, 156, 161, 165–66, 176–77, 185; on postwar mood, 219–20, 234, 236–37

Wilhelm of Hohenzollern, kaiser: asylum in Holland, 213, 244; and deportations, 187–88, 191; indictment of, 122, 172, 208–9, 213–15, 227–30, 239–40, 242, 244, 248, 273; mentioned, 7, 16, 18–19, 39, 51, 90, 180, 186, 205, 207; telegram to Wilson, 66, 67, 68. *See also* Germany

Wilson, Woodrow: and Albert, 88, 160, 193; and Belgian mission of 1914, 62, 64–66, 68–72, 75; and deportations, 162–63, 180–82; fears Allied aims, 88, 212–13, 225; Fourteen Points of, 200–202, 238; and Lansing, 130, 180–82, 206, 229; and *Lusitania*, 131; mentioned, 94, 129, 136, 161, 185, 206–7, 209, 261, 273; at Paris Peace Conference, 221, 222, 225, 228–31, 232–34, 236, 237, 239–40, 275; peace initiative of, 180–82, 273. *See also* neutrality, U.S.; United States; war crimes

Woeste, Charles, 16–17, 169

About the Author

LARRY ZUCKERMAN is the author of *The Potato: How the Humble Spud Rescued the Western World,* which has been translated into four languages and won Great Britain's André Simon Special Commendation Award, given annually to a book about food. A former editor and freelance writer, he lives in Seattle with his wife and their two sons.